# STREET KIDS

# STREET KIDS

## The Lives of Runaway and Thrownaway Teens

R. Barri Flowers

McFarland & Company, Inc., Publishers
*Jefferson, North Carolina, and London*

LIBRARY OF CONGRESS CATALOGUING-IN-PUBLICATION DATA

Flowers, R. Barri (Ronald Barri)
    Street kids : the lives of runaway and thrownaway teens /
R. Barri Flowers.
        p.      cm.
    Includes bibliographical references and index.

    ISBN 978-0-7864-4137-2
    softcover : 50# alkaline paper

    1. Street children — United States.    2. Street youth —
United States.    3. Homeless children — United States.
4. Homeless youth — United States.    I. Title.
HV875.55.F53    2010
362.74 — dc22                                    2010009816

British Library cataloguing data are available

Front cover ©2010 Shutterstock

Manufactured in the United States of America

*McFarland & Company, Inc., Publishers
    Box 611, Jefferson, North Carolina 28640
    www.mcfarlandpub.com*

To H. Loraine, as always,
and to the Rev. Jacquelyn V. White,
who never gave up on her dream,
and to Michigan State University students,
alumni and memories of life on campus.

# Table of Contents

**PART VII : COMBATING THE PROBLEM**

# Preface

A serious problem in the United States is missing children. An estimated two million run away from or are forced out of their homes each year. Many have escaped from sexual, physical or mental abuse, domestic violence, family conflict, and dysfunctional homes, or have been lured away by pimps or Internet predators. Others have fled or been driven away because of behavioral or mental health problems, substance abuse, or sexual orientation or gender identity issues. Though some leave home as an act of rebellion, to seek adventure or romance, to ease loneliness, or to discover themselves, for the vast majority of runaways, leaving home is an escape from an unsafe and unstable environment. Some are repeat runners, finding that the conditions that drove them away before still exist and running away again seems like the only option.

Though most runaways return home within a short period of time and are able to readjust with no lasting effects, a growing number do not and become homeless. Unfortunately, most of these kids will become involved in the dynamics of street life simply to survive — they will engage in survival sex, prostitution, substance abuse and drug dealing. They may also commit property crimes or join gangs. Risky behaviors expose them to all types of health hazards, including sexually transmitted diseases such as HIV, and problems resulting from poor nutrition and unsanitary living conditions. Most runaway and thrownaway youth become victims of or witness to violence such as forcible rapes, physical assaults, hate crimes, verbal attacks, and even death.

This work examines the pathway from home to homeless for runaways and thrownaways, including precursors to life on the street such as child abuse and neglect, sexual abuse, substance abuse, mental health problems, promiscuity, behavioral issues, and sexual orientation/gender identity problems. Also explored are the consequences of homelessness, such as survival sex and commercial child sexual exploitation by pimps, pornographers, pedophiles, and others who prey on minors; sexually transmitted diseases such as HIV and other health concerns; and violence experienced by runaway, thrownaway and homeless youth. The book will also discuss efforts to curb running away and to combat the victimization of runaway and thrownaway youth.

My sincerest gratitude goes out to my loving wife of thirty years, Loraine, for her professionalism and patience in providing invaluable assistance along the way.

# PART I

## RUNAWAY YOUTH

# 1

# Identifying the Runaway

Children who leave home of their own volition or are coerced into leaving is generally given inadequate attention in this country as a serious social concern. They differentiate from another category of missing children who are abducted and given top priority to locate through Amber Alerts and other means. Runaway youth tend to fall between the cracks in terms of recognition, response, and recovery but are far more prevalent. Each year hundreds of thousands of kids are classified as runaways. Many of these kids wind up on the dangerous streets and are forced to fend for themselves through any means necessary for survival, including dealing in drugs, prostitution, petty crimes, and other high-risk behavior. Runaways typically have been victims of child abuse and neglect, sexual abuse, domestic violence, family dysfunction, and other intolerable or stressful conditions. Some cope with mental issues, disciplinary problems, broken homes, peer pressures, struggles in school, substance abuse, and economic woes that can lead to running away. Identifying runaways can lead to a better understanding of the dynamics and confronting the problem.

## Defining the Runaway

What is a runaway? Definitions of runaways can vary greatly based upon various criteria from source to source, such as "the duration of time absent from the home, the nature of the running way, and parental knowledge of the missing youth's whereabouts."[1] The runaway youth is generally seen as a minor who leaves home, a living arrangement where there is guardianship, juvenile detention, or another place of residence for a period beyond that which is considered acceptable by those caring for; or whereby the juvenile fails to return home by a reasonable time with no indication that he or she is in harm's way or prevented from returning. A primary component of running away is the voluntary nature of leaving as opposed to being forced out of the home (see Chapter 3 for more discussion on thrownaways) or taken out against their will. However, because leaving home of one's own free will is often the result of serious precipitating factors, relatively few runaways truly leave home voluntarily as opposed to as a last resort, personal safety, or as a cry for help.

According to the 2007 National Symposium on Homelessness Research, the National Runaway Switchboard (NRS) definition of a runaway is "any youth who, without permission, leaves home and stays away overnight, or, if away from home, chooses to not to come home when expected."[2] The U.S. Department of Justice's *Juvenile Offenders and Victims: 2006 National Report* defines the runaway as "a child who left home without permission and stayed away at least overnight or who was already away and refused to return home."[3]

These are consistent with a definition of running away by the National Center for Health Statistics as "leaving or staying away on purpose, knowing you would be missed, and intending to stay away from home for at least some time."[4]

Similarly, the Office of Juvenile Justice and Delinquency Prevention (OJJDP), definition of a runaway is a "child/youth who has left (or not returned to) a parent's or caretaker's supervision without permission."[5] Runaways are defined by the OJJDP as a subcategory group of missing persons age seventeen or younger who have been reported as missing to local law enforcement agencies.[6]

The Second National Incidence Studies of Missing, Abducted, Runaway and Thrownaway Children (NISMART-2), published in 2002, define a runaway episode as involving any of the criterion as follows:

- A child leaving home without the permission to do so and remains away overnight.
- A child under the age of fifteen (unless older and mentally incompetent) who is not at home and decides not to return when expected and remains away for the night.
- A child age fifteen and up who is away from home, decides not to return, and remains away for two nights.[7]

Legally, running away from home, institutional care, or another place of residence is a status offense, or applicable to persons usually under the age of eighteen. Arrests of runaways is defined by the Federal Bureau of Investigation's Uniform Crime Reporting Program as "juveniles taken into protective custody under provisions of local statutes."[8] However, there is a gray area here. Runaways, as a consequence, find themselves engaging in criminal violations of the law such as substance abuse and prostitution and, as such, may be taken into custody as a status offender and juvenile delinquent.[9] (See also Chapter 11.)

## Defining Other Missing Children

Runaways represent one category of children who are missing from home, but are often incorrectly grouped with or differentiated from other missing youth, though the general circumstances are the same. The sometimes complex overlapping, defining, and/or understanding of missing youth and their motivations or reasons for being away from home can have an effect on identifying, locating, and aiding runaways and other missing children, such as thrownaways, street kids, homeless youth, and abducted children.

Thrownaway children are typically aligned with runaway children and have been defined by the OJJDP as youth who have left their homes involuntarily and not allowed to return.[10] Thrownaways or discarded children are forced to leave home by parents or guardians in relation to behavioral problems, major disagreements, substance abuse issues, abuse, and other family dysfunction, as well as financial woes, with no desire for them to return. Part II will focus more in depth on thrownaway youth.

Homeless youth, also known as "street youth" and "street kids," have been defined by the Runaway and Homeless Youth Act as a person between the ages of sixteen and twenty-one "for whom it is not possible to live in a safe environment with a relative and who has no other safe alternative living arrangement."[11] Many homeless youth are, in fact, runaways and thrownaways, forced to live on the street and find food or shelter wherever possible or do without.

The Children's Society describes as "detached" such youth who have "left or been forced to leave parents or careers and has been detached from parents, careers or relatives, for a period of four weeks or more" with the term reflective of "the over-arching themes of living outside key societal institutions, self-reliance, and a dependence upon informal support networks."[12]

The National Network for Youth uses the term "unaccompanied youth" to include "children and youth through age seventeen, who are living apart from their parents or guardians" and are "economically and/or emotionally detached from their families and are experiencing homeless situations."[13]

Runaways and homeless children have also been referred to as "disconnected youth," a term that relates to the "youth's separation from societal institutions such as family, school, etc., which is indicative of their socioeconomic instability."[14] (See also Chapter 2).

NISMART-2 definitions of missing children other than runaways include the following[15]:

- Family Abduction — when a noncustodial family member or someone acting on their behalf abducts a child or intentionally fails to return, hides, or transports from state unlawfully.

- Kidnapping — when a child is abducted by a stranger or nonfamily member, held overnight and/or for ransom, transported fifty miles or more, with the intention to keep forever, or killed.

- Missing Involuntarily — when a child is absent unwillingly, lost, or injured and whereabouts is unknown to parents or caretaker, who is alarmed for an hour and seek to locate.

- Missing for Benign Reasons — when a child's location is unknown to parent or guardian, causing alarm, attempt to locate, and contact the police, so long as missing child does not fall under the aforementioned reasons, including runaway or thrownaway.

- Nonfamily Abduction — when child is taken away by force or threat of by a nonfamily member and detained for an hour or more without permission of a parent or otherwise unlawfully; or when a child age fourteen and under or mentally incompetent is abducted or accompanies willingly, while hiding whereabouts, seeking ransom, or with no plans to return child.

Some runaway youth could, in fact, fit into any of these categories, such as running away from a family or nonfamily abductor or kidnapper. Most runaway and thrownaway youth tend to be missing because of leaving the home willingly, if not under duress, or were made to leave against their wishes. Any such children can fall prey to being the victims of abduction along with other hazards of being away from home.

## Types of Runaways

In spite of a general labeling of runaways as a group in their actions, children who run away from home or other guardianship are not homogeneous. They run from unstable environments, sexual abuse, physical violence, poverty and, at times, an inability to respond properly to authority; while some are forced from the home by those who no longer want them there. In each instance, the runaway is thrust into an environment that challenges at every turn, even if returning home no longer seems a viable option.

There are basically five kinds of runaways, though there may be variations and overlapping within: (1) situational, (2) recidivist, (3) chronic, (4) street, and (5) thrownaway.

- *Situational runaways* constitute the largest group of youth who leave home. They usually are away for a day or two following a quarrel with parents before returning home.
- *Recidivist or repeat runaways* leave home more than once, sometimes staying with friends, others living on streets or shelters. Studies show that recidivist runners are more likely than non recidivist runaways to leave home due to problems involving family dynamics, substance abuse, transportation, and the judicial system, among others.[16]
- *Chronic runaways* constantly run from home and remain away for longer stretches of time, often progressing to street youth.
- *Street youth runaways* leave home permanently and as the term suggests, tend to literally live on the street and must fend for themselves. Some street kids also spend time staying in transitory housing, such as shelters or abandoned buildings, and are most at risk for victimization.[17]
- *Thrownaways* leave home involuntarily, often as a result of a dispute with parents/guardians, or are abandoned. Some thrownaway youth also fall into other categories of runaways.

Researchers have further classified four types of runaways: (1) running to, (2) running from, (3) thrown out, and (4) forsaken.[18] These are described as follows:

- Running to: youth in search of adventure and excitement away from the restrictive nature of home.
- Running from: those looking to escape a negative home environment, such as emotionally or sexually abusive.
- Thrown out: youth who are forced into leaving home due to strong alienation there in the community, or and/or school.

- Forsaken: children who run away from home due to parents being unable to support financially with weak family ties and peer group bonds.

Another breakdown of runaways was established by Clifford English, who based four types upon the commitment to stay away from home and the situational factors present in running away:

- Floaters: youth who run away from home for only a short while, usually returning once things cool down.
- Runaways: those who remain away from home for a long stretch of time (frequently weeks or months), in many instances because of an unsteady family environment or a serious personal issue.
- Splitters: youth who seek pleasure and status among their peers.
- Hard-Rock Freaks: runaways who leave home for good, having chosen to be on their own, often as a result of serious family issues.[19]

The NISMART-1 identified three types of "runaway phenomena," defining runaways as (1) Broad Scope Runaways, (2) Policy Focal Runaways, and (3) Runaway Gestures.[20]

- *Broad Scope Runaways* are youth who leave or stay away from home without parental consent for at least one night. An exception is teens over the age of fourteen who have permission to be out, but fail to return home at an agreed upon time, such as those violating curfews while at parties or on dates. These teenagers would need to be away from home for two or more nights in order to be viewed as Broad Scope Runaways.
- *Policy Focal Runaways* are youth who, in addition to being defined as Broad Scope Runaways, are put in danger from being in an unfamiliar, unsafe place away from home. An example of a Policy Focal Runaway is a child who runs away and lives on the street, in a shelter, or car. This type of high-risk runaway represents the greatest concern for police and policymakers.
- *Runaway Gestures* are youth who run away from home for only a few hours, while not staying away overnight, including those who leave a "runaway note." Runaway Gestures include older teenagers whose overnight stay without parental consent was not seen as a serious concern. Though runaway youth in this category typically have family problems, they are usually not included in national figures on the number of runaways.[21]

Other research on runaways have produced further breakdowns, such as a study by Franklin Dunford and Tim Brennan, which placed runaway children into six groups: (1) self-assured, (2) well-adjusted, (3) strong delinquent behavior, (4) escaping, (5) harmfully influenced, and (6) uncontrolled.[22]

The NRS reported that many runaways are away from home for only a little while, yet are gone long enough to be considered a runaway by family, though not necessarily law enforcement.[23] An estimated 40 percent of teenagers who leave home stay away for one to three days.[24] More than half of runaways believed their home crisis could not be resolved by social service agencies.[25]

## RUNAWAYS FROM SUBSTITUTE CARE

While most runaway youth run from home and family settings, some leave other types of accommodations. The NISMART distinguishes household runaways from those leaving non-household settings. Non-household runaways include those who run from juvenile facilities or substitute care such as boarding schools, detention centers, foster care, group homes, hospitals, and mental health institutions.[26]

Studies show that youth who live in substitute care housing are more likely to become runaways than those who live with their parents.[27] Teenagers who run from substitute facilities are more often repeat runaways than runaway teens from home.[28] The likelihood of running away from substitute care is highest within the first few months upon being placed.[29] Older teenagers tend to run away more often from substitute care than younger teenagers; while runaway youth from non-household settings are more likely than runaways from home to stay away for longer periods of time and travel greater distances.[30]

In spite of representing only a small proportion of all runaway youth, substitute care runaways tend to disproportionately involve law enforcement resources and manpower.[31]

## *The Extent of Runaway Youth*

How many children run away from home? It is difficult to assess the true number of youth who go on the run as definitions of runaways vary as well as differentiate by type and from other missing children, along with reporting mechanisms. However, most experts believe that anywhere from hundreds of thousands of youth to a few million children run away from home in the United States for some period of time in a given year.[32] A youth runs away or is thrown out of the home every twenty-six seconds.[33] One in seven youth between ten and eighteen years of age will have a runaway episode at one time or another[34]; with a National Longitudinal Survey of Youth reporting that more than one in ten youth had ever left home as a runaway.[35] An estimated 300,000 youth are considered hard core street kids who are habitual runaways;[36] while over half of runaway children had left home on at least three occasions.[37] According to a national survey, more than half a million families are affected by children running away annually.[38]

According to the NRS, between 1.6 and 2.8 million youth run away from home every year.[39] The NISMART-2 estimated that around 1.7 million youth were runaways or thrownaways in 1999.[40] Only around four in ten of these runaway/thrownaway youth were considered to be caretaker missing children — or those for whom parents or caretakers were unaware of their whereabouts and worried as a result for at least sixty minutes while trying to find them. About one in five of such absences were reported to law enforcement or a missing children's agency with the desire to locate the runaway. More than seven in ten of all runaways/thrownaways could have been placed in danger during the episode as a result of substance abuse or dependency, physical or sexual abuse, in a location where criminal behavior was taking place, or being very young or under the age of fourteen.[41] The Office of Applied Studies reported that in 2002, 1.6 million American youth between the ages of twelve and seventeen had run from home and been forced to sleep on the streets.[42] In all, up to three million runaways and homeless children are believed to be street kids in the United States.[43]

The NISMART-1 estimated that there are 446,700 Broad Scope Runaways from households and another 4,000 who run from juvenile facilities in the United States each year.[44] Of these in total, 133,500 are Policy Focal Runaways. An estimated 8,800 youth run away from households and juvenile facilities annually.[45] Additionally, some 173,700 children are defined as Runaway Gestures every year.[46]

Other findings from NISMART are as follows[47]:

• About one in four runaways traveled at least fifty miles from home.

• Nearly one in ten runaway episodes resulted in leaving the state.

• More than three out of four runaway youth were back at home in less than a week.

- Seven percent of runaways were away from home for more than a month.
- One in ten Broad Scope Runaways traveled more than 100 miles from home.
- Three in ten runaways traveled eleven to fifty miles from home.
- Seven percent of household runaways leave the state.
- Over one in four runaways stay away from home overnight, though for twenty-four hours or less.
- Nearly one in four runaways is away from home for one to two days.
- One in ten runaway youth never return home.
- More than one in three runaways leave home more than once over a twelve-month period.
- Juvenile facility runaways are most likely to run away from group foster homes, mental health facilities, and residential treatment centers.
- In nearly half the juvenile facility runaway cases, the institution does not know the whereabouts of the runaway.
- About four in ten ran away more than once from the same juvenile facility within the previous twelve months.
- Almost half the juvenile facility runaway youths were in the company of others when running away.
- Six in ten Broad Scope Runaways initially go to a friend's house.
- Eight in ten runaways run to a friend's house at any time.
- More than one in ten runaways has no place to sleep any night.
- Only 2 percent of runaways go to runaway shelters.
- Nearly eight in ten runaways are accompanied by others.
- One-third of runaways were involved in an argument prior to leaving home.
- Nearly seven in ten children run away during a weekday.
- Around four in ten runaway episodes occur during the summer.
- Six in ten runaway episodes take place in the winter, spring, or fall.
- Almost four in ten caretakers know the whereabouts of the runaway youth most of the time.
- More than one in four caretakers does not know the whereabouts of runaways.

- The most common type of endangerment faced by runaways is physical or sexual abuse at home or thereof when returning home.
- Almost all runaways eventually return home or to substitute care.

Though most runaway youth do not remain away from home permanently, those who do will likely end up as street kids, where each day can become an exercise in survival.

# 2

# Characterizing Runaway Youth

In spite of the view of many, perhaps perpetuated and glamorized by Hollywood and fiction, that runaways tend to flee home for a life of adventure, an unwillingness to bend to authority, or misguided feelings of love, the reality is often quite different. They run away more often than not due to an atmosphere that may be abusive, neglectful, stressful, or otherwise unbearable to live in. Runaway youth are often misunderstood by those in their home, creating conditions that can lead to leaving an uncomfortable situation. And, unlike dramatized portrayals of runaways as typically attractive, white teenage girls who leave home for life on the streets and/or selling their bodies, not all runaways fit this mode. Children who leave home as runaways, detached, and disconnected youth, come in all racial and ethnic groups, are male as often as female, from every socioeconomic background and family structure, and run away or are forced out of the house for usually multiple reasons. Runaway youth bring with them various issues such as emotional scars or substance abuse that tend to be exacerbated when homeless. Though most runaways will return home to confront their issues or because of the harsh realities of life on the streets, some will run away again; while others never come home, disappearing into the abyss of a dark world with no one to trust or find safety in.

## Runaways and Gender

Runaway youth is not a gender-specific phenomenon; though more attention tends to be paid to female runaways and issues they run from and run into. Male and female juveniles flee from home for various and similar reasons. Earlier studies indicated that more girls ran away than boys. The

Office of Juvenile Justice and Delinquency Prevention (OJJDP) found that females accounted for 58 percent of runaways from home and males 42 percent.[1] Other data supported this finding, contending that roughly six girls run away for every four runaway boys.[2] Similarly, about 53 percent of runaways from juvenile facilities were found to be female compared to 47 percent male.[3]

Some recent studies indicate that girls and boys run away from home in approximately equal numbers. According to the Second National Incidence Studies of Missing, Abducted, Runaway and Thrownaway Children (NISMART-2), half of runaways across the country in 1999 were estimated to be female (841,600) and half male (841,300).[4] A National Longitudinal Survey of Youth (NLSY97) found that 11 percent of the female respondents and 10 percent of the male respondents had run away from home at some point in their lives.[5]

However, two comprehensive studies of street kids cited at the 2007 National Symposium on Homelessness Research gave mixed results on runaways and gender. The Midwest Homeless and Runaway Adolescent Project (MHRAP) reported that 60 percent of the participants were female and 40 percent male[6]; whereas in the Seattle Homeless Adolescent Research Project (SHARP), 55 percent of those involved in study were male and 45 percent female.[7]

According to the National Runaway Switchboard (NRS), whose mission is to help runaway and street youth and prevent children from running away, between 2000 and 2005 more than two-thirds of runaway callers were female, while just under one-third were male.[8] The breakdown was virtually the same for thrownaway callers to the NRS. For youth who were thinking about running away, nearly eight in ten callers were female and around two in ten male.[9]

Arrest data show that about 56 percent of those arrested as runaways are female and 44 percent male, which may reflect police discretion and other factors as much as the incidence of running away for boys and girls.[10] (See Chapter 6 for more discussion on runaways and arrest).

Research has generally shown runaway youth to be disproportionately female relative to their population figures.[11] Authorities on missing children believe this may be a reflection of a greater propensity by runaway girls to seek help outside the home in addressing their problems. Female adolescents are also seen as maturing much earlier than male adolescents, increasing the likelihood of wishing to leave home ahead of reaching adulthood.[12] Further, a correlation has been shown between greater numbers of runaway females and a rise in girl delinquency.[13]

# Runaways and Age

Runaway youth include teenagers and preteens who are roughly divided between female and male and of various racial and ethnic groups. The majority of runaways are older teenagers, who may have more reasons built up for leaving home, problems relating to authority, and greater resources initially for being on their own. According to the NISMART-2, as shown in Figure 2.1, 68 percent of children having runaway episodes during the study year were between the ages of fifteen and seventeen. Twenty-eight percent of the runaways fell between twelve and fourteen years of age, while 4 percent were ages seven to eleven.[14]

This is consistent with findings from the 1990 published study on missing youth, *Missing, Abducted, Runaway, and Thrownaway Children in America, First Report: Numbers and Characteristics, National Incidence Studies* (NISMART-1), which concluded that sixteen and seventeen year olds constituted over two-thirds of Broad Scope Runaways, with fourteen and fifteen year olds making up almost one-fourth of the total.[15]

Other researchers have reported similar results. The NRS found 86 percent of runaway youth to be fourteen to seventeen years of age.[16] In the

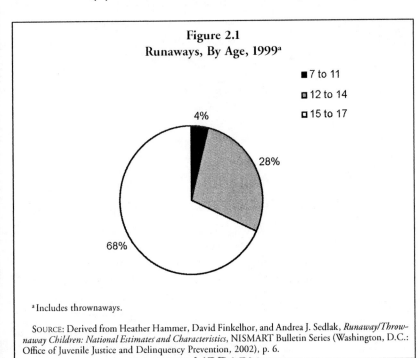

**Figure 2.1**
**Runaways, By Age, 1999[a]**

■ 7 to 11
▣ 12 to 14
▢ 15 to 17

4%

28%

68%

[a] Includes thrownaways.

Source: Derived from Heather Hammer, David Finkelhor, and Andrea J. Sedlak, *Runaway/Thrownaway Children: National Estimates and Characteristics*, NISMART Bulletin Series (Washington, D.C.: Office of Juvenile Justice and Delinquency Prevention, 2002), p. 6.

MHRAP study, the mean age of runaways was 16.24[17]; while the mean age in the SHARP study was 17.15.[18] According to the NLSY97, 17 percent of the sixteen-year-olds had ever run away, compared to 12 percent of fourteen to fifteen year olds, and 6 percent of respondents twelve to thirteen years of age.[19]

Studies have shown a relationship between age and gender of runaway youth, with motivation often being a stronger indicator than gender. In one study, for example, girls tended to run away from home more often than boys, while more than one-third of total runaways were thirteen to fourteen years of age. However, for runaways younger than fifteen, males ran away at a rate higher than females. Beginning at age fifteen, runaway females outnumbered runaway males with the total number of runaways for both sexes declining with age as a reflection of the loosening of parental restrictions as the youth grow older.[20]

Younger runaways have been described as junior adventurers, whereas older runaways are characterized as wanting to establish themselves as adults. The higher number of girl runaways age thirteen and above appears to be related to a greater propensity to "look for action" during those years, increasing the likelihood they will leave home.[21] Many older female teenagers may run away more often than their male counterparts as a result of more severe issues at home, such as physical and sexual child maltreatment.[22]

In a typical scenario of a sixteen-year-old female runaway named "Jean," leaving a dysfunctional and violent home became a matter of survival:

> I ran away from my parents' house about two years ago, when I was 13 years old. It was very abusive at my mom and dad's house — physically, emotionally abusive. My stepfather is crazy. He's like this total alcoholic and a big pothead. Whenever he was drunk, he'd chase after us with guns![23]

## Runaways and Race/Ethnicity

Runaway youth are predominately white, non–Hispanic; however minority youths are overrepresented as runaways, according to some studies.[24] The NISMART-2 reported that in 1999, white, non–Hispanics accounted for 57 percent of runaways in this country, while black, non–Hispanics made up 17 percent, Hispanics 15 percent, and others 11 percent of runaways (see Figure 2.2).

The NISMART-1 found that among Broad Scope Runaways, three in every four were white, with two out of ten black. Around 4 percent of Broad Scope Runaways were Hispanic and 2 percent other racial/ethnic groups.[25]

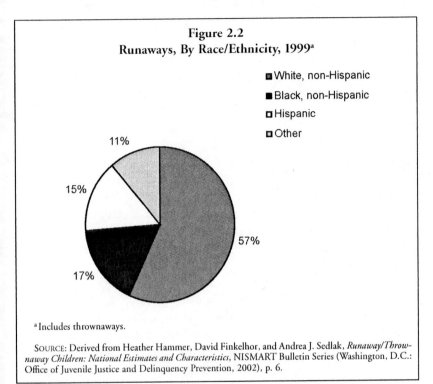

**Figure 2.2**
**Runaways, By Race/Ethnicity, 1999[a]**

◼ White, non-Hispanic

◼ Black, non-Hispanic

◻ Hispanic

◻ Other

11%

15%

17%

57%

[a] Includes thrownaways.

SOURCE: Derived from Heather Hammer, David Finkelhor, and Andrea J. Sedlak, *Runaway/Throw-naway Children: National Estimates and Characteristics*, NISMART Bulletin Series (Washington, D.C.: Office of Juvenile Justice and Delinquency Prevention, 2002), p. 6.

Self-report surveys reveal that slightly more minorities (11 percent) than whites (10 percent) ever ran away from home.[26]

Other findings have emerged producing similar results on the racial breakdown of runaways. The MHRAP reported that 61 percent of the participants were white and 25 percent black[27]; while the SHARP found that 53 percent were white and 18 percent black.[28] In both instances, black runaways were disproportionate to their percentage of the general population. A report from the Federal Bureau of Investigation further supported the overrepresentation of black youth as runaways, showing that one-third of missing children in 2005 were black.[29]

Research shows that the percentage of white youth who run from substitute or away from home care facilities is higher than those who leave home. More than 80 percent of juvenile facility runaways are white, compared to about 10 percent black.[30] Hispanic runaways are more likely to flee from juvenile facilities than households; whereas other racial and ethnic minorities are equally likely to run away from home or out of home care for juveniles.

Among runaway girls, an estimated seven in ten are white, while two in ten are black, and around one in ten are Hispanic or youth from other ethnic or racial minorities.[31]

## Runaways and Class/Income

The socioeconomic constituents of class and income have been linked to runaway behavior. Much attention has been paid, in particular, to the relationship between impoverishment and runaways with the assumption that poor children are more likely to run away from home. The Family and Youth Services Bureau estimated that 40 percent of runaway youth living in shelters or homeless came from families living below the poverty line.[32] In a study of female runaways, Louise Homer found that most were from lower and lower middle class backgrounds, with seven out of ten families living on welfare.[33]

Most research has indicated that runaway youth are more likely to run from middle class than lower class families. In. James Hildebrand's study, the "vast majority" of runaways were from the middle class;[34] while in a study of suburban runaways, Robert Shellow found that more than half were middle class and working class youth.[35]

According to findings from the NISMART-1, there appears to be no significant correlation between running away and household income. Broad Scope Runaways were more likely, however, to come from middle and upper class families than lower class ones. Forty percent of runaways fled families with household incomes between $20,000 and $40,000, while 24 percent ran away from families with a household income of $10,000 to $20,000, and 24 percent from families with a household income of $40,000 or more. Only 13 percent of runaway youth left homes with a household income of $10,000 or less.[36] The positive association between runaways and all household income levels has been supported through other studies.[37]

## Runaways and Broken Homes

Runaways are most likely to run from broken homes, defined as "homes in which one or both parents are missing, usually due to divorce, separation, or desertion."[38] In the NISMART-1, almost half of Broad Scope Runaways were living with a single parent without a partner or a single parent who had a partner. Less than three in ten Broad Scope Runaways lived with both parents when they left home. Seven percent of the runaway youth ran from homes where both parents were absent, while 15 percent of the runaways left homes were the parental structure was uncertain.[39] Studies have found that children who live in households with both natural or adoptive parents are less likely to run away from home than those living in households with stepparents or live-in partners.[40]

Juvenile or substitute care facility runaways tend to come from households most often with a single parent or one natural parent and partner prior to their stay at an away from home facility. Over half the runaways in the NISMART studies fell into this category.[41] Just over one-fourth of the runaway youth had both parents living in the household before being placed in a juvenile facility.

Research on juvenile delinquency has supported the correlation between broken homes and aberrant behavior, including running away. For instance, in a study of 1,517 male youths and delinquency, Rolf Loeber, Ann Weiher, and Carolyn Smith found that juveniles from single parent families were more likely to increase their rate of delinquency as they go through adolescence compared to juveniles who lived in homes where both parents were present.[42]

## Runaways and Family Structure

Family structure has been examined by researchers in relationship to running away and other delinquent behaviors.[43] Larger families have proven to be a strong predictor of running from home. In N. S. Johnson and Roxy Peck's study of adolescent runaways, they were more likely to come from large families rather than average sized families.[44] The study also found that more than half the runaway youth were from families with their siblings all of the opposite sex or with a very young brother or sister.

A strong correlation between large family size and delinquency was found in studies by Israel Kolvin and colleagues[45] and Newson, Newson, and Adams.[46] Self-report surveys of juvenile and adult deviant behavior have shown large families to be significantly predictive of antisocial behavior.[47]

A cause and effect association to juvenile status offending and delinquency has also been made to the ordinal position in the family with intermediates — or children with older and younger siblings — finding them to be overrepresented among troubled youth. Researchers have posited that the attention paid by parents to their youngest and oldest progeny often squeezed intermediates out of the family and pushed them into a life that may include running away or other aberrant behavior.[48]

Other research has explored the family structure of runaway females, concluding it to be dysfunctional, while noting that the functional level within "family roles, problem solving, and emotional responsiveness" were lower than norms of society.[49] Family structure and juvenile offending has also been linked to family dynamics such as divorce, unemployment, and substance abuse.[50]

## Runaways as Disconnected Youth

Runaways and homeless teenagers have been characterized as being disconnected youth. They are seen as having "weak social networks of family, friends, and communities that provide assistance such as employment connections, health insurance coverage, tuition, and other financial assistance, and emotional support."[51] An estimated two to three million young adults are believed to be disconnected.[52]

Experts on runaway and homeless young people have used two quantifiable characteristics in ascertaining that certain youth groups fallen into the category of disconnected: (1) not attending high school and/or college, and (2) being unemployed for a year or more. Weak academic and employment results have been found to correlate with "concentrated poverty, community insecurity, and unstable family structures."[53] Urban minority runaways and street kids are disproportionately seen as disconnected youth.[54]

Runaways and homeless young adults are considered high-risk for becoming disconnected due to being separated from family and friends, school absence, and not participating in the economy.[55] Disconnected youth often find themselves becoming involved in delinquency or criminality as a means to survive and compensate for the lack of familial support, education, or employment.[56]

Juveniles in the foster care system and other substitute care are especially prone to disconnection from family and school, contributing to the likelihood that they will become runaways and homeless, along with the other negative consequences inevitable as disconnected youth.[57]

# PART II

## THROWNAWAY YOUTH

# 3

# Identifying the Thrownaway

A subgroup of runaways that is often overlooked or combined with other homeless children and young adults in the research and national consciousness is the thrownaway youth. Also referred to as "throwaways," "push outs," "cast outs," and "castaways," unlike most runaways who leave home voluntarily, thrownaways are literally forced to leave the residence. Or they are otherwise abandoned by parents or caretakers. These youth tend to be tossed out of their home and comfort zone for reasons ranging from behavioral problems, family dysfunction, school failure, substance abuse, money problems, and sexual identity issues. Some return home only to be thrown away again. Many are victims of child abuse. Others have been placed in the foster care system only to end up on the streets as homeless and disconnected youth. Like other teenagers who no longer have a stable place to call home, thrownaways tend to divide their time between homelessness and transitional housing. Along the way they are especially susceptible as prime targets for exploiters, pimps, pedophiles, gangs, and others who see them as easy prey with often nowhere to turn.

## Defining the Thrownaway Youth

What are thrownaway youth? The term largely refers to children who have been made to leave home against their wishes, usually at the behest of parents of guardians. Most definitions of thrownaways tend to differentiate them from other types of missing children. However, in some definitions and statistics, thrownaway youth are defined as a branch of runaways, thereby failing to recognize them as a distinct population of youth who have been banished from their homes.

The National Network for Youth defines the thrownaway as youth who "were induced by their parents to leave against their will and no effort was made by the parents to find them once they left home."[1] Thrownaways are defined by The Focus Adolescent Services as "youth who have left home because their parents have abandoned them, asked them to leave, or subjected them to extreme levels of abuse and neglect."[2]

The term *thrownaway* is described by the National Incidence Studies' *Missing, Abducted, Runaway, and Thrownaway Children in America* (NISMART-1) as "unambiguously conveys what has been done to the child."[3] In a report to Congress, thrownaway youth are seen as "part of the homeless population if they lack alternative living arrangements."[4] Many of these children may have lived with other relatives at some point or spent time in the foster care system.[5]

There are instances where thrownaways and runaways are the same individuals with the difference being a matter of interpretation, dependent upon the source, or perhaps these youth may have actually run away and been thrown out of the home at one point or another. Recidivist runners and thrownaways are not uncommon, often victims of family dysfunction, family violence, and other issues that make their absence from home a recurring theme.

In the Second National Incidence Studies of Missing, Abducted, Runaway and Thrownaway Children (NISMART-2), in particular, dissimilarities between thrownaways and runaways have been deemphasized "because many youth experience both circumstances, and the categorization of a runaway or throwaway episode frequently depends on whether information was gathered from the youth (who tend to emphasize the throwaway aspects of the episode) or their caretakers (who tend to emphasize the runaway aspects)."[6]

The concept of thrownaway children began in the 1970s as researchers and child welfare experts recognized that many "runaways" did not leave home of their own accord as the term implied, but instead "were manipulated into leaving, compelled to leave due to intolerable conditions at home, or outright forced onto the street by parents or guardians."[7] Other youth falling under the banner of missing children were, in fact, abandoned by parents or caretakers, while not reporting them missing or labeling them as runaways to authorities.

In discriminating thrownaways from runaways and other missing children, one researcher, recognizing the vulnerability faced by thrownaway youth turned street kids, noted soberly: "These are the children most preyed upon and exploited, the children most likely to be lying in John and Jane

Doe graves all over the United States, unidentified because no one has reported them missing."[8]

## The Extent of Thrownaway Youth

Establishing an accurate estimate on the number of children thrown away in this country is difficult as most national statistics combine thrown-aways with runaways, often classifying them as street kids and homeless youth. The National Runaway Switchboard (NRS) estimates that between 1.6 and 2.8 million youth run away from or are thrown out of the house annually.[9]

According to NISMART-2, there were approximately 1.7 million youth who had a runaway or thrownaway episode in the United States in 1999.[10] Seventy-one percent of these youth were felt to be endangered as a result of being away from home by such things as child physical or sexual abuse, substance dependency, criminality, and being under the age of fourteen.[11]

NISMART-1 differentiated thrownaways from runaways in its study. It estimated that there are 127,100 Broad Scope Thrownaways (youth who are away from home overnight involuntarily, not allowed to return home, missing through parental neglect or desertion) each year. Of these 59,200 are Policy Focal Thrownaways, who are absent of a secure and familiar environment at some point while away from home (see Chapter 1).[12] Almost 15,000 of these thrownaways are estimated to be children who were abandoned or "whose parents or caretakers had gone off and left them (rather than kicking them out)."[13] The report classified 45,900 missing youth annually as runaways and thrownaways.

Other NISMART findings on the nature and compass of thrownaway episodes are as follows:

- Over eight in ten Broad Scope Thrownaways were living at home before being thrown out.
- More than four in ten thrownaways were asked to leave home.
- Mothers are more likely than fathers to throw away their children.
- Almost six in ten thrownaways got into an argument prior to being forced out of the home.
- Nearly three in ten thrownaway episodes involved physical violence in the household.
- In almost three in ten runaway episodes, parents made no attempt to bring the missing child back home.

- Six in ten thrownaways' first destination upon leaving home is a friend's house.
- More than eight in ten thrownaway youth are accompanied by others when leaving home.
- Over half of thrownaways travel between one and nine miles from home.
- Only one percent of thrownaway youth leave the state.
- Over two in ten thrownaways are absent from home for a day or less.
- One in five thrownaways is away from home for less than two weeks.
- One in five thrownaway youth never return home.
- More than one in ten youth thrown away do not have a place to sleep.[14]

According to data from the NRS, between 2000 and 2005, 5.3 percent of callers to their crisis line were identified as thrownaway youth (see Figure 3.1). By comparison, 37.7 percent of callers were classified as runaways, representing the largest group of callers; followed by 33.3 percent of youth having a general crisis. Homeless youth comprised 6.6 percent of the callers, with 17.1 percent considering running away. Only around 5 percent of all runaways, thrownaways, and/or homeless youth in this country call the NRS.[15]

Some research suggests that thrownaway youth may constitute a large proportion of runaways and homeless teenagers, in spite of available data to that effect. Many experts on missing children believe that thrownaway youth are underreported among runaways. Surveys of youth at runaway shelters have shown that thrownaways comprise from 10 percent,[16] to one-third,[17] to as many as 50 percent of children living on the streets.[18] An estimate by the Youth Development Bureau placed the number of runaway youth in this country who were actually forced to leave home at 30 to 35 percent.[19] Likewise, it was estimated by the National Network of Runaway and Youth Services that 40 percent of the nation's 1.5 million homeless youth were in fact thrownaway children.[20] A survey of homeless youth found that 51 percent were no longer living at home as a result of being thrown out by parents or guardians.[21]

In a Family and Youth Services Bureau (FYSB) funded study, *Youth With Runaway, Throwaway and Homeless Experiences: Prevalence, Drug Use, and Other At-Risk Behaviors*, the term "runaway" was described as misleading where it concerned homeless youth. The study approximated that around half of those staying in shelters and sleeping on the streets had either been compelled to leave home by a parent or caretaker or such person made no

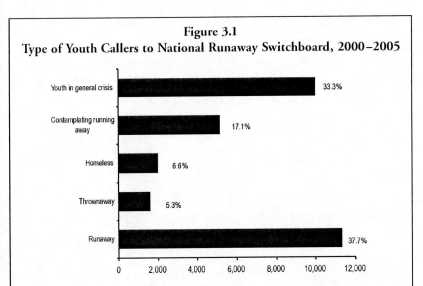

**Figure 3.1**
**Type of Youth Callers to National Runaway Switchboard, 2000–2005**

Youth in general crisis — 33.3%
Contemplating running away — 17.1%
Homeless — 6.6%
Thrownaway — 5.3%
Runaway — 37.7%

SOURCE: Derived from Alma C. Molino, "Characteristics of Help-Seeking Street Youth and Non-Street Youth," 2007 National Symposium on Homelessness Research, March 1–2, 2007, http://aspe.hhs.gov/hsp/homelessness/symposium07/molino/index.htm.

attempt to stop them from leaving the household.[22] In one study, it was put forward that the difference between runaways and thrownaways was dependent to a large extent on who returned home, finding that runaway youth were more than two times as likely as thrownaway youth to come back home.[23] According to researchers Carolyn Males and Julie Raskin, thrownaway youth "crash" wherever they can, illustrating the difficulty of locating and gathering information on this segment of the runaway population nationwide.[24]

## Types of Thrownaways

Thrownaway youth, like other missing children, have been broken down into types by researchers, based upon the circumstances of their being out of the home, length of time away, lack of parental arrangements for appropriate substitute housing, and the parents' or guardians' unwillingness to allow for a safe return.

In the Department of Justice's *Juvenile Offenders and Victims 1999 National Report*, four types of thrownaway youth were identified:

• Youth told emphatically by parents or parent figures to leave home.
• Youth whose parents or guardians refused to allow them to return home after being absent.

- Youth whose parents or caretakers made no attempt to locate and return home after running away.
- Youth who were victims of parental abandonment or dessertion.[25]

The NISMART-1 divided thrownaways into Broad Scope Thrownaways and Policy Focal Thrownaways as follows:

- *Broad Scope Thrownaways* are youth who are thrown out of the household for at least an entire night. These thrownaways typically stay with a friend while away.
- *Policy Focal Thrownaways* are youth thrown out of the home without a safe place to stay while absent.[26]

For Broad Scope and Policy Focal Runaways, the missing youth are regarded as thrownaways due to lack of supervision or custody by parents or caretakers.

In the NISMART-2, a thrownaway episode is described as fitting one of the criteria as follows:

- The child is told by a parent or parent figure to leave home, no sufficient substitute care has been set in place by the parent or caretaker, and the youth is away from home for the night.
- The child away from the household is barred from returning home by a parent or parent figure, alternative housing has not been secured by the guardian, and the youth is away from home all night.[27]

Teenage homosexuals are particularly vulnerable for being thrownaways as youth "whose parents or guardians evict them from their homes, most often because they are gay or lesbian ... or otherwise considered ... as just too much trouble to deal with."[28] Over four in ten thrownaway or homeless youth are lesbian, gay, bisexual, or transgender (LGBT), according to one report. Gay teenagers are twice as likely to attempt suicide than heterosexual teenagers and much more likely to indulge in such risky behavior as alcohol and drug use — all of which makes life as a runaway or thrownaway that much more difficult for this population of youth.[29] (See Chapter 9 for further discussion on gay and lesbian runaways/thrownaways).

## Characterizing Thrownaway Youth

As with runaway youth, thrownaways tend to reflect children from all demographic groups and backgrounds. The risk of becoming a thrownaway is based less on particular characteristics of the individual forced to leave a household than on the relationship (or lack of) between the thrownaway and parents or guardians, and the willingness of caretakers to push out or desert their progeny or deny them reentry back into the household.

## THROWNAWAYS AND GENDER

Most available data does not differentiate thrownaways by gender. In NISMART-2, runaways and thrownaways were almost evenly divided between males and females in 1999, which is generally consistent with some other studies.[30] However, in the NISMART-1 findings based on 1988 data, thrownaways are studied apart from runaways; whereas girls are seen as more likely to be thrown out of the home than boys. In its household survey of Broad Scope Thrownaways, 53 percent were disproportionately female, with 47 percent male (see Figure 3.2).

Female thrownaways are most likely to be tossed out of their homes due to disputes with their mothers and behavioral problems. In a *San Diego Union Tribute* article, one account of a sixteen-year-old thrownaway named "Honey" is told:

> The fights with her mother started two years ago. When her mother [asked her] to help ... with household chores, she would refuse. "Then she'd go into

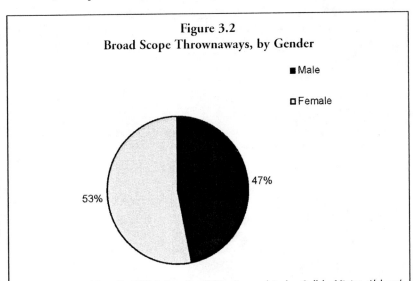

**Figure 3.2**
**Broad Scope Thrownaways, by Gender**

■ Male

□ Female

53%        47%

SOURCE: Derived from David Finkelhor, Gerald Hotaling, and Andrea Sedlak, *Missing, Abducted, Runaway, and Thrownaway Children in America, First Report: Numbers and Characteristics,* National Incidence Studies (Washington, D.C.: Office of Juvenile Justice and Delinquency Prevention, 1990), p. 145.

a tizzy and throw trash bags at me and tell me to pack up and get out," Honey recalls. So she did. "Once [my mother] put me on a bus to El Centro with $300 and told me to get a job and not come back.... I've been kicked out about six times."[31]

Male juveniles are more likely to be abandoned than female juveniles. According to the National Incidence Study's Community Professionals Study (CPS) of abandoned children, 52 percent of the thrownaways were boys, compared to 48 percent girls.[32] Abandonment is a form of child abuse and neglect, alongside "many other types of throwing away behaviors."[33] Estimates of child abandonment are thought to be fairly conservative due to the nature of this type of child maltreatment and insufficient knowledge by child health and law enforcement practitioners.[34]

## Thrownaways and Age

Most thrownaway youth are older teenagers. The NISMART-2 found that in 1999, 68 percent of runaways/thrownaways fell between the ages of fifteen and seventeen, while 28 percent were ages twelve to fourteen. Only 4 percent were under the age of eleven.[35] Other research has supported these findings, such as two comprehensive studies on street youth, which most experts on missing children contend are largely comprised of runaway and thrownaway children and young adults. The mean age of street youth in the Midwest Homeless and Runaway Adolescent Project (MHRAP) was 16.24,[36] while the Seattle Homeless Adolescent Research Project (SHARP) placed the mean age for street kids at 17.15.[37]

Similarly, in the NISMART-1, 84 percent of Broad Scope Thrownaways were ages sixteen and seventeen, with 16 percent of thrownaways falling between the ages of thirteen and fifteen (see Figure 3.3). There were no cases of thrownaway children age twelve or younger in the findings. However, other studies have found that some younger children are forced out of their homes by parents or guardians — often due to such issues as finances, substance abuse, mental problems, and illness as seen in the following example.

> Because of all the arguing and fighting between Jade and her older sister, their mother would have an asthma attack and sometimes end up in the hospital. This played a large part in the father's decision that one of the sisters should leave home and resulted in Jade being thrown out of home at the age of fourteen.[38]

Thrownaway youth who are abandoned by parents or guardians tend to be younger than those who are made to leave home. In the CPS, over half

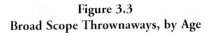

**Figure 3.3**
**Broad Scope Thrownaways, by Age**

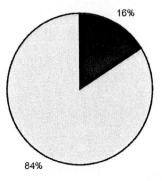

□ 16-17

SOURCE: Derived from David Finkelhor, Gerald Hotaling, and Andrea Sedlak, *Missing, Abducted, Runaway, and Thrownaway Children in America, First Report: Numbers and Characteristics,* National Incidence Studies (Washington, D.C.: Office of Juvenile Justice and Delinquency Prevention, 1990), p. 145.

the abandoned children were under the age of five. Almost half were between five and fourteen years of age, with just 1 percent age fifteen to seventeen.[39]

## THROWNAWAYS AND RACE/ETHNICITY

Thrownaways tend to be overwhelmingly white; however, minorities are overrepresented in data on runaways, thrownaways, and homeless youth. The NISMART-2 reported that 57 percent of the combined runaways/ thrownaways in 1999 were white, with blacks making up 17 percent, Hispanics 15 percent, and other groups 11 percent. In the NISMART-1 results, over 60 percent of the Broad Scope Thrownaways were white, with 24 percent black. Hispanics comprised 11 percent of thrownaways and others 3 percent (see Figure 3.4).

The CPS revealed that approximately half of the abandoned youth were white, including Hispanic whites. Thirty-one percent of youth abandoned were non-white, with race of the thrownaways unknown in 18 percent of the cases of abandonment.[40]

Supporting these results are a National Network for Youth (NN4Y) report that demonstrates the overrepresentation of racial and ethnic minority youth among the unaccompanied youth population, which includes minors who are not living with parents or caretakers. It cites a study of unaccompanied young people staying in youth shelters, in which 40.7 percent

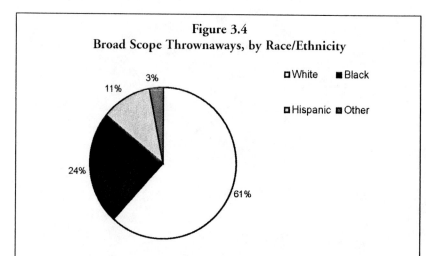

**Figure 3.4**
**Broad Scope Thrownaways, by Race/Ethnicity**

□ White    ■ Black

□ Hispanic ▨ Other

3%

11%

24%

61%

SOURCE: Derived from David Finkelhor, Gerald Hotaling, and Andrea Sedlak, *Missing, Abducted, Runaway, and Thrownaway Children in America, First Report: Numbers and Characteristics*, National Incidence Studies (Washington, D.C.: Office of Juvenile Justice and Delinquency Prevention, 1990), p. 250.

were black, 19.7 percent Hispanic, 31.7 percent white, and 7.9 percent of other groups.[41] Further NN4Y findings from street youth are consistent, revealing that blacks made up 27.4 percent and Hispanics 17.7 percent of the total, with whites accounting for 45.9 percent, and others 9 percent.[42]

The out of proportion rate of thrownaway and runaway minority youth as part of the homeless population relative to their numbers in the general population indicates greater at-risk factors for minorities that needs to be better understood to more effectively deal with the problem.

## THROWNAWAYS AND CLASS/INCOME

Research on thrownaways, in particular, relative to social class and family income is fairly limited. In general, children who are thrown out of the home come from families with any level of household income. However, according to NISMART-1, thrownaways are disproportionately likely to come from low income and high income families. As shown in Figure 3.5, 40 percent of Broad Scope Thrownaways came from families with a household income of $20,000 or less, while 35 percent had families with a household income of $40,000 and up. One-quarter of all thrownaways came from families where the household income was $10,000–$20,000, with just over one-quarter coming from families with a household income of $20,000–$40,000.

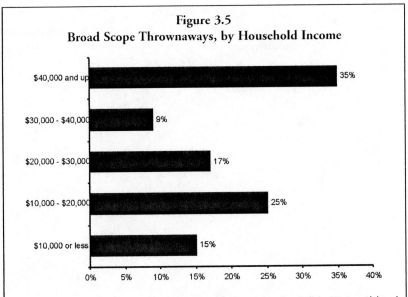

**Figure 3.5**
**Broad Scope Thrownaways, by Household Income**

SOURCE: Derived from David Finkelhor, Gerald Hotaling, and Andrea Sedlak, *Missing, Abducted, Runaway, and Thrownaway Children in America, First Report: Numbers and Characteristics*, National Incidence Studies (Washington, D.C.: Office of Juvenile Justice and Delinquency Prevention, 1990), p. 250.

Children who are abandoned as thrownaways tend to come from families with low household incomes. The CPS reported that 46 percent of abandoned children came from families where the household income level was $15,000 and under, with the household income level of 56 percent of abandoned youth unknown.[43]

## THROWNAWAYS AND FAMILY STRUCTURE

Though thrownaway youth come from broken and whole families, they tend to be tossed out of homes where there is only one parent or guardian more often than when both parents are present. NISMART-1 found that 29 percent of Broad Scope Thrownaways were pushed out of homes where there was only a single parent without a partner. In 12 percent of cases, thrownaways had neither parent present when forced to leave home. In 19 percent of instances of thrownaway youth did the thrownaway come from households where two parents were at home.[44]

When looking at abandoned thrownaways, the likelihood is greater that they will come from homes with both parents present. In the CPS, 37 percent of the abandoned youth lived at home with both parents before being discarded.[45] This group of thrownaways is underrepresented in relation to their population figures. Twenty-five percent of the abandoned youth resided in households with a mother only, and in 14 percent of the cases there was only a father present. In one out of four episodes of abandonment, the family structure was unknown (see also Chapter 2).

# Part III

## Why Youth Run Away

# 4
# Reasons for Running Away

An image of a rebellious, disrespectful, drug abusing, adventure seeking runaway is often portrayed in film and fiction. In reality, few runaways leave home for uncharted territory or thrills based on such reasoning. Most teenagers flee what should be a comfort zone due to problems that become intolerable or even life threatening. These include sexual abuse, physical violence, emotional abuse, neglect, family dysfunction, parental or guardian mental issues and/or substance abuse, economic distress, and other negative issues. Some youth termed runaways are, in fact, thrown out of the house by parents or caretakers for such reasons as teen substance abuse, disciplinary problems, and sexual orientation. Other teenagers leave home due to disagreements with parents over boundaries or independence, and conflicts with other family members. School problems can also be a strong factor in prompting youth to run away, as well as romantic involvement or friendships/associations that parents may dislike. Most teens leave home for more than one reason and often find that life away from home can be just as difficult and often worse. Yet repeat runners or those who fare poorly upon return home illustrate that a home life fraught with the same factors precipitating running away can put the youth at high risk to run again, in spite of the consequences.

## Precursors to Leaving Home

Children who leave home as runaways do so for a number of reasons. However, most runaways flee their households for multiple reasons that bring them to the pivotal point of departure. Though many youth run away on impulse, the causal elements for running away usually do not occur overnight, but rather build up over time, leading to the runaway episode.

Running away is most often associated with sexual and physical abuse at home. In one study, 47 percent of youth detached from parents or caretakers reported leaving home after being sexually abused, while 31 percent fled parental physical abuse.[1] A U.S. Department of Health and Human Services (HHS) report found that 46 percent of runaway and homeless youth had been the victims of physical abuse and 17 percent were victims of sexual abuse while at home.[2] According to the Justice Department's Second National Incidence Studies of Missing, Abducted, Runaway and Thrownaway Children (NISMART-2), in 1999, more than one in five runaway/thrownaway youth had been victims of physical or sexual abuse in the year preceding the episode of leaving home or were fearful of such maltreatment upon their return.[3]

A study of abused runaways found that females accounted for nearly 84 percent of those physically and sexually abused.[4] Research done at a runaway shelter found that the biological fathers tended to be the perpetrators most often for physical abuse, whereas stepfathers were more likely to be the sexual abuse offenders.[5] In another study, almost nine in ten sexually or physically abused runaway and homeless youth and nearly four out of ten youth who were victims of sexual abuse only while at home were victimized by a member of their own families.[6]

Teenage victims of both sexual and physical mistreatment at home tend to experience more personal, family, and school-related issues that can lead to running away than teens who were victims of only one type of abuse or the other, or were not abuse victims.[7] Runaway victims of sexual and physical abuse have been shown to be more likely to engage in substance abuse, suicidal behavior, require hospitalization for mental problems, and become prostituted youth.[8] Teenagers who experience physical and sexual maltreatment tend to be repeat runners and remain away from home for longer stretches of time than youth who are not abuse victims.[9]

Emotional abuse is also seen as a significant contributory factor for runaway behavior. According to an HHS study, 38 percent of youth who were runaways or homeless had suffered emotional abuse from a parent or guardian.[10] Such abuse can include psychological maltreatment and is often accompanied by physical and/or sexual abuse.[11]

Researchers have identified a number of other precursors to running away from home that relate to parent-child disagreements, poor or authoritarian parenting, family structure, teen pregnancy, promiscuity, child misbehavior and/or abuse of alcohol or drugs, schooling, and lifestyle, including:

- Mental illness such as severe depression and conduct disorder.[12]
- Serious conflicts involving one or more family members.

- Breakup of family through divorce or death.[13]
- Inability to get along with a stepparent or foster parents.[14]
- Rejection of a blended family or foster family.[15]
- Disagreements with parents over friendships, going to parties, staying out late, etc.[16]
- Overly strict rules that inhibit normal child development and interaction with peers.[17]
- Sexual orientation.[18]
- Parent neglect or abandonment.
- Parental failures to set acceptable boundaries, take necessary disciplinary measures, and gain proper respect.[19]
- Physically or mentally ill parents or guardians and related issues such as stress and medical expenses.[20]
- Negative parenting such as abusing drugs, domestic violence, and association with other abusive or deviant persons.[21]
- School problems such as fighting, poor grades, truancy, suspension, and dropping out.[22]
- The influence of persons outside the family, such as girlfriends or boyfriends, other runaways or delinquents; adult sexual exploiters, predators, or criminal elements.[23]

## SEXUAL ABUSE

The strong correlation between runaway youth and sexual abuse has been well documented.[24] Child sexual abuse can encompass a number of unlawful interfamilial or non familial sexual acts or circumstances involving a minor, including incest, molestation, rape, statutory rape, exhibitionism, voyeurism, and other forms of sexual exploitation. Children who are the victims of sexual abuse by parents, guardians, siblings or others within the household are much more likely to run from such maltreatment than juveniles who are not victimized by sexual abuse.[25]

Studies reveal that prevalence rates for sexual abuse are somewhere between 20–25 percent to more than 70 percent.[26] In the Midwest Homeless and Runaway Adolescent Project, 21 percent of the youth sampled had been the victims of sexual abuse prior to leaving home.[27] According to the Street Youth at Risk for AIDS (SYRA) study, 34 percent of the respondents reported having been sexually abused when at home.[28] Forty-two percent of the female and male youth in the Seattle Homeless Adolescent Research Project were victimized by child sexual abuse.[29]

Other research has supported the high incidence of sexual abuse victimization among runaways. The National Network of Runaway and Youth Services reported that 70 percent of runaways in shelters had been sexually molested or abused at home.[30] Ann Hayman, who created the Mary Magdalene Project in Los Angeles, asserted that female runaways, in particular, were often subjected to "lots of incest ... [and] lots of sexual battery."[31] Thirty-two percent of the girl runaways in Kimberly Tyler and associates' study of the effects of sexual abuse on runaway youth had been sexually molested before leaving home.[32] Two out of three prostituted runaways in Mimi Silbert's study were child abuse and incest victims[33]; while more than two in ten boys and girls in the Seattle Homeless Adolescent Research and Evaluation Project (SHARP) had been victimized by one type of sexual abuse or another while living at home.[34]

Not all sexually abused runaways left home specifically for that reason; though in most cases the molestation plays a big role in the decision to flee the unsafe and troubled environment. In a study analyzing the SYRA research, sexual abuse or rape was given as the reason for fleeing home for 34 percent of the street youth.[35] Thirty-eight percent of the female runaways and 16 percent of the male runaways in Nathanial Terrell's study said they ran away because of being sexually abused.[36] Though 17 percent of the youth in Les Whitbeck and Ronald Simons' study reported leaving home due to sexual abuse, almost 25 percent of the runaways indicated having actually been sexually abused.[37]

In many instances, sexual and physical abuse go hand in hand, often with other forms of maltreatment such as emotional or verbal abuse and neglect, increasing the odds that the victimized youth will run or be a repeat runner to escape or flee again from these damaging issues.

## VIOLENCE IN THE FAMILY

Family violence including child physical abuse, domestic violence, parent abuse, sibling abuse, and other forms of aggression have been linked to running away or being thrown out of the home. In particular, abusive behavior toward children increases the likelihood that such victims will leave home to escape the violence. In one study of runaways, 90 percent or more were said to have been the victims of severe child abuse.[38] Another study of teenage runaways found that 77 percent had been victimized by physical abuse before leaving home.[39] In an investigation of runaways and street kids staying in shelters, nearly half reported "physical harm or intense conflict by a family member as a chief contributing factor to becoming homeless."[40] Abuse and neglect are commonly cited by runaway and homeless youth as reasons for leaving home.[41]

Child physical abuse is often a persistent theme in runaway episodes and youth may run to keep from striking back at a loved one or having to endure more abuse. Such is the example of fourteen-year-old "Amy," who said candidly: "I ran away from home because I have a lot of problems with my mom — we fight a lot. And we get in physical fights, but I don't hit her because she's my mom."[42]

Youth who witness or experience domestic violence, which is often present in households where child abuse is ongoing, are also at high risk of becoming runaways. Domestic violence is defined as "a pattern of assaultive and coercive behaviors, including physical, sexual, and psychological attacks, as well as economic coercion, that adults or adolescents use against their intimate partners."[43] According to the American Medical Association, an estimated four million spouses are battered in the United States each year.[44] Murray Straus estimated that 65 percent of all married couples experienced intimate violence as victims or offenders, with 25 percent of a serious nature.[45]

Runaways who have been victims of domestic violence or abuse have a high risk of becoming prostituted youth. Researchers have reported that 44 percent to 77 percent of young streetwalkers left their households to escape violent homes or violence in the community.[46] Gary Yates and colleagues found that most female runaways who turned to prostitution had histories as victims of child abuse[47]; while Les Whitbeck and Danny Hoyt found a high rate of youth running away from home due to abuse, domestic violence, and neglect.[48]

Experts on runaway and homeless youth concur that abuse and other violence in the home are the biggest contributory factors in children making the decision to run from this environment.[49] In *Runaway Kids and Teenage Prostitution*, one instance of the devastating effect of domestic violence on runaway youth is described:

> Meet Julie.... She ran away from home when she was 12. She saw her dad beat and almost kill her mother, and two more wives after that.... She's seen the women in her father's life thrown down stairs, punched, choked. Good old dad also molested Julie. So much for a chance at life....[50]

## SUBSTANCE ABUSE

The use of alcohol and/or drugs by teenagers while living at home has been shown to be an important factor in circumstances that prompts them to run away or be thrown out of the home. According to a report from the National Survey on Drug Use and Health (NSDUH) in 2002, juveniles between the ages of twelve and seventeen who had left home as runaways within the past year were more likely than juveniles who had not to have consumed alcohol, used marijuana, or other illegal drugs such as cocaine/crack, heroin, hallucinogens, inhalants, or prescription drugs for nonmedical purposes.[51]

As shown in Figure 4.1, use of alcohol or illegal drugs over the past year was substantially higher among twelve to seventeen year old runaways than non runaways. The rate of alcohol use for runaways during the past twelve months was 50 percent, compared to 33 percent for youth who did not run away. Regarding illicit drug use, nearly twice as many runaways (27.8 percent) used marijuana within the past year as non-runaways (14.3 percent). A similar discrepancy existed for use of any illicit drugs aside from marijuana, with past year runaway use at 23.2 percent versus youth who did not run away from home at 12.4 percent.

Female runaways' past year use of alcohol, marijuana, and other illicit drugs tended to be higher than male runaways; while older teens (sixteen to seventeen) had the highest rate of marijuana or any other illegal drug use in the previous twelve months, followed in descending order by fourteen to

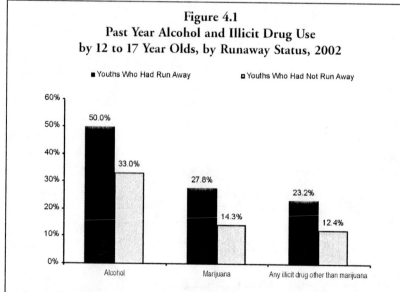

**Figure 4.1**
**Past Year Alcohol and Illicit Drug Use**
**by 12 to 17 Year Olds, by Runaway Status, 2002**

■ Youths Who Had Run Away          □ Youths Who Had Not Run Away

SOURCE: National Survey on Drug Use and Health, *The NSDUH Report*, "Substance Abuse Among Youths Who Had Run Away From Home" (July 2, 2004), http://www.oas.samhsa.gov/2k4/run Aways/runAways.htm.

fifteen year olds and twelve to thirteen year olds. When considering gender and age range, runaways had a higher rate of past year illicit drug use than juveniles who did not run away.[52]

Other research further reflects the strong relationship between runaway youth and substance abuse. As many as seven out of ten teenage runaways used drugs while living at home, according to one study.[53] Another study found that almost half the prostituted runaways were alcohol users prior to selling sexual favors.[54] Many runaway teens had already become dependent on alcohol or drugs before becoming street kids.[55] For some runaway substance abusers, drugs or alcohol enabled them to cope with serious problems while living at home, such as sexual abuse and physical abuse.[56]

Substance abuse by family members can also lead to a youth running away from home. A study by the Family and Youth Services Bureau (FYSB) of homeless runaways or those living in shelters found that 45 percent of the homeless runaways and 31 percent of the shelter runaways reported drug use by a member of the family in the month prior to the youth running away.[57] Among homeless runaways, about 24 percent of the drug users were biological fathers, 33 percent biological mothers, and around 35 percent were said to be stepparents. For the shelter runaway youth, about 19 percent of their biological fathers used drugs, 18 percent of their biological mothers, and around 27 percent of the stepparents. In a study of runaway prostitutes, parental substance abuse was listed by respondents as among the main problem experienced at home, significantly affecting their lives.[58]

## MENTAL ILLNESS

Mental illness such as anxiety, severe depression, conduct disorder, schizophrenia, and suicidal behavior have been seen as contributory factors in runaway behavior, though often in combination with other problems such as child abuse and neglect, sexual abuse, and substance abuse.[59] According to Carol Canton and David Shaffer's study of youth shelter runaways, 41 percent were characterized as depressed and antisocial, while 30 percent were seen as depressed, and 18 percent were considered antisocial.[60] In a study that compared runaways and non-runaways, 85 percent of the runaways were found to have suffered from clinical depression, with 21 percent of the runaways having serious mental health problems.[61] The runaways were four times as likely as non-runaways to have emotional problems.

In a survey of 455 teenage runaways in the Midwest, the researchers found that runaway youth were much more likely than teens who did not run away to suffer from conduct disorder, severe depression, post–traumatic stress disorder, and other mental health problems.[62] The study noted that 74 percent of the runaway males and 57 percent of runaway females had conduct disorder, well above the 15 percent teenage population at large. Furthermore, 43 percent of the females and 23 percent of the males exhibited post–traumatic stress disorder symptoms.

An FYSB study of shelter and homeless runaway youth found that 71 percent of the homeless runaways and 58 percent of the shelter runaways had spent some time in a psychiatric or mental facility.[63] In a study of 576 mostly black and Hispanic runaways at four publicly funded New York City residential runaway shelters, 37 percent had attempted suicide at some point, with 44 percent of this group having attempted to kill themselves within the past month.[64]

A number of studies on runaways have examined the relationship between child sexual abuse and suicide ideation or attempts. It has been found that runaway and homeless youth who had been victims of sexual abuse were two to four times more likely to attempt or conceive the notion of suicide than youth who had not been victimized by sexual abuse.[65] One study reported, based on findings from the AIDS Evaluation of Street Outreach Project Street Intercept, that street youth who had a history of being sexually abused had a three times higher likelihood of reporting suicide ideation or attempting suicide than non sexually abused youth.[66] Other studies found sexual abuse of runaway and homeless youth to be "a significant predictor in regression models predicting suicidal behavior."[67]

In research on maltreated runaways, P. David Kurtz contended that those who were victims of sexual and physical abuse were much more susceptible than runaway youth who were only physically abused and tended have lower self-esteem, depression, and suicidal tendencies.[68]

## Foster Care

Runaways from foster care do not always run away for the same reasons that other youth flee their homes, though many such teenagers may end up in foster care as a result of being repeat runners or other circumstances that often lead to running away such as being abused, displaying aggressive behavior or otherwise considered unmanageable. Foster care runaways typically have a history with the foster care system. As such, it is not unusual for youths to be placed with multiple foster homes, which can result in them "feeling disempowered and detached," increasing the chances of running away.[69]

According to a Congressional Research Service report on runaway and homeless youth, the three main reasons juveniles run away from foster care facilities are: (1) to "reconnect or stay connected to their biological families," irrespective of health or safety issues that may be present, (2) to "express their autonomy and find normalcy among sometimes chaotic events," and (3) to "maintain surrogate family relationships with non-family member."[70] The study found that youth care runaways were more likely than their non-runaway counterparts to be drug abusers and suffer from certain mental illnesses.[71]

In *Juvenile Runaways*, researcher Kelly Dedel identified a number of reasons why juveniles in the foster care system run away, including:

- To go home or to their communities to be amongst family, friends, and significant others.
- To get away from crowded conditions or find time alone.
- To draw attention and/or reinforce that caretakers are sincere in their concern.
- Flee from abusive personnel.
- Run from bullies or sexual harassers.
- As a protest against social worker's insufficient focus on their needs.
- As resistance to compulsory restrictions under the care system.[72]

Dedel suggests that the placement's environment itself within the substitute care can provide an inducement for residents to flee:

> Placements lacking structure and activities and those with overwhelmed staff who do not exercise their authority properly have higher rates of runaways than facilities with strong leadership, staff support, and juveniles involved in activities and setting rules.[73]

Many youth who run away from foster care end up in shelters. In a National Association of Social Workers survey, it was found that more than one out of five youth arriving at shelters came straight from foster care and over one in four youth had been in the care system the year before.[74] Nearly six in ten of the youth in shelters and more than seven in ten of the street youth had been in one or more of the following institutional facilities: foster care, group home, psychiatric hospital, juvenile detention, or jail.[75] One in four foster children will become homeless at some point within two to four years upon leaving foster care.[76]

## SEXUAL ORIENTATION ISSUES

Some youth run away or are thrown out of the home due to problems associated with sexual orientation/gender identity. Youths who identify themselves as lesbian, gay, bisexual, or transgender (LGBT) are especially vulnerable to become runaways, thrownaways, and street kids. Though there is no consensus on the number of LGBT teenage runaways, most experts believe that they constitute a large proportion of youth considered homeless in the United States. Some estimates from the mid 1980s to mid 1990s, placed the number of homeless youth who were gay or lesbian at between 3 percent and 10 percent.[77] However, researchers have since estimated that anywhere from 15 percent to as many as 50 percent of homeless youth may be LGBT.[78]

According to the National Gay and Lesbian Task Force, in conjunction with the National Coalition for the Homeless, of an estimated 1.6 million homeless youth in this country, "up to 42 percent identify as lesbian or gay, and a disproportionate number identify as bisexual or transgender."[79] In a study of "street-involved" and homeless youth, Michael Clatts and colleagues estimated 35 percent to be LGBT, with up to 50 percent of those labeled street youth identified as LGBT.[80]

Some city estimates of homeless lesbian, gay, or bisexual (LGB) youth correspond with national figures. In Seattle, the Commission on Children and Youth placed the number of homeless youth who identify as LGB at approximately 40 percent[81]; while in Decatur, Illinois, 42 percent of homeless youth surveyed were LGB.[82] Similarly, in Los Angeles, 25 percent to 35 percent of homeless youth identified as lesbian or gay, according to youth service providers.[83]

There is some debate over whether more LGBT youth leave home on their own or are thrown out. One study reported that more than one in four gay or lesbian teenagers were forced to leave home as a result of gender identity/sexual orientation.[84] Another study found that half of gay male teens received an adverse reaction from parents when coming out, with more than one-quarter of the youth being thrown out of the house as a consequence.[85] In her essay on homeless gay youth, Jenny Gable found that many "'out of the closet' teens face angry homophobic parents who throw them out of the house when they are fourteen or fifteen. These youths ... then end up in gay homeless shelters or counseling centers."[86]

However, other researchers have found that most teenagers with sexual orientation issues chose to leave home. For example, in a survey of 775 gay homeless teenagers in New York, San Francisco, and Denver, about 78 percent reported leaving home of their own accord, with only 16 percent being thrown out.[87] The survey did reveal that almost six in ten of the teens ran away from home as a result of family conflicts, and more than two in ten after being victims of abuse or rape.

While the majority of runaways leave home due to physical and sexual abuse and neglect, LGBT youth tend to be especially susceptible to such forms of victimization. One study found that around one in three lesbian or gay identified youth were victims of physical abuse perpetrated by a member of their family.[88] Other research has produced similar conclusions on familial physical and sexual violence aimed at LGBT youth, in relation to disclosure of their gender identity and sexual orientation.[89]

Other reasons attributed to gay and lesbian youth leaving home include[90]:

- Broken home or blended family issues.
- Uncaring or loving parents.
- Family instability and dysfunction.
- Substance abuse within family.
- Criminality or criminal justice issues in family.
- Autonomy.
- Religious beliefs.

## SCHOOL-RELATED ISSUES

Issues involving school can play a big role in a juvenile's decision to run away from home or substitute care. These include poor school performance, fighting, truancy, bullying, peer pressures, disciplinary measures, depression, substance abuse, gender identity, family pressures, and dropping out. Studies reveal that 13 percent of high school students have run away from home at some point in their lives,[91] while another 20 percent have seriously considered running away.[92] Poor school performance was found to be an important factor in the decision to run away for 12 percent of homeless youth living in Los Angeles.[93] Other research has indicated that more than one-third of street youth were forced to repeat a school year.[94]

In a study of homeless youth, it is noted that "educational failure can lead to either being kicked out for not having done well enough, or walking out for fear of being seen as a failure."[95] Either can lead to a child running away. In Emilie Smeaton's study of detached runaways, almost half the respondents had dropped out of school before the age of sixteen.[96] Some of the sample group were expelled from school and had not participated in any other type of schooling. A government-funded study found that 41 percent of the homeless youth respondents had dropped out of school prior to finishing high school.[97] Around 12 percent of school dropouts in the United States ran away from home on one or more occasions.[98]

Bullying in school can be harmful in many ways and result in the victim running away. In *Kids Who Commit Adult Crimes*, it was pointed out that about 5 percent of students between the ages of twelve and eighteen reported being bullied at least once within the past six months.[99] Such youth are more likely than students not being the victims of bullying to withdraw from school and leave home; with the risk higher for running away and becoming homeless when compounded with other school-related conflicts and problems such as child physical or sexual abuse, or sexual orientation troubles.[100]

## DESIRE FOR INDEPENDENCE AND ADVENTURE

Though most youth who leave the comfort and security of home do so to run from abuse, violence, neglect, and other problems; not all runaways are escaping intolerable or strained circumstances. Some run to be independent from their parents or guardians, and/or for the adventure that running away and being on your own may conjure up. Most children who fit into this category are older, more mature teenagers, who may have trouble with authority and constraints placed on their freedom of movement and activities.

In a study by Pamela Miller and colleagues of street youth, independence was identified as a significant dynamic in their becoming homeless.[101] Another study of runaway teenagers found that their initial aim was to "acquire a place to sleep and then look for adventure — get a crash pad and some kicks."[102] According to Les Whitbeck and Danny Hoyt, with respect to autonomy-minded homeless youth, "Precocious independence and early dependence on themselves rather than caretaker adults often occurred prior to youth running away."[103]

For many runaway adventurers, they seek the camaraderie, reassurance, and acceptance they often lack at home. This is typically accompanied by other things that increase the likelihood of one becoming a runaway or thrownaway, such as substance abuse, behavioral or disciplinary issues, physical or sexual abuse, and promiscuity. Unfortunately, most who fall in this category of runaway find they have left one problematic world only to enter another. This is aptly conveyed by prostitution researcher Robin Lloyd:

> The children who run look for companionship, friendship, and approval from those they meet. Many such youths are easy marks for gangs, drug pushers and pimps. Runaways often sell drugs or their bodies, and steal to support themselves.[104]

# Part IV

---

# After Leaving Home

# 5

# Where Runaway Youth Journey To

When children leave home, they do not always become street kids as is often portrayed in the media or Hollywood. Indeed, most youth who decide to leave home or are forced to leave do not wind up on the streets and turn to prostitution and other forms of delinquency and criminality in order to survive or fit in with their surroundings. Runaways tend to stay with those they know or can trust — usually peers or other family members. They typically return home after a short absence once things cool down. But if the issues that drove them away from what would normally be considered a comfort zone and warm environment are not adequately resolved, the youth is at risk to run away again. This could lead to repeat or chronic running away, street life, prostituted youth, and other negative consequences of being away from home, whether voluntarily or imposed upon them. Children who run away from home rarely have the luxury of charting their own course without potentially hazardous or life altering pitfalls along the way

## Staying Close to Home

Most children who leave home, whether voluntarily or involuntarily, do not go very far, choosing the comfort of familiarity over somewhere unknown or more frightening. According to the Second National Incidence Studies of Missing, Abducted, Runaway and Thrownaway Children (NIS-MART-2), 83 percent of runaways/thrownaways in 1999 never left the state.[1] Nearly seven in ten traveled fifty miles or less from home, while almost eight in ten youth during runaway/thrownaway episodes traveled no more than a

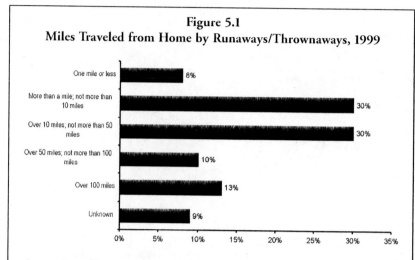

**Figure 5.1**
**Miles Traveled from Home by Runaways/Thrownaways, 1999**

SOURCE: Derived from Heather Hammer, David Finkelhor, and Andrea J. Sedlak, *Runaway/Throw-naway Children: National Estimates and Characteristics*, NISMART Bulletin Series (Washington, D.C.: Office of Juvenile Justice and Delinquency Prevention, 2002), p. 7.

hundred miles from their house (see Figure 5.1). Only 13 percent traveled more than a hundred miles away from home during a runaway or thrown-away episode.

Other research has found similar results on runaways remaining proximate to home. In Laurie Schaffner's quantitative study of teenage runaways, 88 percent had fled less than a hundred miles.[2] Similarly, in a survey of young people at seventeen runaway and homeless youth programs across the country, Therese van Houten and Gary Golembiewski found that 72 percent of the respondents lived in the same locality before leaving home.[3] In one such example, the *Oregonian* newspaper reported that a fourteen-year-old boy ran away with his six-year-old sister overnight, stealing their father's pickup, before they were caught by police and taken into custody.[4]

Some research suggests that runaways who stay close to home indicates they did not want to leave home and their comfort zone in the first place, and hope to reconcile differences with their parents or caretakers. Indeed, Schaffner found that the majority of runaways "tried not to run away" and resisted fighting with parents and breaking rules, preferring to preserve family bonds, but a lack of love between the runaway and parent(s) made it difficult to stay.[5]

For some runners, leaving home is less about truly wanting to get away from family problems per se, but rather is an attention-seeking move to get a response out of parents when feeling lonely, ignored, neglected, or unwanted.[6] Robert Emerson spoke of running away as a "last resort" for many teenagers, when all other avenues for remaining at home had failed.[7] Tim Brennan and colleagues held that the breakdown of the family bond was significant in the behavior or runaways,[8] while Schaffner argued that runaways were seeking relationships and an atmosphere that offered safety, describing it as a "'phoenix of connection' rising out of the ashes of disintegrating family relationships."[9]

## Running Far from Home

Though the vast majority of runaways stay within close proximity to their families when they leave home, some venture far away, even to other states. Of an estimated 1.7 million runaway/thrownaway episodes reported by NISMART in 1999, only around 210,000 involved journeying farther than one hundred miles from home.[10] These youths are typically older and often run away for independence, adventure, partying, and romance; but also leave home to escape abuse, family dysfunction, and other circumstances deemed intolerable.[11]

Many teenagers who run far from home make their way to big cities were runaway and other homeless youth congregate such as New York, Los Angeles, Portland, and San Francisco.[12] They find varying degrees of support and camaraderie, as well as encountering street-wise youth, some of whom have become hardened enough to show them the ropes and recruit the runaway into a street life that can include substance abuse, drug dealing, prostitution, and other self-destructive behavior and victimization.[13]

A typical example of a long distance rebellious runner can be seen as follows:

> With only a Swiss Army knife and the clothes on his back, fourteen-year-old Jascha Ephraim made a ... "spur of the moment" decision — a hasty, impulsive beginning to the days of "total debauchery and mayhem" that would follow. Fueled by a flare for rebellion, Ephraim, a freshman at the time, decided to run away from home in the fleeting moments before an Amtrak train would begin its journey to New York City, more than 200 miles away.[14]

## Where Do Runaways Go?

Unlike the stereotype that runaways automatically take to the street as homeless individuals upon leaving home, become streetwalkers or live under bridges, the reality is that most youth who run from or are thrown out of their homes find refuge with friends and relatives. In Emilie Smeaton's study of twenty-three runaways, all but two stayed with friends in their own age group or with adults, while away from home.[15] For the most part, these individuals with whom the runaway is acquainted are accommodating, at least on a temporary basis. This generally gives the runner a safe place to stay while assessing the situation and what happens next. In many of these runaway cases, the parents or guardians are aware of where the runaway is located and, as such, may not consider them to be missing to the level of notifying authorities.[16]

Not all "friends" who give a runaway shelter are above board with the person's health and welfare in mind as illustrated in the following account:

> Jason, aged fourteen, moved in with older friends who took his wages off him, involved him in a situation where he was beaten up by five adult men and locked him in a cupboard under the stairs when they wanted him out of the way.[17]

For runaways who do not return home soon or otherwise wear out their welcome, they may wind up staying at shelters temporarily or off and on. Some teenagers, by choice or circumstances, become literally homeless and live in abandoned buildings, alleys, parks, under bridges, and on the streets, where survival can lead to taking drastic measures including panhandling, "survival sex," theft, dealing in drugs, and other high-risk behaviors.[18] In some instances, runaways or thrownaways find shelter with people who do not have their best interests at heart, such as pimps, pedophiles, and drug dealers.[19]

## How Do Runaways Get Where They Are Going?

There is no uniform way for a child planning to run away in terms of getting from point A to point B. On the contrary, as the vast majority of runaways decide to break from home impetuously, albeit usually with one or more precipitating actions, typically little forethought goes into the means for running away. As such, runaways depart from home in every possible way, including by foot, stealing (or borrowing) the family automobile, taking a bus or train, and even flying.[20] Some runaways count on rides from friends who they may stay with or help facilitate the runaway episode. Many runaways may use multiple modes of transportation to get around, especially the longer staying away from home persists.

Whether the ultimate destination is near or far, or even unknown at the time of departure, for most runaways there is only the desire to bolt from their troubles, looking more toward the past or present than future. Such future is often fraught with perils and struggles to make ends meet. Not too surprisingly, most runaways leave home with little money or a clear plan for making enough to sustain them. Without the support of others, they may have to resort to any means necessary to feed themselves and provide shelter. The same is true as it relates to the runaway getting from place to place during the occurrence of running away and returning home.

## How Long Do Runaways Remain Away from Home?

Whatever their reasons for leaving home, the vast majority of runaways return home within one week's time. According to NISMART-2, 99.6 percent of the runaways in their research had returned home by the time the data for the study was amassed.[21] More than three-fourths of runaways/thrownaways were back at home or in substitute care such as foster homes in less than a week (see Figure 5.2). Around one in five runners or thrownaways returned home in under twenty-four hours. Fifteen percent were gone

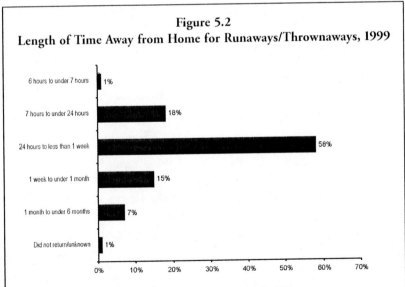

**Figure 5.2**
**Length of Time Away from Home for Runaways/Thrownaways, 1999**

- 6 hours to under 7 hours — 1%
- 7 hours to under 24 hours — 18%
- 24 hours to less than 1 week — 58%
- 1 week to under 1 month — 15%
- 1 month to under 6 months — 7%
- Did not return/unknown — 1%

(0% to 70%)

[a] Estimate is the result of too few sample cases to be considered reliable.

Source: Derived from Heather Hammer, David Finkelhor, and Andrea J. Sedlak, *Runaway/Thrownaway Children: National Estimates and Characteristics*, NISMART Bulletin Series (Washington, D.C.: Office of Juvenile Justice and Delinquency Prevention, 2002), p. 7.

for between one week and less than a month, while 7 percent of the runaway/thrownaway episodes lasted for between one month and under six months in duration. There were less than 1 percent of runaways who never returned home or for which there was no information.

Another study found that half of runaway teens came back home in less than a day, with most of the runaways home within a few days.[22] According to writer Kelly Dedel, runaways who remain away from home "for longer periods of time tend to cycle through a series of temporary stays with friends and relatives, a practice called 'couch surfing.'"[23] The longer children on the run are away from home, the more likely they are to become homeless, live in squalor, and encounter various obstacles to their health and welfare, as well as staying on the right side of the law.

Such is the case of "Kevin," who started running away at age thirteen and found shelter in

> trash bins, abandoned buildings, electrical meter rooms, in strip malls and under bridges.... He slept in an abandoned warehouse in Liberty City, next to railroad tracks strewn with garbage, and on the roof of a Lauderhill strip mall.... He bathed in pools at apartment complexes when no one was around and befriended other homeless people.... He also stole to buy food or drugs.... He was beaten in the head and knees with a shotgun in a fight with drug dealers in Lauderhill when he was 17.[24]

Researchers have found that after being on the streets for two weeks, three out of four runaways will find themselves involved in high-risk behaviors, situations, and exploitation such as prostitution, pornography, substance abuse, and other criminality and victimization.[25]

## Repeat Runaways

Some runaways leave home or institutional care more than once and often a number of times. These are called repeat runners and can result in chronic leaving home or running away for good to become street kids or homeless youth. Researchers have found that recurring runaways are more likely than single time runaways to leave home related to such unresolved issues as family dysfunction, school problems, substance abuse, neglect, and the judicial system.[26] The fact that these youth return home only to run away once more illustrates that their needs are not being met within the household and problems may actually get worse, often propelling them to leave home again.

In a study by Ruby Martinez of twenty-three teenage runaways from the Midwest who were being held in a detention center and had run away from home for a minimum of two nights more than once, three major factors were identified in their habitual running away: (1) changing their present circumstances, (2) establishing new associations, and (3) learning from their experiences.[27] All the participants in the study had run away to escape a disagreeable or dangerous environment, while most had experienced violence, substance abuse, and neglect at home.

According to data from the National Runaway Switchboard for the years between 2000 and 2005, nearly three in ten callers were repeat runners, having run away from home an average of four times (see Figure 5.3). Comparatively, nearly six in ten runners had not run away from home previously, while the previous experience of the caller was unknown for more than one in ten calls to the hotline.

An all too familiar scenario is the account of "Eva," a habitual runaway who, at fourteen, had fled from an abusive, alcoholic mother and then from a sexually abusive crack house of a friend:

> I had gone down to the police station to turn in this guy for raping me and ... they pulled out my CHINS warrant [CHINS is the Department of Social Service acronym for child in need of services; in some states it is termed PINS, person in need of services], so my parents came down and got me. I went back

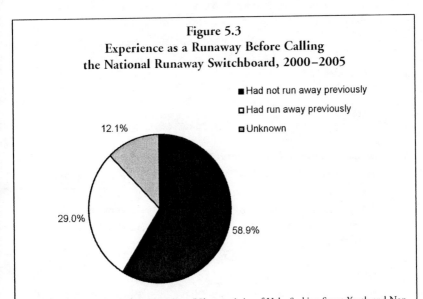

**Figure 5.3**
**Experience as a Runaway Before Calling**
**the National Runaway Switchboard, 2000–2005**

■ Had not run away previously
□ Had run away previously
▨ Unknown

12.1%

29.0%

58.9%

SOURCE: Derived from Alma C. Molino, "Characteristics of Help-Seeking Street Youth and Non-Street Youth," 2007 National Symposium on Homelessness Research, March 1–2, 2007, http://aspe.hhs.gov/hsp/homelessness/symposium07/molino/index.htm.

to my house and I wasn't there for very long. I was there for a few days ... and then I ran away again.[28]

Children who run away repeatedly from home for issues ranging from behavioral to drug use to abuse are often placed in juvenile facilities or substitute care such as foster homes, boarding schools, or juvenile detention centers. Studies show that, in fact, juveniles living in institutional facilities are much more likely to run away than those who live at home, and comprise as many as half of the repeat runners that law enforcement are aware of.[29]

In a study by the Vera Institute of Justice of youth who were recidivist runaways from foster care in New York, referred to as "going AWOL," it was found that the AWOLs were "concentrated among a small group of adolescents who run more than once, and that most AWOLs are from congregate care settings."[30] Another Vera study of chronically AWOL youth in foster care found that most stayed with friends without revealing their AWOL status, and ran away due to real or imagined placement issues.[31]

The instability and detachment of living in an institutional setting increases the risk of such juveniles running away time after time. Schaffner points out that "youths who come under the jurisdiction of the juvenile social service system face a great deal of shuffling. Caseworkers, probation officers, social workers, and counselors change constantly [with runaways typically expressing] frustration and feelings of impermanence and disconnectedness."[32] The lack of strong emotional attachment to those caring for them in juvenile facilities makes recurrent running away by juveniles in substitute care easier.[33]

## When Runaways Return Home

Fortunately almost all runaways return home sooner or later, though not always willingly. Some return home with the same behavioral or other issues that drove them away, while others are brought back to a household where they have been abuse victims. Other runaways come back to juvenile care facilities and find that problems have not changed since they left. Consequently, such runaways are at risk of becoming repeat runners, should the causes for running away be ignored or downplayed by parents, caretakers, or authorities.

Further, even runaway youth who have been absent for only a short time may still have gone through various negative experiences such as hunger, sleeplessness, mental issues, substance abuse, sexual assault, survival sex, exploitation, and fear. These areas must be addressed in getting the runaway back to a point of health and normalcy, along with confronting the precursors to running from home through communication, counseling, support, not affixing blame, and mutual cooperation in reducing the possibility of a recurrent runaway episode.

# 6

# Runaways and Police Contact

Runaway youth often manage to avoid law enforcement as they navigate a path fraught with potential hazards and unpredictability. Around one-third of runaways come into contact with police, meaning that roughly two-thirds of runaway youth have no such contact. Less than one in ten children are taken into custody as runaways; though others are arrested for such things as prostitution, drug- or alcohol-related offenses, truancy, curfew and loitering law violations, or other offenses Though the welfare of missing children is of concern to the police, the reality is that runaway children are not a high priority like abducted children, abused children, or other types of police duties. There is quite a bit of discretion where it concerns police involvement in runaway cases, based on such issues as youth reported missing and degree of risk for victimization or criminality. Police perception, community involvement, personal biases, other investigations, and resources can also play important factors. Police are disproportionately more likely to be involved in runaway cases where youth flee from substitute care or juvenile facilities than those who run from home. Moreover, the police are often unaware that children have run away, been discarded by parents or caretakers, or the circumstances involved, such as child abuse or other endangerment, making the task of locating runaways and returning them to a safe environment that much more difficult.

## Runaways and the Police

The relationship between runaways and the police can be complicated. A runaway youth's contact with law enforcement generally comes through the police looking into cases of missing children, discovering them during regular patrols, investigating delinquency and criminal behavior, and intervening in instances where a runaway has been victimized or is in danger of such. Actions taken on the part of the police in dealing with a runaway include taking the youth into custody for the purpose of returning them home or placement in a juvenile facility, or arresting them for violating criminal laws or committing status offenses, which apply only to juveniles. The nature of police-runaway contact depends upon a number of factors such as reports of missing youth, type of runaway episode, desire of parents or guardians for locating and returning the youth home or placing elsewhere for the child's safety, the type of runaway episode, police department size, and the local laws that deal with runaways.

About one in three runaways have contact with police at some point. According to the Second National Incidence Studies of Missing, Abducted, Runaway and Thrownaway Children (NISMART-2), based on data gathered from the National Survey of Adult Caretakers, National Household Survey of Youth, and Juvenile Facilities Study, an estimated 539,100 runaways/thrownaways had police contact in 1999. Sixty-eight percent of runaways/thrownaways, or more than 1.1 million, had no contact with law enforcement.[1]

The NISMART-2 reveals the characteristics of police contact with runaway and thrownaway youth. In nearly three in ten cases, the reason for contact was locating a missing child. The main reasons given for not contacting police include knowing the runaway's location, did not believe the police were needed, the child had not been missing long enough, the runaway was expected to return home, and fear that the child would get in trouble or be arrested.[2] It has also been found that some parents do not report their child running away because of a negative experience associated with reporting a previous runaway incident to the authorities.[3]

## REPORTING OF RUNAWAY YOUTH

Police investigations and taking runaway youth into custody often depend on reports of missing children by parents or caretakers. The National Incidence Studies found that an estimated 40 percent of police involvement in runaway cases is the result of reports of runaway children by their parents or guardians.[4] Law enforcement agencies investigate runaway cases much more often than family abductions, another form of missing children. In a study of police file reports of youth who are missing from home, the ratio of runaway cases to family abductions was 55 to 1.[5] Because many runaways are, in fact, thrownaways, these children are generally not reported to be missing by parents who do not wish for them to be located. Consequently, these runaways are often unknown to police and are more likely to run into trouble as crime victims or be arrested for prostitution, alcohol or drug violations, or other offenses apart from running away.[6]

## RESPONDING TO RUNAWAY CASES

The police response to reports of runaway children is contingent on a number of factors, including the extent of parental concern, information given on the runaway, other police investigations, police department policies, subjectivity, and risk assessment. In many instances, police may see a runaway case as less of a police matter and more of a social work investigation. As a result, unless the runaway episode is perceived to be an immediate crisis, it may be given lower priority than other duties by some law enforcement agencies.[7] The bigger the police department, the more likely it will have policies and procedures in place for dealing more efficiently with runaway cases.[8] In most police agencies, a higher priority is given to reports of missing children who are very young or thought to be victims of kidnapping or foul play.

Studies indicate that most reports of runaway youth can be officially made without waiting periods. A survey of police departments found that only 2 percent of large police agencies had waiting periods before reports of children running away became official.[9] In more than 75 percent of reported runaway cases, a police officer is sent to the house of a suspected runaway to take a report.[10] The police response from there can vary from department to department. Findings on police procedures and policies in responding to cases of runaways can be seen as follows:

- Sixty-three to 75 percent of police request a photograph of the runaway, names of friends or acquaintances, and other pertinent information.
- Twenty percent of runaway cases lead to an APB (All Points Bulletin).
- In around 75 percent of the runaway cases, police make at least one other contact with the parent or guardian after the initial report.
- Fifty-eight percent of the time parents of runaways are given a case number by police.
- Ten percent of the initial police response results in other officers being brought in on the runaway or missing person investigation.
- Family characteristics such as gender, race, ethnicity, class, and income have little relative impact on police handling of runaway cases.[11]

## Homeless Youth and the Police

Police contact with homeless youth is somewhat limited, given the number of street kids and insufficient police resources for investigating the nature of their homelessness. In general, law enforcement agencies are more inclined to refer runaway and thrownaway youth cases to social service agencies more equipped to deal with them. These include foster homes and group homes for abandoned or thrownaway children. Only around two out of ten police departments report having written policies for handling cases involving homeless youth.[12]

Police most often make contact with unreported street youth while on patrol, or if the homeless children have been victimized or committed a crime, or need medical attention.[13] Difficulties occur for many police departments in deciding what to do with homeless runaways when taken into custody, given that the circumstances for their becoming homeless are often unclear or suspect. Nearly two-thirds of police departments surveyed reported a number of obstacles to either returning runaway youth home or placing them in protective care facilities. These include:

- A runaway youth's individual characteristics such as age, mobility, and independence.
- Running away is a status offense rather than a criminal offense.
- Thrownaway children's parents or caretakers often tend to be uncooperative.
- There is a lack of shelters for homeless youth.
- Returning a runaway or thrownaway to an abusive environment.
- The runaway youth's involvement in criminal activities.[14]

## Runaway Laws and Youth in Custody

Police arrest of runaways and keeping them in custody are subject to various and sometimes disparate local, state, and federal laws, impeding the effectiveness of handling runaway cases. Some laws, for example, prohibit police questioning of juveniles without the presence of parents or legal guardians, who may be the root of problem for a runaway, such as child sexual abuse.[15] In most states, runaway children can only be detained for a limited amount of time. This usually ranges from three to twelve hours for in-state custody of runaways and up to seventy-two hours for out of state runaways.[16]

About 40 percent of police departments report the lack of ability to hold runaway youth to be a significant factor in the successful disposition of such cases.[17] This is particularly true for recidivist runaways and runaway youth from other jurisdictions where correct identification or return of a runaway might be all but impossible in the time allowed. Most law enforcement departments prefer to be selective in holding runaway children on a case by case basis, if they were legally permitted to, due to a lack of police personnel and inadequate resources.[18]

## Arrests of Runaway Youth

Though the majority of runaways never have any contact with police and even less are arrested, tens of thousands of runaway youth are arrested each year, with other runaway teenagers arrested for related offenses such as prostitution, substance abuse related offenses, and petty crimes.[19] Bringing runaway youth into the juvenile justice system through arrests and taking them into protective custody or detention has proven to be problematic, often doing more harm than good in adversely affecting the runaway through labeling, racial profiling, suicidal tendencies, interaction with delinquent youth, and other implications.[20]

According to the Federal Bureau of Investigation's (FBI) annual online publication, *Crime in the United States, 2007 (CIUS)*, its data drawn from the Uniform Crime Reporting Program (UCR), there were an estimated 108,879 arrests of persons under age eighteen as runaways in this country in 2007.[21] Since some of the runaways were recidivists, the *CIUS* statistics compile the number of arrests reported by law enforcement agencies instead of number of persons arrested. The rate of runaway arrests was 36.6 per 100,000 inhabitants — exceeding that of some crimes commonly associated with running away, such as prostitution and commercialized vice, and vagrancy.[22]

The potential harm in arresting a runaway and failure to adequately deal with them can be seen in the following example of a teenage victim of suicide:

> On a Saturday night ... Kathy Robbins, a 15-year-old girl [runaway] from Glenn County, California, was arrested.... She was taken in handcuffs to a 54-year-old cell in Glenn County's adult jail. Four days after she was arrested, at a juvenile court hearing, a judge refused to release her to a juvenile detention facility. On that day, still isolated and alone in an adult jail cell, Kathy Robbins twisted a bed sheet around her neck, and hanged herself from the rail of the top bunk bed.[23]

## ARRESTS OF RUNAWAYS BY AGE

All individuals arrested as runaways are minors under the age of eighteen. Arrest data on runaways is consistent with other findings on runaway youth and age. Arrests as runaways tend to be lowest among younger teenagers and highest for older teenagers, declining at age seventeen with adulthood approaching. Most arrestees are fifteen- and sixteen-year-olds, according to the *CIUS* (see Figure 6.1). In 2007, 53 percent of runaway arrestees totaling 43,735 were age fifteen to sixteen. Nearly 32 percent of runaway arrestees, or 26,250, were under the age of fifteen. Arrests for running away peaked at age sixteen. Just over 15 percent of all persons arrested as runaways, or 12,474, were seventeen years of age.

Though the bulk of arrests for running away from home at 65,584 were of juveniles age thirteen to sixteen, there were still more than 4,400 youths age twelve and under arrested as runaways, including over 600 who were under ten years of age in 2007.[24] This illustrates that the circumstances that compel juveniles to flee a home environment can begin early in life, making youth of all ages susceptible to running away and facing the hardships associated with being homeless, including arrest.

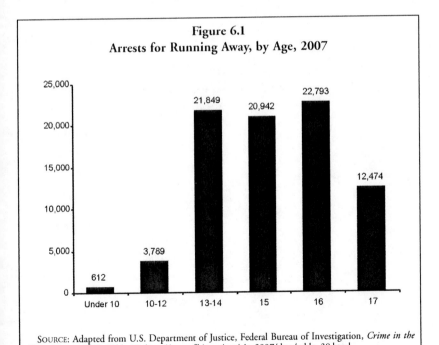

**Figure 6.1
Arrests for Running Away, by Age, 2007**

SOURCE: Adapted from U.S. Department of Justice, Federal Bureau of Investigation, *Crime in the United States, 2007*, Table 38, http://www.fbi.gov/ucr/cius2007/data/table_38.html.

## ARRESTS OF RUNAWAYS BY SEX

In spite of the fact that roughly the same number of males and females run away from home, female runaways are more likely to face arrest than male runaways. In 2007, there were 46,265 arrests of females for running away, compared to 36,194 arrests of male as runaways.[25] Females made up 56.1 percent of total arrests as runaways, while males comprised of 43.9 percent of the runaway arrests (see Figure 6.2). The percentage of overall arrests was more than four times as high for female runaway arrestees as males arrested as runaways.[26] The ratio of female-to-male arrests for running away was 1.3 to 1.

When considering age and sex of runaway arrestees, older females are more likely to be arrested than older males; while younger males are more likely to be arrested for running away than younger females. The *CIUS* data indicates that for runaway arrestees age thirteen and up, more females were arrested than males; whereas males were arrested more often as runaways under the age of thirteen than females. Both male and female runaways were arrested most often at age sixteen.[27]

Experts in juvenile deviant behavior attribute the overall disparity in female-male arrests as runaways to various reasons, including a higher incidence of child victimization experienced by runaway girls than runaway boys, a stronger desire for female teenagers to want to strike out on their own than male teens, police discretion in arrests that favors targeting female

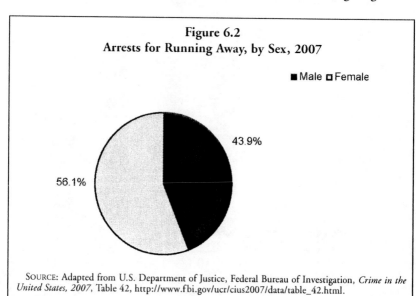

**Figure 6.2**
**Arrests for Running Away, by Sex, 2007**

■ Male □ Female

43.9%

56.1%

SOURCE: Adapted from U.S. Department of Justice, Federal Bureau of Investigation, *Crime in the United States, 2007*, Table 42, http://www.fbi.gov/ucr/cius2007/data/table_42.html.

runaways more often in order to rescue them from an unsafe environment, and more juvenile male runaways being arrested for other offenses than juvenile female runaways.[28]

Female youth are much more likely to have run away from abusive homes than male youth. A recent survey of females in runaway shelters found that over 70 percent admitted to running away from home as a result of sexual abuse, compared to almost 40 percent of the male runaways at the shelter.[29]

## ARREST OF RUNAWAYS BY RACE

Most juveniles arrested as runaways are white; however black juveniles are disproportionately likely to be arrested as runaways. The *CIUS* reveals that in 2007, 69.3 percent of persons under the age of eighteen arrested in this country for running away were white (see Figure 6.3). Blacks younger than eighteen constituted 27.2 of the runaway arrestees, compared to their 15 percent share of the juvenile population in the United States. Native American juveniles, consisting of American Indians or Alaskan Natives, represented 2.1 percent of those arrested as runaways, with Asian or Pacific Islander minors accounting for 1.4 percent of the total. The rate of white

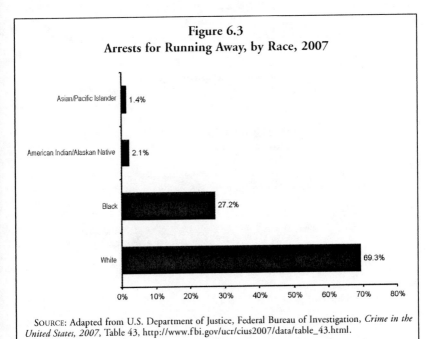

**Figure 6.3**
**Arrests for Running Away, by Race, 2007**

SOURCE: Adapted from U.S. Department of Justice, Federal Bureau of Investigation, *Crime in the United States, 2007*, Table 43, http://www.fbi.gov/ucr/cius2007/data/table_43.html.

juvenile arrests as runaways tends to be higher in nonmetropolitan counties than metropolitan counties, whereas the reverse is true for black juvenile arrests.[30]

The *CIUS* does not offer arrest data on Hispanic runaways. However, some research has suggested that Hispanics in general have a high rate of arrest and incarceration.[31] Studies indicate that around 15 percent of runaway youth are Hispanic, slightly above their population figures.[32]

## ARRESTS OF RUNAWAYS BY COMMUNITY SIZE

Runaway youth have the highest rate of arrests in cities among community sizes. As seen in Figure 6.4, the rate of runaway arrests per 100,000 persons in 2007 was 40.4 in cities, compared to 32.2 in metropolitan counties, 29.4 in suburban areas, and 17.4 in nonmetropolitan counties. This is not particularly surprising, given the larger population groups in cities and metropolitan counties. It does give some perspective, though, on the differential rates for comparison and consideration of influential circumstances, such as police discretion and precursors for running away that may be greater in one type of community size than another.

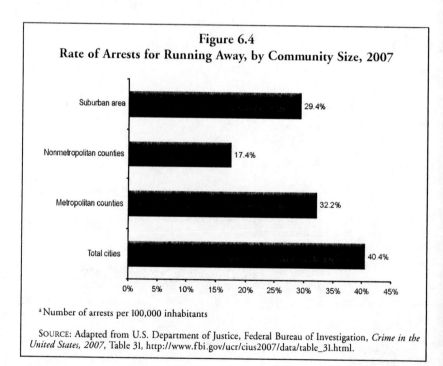

**Figure 6.4**
**Rate of Arrests for Running Away, by Community Size, 2007**

[a] Number of arrests per 100,000 inhabitants

SOURCE: Adapted from U.S. Department of Justice, Federal Bureau of Investigation, *Crime in the United States, 2007*, Table 31, http://www.fbi.gov/ucr/cius2007/data/table_31.html.

The majority of runaways, regardless of the community type they ran away from, have in common "running into a myriad of problems and illegal situations while away from home."[33] In one such example of a fourteen-year-old who fled from a suburban household, his take on the experience was: "We got into this group made up of runaway and homeless kids where there were a lot of hallucinogens offered. There was a lot of violence, most of it deliberate. There were a lot of drugs and just brain-numbing noise."[34] This runaway was ultimately arrested by police and returned home.

## Trends in Arrests for Runaway Youth

Official data indicates that overall arrests for running away are on the decrease in the United States. According to the *CIUS* ten-year arrest trends, between 1998 and 2007, runaway arrests fell more than 36 percent (see Figure 6.5). However, the decrease in arrests for running away was only 9.4 percent for the five-year arrest trends between 2003 and 2007, indicating the rate of decline was slowing (see Figure 6.6).

Arrest trends by sex reveal that the decrease in runaway arrests is higher for females than males. As shown in Figure 6.7, between 1998 and 2007,

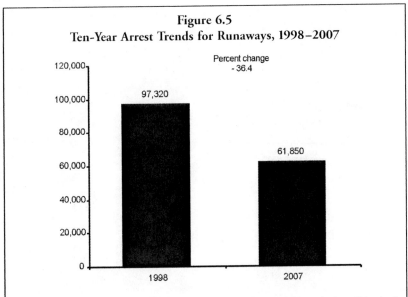

**Figure 6.5**
**Ten-Year Arrest Trends for Runaways, 1998–2007**

SOURCE: Adapted from U.S. Department of Justice, Federal Bureau of Investigation, *Crime in the United States, 2007*, Table 32, http://www.fbi.gov/ucr/cius2007/data/table_32.html.

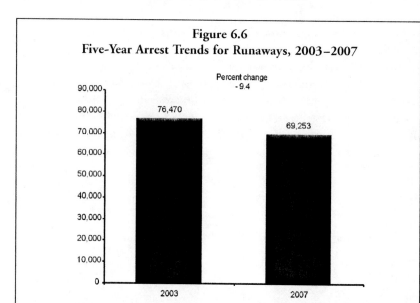

**Figure 6.6**
**Five-Year Arrest Trends for Runaways, 2003–2007**

SOURCE: Adapted from U.S. Department of Justice, Federal Bureau of Investigation, *Crime in the United States, 2007*, Table 34, http://www.fbi.gov/ucr/cius2007/data/table_34.html.

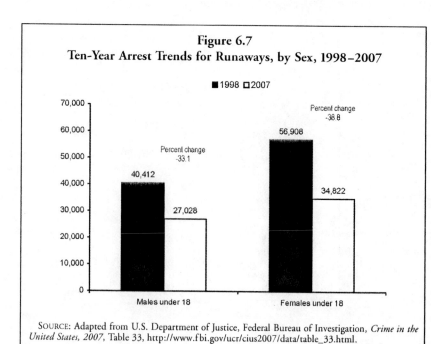

**Figure 6.7**
**Ten-Year Arrest Trends for Runaways, by Sex, 1998–2007**

SOURCE: Adapted from U.S. Department of Justice, Federal Bureau of Investigation, *Crime in the United States, 2007*, Table 33, http://www.fbi.gov/ucr/cius2007/data/table_33.html.

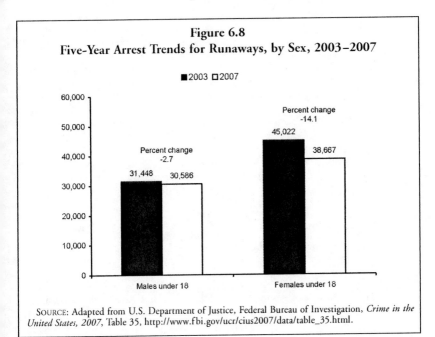

**Figure 6.8**
**Five-Year Arrest Trends for Runaways, by Sex, 2003–2007**

■2003 □2007

SOURCE: Adapted from U.S. Department of Justice, Federal Bureau of Investigation, *Crime in the United States, 2007*, Table 35, http://www.fbi.gov/ucr/cius2007/data/table_35.html.

female arrests as runaways dropped nearly 39 percent, compared to a decrease of male arrests by just over 31 percent. The differential is even greater for the five-year arrest trends. From 2003 to 2007, runaway female arrestees fell by more than 14 percent, while runaway male arrests declined by less than 3 percent (see Figure 6.8).

The higher rate of decrease in female arrests for running away might indicate that more females are beginning to find alternative means for dealing with such issues as family dysfunction and disciplinary problems. Conversely, some studies indicate that overall females are more likely to run away from home than males due to perhaps having a lower threshold of tolerance for such issues as sexual and physical abuse.[35]

## Arrests for Offenses Related to Running Away

Runaway youth are represented in arrest data in other offense categories besides runaways. Many teenagers who flee home or are thrown away become involved in prostitution, alcohol and drug use, property crimes, petty offenses, and violations of curfew and loitering laws. Table 6.1 shows juvenile arrests for offenses often associated with runaways in 2007. The high-

### Table 6.1
### Arrests for Runaway-Related Offenses, 2007

| Offense | # of Arrests |
|---|---|
| Curfew and loitering law violations | 109,815 |
| Disorderly conduct | 153,293 |
| Drug Abuse Violations | 147,382 |
| Drunkenness | 12,966 |
| Liquor laws | 106,537 |
| Prostitution and commercialized vice | 1,160 |
| Suspicion | 303 |
| Vagrancy | 2,924 |
| Vandalism | 84,744 |

SOURCE: Adapted from U.S. Department of Justice, Federal Bureau of Investigation, *Crime in the United States, 2007*, Table 38, http://www.fbi.gov/ucr/cius2007/data/table_38.html.

est numbers were for disorderly conduct, drug abuse violations, curfew and loitering law violations, liquor laws, and vandalism. There were over 100,000 arrests for all but vandalism, with over 147,000 arrests of persons under eighteen for drug abuse violations. Other offenses with lower arrest figures for juveniles include drunkenness, prostitution and commercialized vice, vagrancy, and suspicion. Though many of the arrests for these offenses may have been non-runaway related, studies show a strong correlation between runaway youth and juvenile delinquency.

Prostitution has been particularly associated with runaways and street kids, who often must turn to selling their bodies for food and shelter. There were only 1,160 arrests in 2007 for prostitution and commercialized vice, compared to nearly 109,000 arrests for running away. The significant disparity may be a result of more prostituted youth being arrested and processed as a status offender or for other offenses such as drug abuse violations.

In spite of the relatively low numbers of juvenile arrests for prostitution, ten-year arrest trends for prostitution and commercialized vice reveal that there has been a significant increase in female juvenile arrests for prostitution. Between 1998 and 2007, arrests of females younger than eighteen for prostitution rose by more than 56 percent, compared to a decline of arrests for males under eighteen by over 51 percent (see Figure 6.9). This difference could suggest more female runaways turning to prostitution to survive or more male runaways supporting their life on the streets through other activities such as drug crimes and theft. See Part VI for more detailed discussion on the relationship between running away from home and juvenile prostitution.

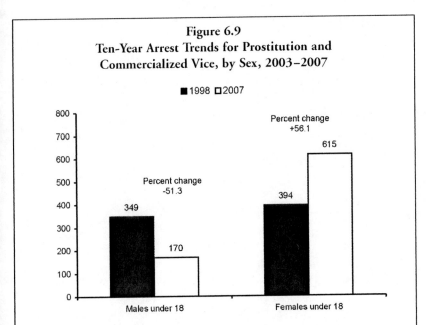

**Figure 6.9
Ten-Year Arrest Trends for Prostitution and
Commercialized Vice, by Sex, 2003–2007**

■1998 □2007

SOURCE: Adapted from U.S. Department of Justice, Federal Bureau of Investigation, *Crime in the United States, 2007*, Table 33, http://www.fbi.gov/ucr/cius2007/data/table_33.html.

# Part V

---

# Life on the Streets for Runaways

# 7

# Homeless Youth

As has been discussed, juveniles run away or are made to leave home for various reasons ranging from abuse/violence to substance abuse to neglect and more. The vast majority of these youth eventually return home, in spite of the reasons for leaving. In fact, according to a government study on runaways and thrownaways, 99 percent will make their way back at home, with less than 1 percent staying away indefinitely.[1] Most runaways spend their time away from home with friends and relatives, while encountering relatively few difficulties in terms of having a roof over their heads, food to eat, and a safety net to protect them from danger. However, some of these youth will wind up on the streets in big and small cities and towns across the United States. Being homeless can present runaway and thrownaway youth with a myriad of problems on multiple levels. These include having to endure harsh elements, being reduced to begging, stealing, survival sex, and other acts of desperation for food and shelter; exposure to crime and violence, becoming involved with alcohol and drugs, gangs, pimps, pornographers, and other sexual exploiters. Furthermore homeless runaways are at greater risk for various health issues such as drug addiction, disease, mental illness, sexually transmitted diseases, and HIV infection. For most runaways turned street kids or homeless, the upside such as independence and escapade is minimal at best, whereas the downside can be especially bleak around virtually every corner.

## Defining the Homeless Youth

What constitutes a homeless youth and how does it differentiate from non homeless or street youth? Unlike runaways and thrownaways who find

refuge with relatives, friends, or someone other than their parents or caretakers, those who have no place reliable to call home for a certain period of
time are considered homeless. These youth often live wherever they can,
including under bridges, in dilapidated or abandoned buildings, on rooftops,
in cars, parks, and alleys. Most homeless youth tend to live where circumstances warrant for survival and try to make the best out of a bad situation.

Experts on missing and runaway youth differ on the parameters of what
it means to be called homeless youth, with varying definitions and criteria.
The Runaway and Homeless Youth Act's definition of homeless youth is
"individuals under eighteen who are unable to live in a safe environment
with a relative and lack safe alternative living arrangements, as well as individuals ages eighteen to twenty-one without shelter."[2] In the U.S. Department of Health and Human Services publication, *Incidence and Prevalence
of Homeless and Runaway Youth*, homeless youth are defined as "those who
are unaccompanied by their families and lack stable housing, such as those
living on the street, in shelters, or in unstable residences with friends or
acquaintances."[3] Other researchers have similarly defined homeless youth as
"those who live on the streets, in shelters or other system-based institutions."[4]

A number of key studies on youth and homelessness have defined this
population according to their own methodology, such as AIDS Evaluation
of Street Outreach Project Street Intercept (AESOP), which defines a youth
as homeless if he or she does not

> have a fixed, regular, and adequate night-time residence or the primary resi-
> dence was a supervised public/private shelter, an institution providing tem-
> porary assistance, or a public/private residence not typically used for sleeping
> accommodations.[5]

The definition also required that the youth either lived on the street or a
shelter for two straight months while being apart from families, or were
engaged in the street life for any amount of time away from home, such as
survival sex, theft, or panhandling.

Other studies define a homeless youth as follows:

- *Street Youth at Risk for AIDS (SYRA)*— youth living on the streets for
  three or more months, and had not lived with parents or guardians
  for more than two weeks within that span.[6]
- *Midwest Homeless and Runaway Adolescent Project (MHRAP)*— youth
  who have been away from home for the night without a parent or
  caretaker's consent or knowledge.[7]

- *Seattle Homeless Adolescent Research and Evaluation Project (SHARP)—* youth who have no stable home and are without a feasible residence to return to.[8]

Homeless youth have also been classified by researchers in terms of their specific actions and location. These include youth who stay overnight in[9]:

- An official shelter
- An ad hoc shelter such as an automobile or deserted building
- Walk up and down the streets
- An all night diner
- A train or bus station
- A park
- A hotel

Time away from home has also been used to define the homeless youth. Alan Lifson and Linda Halcon categorized them as youth who were without shelter for two or more weeks within the past year[10]; while John Noell and colleagues defined homeless youth as those not living with parents or caregivers for longer than a month within the last six months, or had not lived with parents or caretakers within the past month.[11]

Sometimes homeless youth are used interchangeably with runaway youth. Though they are technically different (see Chapters 1–3), most homeless youth consist of teenagers and young adults who have run away or been thrown out of their homes. Indeed, the American Medical Association Council on Scientific Affairs asserts that "the distinctions between the two groups are artificial and may be counterproductive," contending that "most youth on the streets are both runaways and homeless because they have no home in which they are willing or able to return."[12]

Within this context, researchers have also added the terms of "street youth" and "street kids," as well as "street active youth" and "street involved youth" in reference to runaway and homeless youth who "reside in high-risk, nontraditional locations such as under bridges or in squats." Street youth have been defined by the federal government as:

> those who run away or who are indefinitely or intermittently homeless, and spend a significant amount of time on the street or in other areas that increase their risk for sexual abuse, sexual exploitation, prostitution, or drug abuse.[13]

Some definitions of street youth have focused on the kind of locations in which shelter was sought, such as living on the street, in a vehicle, an abandoned dwelling, or "another transient domicile for at least two days in the past thirty days."[14] Others have defined street kids as being without a stable home in relation to the activities they participated in, such as panhandling, drug dealing, prostitution, and child pornography.[15]

## The Extent of Homeless Youth

The precise number of runaway and homeless youth in the United States is unclear because of inconsistent definitions and methodological differences in defining this population and subgroups such as thrownaways; as well as the transitory nature of youth who are living on the streets or in temporary housing. According to a Congressional Research Service Report for Congress, "These youth often eschew the shelter system for locations or areas that are not easily accessible to shelter workers and others who count the homeless and runaways."[16] The report further notes that "youth who come into contact with census takers may also be reluctant to report that they have left home or are homeless."[17]

Runaway, thrownaway, and street youth tend to be hidden in plain view as a result of "their high residential mobility, diffusion throughout communities, and movement into and out of domiciles, public institutions, and the streets."[18] Many such youth often shy away from contacting shelters, law enforcement, or the medical community, making it that much tougher to get at their numbers.[19]

These issues notwithstanding, indications are that the number of homeless youth in society is on the rise.[20] Estimates of runaway and homeless youth have varied from tens of thousands to nearly two million living on the streets or away from home at any given time.[21] A National Health Interview Survey of persons between twelve and seventeen years of age found that 5 to 7.6 percent of this age group — or as many as 1.6 million — had been homeless at least one night within the last year.[22] This included spending one or more nights on the street, in an abandoned building, park, under a bridge, public places such as a subway or bus station, a stranger's residence, or elsewhere away from home. Male youth were more likely to go through a homeless episode than female youth. However, other surveys have indicated that males and females were equally likely to experience homelessness, or female youth were more likely to become homeless.[23]

An examination of data from the Homeless Youth Management Information System found annual estimates of runaway and thrownaway youth ranging from 575,000 to one million.[24] According to a study by the U.S. Department of Housing and Urban Development, approximately 1.6 million youth run away or are homeless annually[25]; while a U.S. Department of Health and Human Services (HHS) study done by the Research Triangle Institute reported that an estimated 2.8 million youth between the ages of twelve and seventeen had at least one occasion of running away from home.[26] Studies show that shelter youth have a tendency to undergo "short periods of homelessness and have not experienced prior homeless episodes, while youth living on the streets are more likely to demonstrate patterns of episodic ... or chronic homelessness."[27]

How many runaways end up becoming homeless? The number of homeless youth who ran away from home or were thrown out of home or substitute care is unclear. According to the HHS Administration for Children and Families' *FY2004 Justification of Estimates for Appropriation Committees*, there are an estimated 500,000 to 1.5 million youth who flee their homes every year; and roughly 300,000 youth who become homeless annually.[28] The Second National Incidence Studies of Missing, Abducted, Runaway and Thrownaway Children (NISMART-2) combines runaway and thrownaway episodes in its data, finding that approximately 1.7 million youth are runaways/thrownaways per year.[29] Though the vast majority of these youth are believed to return home eventually, there are those who never find their way back home.

Much of the literature suggests that homeless youth are largely composed of runaway and thrownaway teenagers. Researchers have found that running away or being put out of the house and home "are among the pathways most commonly identified by public policy and research as leading to youth homelessness."[30] Others have supported this contention, suggesting that running away may turn youth into street kids, and result in their becoming homeless."[31]

It is estimated by Les Whitbeck and Ronald Simons that one out of every eight children will be a runaway at least once prior to reaching the age of eighteen, of which 40 percent will never return home.[32] The strong correlation between runaway youth and homeless youth is such that in many studies no distinction is made between the two.[33]

## Perils for Homeless Youth

Though most runaway youth seek to escape an unsafe, unstable, or neglectful environment, those who wind up homeless often find themselves in an even more perilous world where they face a plethora of risks and uncertainties. These include hunger, cold, fear, intimidation, sexual exploitation, sexual maltreatment, substance abuse, robbery, violence, mental illness, diseases, other health issues, sexual orientation/gender identity concerns, lack of adequate educational and employment opportunities, and countless other dangers and challenges, including death. Few, if any, teenagers who find themselves suddenly without a real home are equipped mentally, physically, or financially to deal with the circumstances most are destined to encounter on the streets. For some repeat runners, they would have a better sense of what to expect being homeless, but may still feel compelled to run away due to the often dire situation at home, such as physical and sexual abuse, neglect, domestic violence, dysfunctional family, changes in the family structure, and other drawbacks to remaining home.

There is a high rate of victimization experienced by homeless youth.[34] It is not uncommon for runaways who become street kids to witness or be a victim of various kinds of sex crimes, violent crimes, drug crimes, property crimes, and other criminal acts and harmful experiences. In Pamela Miller and associates' study of homeless youth in Calgary, it was concluded that the majority were victims of one type of violence or another every day.[35] Another study of runaway and homeless youth in Seattle found that sexually abused youth involved in promiscuity and other unsafe sexual behavior such as prostitution had a greater risk for being sexually victimized.[36]

In NISMART-2, endangerments as a consequence of runaway/thrownaway episodes were listed (see Table 7.1). The most common type of endangerment was sexual or physical abuse experienced at home or the fear of such maltreatment upon returning home. More than one in five runaway/thrownaway episodes involved this factor, which could have put youth in further jeopardy of victimization. Substance dependency was the second most common endangerment for runaway/thrownaway youth, with nearly one in five reporting substance dependence during their runaway or thrownaway episode. Similarly, almost one in five runaways/thrownaways were using hard drugs while as a runaway/thrownaway; with around the same percentage in the company of a known drug abuser.

Other key areas of endangerment included nearly one in five runaways/thrownaways who were thirteen years of age or younger and the greater risks for victimization faced as a result; youths who spent time where criminality was known to take place, youths who became involved in delinquency/criminal behavior; and where runaways and thrownaways were in the company of a violent individual.

Interestingly enough, NISMART-2 found that only around 4 percent of these youth during their homeless episode were with a sexually exploitative person, victim of a sexual or attempted sexual assault, or traded sex for

**Table 7.1**
**Endangered Runaways/Thrownaways, by Type of Episode**

| Characteristic of Episode | Percent |
|---|---|
| Child had been physically or sexually abused at home in the year prior to the episode or was afraid of abuse upon return | 21 |
| Child was substance dependent | 19 |
| Child was 13 years old or younger | 18 |
| Child was in the company of someone known to be abusing drugs | 18 |
| Child was using hard drugs | 17 |
| Child spent time in a place where criminal activity was known to occur | 12 |
| Child engaged in criminal activity during the course of the episode | 11 |
| Child was with a violent person | 7 |
| Child had previously attempted suicide | 4 |
| Child who was enrolled in school at the time of the episode missed at least 5 days of school | 4 |
| Child was physically assaulted or someone attempted to physically assault child during the course of the episode | 4 |
| Child was with a sexually exploitative person | 2[a] |
| Child had a serious mental illness or developmental disability at the time of the episode | 1[a] |
| Child was sexually assaulted or someone attempted to sexually assault child during the course of the episode | 1[a] |
| Child's whereabouts were unknown to the caretaker for at least 30 days (and the episode was unresolved or no information was available) | <1[a] |
| Child engaged in sexual activity in exchange for money, drugs, food, or shelter during the episode | <1[a] |
| Child had or developed a serious or life-threatening medical condition during the course of the episode | [b] |

[a] Estimate is unreliable as a result of too few sample cases.
[b] There were no cases identified.

SOURCE: Adapted from Heather Hammer, David Finkelhor, and Andrea J. Sedlak, *Runaway/Thrownaway Children: National Estimates and Characteristics*, NISMART Bulletin Series (Washington, D.C.: Office of Juvenile Justice and Delinquency Prevention, 2002), p. 8.

money, food, drugs, or shelter. Numerous studies on runaway and homeless youth contradict these findings, indicating that the correlation between runaway/thrownaway street youth and prostitution, pedophilia, sexual assaults, and other forms of sexual exploitation is considerable.[37] (See also Part VI). Homeless youth are often victims of repeat kinds of sexually exploitative treatment, as well as related victimization and pressures to involve themselves in risky behavior and dangerous situations.

More often than not, homeless youth who are the victims of crimes are unlikely to report this to anyone, compounding their bleak situation and propensity to be targeted again and again. In Stephen Gaetz's study of homeless youth, only about one-third ever told someone after becoming a crime victim.[38] Just over 12 percent reported the worst victimization they had experienced to law enforcement authorities. Reasons for not reporting include fear of being viewed as a snitch, and involvement in criminality concurrent to their victimization.

## Delinquency and Criminality by Homeless Youth

Though runaway and homeless youth are often victims of crime and violence while living on the streets and in transient housing, their circumstances (including the need for money to buy food or shelter, drug addiction, and mental illness) can also lead to involvement in delinquent activities and criminal behavior. Each year thousands of runaways face arrests and detention, not only for the status offense of running away from home, but for criminal violation of the law such as alcohol- and drug-related offenses, prostitution, property and violent crimes, and curfew and loitering law violations.[39] In most instances, experts believe the delinquency or criminality is inexorably tied to being homeless and survival.[40]

Studies show that running away or being thrown out of the home puts youth at increased risk for becoming law violators. In a study examining the relationship between child abuse and neglect, running from home, and delinquency, Jeanne Kaufman and Cathy Widom found that youth who experienced child maltreatment were more likely to become runaways than those who did not have such experiences, and that there was a significant correlation between being a runaway and arrested as a minor.[41] The association between runaway youth and juvenile delinquency was strong as well when including such variables as gender, race, ethnicity, and social class. In relating homelessness with delinquent behavior and other negative effects, the researchers contended that a "critical point for intervention" existed the moment the runaway left home.[42]

According to homeless youth researcher Nicholas Ray, "The street economy is fertile ground for increased risk and violence. Integration into the street economy often occurs if a youth's only sources of income" are derived from involvement in theft, panhandling, drug dealing, prostitution, pornography, and other forms of deviant behavior or sexual exploitation.[43] One study suggested that once homeless, peer pressure from other street kids could increase the chances for a runaway youth becoming delinquent and suffering from depression.[44] Other research links the aberrant behavior of homeless youth to conditions they face, such as hunger, desperation, illness, mental health problems, pressure from pimps, drug dealers, other adults, and substance abuse.[45]

The following account is an example of a runaway teenager who wound up dealing drugs and processing crack cocaine while away from home:

> I made my money. I sold my dope, my crack.... I made it and I cracked it up.... He [boyfriend] told me one day did I know how to chop up crack. I was like "no." So he [taught] me and just made me start chopping up crack and putting it in the vials. He made me grind the dope and shit and make it.[46]

There is evidence to indicate that "the constant witnessing of bad behavior by street contemporaries may lead homeless youth to copy such activity."[47] In one study, the researchers found that "58.6 percent of the difference in likelihood to commit a crime is explained by youth's experience on the streets."[48] As explained, when the commission of such criminal acts becomes habitual rather than as a necessary means for survival, "theft activity often moves from the level of innovation to avocation."[49]

Another problem faced by homeless youth with respect to crime and victimization is the "criminalization of many life-sustaining activities associated with homelessness."[50] The National Coalition for the Homeless and National Law Center on Homelessness and Poverty have noted a recent trend in cities and towns across the country toward cleaning up downtown areas and some other places where the homeless congregate, by passing laws prohibiting sleeping, lying, or hanging out in particular areas under specific circumstances.[51] This has been shown to lead to dislocation, arrest, and an increase in violent criminality and hate crimes against the homeless.[52]

## Why Homeless Youth Fail to Return Home

Since the majority of youth who run away return home in due course, given the difficulties inherent in and experienced by homeless youth, one might wonder why all runaways simply do not return home as well. There are various factors in play that keep many runaway and thrownaway youth amongst the homeless. The obvious ones are that such youth have left homes where there was abuse, neglect, and other serious issues and feared having to relive it were they to return; or they were kicked out of the house and not welcome back. Some homeless youth are involved in illegal activities, drug addiction, promiscuity, gangs, romantic or adult relationships, arrests or detention, or other situations that may prevent or discourage them from returning home.[53] Children also leave home to escape authority and for independence, and may be reluctant to give this up, even if their circumstances away from home are dire. In one study of homeless youth in Minnesota, over half mentioned their freedom as an important reason for staying on their own.[54]

According to Michael MacLean and associates, long term runaway and homeless youth live on the streets rather than home by choice, suggesting that such choice is an indication that these "youth have left a particularly aversive family environment and are confident in their ability to survive on the street."[55] One authority on homeless youth held that by leaving a bad environment, some runaway youth are putting themselves in control of their lives, for better or worse.[56] Another researcher found that "many young people 'gravitate' towards the streets because they feel their 'street family' is able to look after their needs."[57]

A study of homeless youth in San Francisco listed four reasons why they remain homeless[58]:

• The scarcity of affordable lodging.
• Lack of adequate schooling, making it difficult to obtain well-paying employment.
• The difficulty in a tough economy to find employment.
• Substance abuse.

Studies indicate that youth who ran away from sexually and physically abusive households have the least desire to give up the harsh realities of street life for returning home, where often the same dynamics remain in place that caused the youth to leave in the first place.[59]

# 8

# Implications for Runaway and Homeless Teens

Once a youth decides or is forced to leave home and joins the ranks of the homeless, new issues and circumstances often develop that can have a detrimental effect upon their mental and physical health, living conditions, associations, and day-to-day survival. Though children, mostly older teenagers, become runaways or thrownaways for various and common reasons, they usually become street youth for the same reasons. These include having nowhere else to go, no one trusting enough to turn to, no other viable choices for things most youth take for granted such as food, shelter, education, love and support; and being thrust into a street world where adaptability and growing up prematurely becomes essential if one is to get through it with any chance to still have a meaningful life afterwards. Typical issues runaway and homeless youth must deal with are trying to meet basic necessities in an atmosphere where there are no easy means to achieve such, poor nutrition, poor hygiene, promiscuity, teen pregnancy, survival sex, sexual assaults, substance abuse, gangs, and health crises including severe depression, sexually transmitted diseases, HIV infection, and sometimes a life cut short when all other options to get off the street come too late.

## Lack of Basic Necessities

Runaway and thrownaway youth who become homeless tend to find themselves lacking the basic necessities of life most take for granted, such as food, shelter from the elements, a bed to sleep in, and the proper guidance and support of parents or guardians. In a study by the Family and Youth

Services Bureau, two-thirds of street kids and one-third of youth staying in shelters found it difficult to acquire food, clothes, shelter, and medical attention.[1] A high percentage of homeless youth also reported lacking other basic needs including the support and encouragement of family, or were the victims of child sexual abuse, violence, mental abuse, and/or neglect.[2]

According to a U.S. Department of Health and Human Services report, "Once on the street, young people lack support and guidance in dealing with the negative feelings resulting from their family experiences and in obtaining and retaining a job. With no source of income, many cannot acquire basic necessities like food, clothing, and shelter."[3] As most runaways have also dropped out of school and find roadblocks in completing basic education, their ability to gain meaningful employment is also impaired, making it that much more challenging for them to make ends meet while homeless.

The degree of vulnerability and victimization as it relates to basic necessities and other issues common to runaway and homeless youth depends upon where one ends up on the street, the resourcefulness in adjusting to the circumstances presented, the associations formed, maturity level, background, and willingness to take extreme or high-risk measures to meet the requirements for day-to-day survival. For most street youth, there are no easy solutions to their predicament, but rather a series of difficult choices that will harden or numb them, or weaken them to further susceptibility and exploitation.

## Promiscuity and High-Risk Sexual Relations

A high percentage of runaway and homeless youth engage in risky consensual sexual relations with multiple partners.[4] Though much of this is tied to their circumstances which often encourage sexual activity with other homeless youth and adults and exploiters, along with substance abuse, stress, low self-esteem, and other experiences common to street life, some youth were sexually active before running away or being thrown out of the house.[5] In both instances, the consequences of unprotected sexual relations for homeless youth include pregnancy, sexually transmitted diseases, and exposure to the HIV virus.[6]

Teenage involvement in sexual activity is a serious concern in the United States whether youth remain at home or leave before reaching adulthood. In 2007, some 35 percent of high school students were sexually active in the

United States, with about 48 percent engaging in sexual intercourse, according to the Centers for Disease Control and Prevention.[7] Around two-thirds of females and males have had sex upon becoming seniors in high school[8]; while half of persons between the ages of fifteen and nineteen have engaged in oral sex.[9] Eight in ten males and seven in ten females will be sexually active prior to reaching the age of twenty.[10] The incidence of teen sex is even higher for runaway and homeless youth, who often "engage in sexual relations without pay as a natural part of increased independence, puberty, and sexual experimentation."[11]

A survey on sexual practices of runaway youth in New York, Denver, and San Francisco, found that the average age a female runaway lost her virginity was under age fourteen and the average age for a male runaway losing his virginity was under thirteen years of age.[12] Group sex tended to be a common occurrence among teenage runaways. One-third of the male runaways and one-fourth of the female runaways had engaged in sexual activity that involved more than two persons. Among lesbian and gay runaways, the survey reported that nearly four in ten girls and almost one in four boys admitted to having oral sex. In another study, half the male runaways younger than fourteen were sexually active.[13]

According to Doreen Rosenthal and Susan Moore, homeless youth get involved in high-risk sexual practices as a coping mechanism due to the dereliction of their primary needs.[14] Cathy Widom and Joseph Kuhns reported a relationship between childhood sexual abuse and neglect and promiscuity, pregnancy, and prostitution.[15] In a study on newly homeless youth, it was found that they had a higher rate of involvement in dangerous sexual activity such as multiple sexual partners and drug abuse than other homeless youth, though homelessness among young people in general and risky sexual relations were considered high relative to non homeless youth.[16] The study found that while 77 percent of the respondents were sexually involved at the onset of the examination, this number had risen to 85 percent when the study was completed two years later.

Other studies have shown that promiscuity and substance abuse in combination among homeless youth increases the risk of developing mental and physical problems. Susan Ennett and associates put forward that runaways without a social network had a greater likelihood than those with a strong social network to participate in illicit drug use, sexual relations with multiple partners, and survival sex.[17] In Linda Halcon and Alan Lifson's study of homeless youth, a strong correlation was found between heavy drinkers and multiple sex partners; and female intravenous drug users and multiple sexual involvements.[18]

## SURVIVAL SEX

As part of the street culture and its harsh reality, many homeless youth find themselves engaging in *survival sex*. The term generally relates to use of sexual relations by homeless youth to survive in the absence of a stable and loving home. Survival sex has been defined as "the commercial sexual activity of young people as a way of obtaining the necessities of life, including food, drugs, clothing, transport, or money to purchase these goods and services."[19] Lynn Rew and colleagues referred to survival sex as the exchange of "sex for anything else needed, including money, food, clothes, a place to stay, or drugs."[20]

In a study of the prevalence of survival sex involving homeless and runaway youth, Jody Greene, Susan Ennett, and Christopher Ringwalt referred to it as "selling of sex to meet subsistence needs."[21] The researchers further stated: "The dangers inherent in survival sex make it among the most damaging repercussions of homelessness among youths."[22]

Though survival sex is often used interchangeably with prostitution, especially juvenile prostitution, studies show that "many youth involved in the exchange of sex for money or other considerations ... do not perceive themselves as engaging in prostitution, but rather as doing 'whatever is necessary' to ensure their survival."[23] Furthermore, not all "survival sex" is a matter of life or death, per se, or where compensation is in the form of cash payment, as is usually identified as prostitution. Some homeless youth engage in consensual or recreational sexual relations as a reflection of their independence, past sexual experiences, promiscuity, and shared experiences among peers within the street life. According to child prostitution researcher Pam Oliver, "The term 'sex for favors' suggests that sex may also be carried out to make life more enjoyable or tolerable in terms of material goods or accommodation, or for emotional security, approval, attention, or affection."[24]

Many runaway and homeless youth are the victims of forcible rape and statutory rape, and other means of child sexual exploitation by pimps, customers, pedophiles, drug dealers, gangs, and other opportunists.[25] This indicates that survival sexual acts often go well beyond being a willing participant as a measure of the hazards typically faced by runaways and thrownaways as street kids.

How many homeless youth resort to survival sex? The proportion of runaway and homeless youth engaging in survival sex has been estimated to vary from 10 percent to 50 percent.[26] One study estimated that between one-fourth and one-third of homeless youth have turned to survival sex at some point.[27] Greene and associates found that 27.5 percent of their sample living on the streets and 9.5 percent of those staying in shelters had ever been involved in survival sex.[28] In a study of homeless youth in New York City, over one-third had engaged in survival sex[29]; while 27.7 percent of homeless youth in a Montreal study had participated in sexual activity as a survival mechanism.[30] Similarly, a study of ninety-three homeless youth in San Francisco found that 31 percent had prostituted themselves to survive living on the streets.[31]

The relationship between survival sex and homeless youth is a given when considering the circumstances that inexorably cause the two to converge. According to Nicholas Ray, survival sex "is a desperate and risky behavior borne out of isolation and the lack of any tangible resources."[32] See Part VI for further discussion on the dynamics of runaways and juvenile prostitution.

## SEXUAL ASSAULT

Aside from recreational sex or consensual survival sexual activities, runaway and homeless youth are commonly the victims of sexual assaults. Child sexual assault (CSA) is defined in a report on commercial child sexual exploitation in the U.S. Canada, and Mexico as "any sexual act directed against a person younger than eighteen years of age, forcibly and/or against that person's will; or not forcibly or against that person's will where the victim is incapable of giving consent because of his/her temporary or permanent mental or physical incapacity."[33] CSAs include such sexual mistreatment as "forcible rape, forcible sodomy, sexual assault with an object, and forcible fondling," among other nonconsensual sexual acts.[34] Perpetrators are often adults, pimps, customers, pedophiles, members of gangs, substance abusers, and other homeless youth and young adults, and street persons.[35]

It is unclear how many homeless youth are the victims of sexual assaults each year in the United States; however, by most indications, the number is high. In a Seattle study of runaway and homeless youth, 31 percent of female and 13 percent of male youth reported being victims of sexual assaults.[36] A study of young streetwalkers found a high rate of rape and violence against the sex workers while in the midst of plying their trade.[37] Other studies have found homeless youth to be much more likely to be victims of sexual violence than their non homeless counterparts.[38] Sexual violence against homeless youth is a sad and inescapable reality in every state.

According to Nancy Walker of the Institute for Children, Youth and Families, more than two in three teenage prostitutes have been the victims of rape, often multiple times.[39] In one instance reported in the government publication *Female Juvenile Prostitution: Problem and Response*, a young woman who had entered prostitution at the age of thirteen, claimed she had been raped by customers on "approximately fifteen to twenty occasions."[40] She described experiencing "intrusive images of being raped, beaten, and humiliated."[41]

Some homeless and prostituted youth have reported being the victims of gang rape and other acts of sexual violence. In many instances, being under the influence of alcohol or drugs, or having mental health issues makes such youth even easier prey for assaults or what may seem to be consensual sexual relations to the victim. In the homeless world, street kids often find themselves having to move regularly between survival sex and forced sexual relations as part of the subculture they have become a part of.

## Substance Abuse

Runaway and homeless youth commonly find themselves using and abusing alcohol and drugs, which are woven into the street life and its dynamics. A plethora of studies have illustrated the strong correlation between homeless youth and substance abuse.[42] Many street kids were using alcohol and/or drugs prior to leaving home. Others were introduced to these substances while living on the street, often abusing them as part of the subculture of conforming, survival, selling sexual favors and drugs, and numbing oneself to the brutal realities of homeless life. A high degree of homeless youth have past and present experiences with alcohol and drugs, often in relation to childhood sexual abuse, survival sex and sexual assaults, and other precursors and consequences of homelessness.[43]

In Shelly Mallett and associates' study of 302 homeless youth, 38 percent had become homeless as a result of alcohol and drug related issues, while 17 percent of the respondents using drugs since becoming homeless attributed this in part to conflicts within their families.[44] The rate of chemical dependence among homeless youth in five different studies in Minnesota had a range of 10 to 20 percent.[45]

A much higher percentage of substance abuse among homeless youth has been reported in other research. In a study of 432 homeless youth living in Los Angeles found that 71 percent had substance abuse disorders[46]; and in a national survey of 600 homeless youth, half of those who had attempted suicide reported that alcohol or drug use was a precipitating factor.[47] A high rate of drug and alcohol abuse by homeless youth was also found in a public health survey that covered eight cities, including Chicago, Denver, Minneapolis, and St. Louis.[48]

Homeless youth who ran away from institutional care, such as foster and group homes, have been found in studies to be prone to substance abuse either in relation to their previous use of prescription drugs or their current unstable environment, mental health issues, peer group pressures, and other risky involvements.[49]

Alcohol and marijuana are the drugs most frequently used by runaway and homeless youth.[50] However, many also use cocaine, crack, amphetamines, heroin, inhalants, and misuse prescription drugs.[51] Over three in four juvenile prostitutes are substance abusers, according to one study.[52]

In *Runaway Kids and Teenage Prostitution*, one disturbing account of a homeless and drug-addicted runaway is described:

> At 9, Diane ran away from home.... By age 12, she was smoking pot.... By 16, she was a hooker and a junkie, sleeping under benches on the streets.... Everything had become incidental to the drugs — sex, friendships, plans, promises, security.... The first thing on her mind when she woke up was how long she would have to work for her first fix. On cocaine, she could turn tricks for 12- or 14-hour days, the most intense part of the high lasting 15 or 20 seconds.[53]

Use of crack cocaine by prostituted youth in many impoverished inner cities has been a serious problem. In the *Prostitution of Children and Child-Sex Tourism* government publication, crack has been described as "the new pimp. And younger girls who get crack from their pimps are seen as willing to do anything to feed their habits."[54] The presence of criminal gangs in the street life poses a further high-risk factor for homeless youth and their involvement in drug abuse, prostitution, and related forms of sexual exploitation, victimization, and criminality.[55]

In an examination of three nationwide surveys of alcohol or drug use by youths who had ever run away or been homeless, the following findings emerged[56]:

- Street youth had a higher rate of drug use for virtually every drug than shelter youth or those living at home.
- Street youth had a higher rate of using such drugs as crack, methamphetamines, heroin, and other intravenous drugs than youth in shelters or who lived at home.
- Among street and shelter youth, there was a higher rate of drug use for most drugs surveyed by older, male, and white youth than younger, female, and black youth.
- Three in four homeless youth were using marijuana.
- One in three homeless youth were using hallucinogens, stimulants, and analgesics.

• One in four homeless youth were using cocaine, crack, inhalants, and sedatives.

Other studies, such as by Lynn Rew and associates, have supported the contention that homeless youth are more likely to be substance abusers than youth who live in transitory housing or at home.[57] Ray suggested that alcohol or drug use could be a "coping mechanism which increases in prevalence as the living situation of homeless youth becomes more stressful and less stable."[58]

Relatively few homeless youth seek treatment for substance abuse. In a survey of substance abusing youth living on the street and in shelters, only 24 percent of the street youth and 18 percent of the shelter youth had ever received any treatment for alcohol or drug abuse.[59]

One study found that 63 percent of adolescent prostitutes who are abusing alcohol and/or drugs were in denial and, as such, did not seek treatment.[60] This reality for many homeless youth with substance abuse issues compounds the problems they face which, along with frequent sexual activity and multiple partners, exposes them to various health concerns, including HIV.

## Health Problems

Homeless youth must deal with a number of health concerns that are directly attributable to living on the street, though some health issues that were present when leaving home are exacerbated upon becoming street kids. These include mental, physical, environmental, and economic issues that can have a detrimental effect on health, even resulting in death. Among the homeless, for example, there are a multitude of "illnesses caused by exposure to the weather, of eating garbage from restaurant dumpsters, and in sleeping in pest and vermin infested areas."[61] Homeless youth routinely suffer from "injuries, malnutrition, and skin infections (such as lice and scabies);" as well as poor hygiene, sleep deprivation, low self-esteem, and diets that are often high in unhealthy fat and carbohydrates.[62]

Substance abuse and survival sex-related involvement further exposes runaway and homeless youth to various emotional and bodily risks such as pregnancy, sexually transmitted diseases, and HIV. Delinquency and criminal behavior, often driven by basic needs and street influences, tend to intersperse with sexual exploitation and victimization, increasing the likelihood that health will be compromised.

A perspective on the dilemma homeless youth face with regard to health and survival can be seen in the following passage from a government study on the subject matter:

> The health-related choices of homeless youth can be easily undermined by the immediacy of their need for food, shelter, and relief from drug or alcohol dependencies. Uninsured homeless adolescents ... very often do not have access to the health services they need. Barriers to obtaining care include confidentiality issues, their status as minors, and a general distrust of adults and the institutions created to help them.[63]

## MENTAL HEALTH PROBLEMS

Being homeless makes runaway, thrownaway, and other street youth susceptible to various mental illnesses or worsens conditions already present prior to leaving home. Homeless youth are more likely than youth who are not homeless to experience depression, anxiety, conduct disorder, thoughts of or attempts at suicide, and other mental health problems. A study of homeless youth found their rates of severe depression, post–traumatic stress syndrome, and conduct disorder was three times that of non homeless youth.[64]

In a study of 432 homeless youth in Los Angeles, the rates of mental health and substance abuse issues were well above rates for community and school youth.[65] More than eight in ten homeless youth surveyed reported having at least one type of mental disorder. Another study found that the prevalence of mental health issues for homeless youth was up to eleven times higher than for the population at large.[66]

Street kids are more prone to clinical depression than other youth and, according to researchers, two times more likely to have a major mental health disorder.[67] One study found clinical depression to be common among homeless youth living in San Francisco and Seattle[68]; while almost two out of three Seattle homeless youth were diagnosed with mental health illnesses, including attention deficit disorder, disruptive behavior problems, post–traumatic stress syndrome, mania, and schizophrenia.[69]

Studies show that homeless youth have a high rate of suicide ideation and suicide attempts compared to other youth. In one study, street youth were nearly two times more likely to be suicidal or have attempted to kill themselves.[70] Another study of prostituted shelter youth found that 71 percent had suicidal ideation, 33 percent a plan to execute the suicide, and 14 percent had attempted suicide previously.[71] As homeless youth consist largely of children who ran away from or were thrown out of homes that were abusive, dysfunctional, and unstable, suicide could be viewed by some as a means to escape their troubled past, according to a report issued by the National Center for Missing and Exploited Children.[72]

The relationship between homeless youth and suicidal thoughts and actions was further supported in a two-year study of largely minority New York City shelter runaways. Thirty-seven percent of the youth had ever attempted suicide, with 44 percent of this group having sought to commit suicide within the past month.[73] Similarly, a high occurrence of suicidal ideation and attempted suicide was reported in San Francisco, New York, and Denver.[74]

Some research has associated loneliness experienced by homeless youth with depression, suicidal behavior, and psychosomatic disorders.[75] In Ami Rokach's survey of 324 youth in Toronto, consisting of 113 homeless youth and 211 youth living at home, she found that homeless youth were more likely to relate their loneliness to developmental shortfalls, unsatisfying intimate associations, relocation or major separation, and social marginality; whereas domicile youth related loneliness more to personal failures.[76] Rew and colleagues suggested that the association between loneliness, despair, negativity, and suicidal behavior among homeless youth put them at greater risk for attempting to end their lives.[77]

## SEXUALLY TRANSMITTED DISEASES

A high rate of sexually transmitted diseases (STDs), which are also referred to as sexually transmitted infections (STIs), exist among runaway and homeless youth whose sexual involvement often includes promiscuity, recreational sex, survival sex, prostitution, multiple partners, rape, pedophilia, sodomy, and other risky sexual contact. Studies show that for street kids there's "an epidemic of old venereal infections, crabs and Chlamydia, secondary syphilis and super-gonorrhea, resistant to penicillin."[78] The Human Immunodeficiency Virus (HIV) also impacts the homeless youth population through sexual contact and intravenous drug use.[79]

In a study by Lisa Wagner and associates of youth center homeless persons, more than half revealed they had contracted one or more STDs.[80] A high incidence of STDs among homeless youth was also found in Rew and associates research, which revealed[81]:

- One out of four of the youth were treated for gonorrhea.
- One in ten received treatment for Chlamydia.
- One out of fourteen was treated for HIV.
- One in twenty received treatment for syphilis.

Studies indicate that runaway and homeless youth are more likely to "initiate sexual activities at an early age, have multiple sexual partners, participate in a variety of risky behaviors including prostitution, and practice safersex techniques less frequently. For these reasons, they are at a high risk for contracting various sexually-transmitted diseases."[82] According to a study of prostituted youth, "many carry the diseases unknowingly and pass it to their customers or contract different strains from johns. Other runaways selling sexual favors 'know they're flirting with disease.'"[83]

Female teen prostitutes are also vulnerable to pelvic inflammatory disease and have "an increased physiological susceptibility to infection."[84] Some studies further suggest that prostituted girls could have more multiple partner sexual relations and be involved with sex partners who pose a greater risk.[85]

Use of condoms in a steady manner may be the key to reducing the risk of exposure among homeless youth to STDs. However, for homeless adolescent female prostitutes, reluctance by customers to take safer sex precautions has proven problematic as these girls are often too immature and defenseless, and intimidated by those they service, to act in their own best interests in reducing the risk of contracting an STD.[86]

Sexual orientation has also been studied in relation to safer-sex practices. Rew and colleagues' study of 325 homeless youth revealed that those who were heterosexual or bisexual tended to use condoms during sexual relations more than gay or lesbian youth.[87] In Elizabeth Saewyc's survey, she found that there was a greater likelihood among lesbian and bisexual homeless female youth than heterosexual homeless females of being more sexually active, a sexual and physical abuse victim, to engage in survival sex, and use contraceptives unsuccessfully.[88] The dangers of multiple (and in many instances anonymous) partner homosexual sexual relations, was summed up in a report as reflective of "a high-risk subgroup among high-risk groups."[89] (See more on gay and lesbian homeless youth in Chapter 9).

Researchers have found that homeless youth involved in high-risk sexual behaviors are apt to be in denial or play this down, while continuing to place themselves in jeopardy. For example, in one study of homeless male youth and their involvement in the sex trade, it was found that they tended to underestimate their survival sexual encounters and the implications thereof.[90]

## HIV/AIDS INFECTION

As noted in the previous section, due to their dangerous sexual involvements, including prostitution and multiple partners for unprotected sex and intravenous (IV) drug use, runaway and homeless youth are at grave risk for contracting HIV, a precursor to Acquired Immune Deficiency Syndrome (AIDS). It is unknown just how many homeless teenagers have developed AIDS or other HIV-related diseases, but the research suggests the problem is a serious one.

According to the National Network for Youth, it is estimated that between 16,859 and 27,600 runaway and homeless youth are HIV-positive.[91] Approximately 5 percent of homeless youth are believed to be HIV-infected in the United States.[92] However, a study in San Francisco reported that 17 percent of the homeless youth were carriers of HIV.[93] Prevalence rates for HIV among homeless youth have been reported by others studies to be 12.9 percent in Houston and 11.5 percent in Hollywood.[94] According to a medical staffer at Covenant House, New York's largest runaway shelter, as many as 40 percent of homeless youth may be HIV-positive.[95] Youth who are homeless have been shown to be seven times more likely to die as a result of AIDS and have sixteen times the likelihood of being HIV-positive as youth in the population at large.[96] Other researchers have advanced that the prevalence rate of HIV among homeless youth could be as high as two to ten times that of other youth sampled in this country.[97]

The risk factors for exposure to the AIDS virus include:

- Unsafe sexual practices.
- Survival sex.
- Multiple sexual partners.
- Limited use of condoms.
- IV drug use.
- Sharing needles.
- Sexual relations while under the influence of alcohol or drugs.
- Sexually active early in life.
- Being homeless, which increases the risk of sexual activity, exploitation, and victimization.

The correlation between homeless youth and HIV or AIDS has been shown in many studies.[98] One study found that 84 percent of homeless youth participated in one or more AIDS-related sexual or drug-involved actions.[99] In another study of homeless youth in New York, over half believed they would ultimately be infected with the AIDS virus.[100]

The convergence of runaway and homeless teenagers and AIDS was put in context by writer Patricia Hersch:

If geography is destiny, runaway and homeless kids gravitate to the very locations around the country where their risk is greatest. Not only are these kids at higher risk with every sexual contact ... but they also have higher levels of sexually transmitted diseases. Often their immune systems are already compromised by repeated exposure to infections.... Sex more than anything puts runaway kids at risk for AIDS.... Their bodies usually become the currency of exchange.... There is ... an epidemic of exposure, and many runaway kids, years hence, may pay horribly for the events of their troubled youth.[101]

Unprotected sexual relations and multiple partners may put runaways and homeless youth at the greatest risk for HIV infection. Studies in New York City[102] and Cleveland[103] found that the risk of developing AIDS increased among runaway male and female youth who had unprotected sex and multiple partners. International research has supported the contention that multiple sexual partners, unprotected sexual relations, and IV drug use places inner city street kids at high risk for contracting HIV.[104]

Because of their status as street kids without the health care access of children who live at home, runaway and homeless youth are further put at a disadvantage in preventing or treating sexually transmitted diseases, including HIV. One report on the HIV risk and homeless youth noted the "barriers to health care due to lack of health insurance and their distrust of 'adult-serving' institutions."[105]

## PREGNANCY

Another consequence of high-risk sexual activity for homeless girls is pregnancy. Studies show that there is a high rate of teenage pregnancy among street youth. According to one study of female runaways, half of those living on the street and 40 percent of shelter runaways had been pregnant at some point in their lives.[106] About one in ten of the street and shelter runaways were pregnant during the time the study was conducted. Less than one in four runaway females used birth control. In another study, over half the homeless teenage girls had become pregnant since becoming street youth[107]; while in Halcon and Lifson's research on the prevalence of sexual risks for homeless youth, half the homeless girls had at least one pregnancy and more than one-fourth had experienced two or more pregnancies.[108]

According to a nationwide study, the rate of pregnancy for homeless girls thirteen to fifteen years of age was 14 percent, compared to a rate of 1 percent for girls who were not homeless.[109] Survival sex and multiple sexual partners are strongly associated with unplanned pregnancies among homeless female adolescents, as well as childhood sexual victimization and substance abuse.[110] Some research has found that many homeless female youth engage in "risk clustering," or multiple perilous sexual involvements simultaneously, putting them at even greater risk for pregnancy, STDs, HIV, and other circumstances detrimental to their health.[111]

The relationship between runaway and homeless youth and pregnancy has also been examined in relation to males who father children. Thirteen percent of teenage males who had ever run away admitted to getting a girl pregnant in one study, compared to just 2 percent of the male teenagers who had never run away from home.[112] In Wagner and colleagues' study, more than one in five homeless male youth said they had fathered a child.[113] According to another study, half the runaway males younger than fourteen were sexually active, thereby increasing the probability of impregnating a female and putting them at risk for other consequences such as contracting an STD or HIV.[114]

## Death

For runaway and homeless youth, the risky confluence of a unprotected sex with multiple partners, mental illness, substance abuse, IV drug use, exposure to HIV and other diseases, and regular encounters with violence and threats to physical health and well-being makes dying on the streets a real possibility. No one knows for sure how many homeless youth die as a result of being homeless, as their total numbers in society often remain sketchy. Current estimates suggest that as many as 5,000 homeless youth die each year due to violent victimization, illness, suicide, or accidents.[115] There is reason to believe the numbers could be much higher, given the transitory and hard to track nature of the homeless, repeat runners who may return home with a fatal disease such as HIV and no longer be counted as a runaway or homeless youth, and the reality that many homeless youth never show up in the statistics and news for one reason or another, meaning that whether they live or die, it goes undocumented.

Homeless and runaway youth are especially easy targets of those who might wish to do them mortal harm, often using and abusing them through street contact, child prostitution, the Internet as a vehicle to coerce a susceptible child to run away from home, or other means where the homeless youth is most vulnerable to being victimized and murdered. An example of a homeless runaway fatality as the worst case scenario of health consequences of street life can be seen in the following newspaper account:

> The 17-year-old runaway girl found dead in a shallow grave in a remote desert area northwest of Las Vegas has been identified.... [She] died of asphyxiation,

the coroner's office said. She had no known address. Her 18th birthday would have been this coming Friday.... Metro Police arrested a man and a woman on charges of kidnapping and murder.... They are being held without bail.... Detectives said their investigation led them to a remote desert area south of the Snow Mountain Paiute Indian Reservation, where they found [the victim's] body in a shallow grave east of the intersection of U.S. 95 and State Route 157.[116]

# 9

# Sexual Minorities' Homeless Youth Concerns

Though all runaway and thrownaway youth who become street kids face serious challenges on a daily basis to their health, well-being, and survival, those with sexual orientation and gender identity issues are even more vulnerable to hardship and victimization. Youth who identify themselves as lesbian, gay, bisexual, or transgender often are victims of sexual and physical abuse, discrimination, neglect, insensitivity, and other negative treatment while still living at home. Many such youth run away to escape this atmosphere, while others are tossed away by parents or caretakers who choose to reject them rather than embrace their sexual orientation. Whatever the reason for leaving home, most of these runaways/thrownaways find life on the street replete with a new set of problems or carryovers from home. These include physical and sexual mistreatment, substance abuse, mental illness, and being forced into survival sex, prostitution, pedophilia, pornography, and other forms of sexual exploitation. The health effects of homelessness for this population group can be sexually transmitted diseases, HIV infection, severe depression, a breakdown of the immune system, starvation, malnutrition, and more. In exploring their experiences as homeless youth apart from those of heterosexual runaways and thrownaways living on the street, the unique dynamics can be better understood.

## The Scope of Lesbian, Gay, Bisexual, and Transgender Homeless Youth

Homeless youth are generally viewed as a homogenous group in the literature when assessing their scope in society. As such, much of the focus tends to be on the entire homeless youth population regardless of sexual orientation. In this context, the estimates of youth who are considered homeless at any point in time vary between tens of thousands to millions.[1] According to the Second National Incidence Studies of Missing, Abducted, Runaway and Thrownaway Children (NISMART-2), an estimated 1.7 million youth had a runaway or thrownaway episode in the United States in 1999.[2] Similarly, based on a National Health Interview Survey of individuals twelve to seventeen years of age, it was approximated that up to 1.6 million of this group, or 7.6 percent, had experienced homelessness at least one night within the past year.[3] The *FY2004 Justification of Estimates for Appropriation Committees*, from the HHS Administration for Children and Families, gave an approximate range of 500,000 to 1.5 million youth who ran away from home each year; with about 300,000 youth who become homeless annually.[4] A study by the Research Triangle Institute gave a much higher estimate of as many as 2.8 million youth who run away or are put out of home in a given year.[5] Other research has postulated that one in eight youth will leave home at least once before turning eighteen, with 40 percent remaining homeless indefinitely.[6]

The precise number of homeless youth who are lesbian, gay, bisexual, or transgender (LGBT) is uncertain. However, the indication is that they constitute a large share of the homeless youth population. Studies have found that 20 to 40 percent of the total homeless youth in the United States are LGBT, with the figure more often falling on the high end.[7] In a study by Michael Clatts and associates of street and homeless youth, an estimated 35 percent were sexual minorities, with up to 50 percent of street youth alone thought to be lesbian, gay, bisexual, or transgender.[8] City estimates of homeless youth who identify as LGBT include 23.1 percent in Chicago[9]; 25 to 30 percent in Los Angeles[10]; 30 percent in Portland[11]; 40 percent in Seattle[12]; and 42 percent in Decatur, Illinois.[13] Researcher Nicholas Ray noted that some studies and anecdotal information indicated a much larger proportion of LGBT in the homeless youth community than the population at large in this country.[14]

The National Gay and Lesbian Task Force, along with the National Coalition for the Homeless, estimated that as many as 42 percent of homeless youth identify as gay or lesbian, with bisexual or transgender youth disproportionately represented among the homeless.[15] According to San Francisco's Larkin Street Youth Center, though three out of four street kids were heterosexual, one-quarter identified themselves as lesbian, gay, bisexual, or they questioned their sexual orientation or gender identity.[16] Studies have suggested that two in ten transgender youth are either homeless or in danger of becoming homeless.[17] Many transgender youth face additional problems as a result of gender identity, including being shunned by some outreach agencies that cater to gay, lesbian, and bisexual homeless youth.[18]

## Precursors to LGBT Youth Becoming Homeless

Youth who are lesbian, gay, bisexual, or transgender typically face a number of issues while still living at home that often play a large role in their leaving. These include physical and sexual abuse, mental health problems, substance abuse, rejection, neglect, bullying, discrimination, and other difficulties and confusion related to their sexual orientation and gender identity.[19] Though all homeless youth experienced similar issues at home related to family dysfunction, conflict, neglect, and abusive treatment, LGBT youth may be especially prone to such circumstances, increasing the possibility or reality of their running away or being thrown away.[20]

For instance, research shows that gay and lesbian youth are two times more likely to attempt suicide than heterosexual youth[21]; while also being much more likely to be substance abusers.[22] According to one study, about one-third of lesbian or gay youth were victims of familial physical abuse.[23] Other studies have supported the high rate of sexual and physical abuse perpetrated against LGBT youth in correlation with their sexual orientation or gender identity.[24] Furthermore, youth who are gay, lesbian, bisexual, or transgender are more likely to experience emotional and physical health problems, as well as school-related conflicts than heterosexual youth.[25] Any precursor could trigger LGBT youth into leaving home, though it is usually multiple circumstances that lead to this exit.

It appears as if most LGBT youth run away rather than are thrown out of the house, albeit the evidence supports the notion that even voluntarily leaving home is often due to a stressful and unsafe environment. In one survey of 775 gay homeless teenagers in Denver, San Francisco, and New York, 78 percent reported leaving home by choice, while only 16 percent said they were forced to leave.[26] The survey did find, however, that nearly six in ten of the teenagers ran away from home because of family conflicts and more than two in ten due to being abuse or sexual assault victims.

Some studies have found that a high percentage of LGBT homeless youth were thrown away. One study found that more than one-quarter of gay and lesbian youth were tossed out of the house for sexual orientation or gender identity-related reasons.[27] In a different study, half the gay male youth found unsupportive response from parents when coming out; and around one-fourth of these youth were asked to move out.[28] In her study on homeless gay youth, Jenny Gable found that many had homophobic parents who forced them to leave home, often ending up in counseling centers or homeless shelters.[29]

An all too common account of a thrownaway gay youth named "Daniel," was depicted in a recent newspaper article, as follows:

> Six years ago, Daniel left home. At age 12. His mom and dad ... verbally abused him and his brother. Sometimes the ugly confrontations got physical. Daniel is gay, which he says his mother had a hard time accepting. So ... like thousands of children who feel unwanted, unloved and unsafe at home, [he] took his chances elsewhere, staying at friends' houses or sleeping on San Diego's streets. Daniel describes himself not as a runaway but as a "refugee fighting for his stability."[30]

For some LGBT youth, living in foster care or shelters may worsen the situation that drove them from home. In Sanna Thompson and associates' study, over one in three homeless youth or those relying on social services were victims of physical violence after coming out.[31] Ray suggested that such youth may leave foster care or a shelter as a result in favor of street life, which may seem like a less dangerous alternative.[32]

## Life on the Streets for LGBT Youth

Street life can be particularly difficult for homeless youth who are lesbian, gay, bisexual, or transgender. Because of their sexual orientation or gender identity, they tend to be more susceptible to discrimination, victimization, violence and other mistreatment than heterosexual homeless youth. LGBT street kids have a high rate of mental health issues, substance abuse, poverty, unsafe sexual activity, sexually transmitted diseases, HIV infection, and various physical ailments.[33] These issues contribute to a high degree of stress. Studies show that lesbian, gay, and bisexual homeless youth "experience a unique set of stressors related directly to being sexual minorities within a heterosexually oriented society."[34] These stressors include "the stigmatization of being, or being perceived to be, [gay, lesbian, or bisexual] in a society in which homosexuality is negatively sanctioned" and the "internalization of society's stigmatization of homosexuality."[35] LGBT stress often comes from sexual abuse and other physical victimization, abuse verbally, being rejected, and additional negative experiences based largely on their sexual orientation or gender identity. The vicious succession from a troubled home life to the harsh realities of homelessness all but ensures a bleak existence for most LGBT homeless youth as they struggle for survival, often at great cost to their psychological and physical health and well-being.

## MENTAL HEALTH PROBLEMS

Lesbian, gay and bisexual (LGB) homeless youth have a high rate of mental health problems such as depression, suicidal ideation and/or attempted or carried out suicide, and psychopathology.[36] Research by David Fergusson and colleagues supported this contention, finding that LGB youth were at greater risk than heterosexual youth to have serious depression, generalized anxiety disorder, conduct disorder, and be suicidal.[37] In a mental health study of heterosexual and LGB youth, it was found that the latter group had a greater tendency to suffer from serious bouts of depression and post–traumatic stress disorder.[38]

LGB homeless youth are more likely than heterosexual youth to want to take their own lives, a state of mind that for some may have preceded becoming homeless and afterward was exacerbated by living the street life. According to the National Runaway Switchboard, an LGBT youth or one who questions their sexual orientation/gender identity, takes his or her life every five hours, forty-eight minutes.[39] In one study, 73 percent of LGB youth had suicidal ideation versus 53 percent of heterosexual youth; with half the LGB youth attempting to kill themselves on at least one occasion while only one-third of the heterosexual youth attempted suicide.[40] Similarly, 50 percent of the LGB youth in a Massachusetts study had considered committing suicide.[41]

Studies show that mental health problems can differ between male LGB and heterosexual homeless youth, as well as female LGB and heterosexual homeless youth, and any cross comparisons.[42] In a longitudinal study of runaway and homeless youth, Les Whitbeck and associates reported that gay males had a greater likelihood than heterosexual males to show signs of internalization; whereas lesbian youth tended to exhibit more indications of suicidal ideation, attempted suicide, and post–traumatic stress disorder.[43] Another study found a higher rate of mental disorders, as well as sexual and physical maltreatment, among lesbian homeless than other homeless populations.[44]

Relatively few homeless youth with mental health issues utilize or have adequate access to mental health services. Less than one in ten street youth had used mental health services, according to one study, potentially worsening current conditions or developing others that harm their mental health.[45] This finding was supported by the Midwest Homeless and Runaway Adolescent Project, which studied 602 runaway and homeless youth, concluding that such services were being under utilized by this group.[46] LGBT street youth were even less likely to seek help through mental health services, though arguably more likely to have serious mental disorders.

## SUBSTANCE ABUSE

The relationship between substance use/abuse and runaway/thrown-away homeless youth has been solidly established (see Chapter 8). Some studies have suggested that lesbian, gay, bisexual, or transgender youth may be more susceptible to having an ongoing problem with alcohol or drugs prior to becoming homeless and are more likely to develop substance abuse problems after taking to the streets.[47] This is seen largely as a coping mechanism for the burdens they face as a result of sexual orientation or gender identity issues, including confusion, alienation, prejudice, stigmatization, rejection, abuse, violence, neglect, exploitation, and other victimization. LGBT homeless youth, similar to heterosexual street kids, also use alcohol and/or drugs as part of the street culture, peer pressures, dependency, prostitution, delinquency, and additional aspects of surviving while homeless.

Researchers have found higher rates of alcohol and drug abuse among lesbian, gay, bisexual, and transgender homeless youth than those who are heterosexual.[48] In Bryan Cochran and colleagues' exploration of the issues young homeless sexual minorities are confronted with, they found LGBT homeless youth tended to use extremely addictive drugs more often.[49] The researchers also argued that being homeless "often leads to initiation or escalation of substance use."[50] In another study, nearly one in ten impoverished or homeless LGBT youth reported dealing drugs, which is seen as a correlate to drug dependency and substance abuse.[51]

Lesbian, gay, and bisexual youth have a high incidence of lifetime drug involvement. In a study by Margaret Rosario and associates, the rate of ever using illegal drugs or misusing legal drugs for LGB female and male youth was 93 percent and 89 percent, respectively.[52] Almost seven in ten of the female respondents and around six in ten of the male youth admitted to use of an illegal drug. In James Van Leeuwen and colleagues' study of substance use-related issues covering six states, they found that LGB youth were more likely than heterosexual youth to abuse alcohol; and a higher percentage of the LGB youth had enrolled in a substance abuse treatment program than their heterosexual counterparts.[53]

The high rate of substance abuse by homeless sexual minorities, along with other risk-taking experiences such as survival sex, multiple sexual partners, IV drug use and sharing of needles, puts LGBT youth in danger of contracting sexually transmitted infections, HIV, and other diseases.[54] Moreover, use of alcohol or drugs is also a factor in other aspects of street life for LGBT youth, including sexual and physical violence, sexual exploitation, mental health concerns, delinquency and criminality, and arrest and juvenile detention.[55]

## SURVIVAL SEX

Most homeless youth find themselves engaging in survival sex, or consensual sexual relations, in order to receive in return food, shelter, money, or other basic needs; as well as drugs to feed a dependency.[56] This can be in the form of prostitution or sexual activity as part of the street subculture where peer pressure and fitting in make it implicit as a survival mechanism. Some researchers have estimated that as many as one in every three homeless youth have resorted to survival sex during their time as street kids.[57] In a study of homeless youth in Los Angeles, around half the males and one-third of the females acknowledged being involved in survival sex.[58]

Homeless youth who are sexual minorities may be at greater risk for engaging in survival sex, possibly as a result of the added pressures they face in a homophobic society, along with the need to be accepted among the homeless and survive street life. In one study of homeless youth, lesbian, gay, bisexual, and transgender street kids were found to be three times as likely as heterosexual street youth to engage in survival sex.[59] Another study of homeless male youth revealed that nearly one-third had participated in survival sex, with more than four in ten of these being sexually active with other males, and over one in four engaging in survival sex with males and females.[60]

Homeless youth who are transgender are three times as likely to be involved in survival sex as other homeless sexual minorities, according to one study.[61] Transgender male prostitutes at times find themselves more in competition with female prostitutes for customers than other male prostitutes. In an article on male prostitution, one transgender teenage prostitute, who offered only oral sex for pay, spoke openly of walking the streets "side by side" with prostituted girls: "We go wherever the females are because we know we can get [johns] better than them, because we can make ourselves up to look better than them. Wherever you see girls, you might see one or two boys."[62]

Prostituted transgender homeless youth have a high rate of HIV infection as one of the implications they face from survival sex.[63] This subgroup of homeless sexual minority youth are also disproportionately likely to become exposed to sexually transmitted diseases as a result of engaging in unprotected sexual activity and/or sharing contaminated needles.[64]

According to one study, for many LGBT homeless youth, survival sex is seen as a final measure when all else fails in their attempts to continue to exist.[65] Unfortunately, the dynamics of sex for survival often means frequent and unprotected sexual activities with multiple, anonymous, partners, any of whom can pass along to homeless youth sexually transmitted diseases such as HIV. See Part VI for detailed discussion on prostituted homeless youth.

## SEXUALLY TRANSMITTED DISEASES

Homeless young sexual minorities are a magnet for sexually transmitted diseases (STDs) such as genital warts, syphilis, gonorrhea, and AIDS, due to their high-risk sexual habits, IV drug use, involvement with numerous sexual partners in survival sex, and weakened immune systems. Ineffective or inconsistent use of condoms is seen as a key component in the exposure to STDs among this street population. Researchers have found that lesbian and gay homeless youth are less likely to practice safer sex, or use condoms, than heterosexual or bisexual homeless youth.[66] Elizabeth Saewyc and colleagues associated survival sex/prostitution of homeless lesbian and bisexual youth to frequent sexual activity, sexual and physical victimization, poor use of contraceptives, and STDs.[67] Prostituted homeless gay or bisexual male youth have been linked as well to multiple unprotected sexual partners, IV use of drugs, and a high incidence of STDs.[68] In a study of young men sexually involved with men (YMSM), Michael Clatts and colleagues found a number of harmful circumstances related to becoming a drug user, including being a runaway, homeless, prostituted youth, substance abuser, IV drug user, and associated factors.[69]

The risky sexual and drug-related behaviors of LGB homeless youth makes them particularly susceptible to HIV infection. In Rashmi Gangamma and colleagues' comparison study of HIV risks among homeless lesbian, gay, bisexual, and heterosexual youth, they found that the LGB youth were at greater risk for HIV than the heterosexual youth; with the HIV risk highest for bisexual females.[70] Survival sex among the LGB homeless youth was found to be the strongest predictor of risk for HIV infection.

After a meta-examination of surveys constituting around 802,000 adolescent respondents in Canada and the United States, Elizabeth Saewyc and associates concluded that LGB youth were likely to become HIV-positive disproportionately.[71] In a study of transgender homeless runaways, it was estimated that 50 percent were involved in prostitution, with 20 percent testing positive for the AIDS virus.[72]

In describing the plight faced by many LGBT homeless youth, including exposure to STDs, researcher Paul Gibson noted bleakly:

> For many street youth, their struggle for survival becomes the fulfillment of a "suicidal script" which sees them engaging in increasingly self-destructive behaviors including unsafe sexual activity and intravenous drug use. Overwhelmed by the complexities of street life and feeling they have reached the "wrong end of the rainbow," a suicide attempt may result.[73]

# PART VI

## RUNAWAYS, HOMELESS YOUTH, AND PROSTITUTION

# 10
# Prostitution-Involved Youth

Most runaway and thrownaway youth who become homeless inevitably turn to survival sex and prostitution to make ends meet in a street life that often robs them of their youth and forces them into high-risk activities. The thriving sex-for-sale industry in the United States includes a high number of teenage (and even some preteen) and young adult prostitutes who sell their bodies to and for customers, pimps, pedophiles, pornographers, gang members, and other sexual exploiters. Prostituted youth thus become victims and offenders of sex crimes at once, subjecting them to dangerous and often unprotected sexual relations with frequent, anonymous, and known partners, placing them at risk for sexually transmitted infections, including HIV, other illnesses, and arrest. Furthermore, juvenile prostitutes are typically involved with other risky experiences detrimental to their physical and mental health and well-being, such as substance abuse, intravenous drug use, sharing dirty needles, and various delinquencies and criminality. Many prostituted youth have been the victims of sexual and physical abuse at home, both of which have been shown to be strong predictors of running away and prostitution involvement. Though law enforcement has cracked down more on teenage prostitution and those who solicit the sexual services of minors in recent years, runaway/thrownaway youth who have nowhere else to turn continue to find their way into the sex trade as homeless, detached from parents and family, while being amongst other youth who have found themselves headed down the same path.

## Definition of Prostitution

Because prostitution involves various sex acts, forms of payment, and enticement or force to participate; adults and underage prostitutes; and different laws are applicable depending on the participant and circumstances; there is no universal definition of prostitution. How does it differ from survival sex discussed in previous chapters? Or white slavery?

In general, prostitution is defined as "sexual relations that include some form of monetary payment or barter and are characterized by promiscuity and/or emotional apathy."[1] In the book *The Comfort of Sin*, the definition of prostitution is that in which a person "earns a living wholly or in part by the more or less indiscriminate, willing, and emotionally indifferent provision of sexual services of any description to another, against payment, usually in advance but not necessarily in cash."[2]

In the publication *Prostitution of Children and Child-Sex Tourism*, prostitution is defined as:

> performing, offering, or agreeing to perform any act of sexual penetration as defined by state statute or any touching or fondling of the sex organs of one person by another person, for any money, property, token, object, or article or anything of value, for the purpose of sexual arousal or gratification.[3]

While historically prostitution has been largely regarded as gender-specific,[4] or where the prostitute is female, in modern times the definition is gender-neutral and thus applies to females and males plying sexual services for payment. These include oral copulation, sodomy, same-sex prostitution, and that involving adult and child prostitutes.

Juvenile prostitution refers to prostituted minors, or persons age seventeen or younger, and is defined as "sexual acts with adults or other minors where no force is present, including intercourse, oral sex, anal sex, and sadomasochistic activities where payment is involved."[5] The United Nations Economic and Social Commission for Asia and the Pacific (UNECAP) defines child prostitution, also called child sexual exploitation, as "the use of a child for sexual purposes in exchange for cash or in-kind favors between customer, intermediary or agent or others who profit from the trade in children for these purposes."[6]

A definition of child prostitution by the End Child Prostitution, Child Pornography and Trafficking of Children for Sexual Purposes (ECPAT) is:

> the sexual exploitation of the vulnerability of children for cash or some other form of pay, and it may involve an intermediary like a pimp. This exchange is exploitative because it comes about in a relationship of unequal economic, cognitive and psycho-social power and often is physically and emotionally detrimental to the young person's further development.[7]

Survival sex is often viewed as another term for prostitution, particularly among homeless youth. However, while prostitution is legally defined as sexual relations for monetary compensation or something of similar or equal value, survival sex need not require an exchange of money or monetary substitute for the sexual relations to occur. Instead, survival sex refers to providing sexual services in exchange for whatever basic necessities are needed or the means to acquire, including food, clothing, shelter, drugs, or money.[8]

White slavery is a form of prostitution that often involves juvenile and young adult females in the trafficking of persons for sexual exploitation against their wishes.[9] Unlike consensual prostitution (though for most prostituted homeless youth, being in the sex trade is a matter of survival and, as such, can be considered forced participation), white slavery prostitutes are compelled to sell their bodies — usually by pimps, pornographers, pedophiles, or slave traders.[10]

Though white slavery/sex trafficking occurs most often in Southeast Asia and Europe, victims are also trafficked into the United States, working as streetwalkers as well as in houses of prostitution, nightclubs, and massage parlors.[11] In some instances, youth are sexually enslaved within this country and trafficked by pimps, gangs, and child molesters.[12]

## *The Extent of Prostituted Youth*

Just how many youth are prostituted in the United States? The figures have varied considerably, given definitional inconsistencies, methodological differences, hidden child prostitution, reluctance of prostituted youth to disclose this to interviewers, the transitory nature of teenage street prostitutes, and other difficulties. However, there is reason to believe that there may be anywhere from tens of thousands to possibly over a million runaway/thrownaway and homeless youth being sexually exploited or vulnerable to sexual victimization in this country's sex trade industry.[13] These prostituted youth are white, African-American, Latino, Asian, Native American, and come from various backgrounds and household income levels.

According to a U.S. Department of Health and Human Services report, an estimated 300,000 persons under the age of seventeen are prostituted homeless youth in the United States.[14] Some of these juvenile prostitutes are said to be as young as five years old.[15] In a paper published by ECPAT, the estimate of underage prostitutes in this country was placed at 400,000, with as many as 50,000 other youth and women trafficked here from abroad as sex slaves.[16] Law enforcement officials have somewhat conservatively estimated the number of juvenile prostitutes on the streets to be as low as 1,400 and as high as 300,000 (see discussion on prostituted youth and official data later in this chapter).[17]

Some researchers have suggested that there are may be many more prostituted youth on the streets. For example, Nancy Walker, a Professor of Family and Child Ecology at Michigan State University, cited Justice Department data that estimated anywhere from 100,000 to 3 million teenagers are prostituted in America annually.[18] Other experts on juvenile prostitution have put forth that as many as half a million children under the age of sixteen are active in the sex trade[19]; with double or triple that number, depending on the source, when including sixteen and seventeen-year-old prostitutes.[20]

Researchers have also estimated the number of at-risk youth for commercial sexual exploitation. Richard Estes and Neil Weiner, who examined the commercial sexual exploitation of children in the United States, Canada, and Mexico, estimated that there were around 326,000 youth at risk of being sexually exploited commercially, or for purposes of prostitution in this country.[21] A comparable estimate of 293,000 minors in danger of being victims of commercial sexual exploitation was made by the Justice Department's Child Exploitation and Obscenity Section.[22] In a study of sexually trafficked female youth into the United States from eight countries, including Columbia, Ecuador, Mexico, Peru, and Venezuela, Heather Clawson and colleagues, estimated that about 15,000 females younger than nineteen years of age were at risk of becoming victims of sex trafficking.[23]

In spite of the variance in estimates of actual versus at-risk youth becoming prostituted, the relationship between homeless youth and prostitution has been firmly established.[24] Studies show that there are anywhere from hundreds of thousands to well over a million youth living on the streets from year to year.[25] An estimated 1.6 million youth are considered homeless or have run away from home on an annual basis, according to the U.S. Department of Housing and Urban Development.[26] Likewise, results from a National Health Interview Study found that 1.6 million youth between ages twelve and seventeen had been homeless for at least one night within the past year.[27] In a Research Triangle Institute study done on behalf of the U.S. Department of Health and Human Services, an estimated 2.8 million youth twelve to seventeen years of age had ever run away from home.[28] In their study of street life and homeless youth, Les Whitbeck and Ronald Simons put forward that approximately 40 percent of runaways never returned home.[29]

The evidence indicates that for youth who end up homeless, there is a strong likelihood that given their lack of education, marketable skills, and job prospects, along with sexually exploitable vulnerability, selling their bodies may be one of the few options for survival on the mean streets where sexual predators and victimizers are in abundance.[30] Indeed, a recent report in *Newsweek* suggested that teenage prostitution in the United States was on the rise, attributing this to more aggressive recruiting by pimps, with the prostituted youth predominately homeless runaways or thrownaways, illegal immigrants, and poor urban youth (though an increase was seen as well in prostituted middle and upper middle class youth who were not homeless or victims of child sexual or physical abuse as often related to runaways).[31]

## Prostitution-Involved Runaways/Thrownaways

The precise number of runaway or thrownaway youth who become prostitutes or engage in survival sex as part of the homeless population is unknown. According to the Office of Juvenile Justice and Delinquency Prevention's Second National Incidence Studies of Missing, Abducted, Runaway and Thrownaway Children (NISMART-2), less than 1 percent of an estimated 1.7 million youth with runaway or thrownaway episodes in 1999 had prostituted themselves to receive money, shelter, food, or drugs.[32] Another 2 percent were said to have been in the presence of a sexually exploitative individual while away from home.[33] These figures suggest that few runaways/thrownaways resort to prostitution as homeless youth.

Most experts on teenage prostitution believe that runaway and thrownaway youth who actually become homeless (as opposed to staying with a family member or friend) almost inevitably turn to prostitution at some point as a means to meet their basic necessities and often as a result of the coercive powers of pimps and other child sexual exploiters. According to a National Center for Missing and Exploited Children report, as many as one out of three runaway and homeless youth become involved in street prostitution or survival sex; whereas more than three in four prostituted youth have reported running away from home on at least one occasion.[34] In Ruth Dean and Melissa Thomson's study of teenage prostitution, they found that the majority of prostituted youth run away from home or substitute care.[35]

Other researchers have also shown a strong correlation between runaways and prostitution. Walker found that two in three teenage prostitutes were runaways, with more than eight in ten presently or previously homeless.[36] The Klass Kids Foundation reported that an estimated 55 percent of homeless female youth were actively involved in the sex trade industry as prostitutes.[37] In Z. M. Lukman's study of runaway prostituted youth, nearly 78 percent were said to be more likely to become prostitution-involved than participants in other delinquent or criminal behavior.[38] David Barrett posited that being a runaway was a more significant dynamic in youth involvement in the sex-for-sale industry than sexual abuse.[39]

The strong association between runaways and prostituted youth was summed up in an analysis of children in the sex for sale business:

> Prostitution of children is closely tied to life on the streets. Many youth run away from difficult situations at home. They may become involved in prostitution through loneliness and emotional vulnerability as well as homelessness and the need to survive. The children's "young age, lack of education[,] and lack of the necessary street sense to survive alone," contribute to their need to engage in "survival sex" ... that defines many of these young people's lives. [Without viable alternatives,] many turn to prostitution as a means of surviving on the streets.[40]

## Entry into Prostitution

The pathway into the world of prostitution for runaway, thrownaway, and homeless youth often comes with little time to truly digest the implications of selling sex and its associations in the street subculture. Studies show that within thirty-six to forty-eight hours, and sometimes even sooner, after a youth becomes homeless, they will be solicited for sexual favors; persuaded, coerced, recruited, or abducted into prostitution and/or pornography by pimps, customers, gangs, pedophiles, or pornographers.[41] In many cases, the sexual exploiter may pretend to be interested in helping or romancing the new street youth in order to charm and seduce the unsuspecting, naive victim into compliance. Other times, the runaway or thrownaway may be supplied with alcohol or drugs as part of the recruitment and laying the groundwork process. Most newly homeless youth, away on their own for the first time and frightened, are easy marks for those who would take advantage of their desperation and vulnerability.

Researchers have found that the longer runaway/thrownaway youth are without a secure place to call home, the likelihood they will never return to their original home increases, as does the probability of becoming prostituted or otherwise victims of sexual exploitation.[42] Staying homeless for thirty days has been shown to be the single greatest dynamic in leading street youth to become prostitution-involved.[43] However, most homeless youth enter the sex trade much sooner. According to one study, after two weeks of being homeless, three out of four runaways will have participated in prostitution, child pornography, drug, or delinquent activities.[44]

The average age of entrance into prostitution is fourteen, with the median age for prostituted youth 15.5 years.[45] Many prostituted youth have been reported to be under the age of twelve and in some cases as young as nine years of age.[46] The average age for girls to enter prostitution is twelve to fourteen; while for boys and transgender youth, the average age of becoming prostitution-involved is eleven to thirteen.[47]

Most prostituted youth escape from or are forced to leave unsafe or dysfunctional home environments that often include such issues as physical and sexual child abuse, substance abuse, domestic violence, mental illness, and family discord. Many also have school or peer problems that play a role in their leaving home. Unfortunately, the street world they enter provides a host of new troubles, unstable living conditions, dangerous situations, exploiters and victimizers, and negative connotations that few, if any, homeless youth are equipped to deal with.

## Prostituted Youth and Child Sexual Abuse

The relationship between child sexual abuse and prostituted youth has been well documented in the literature.[48] One report noted that sexual abuse "has a significant impact on the probability that a runaway will become involved with prostitution," further suggesting that "sex abuse appears to indirectly increase the chance of prostitution by increasing the risk of running away."[49]

Most runaway youth who enter prostitution have been victims of physical and sexual abuse, with the latter the strongest indicator of becoming drawn into the sex trade industry.[50] Some studies report that more than half of runaway youth were victims of sexual and physical abuse.[51] An Australian study found that nearly three out of four runaways had been sexual abuse victims prior to reaching the age of fourteen.[52] Similarly, another study found that almost eight in ten prostituted girls had been victims of child molestation, and nine in ten victims of physical abuse before entrance into prostitution.[53] In Stephen Gaetz's research, homeless street youth were said to be five times more likely than non homeless youth to have been sexually abused while living at home.[54]

Researcher Christina Hoag described such a case of a sexually victimized runaway turned prostituted homeless youth:

> By the time she was eight, Amanda had been sexually abused by her father's friend for four years. At twelve, she was peddling crack. At fourteen, she was selling sex on the sidewalk. Her pimp beat her weekly to keep her working, stitching up her wounds himself to avoid questions at a hospital. Her average

earnings of $600 for a 13-hour day of turning tricks bought him a car.... Caught when a cop stopped one of her customers for a broken tail light, she was sent to Children of the Night, a residential program in suburban Los Angeles that rehabilitates teen prostitutes.[55]

Child sexual abuse has been shown to be a key issue in the backgrounds of lesbian, gay, bisexual, and transgender (LGBT) prostituted youth. A study of LGBT prostitution-involved youth found that most had left home due to sexual or physical abuse.[56] Another study of prostituted male youth in London reported that sexual abuse was the primary reason for running away from home.[57] In his research on homeless LGBT youth, Nicholas Ray cited a study suggesting that the reaction of parents to discovering a child is gay, lesbian, bisexual, or transgender can actually result in sexual or physical abuse, leading to the victim's homelessness and the methods for survival that accompany it.[58]

## Violence Encountered by Prostituted Youth

Prostitution-involved youth are frequently the targets of violence perpetrated by customers, pimps, pedophiles, pornographers, gangs, and others they encounter in the sex trade and street life. The victimization is in the form of physical assaults, rape/sexual assaults, forced sexual perversions, robberies, verbal attacks, intimidation, and other violence, including murder.[59] As most underage prostitutes are neither physically nor mentally equipped to defend themselves against attackers, while being in a high-risk environment for violence, they face potential threats to their health and well-being at every turn. According to studies, around two in three prostituted youth are the victims of violence perpetrated by pimps and customers.[60] Another study of street prostitutes found a high rate of rape and other violence in the course of prostituting.[61]

Prostituted female youth tend to be the victims of sexual assaults more often than prostituted male youth in the street environment, given their greater association with pimps and physically superior violent johns and other victimizers. However, boy prostitutes are still vulnerable to sexual and physical assaults by older males, gang members, and others who prey on children. One study found that prostituted males tended to be victimized through assaults and robberies most often by "homophobic male onlookers" than customers.[62]

All young prostitutes are at risk of being murdered. Apart from the everyday threats of potential fatal violence from customers, pimps, and drug addicts prostituted youth face, they are also a prime target of sexual and serial killers.[63] For instance, the so-called Green River Killer murdered at least forty-eight females during the 1980s and 1990s in Washington and Oregon. Most of the victims were runaways and teenage prostitutes.[64]

Though prostitution-involved youth are prone to every type of violence that exists in the homeless world, most shy away from reporting their victimization to the authorities for fear of being disregarded, retribution from their attackers, and/or being arrested themselves as runaways and returned to an abusive home environment or put in juvenile detention.[65] Unfortunately this reality only compounds the situation while increasing the risk teenage prostitutes face for further victimization.

In an examination of the culture of violence homeless prostituted youth are immersed in, B. Schissel and K. Fedec found not only a high degree of child sexual and physical abuse experienced by the prostitute, but proposed that prostitution itself "creates a context in which those youth who are involved will run a high risk of being damaged by a predator or by themselves — whether directly through assault and self-injury or indirectly through high-risk behavior."[66] Similarly, in another study of streetwalkers in Vancouver, Canada it was found that most had been physically and sexually abused prior to and after entering prostitution, and a very high percentage had been victims of dating violence.[67]

## Prostituted Youth and Child Pornography

Prostitution-involved youth and are often lured or forced into child pornography as another disturbing aspect of child sexual exploitation. Child pornography, also known as child porn or kiddie porn, is defined as "photographs, videos, books, magazines, and motion pictures that depict children in sexually explicit acts with other children, adults, animals, and/or foreign objects."[68] Child pornography is a multibillion dollar international business that has moved onto the Internet and other digital devices as a means of further exploiting the innocent minors pornographers and pedophiles target.[69] In the United States alone, child porn takes in as much as six billion dollars annually, exposing victims as young as five up to well into their late teens to "every form of child sexual exploitation, including molestation, rape, sadism, prostitution, bestiality, triolism, exhibitionism, voyeurism, and even murder."[70]

Child pornographers often set their sights on runaway, thrownaway, and prostituted homeless youth because they are easily accessible, vulnerable to sexual exploitation, desperate enough to engage in survival sex and pornographic activities, and of fairly low risk for detection by law enforcement (though more aggressive efforts are being made these days to go after pornographers and purveyors of child porn and its customers),[71] and often have mental health or substance abuse issues, further making these youth susceptible to victimization. Most victims of child pornography have been sexually abused at home and sexually victimized through prostitution, rape, sexual slavery, sex trafficking, and other sexual mistreatment as street kids.[72] This puts them at even higher risk for sexually transmitted infections such as HIV.[73]

In many instances, pimps and pornographers are one and the same or work in conjunction in sexually exploiting children. According to the *Prostitution of Children and Child-Sex Tourism*, compelling prostituted female youth to participate in pornographic activities is another way for pimps to "control and humiliate the girl and break her resistance," as well as "normalize the practice of prostitution."[74] In today's Internet age, some pimps use pornographic images of the girls in their stable to peddle them, while many clients and pedophiles photograph or videotape prostituted youth for their own perverse pleasures and collecting child porn.[75]

The correlation between juvenile prostitution and child pornography often begins with the runaway or thrownaway turned street youth and homeless. As explained by teenage prostitution researcher Clare Tattersall: "You do not have to be a runaway to be forced into pornography. But because runaways are more likely to become prostitutes, they are also more likely to be forced into pornography."[76] A survey of prostitution-involved teenagers found that about one in three were also involved in child pornography.[77] The percentage of prostituted youth being exploited by pornographers is likely much higher.

In her study of prostituted youth in New York City, Mia Spangenberg reported that child prostitution is

> a continuum both in terms of the age of the young people involved and the range of exploitation.... Some youth work part-time, some full-time, and some are engaged in prostitution while others work in sex clubs, in the pornography business or both.[78]

For many homeless teenagers looking for any means to survive living on the streets or feed a drug addiction, it may be hard to resist the lure of seemingly "easy" money that child pornographers often promise but can never deliver. While most prostituted youth become involved in pornography after entering the sex-for-sale business, others were initially recruited into child pornography before being coerced into prostitution, maximizing the potential for sexual exploitation.

## Prostituted Youth and Police Contact

Though prostituted youth are generally regarded as victims of sexual and physical abuse and troubled histories and sexual exploitation, they are also subject to arrest as violators of prostitution laws that are in effect in every state where it concerns child prostitution. The delicate balance between victim and offender has made it difficult for law enforcement to handle cases of prostituted youth, who are mainly runaways, thrownaways, and/or homeless and often involved in prostitution as an act of desperation, drug addiction, or a lifestyle dictated by the street environment.

Arrests of prostitution-involved teenagers are often looked upon by police departments as a way to rescue or divert the victimized and sexually exploited youth from a difficult life.[79] In many instances, however, police view prostituted youth in a manner consistent with adult prostituted individuals as sex offenders.[80] Other times, the efforts and resources of law enforcement agencies are either inadequate or the reluctance of the prostituted youth too strong to keep them from returning to the streets or going back to an environment they ran from, which includes an abusive domicile or foster care.

According to the Federal Bureau of Investigation's (FBI) annual publication, *Crime in the United States(CIUS)*, in 2008, there were 7,764 arrests of persons under the age of twenty-one for prostitution and commercialized vice in this country (see Figure 10.1). Of these, 1,158 arrests were of persons younger than eighteen years of age. The majority of juvenile arrestees were between the ages of fifteen and seventeen. Female juveniles were more than three times as likely to be arrested as male juveniles on prostitution charges, as shown in Table 10.1. There were 878 arrests of females under eighteen for prostitution and commercialized vice compared to 280 males under eighteen, with older teenagers arrested most often for both females and males.

Black teenagers are disproportionately arrested for prostitution-related offenses, constituting more than 57 percent of the arrests of persons under eighteen for prostitution and commercialized vice in 2008. This is well above their numbers in the juvenile population of around 15 percent (see Figure 10.2) and may reflect greater visibility in inner city areas known for prostitution as well as racial prejudice and police discretion. White teenagers, who comprise the majority of prostituted youth being sexually exploited in this

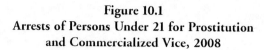

# Figure 10.1
## Arrests of Persons Under 21 for Prostitution and Commercialized Vice, 2008

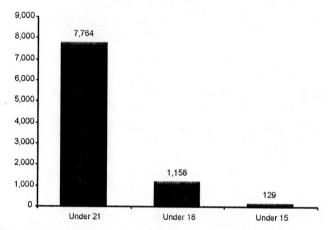

SOURCE: Adapted from U.S. Department of Justice, Federal Bureau of Investigation, *Crime in the United States, 2008*, Table 41, http://www.fbi.gov/ucr/cius2008/arrests/index.html.

# Table 10.1
## Juvenile Arrests for Prostitution and Commercialized Vice, by Gender and Age, 2008

| Age | # of Arrests |
| --- | --- |
| *Females* | |
| 17 | 386 |
| 16 | 25 |
| 15 | 133 |
| 13–14 | 91 |
| 10–12 | 4 |
| Under 10 | 5 |
| Total Under 18 | 878 |
| *Males* | |
| 17 | 142 |
| 16 | 70 |
| 15 | 39 |
| 13–14 | 23 |
| 10–12 | 3 |
| Under 10 | 3 |
| Total Under 18 | 280 |

SOURCE: Derived from U.S. Department of Justice, Federal Bureau of Investigation, *Crime in the United States, 2008*, Tables 39 and 40, http://www.fbi.gov/ucr/cius 2008/arrests/index.html.

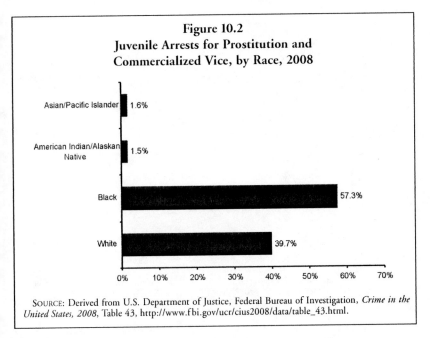

**Figure 10.2**
**Juvenile Arrests for Prostitution and**
**Commercialized Vice, by Race, 2008**

Asian/Pacific Islander  1.6%

American Indian/Alaskan
Native  1.5%

Black  57.3%

White  39.7%

0%  10%  20%  30%  40%  50%  60%  70%

SOURCE: Derived from U.S. Department of Justice, Federal Bureau of Investigation, *Crime in the United States, 2008,* Table 43, http://www.fbi.gov/ucr/cius2008/data/table_43.html.

country, accounted for nearly 40 percent of the arrests of persons younger than eighteen for prostitution and commercialized vice. Asian and Native American juveniles made up around 3 percent of the arrestees. Though official data does not track arrests of Hispanics, evidence suggests that there is a high rate of arrests of Hispanic youth for crimes such as drug and property offenses, and prostitution.[81]

Ten-year arrest trends reveal that from 1999 to 2008, overall arrests of persons under the age of eighteen for prostitution and commercialized vice rose more than 20 percent (see Figure 10.3). For female minors, arrests climbed almost 65 percent during the period, while male juvenile arrests declined by nearly 35 percent. As some studies suggest that there may be as many prostituted male youth as female youth, the differences in arrest rates could reflect greater visibility by prostitution-involved females as well as more efforts to get them off the streets by law enforcement with their discretionary powers.[82]

The total of 1,158 arrests of persons under the age of eighteen for prostitution and commercialized vice in 2008 is low compared to the 57,626 arrests of persons age eighteen and over for prostitution-related offenses.[83] Moreover, the figures pale to the 84,054 arrests of juveniles as runaways in 2008, commonly seen to be the precursor for prostitution-involved youth (see more detailed discussion on runaways and arrest data in Chapter 6).[84]

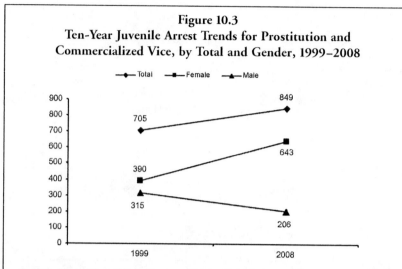

**Figure 10.3**
**Ten-Year Juvenile Arrest Trends for Prostitution and Commercialized Vice, by Total and Gender, 1999–2008**

SOURCE: Adapted from U.S. Department of Justice, Federal Bureau of Investigation, *Crime in the United States, 2008*, Tables 32 and 33, http://www.fbi.gov/ucr/cius2008/arrests/index.html.

The arrest data also falls well short of the estimated number of prostituted youth believed to be active in the sex trade industry in the United States.[85] Many such youth come into contact with or are arrested by law enforcement as runaways or for other related offenses such as alcohol and drug crimes, property and violent offenses, vandalism, and curfew and loitering law violations.[86] As prostitution-involved youth are a transient population and often not a priority for cash strapped police departments, many sexually exploited teens manage to avoid contact with law enforcement officers or are disregarded in favor of other offenders deemed more serious, such as violent criminals, gang members, and drug dealers.

Recent years have seen a greater emphasis by law enforcement agencies on efforts to try and steer prostitution-involved youth away from the streets and/or pimps, as well as the juvenile justice system, while going after pimps, customers, pedophiles, pornographers, sex traffickers, and others who sexually exploit children.[87] In addition to targeting traditional street prostitution, authorities are cracking down on the growing problem of teenage prostitution over the Internet, such as the popular Craigslist.[88]

In an analysis of information taken from the FBI's National Incident-Based Reporting System (NIBRS), which gathers crime data known to law enforcement, for the years 1997 to 2000, David Finkelhor and Richard Ormrod profiled prostitution-involved juveniles.[89] Among their findings were the following:

- The prostitution of juveniles had a greater likelihood of involving multiple offenders than prostituted adults police came across.
- Juvenile prostitution tended to take place more often outside and in large metropolitan areas.
- The likelihood was greater that police would treat prostitution-involved youth as offenders rather than victims of crime and sexual exploitation.
- Prostituted females and young prostitutes were more likely to be considered as victims than males and older prostitutes.
- Female juvenile prostitutes were more likely than prostituted male juveniles to be referred to social service agencies and elsewhere.
- Prostituted youth were less likely to be arrested than prostituted adults.
- More than six out of ten juvenile prostitution incidents involved male offenders.
- More than four in ten male juvenile prostitution incidents consisted of assisting/promoting prostitution.
- Almost nine in ten female juvenile prostitution incidents involved prostitution only.
- Around three in four juvenile prostitution incidents resulted in an arrest.

The researchers also found that among prostituted youth, virtually all the prostitution activities were segregated by gender.[90] This is not too surprising, given that female and male juvenile prostitutes generally operate under different rules with different clientele within the same street subculture, with females typically having pimps who dictate their movement; whereas males tend to work independently, though they too can be controlled by others, such as older prostitutes, customers, pornographers, and drug dealers. See Chapters 11 and 12 for more discussion on female and male prostituted youth, respectively.

# 11

# Prostituted Female Youth

According to many researchers, females constitute the majority of youth involved in teenage prostitution, though some studies have found that male youth are at least equally as active in the sex trade industry. Most of these girls are runaways or castaways, have been victims of child sexual and physical abuse, neglect, mental illness, substance abuse, or otherwise come from homes beset with family conflict and an unsafe environment. As illustrated in the previous chapter, becoming homeless or being forced to live on the street makes it a near certainty that most such youth will resort to survival sex or prostitution to meet basic needs such as food and shelter, or feed alcohol or drug habits. Others are forced into prostitution and/or child pornography by pimps, pornographers, sex rings, and gangs; while many are victims of molestation, rape, sexually perverse acts, and other sexual and physical violence. Prostituted females are especially vulnerable to victimization, with most under the control of abusive pimps and subjected to the violent whims of customers. A high pregnancy rate exists among prostitution-involved girls, who tend to practice unsafe sex with multiple and anonymous partners. This and other risky behavior, such as the sharing of needles for intravenous drug use, also makes prostituted female youth prone to infectious diseases like HIV and pelvic inflammatory disease. The combination of a troubled history, dangerous street life, flourishing child sex-for-sale industry, and few legitimate opportunities for employment leaves most prostituted female youth with few viable options for survival or escape from their predicament.

## The Extent of Female Youth Involved Prostitution

It is unknown just how many prostituted youth in the United States are female. However, some experts believe that females comprise as many as two-thirds of the juvenile prostitution population[1] estimated at anywhere from around 300,000[2] to, in one report, as high as 3 million.[3] Other data also suggest that a high percentage of prostitution-involved youth are female.[4]

The vast majority of prostituted youth in this country are runaways or thrownaways, with more than half thought to be female.[5] According to the 2002 published Second National Incidence Studies of Missing, Abducted, Runaway and Thrownaway Children, there are roughly 1.7 million youth with a runaway/thrownaway episode annually.[6] The National Runaway Switchboard projected that between 1.6 and 2.8 million youth run away or are thrown out of the house in any given year.[7] It is estimated that at least 300,000 of these runaways are seen as hard core or repeat runners who take to the street each year as homeless youth.[8] Studies show that more than two out of every three girl runaways who stay away from home will end up becoming involved in prostitution.[9]

Being homeless is thought to be one of the strongest indicators of a youth turning to survival sex and prostitution to meet their basic needs of food, clothing, shelter, and non essentials such as drugs and transportation.[10] Some studies show that underage females and males are equally likely to become homeless[11]; while others indicate that female youth are more likely than their male counterparts to become homeless.[12] The U.S. Department of Housing and Urban Development reported that approximately 1.6 million youth run away or are homeless every year.[13] Around 2.8 million youth between twelve and seventeen were estimated by the Research Triangle Institute to have at least one episode of being homeless as a result of running away.[14] Researchers Les Whitbeck and Ronald Simons estimated that four in ten runaways will become homeless.[15]

Once a youth is living on the street, it takes virtually no time at all — usually anywhere from thirty-six to forty-eight hours — before she or he is propositioned for sex by strangers in exchange for assisting them in meeting basic necessities.[16] Many youth with nowhere else to turn fall into the trap and thus begin a life of prostitution and sexual exploitation. Within two weeks of being homeless, three-quarters of youth will have been prostituted, recruited into child pornography, or sexually exploited in other ways.[17]

## Entry into Prostitution

Prostituted females often first begin selling sex during their early teen years, though some start prostituting as early as five or six years of age.[18] The average age for girls entering the sex-for-sale business is between twelve and fourteen, according to a number of studies.[19] Researchers Susan Hunter[20] and D. Kelly Weisberg[21] found that the average age for girls to become prostitutes was fourteen; a finding supported by Mimi Silbert and Ayala Pines.[22] In her study of female sex workers, Susan McIntyre reported that fourteen was the mean age of entrance into the sex trade.[23]

One study found that most prostitution-involved girls began plying their trade between the ages of fifteen and seventeen.[24] However, many believe that a high percentage of female prostitutes are entering the business at younger ages. Marcia Cohen's study found that girls started prostituting between the ages of nine and twelve[25]; while 25 percent of the female prostitutes in Miriam Saphira's research were initiated into the business at age thirteen or younger, including 10 percent who were twelve or under.[26] Fifty percent of the prostitutes were fourteen and fifteen years of age. A longtime streetwalker in New York City recently surmised that "half of the girls in the renowned child prostitute tracks in East New York and Long Island City, Queens are between the ages of thirteen to fifteen."[27]

According to Mia Spangenberg, "Many girls physically mature between the ages of twelve and thirteen and are prime candidates for the sex trade.... Since the *average* age for starting out is between twelve and thirteen, there are youth that start even younger."[28] Most of these prostitution-involved females have been victims of familial sexual abuse and other types of victimization prior to and even after entrance into prostitution, making their journey into the sex trade industry that much more difficult.[29]

To put in its proper perspective the terrible toll entering prostitution at an early age can take on a girl's mental and physical state, the following observation was made in a study of the commercial sexual exploitation of youth:

> A girl who begins prostitution at fourteen will have submitted to the sexual demands of four thousand men before she is old enough to drive a car, eight thousand men before she is old enough to vote, and twelve thousand men before she is deemed mature enough to buy a single beer in most states.[30]

## Child Sexual and Physical Abuse

A strong predictor of involvement in prostitution by underage females is a history of sexual and physical child maltreatment. Studies reveal that the vast majority of prostituted girls have been victims of childhood sexual and physical abuse, often perpetrated by parents or guardians, but also by other family members or non strangers.[31] In the Huckleberry House Project's study of juvenile prostitution, 90 percent of the prostituted females had been sexually abused.[32] Two-thirds of the girl prostitutes in Mimi Silbert's study had been incest or abuse victims.[33] Half the prostitution-involved girls Nancy Walker studied were sexually abused before leaving home.[34]

Other research also shows a strong correlation between childhood physical or sexual abuse and teenage prostitution.[35] One study found that nearly eight in ten prostituted girls had been victims of sexual abuse and nine out of ten physical abuse prior to entering prostitution.[36] Another study associated juvenile prostitution to generational prostitution, incest, sexual assaults, substance abuse, and family dysfunction.[37] Daniel Campagna and Donald Poffenberger stressed that a precursor to involvement in prostitution was being sexually abused by a father, stepfather, or other male father figure, such as the mother's romantic partner[38]; which was consistent with conclusions drawn by Ronald Simons and Les Whitbeck[39]; while Weisberg reported that a high percentage of prostituted girls had been victimized by intrafamilial child sexual and physical abuse.[40]

Studies on runaways and homeless female youth further support the connection to child sexual and/or physical abuse and prostitution.[41] It was estimated by the National Network of Runaway and Youth Services that seven in ten runaways in youth shelters have been sexually abused.[42] In one study of abused runaways, more than 87 percent of those sexually abused were female, while girls represented almost 84 percent of runaways who had been sexually and physically abused.[43] According to Susan McClanahan and colleagues, victims of childhood sexual abuse who were runaways were considerably more likely than those who had not left home to have been involved at some point with prostitution or were currently active in the sex trade.[44]

A study of homeless youth found that 47 percent had been sexually abused and 31 percent physically abused while living at home.[45] Homeless girls were much more likely to have been the victims of child sexual abuse than homeless boys. In a study by the U.S. Department of Health and Human Services, 46 percent of runaways and homeless teens had been physical abuse victims, while nearly one in five had been sexually victimized by a family or household member.[46]

In *Runaway Kids and Teenage Prostitution*, it was noted: "Children who are sexually abused are at increased risk to run away from home; in turn, most long-term runaways will become prostituted youth. Girls who are sexually abused are more likely than boys to leave home as a direct consequence and engage in a prostitution lifestyle."[47] Moreover, some researchers such as Deborah Brock[48] and Steven Bittle[49] have written about the redefining of juvenile prostitution as child sexual abuse in and of itself as opposed to a cause and effect relationship.

## Prostitution-Involved Girls and Pimps

For the vast majority of girls involved in prostitution, pimps play a major role in everything from recruitment to where they ply their trade to how much customers are charged for sexual favors. It is estimated that between 75 and 95 percent of all female teenage prostitutes work the streets for pimps, who use a combination of charm, coercion, drugs, violence and street smarts to control their stable of prostituted girls; some of whom can earn up to $500 a day according to law enforcement authorities.[50] Most prostitution-involved female youth are initiated into the sex trade business by pimps or so-called boyfriends (though most pimps are male, there are some female pimps or madams who often were ex-prostitutes), who seek out such vulnerable girls to be sexually exploited. Studies have found that as many as nine in ten prostituted girls entered prostitution as a result of the persuasive abilities and aggressive techniques of pimps.[51] For most of these girls, their ties to pimps will last for as long as they are in the business. One survey reported that virtually every teenage streetwalker reported being connected to a pimp in some capacity.[52]

Runaway/thrownaway and homeless female youth are disproportionately victimized by pimp recruiters for prostitution because of their naïveté, vulnerability, dire straits, and easy manipulation.[53] Pimps and their recruiters or runners (who are often also prostituted teenagers) find these girls at "bus and train stations, shopping malls, coffee shops, arcades, street corners, and anywhere that runaway, wayward, and lost kids hang out or end up."[54] Youth shelters are another popular place for pimps to set their sights on to find vulnerable new recruits for sexual exploitation.[55] Prospective juvenile sex workers are relatively easy to pick out, as they typically are disheveled, look hungry, alone, disoriented, frightened, under the influence of alcohol or drugs, and in need of comfort and friendship. Pimps use all these traits to their advantage in befriending, romancing, or "coming to the rescue" of such youth, who are often unaware of the dangerous path they are being led down.

The typical pattern of seduction pimps often employ in winning teenage girls over was described in an article on pimping:

> It often starts out with romance. Seduced at malls and in schoolyards, courted with restaurant meals and expensive gifts, the girls eventually find themselves cut off from their families and being asked to "return a favor." They are all, after all, very young. But the pimps also choose their targets well — girls from

broken homes, girls living on the streets, girls who are just somehow troubled.[56]

Though prostituted teenage girls are typically associated with pimp controlled streetwalking prostitution, they are also placed by pimps in massage parlors, escort services, topless bars, sex rings, with pornographers and pedophiles, and advertised on the Internet.[57] Pimps also often shift their prostitution stable from city to city to try and evade law enforcement crackdowns as well as maintain a psychological and physical hold on the females they sexually exploit.[58]

Experts on child prostitution have identified different types of pimps. In *Teen Prostitution*, Joan Johnson described three primary kinds of pimps: (1) the *popcorn pimp*, (2) the *player pimp*, and (3) the *Mack pimp* as follows[59]:

- *Popcorn pimp*— recruits primarily runaways, highly competitive with other pimps, most likely to be violent toward their stable of girls, least successful type of pimp with a high turnover rate of prostitutes.

- *Player pimp*— more established and successful than popcorn pimps with one "special" girl among small stable; relies more on psychological manipulation than violence in controlling prostitutes.

- *Mack pimp*— the elite among pimps, often combining street smarts with sharp business acumen; invests profits from sex trade into legitimate businesses; has the largest number of prostituted females in stable.

Rasmusson divided pimps into two categories: (1) *a villain pimp* who "lives off the victim, beats ... and makes false promises," and (2) a *mutual arrangement type pimp*, where he purportedly will protect the prostituted girl from law enforcement and sexual predators or perverts.[60] In the latter instance, it was noted that pimps have little interest in the welfare and safety of prostituted girls, aside from the potential loss of income they provide.

Though most of the pimps who go after gullible teenage or even younger girls (boys are rarely the target of pimps) are initially strangers or associated with other prostitutes who serve as recruiters, that is not always the case. The pimp or procurer is sometimes a member of the prostituted female's own family, such as parent/guardian or brother or sister.[61] According to Parry Aftab of an Internet safety group, when parents are the pimps, "there is almost a 100 percent chance that these kids are already being molested and will continue to be abused."[62]

Gangs have also become involved in the pimping of female youth, targeting runaways, thrownaways, drug dependent or promiscuous girls, school dropouts, and other vulnerable or coerced teenagers. According to one study on prostituted children:

> These girls are under the control of more than one gang member, which places greater restrictions on their freedom. They are also subject to more violence, including sexual assault and rape, and may be at greater risk for STDs and AIDS, since they will likely have more than one gang member as a sexual partner.[63]

Experts believe that as gang recruitment of new members grows, at-risk female youth will most likely continue to be targeted for commercial sexual exploitation and victimization.

Violence or the threat of it is the pimp's most powerful tool in keeping his prostitutes in line. Though studies[64] show that only a small percentage of female youth are actually forced into the sex-for-sale industry per se, once a girl is part of a pimp's stable, "she is generally subject to his rules, regulations, and manipulation which includes falling in love, working for him, believing him, giving him much of her earnings, and violence."[65] Anne Rasmusson echoed this view, pointing out:

> Pimps usually impose quotas of earnings on their girls, give them little money, beat them if they fail to meet their quotas, and often have a "stable" of girls who work for them. Pimps most frequently beat them for not making enough money, being disrespectful to the pimp, violating some rules, or leaving, or threatening to leave.[66]

Prostituted female youth are commonly the victims of violence at the hands of their pimps who use physical assault, sexual assault, verbal abuse, and threats to keep the fear, psychological dependence, respect, cooperation, and loyalty of the girls in their stable. In a study of prostitution-involved female youth, most were found to be the victims of "extreme sexual, physical, and psychological abuse" from pimps and customers.[67] The physical mistreatment includes being hit with closed fists, slapped, kicked, burned, and beaten with "coat hangers to lashings with a six-foot bull whip."[68] In a self-report survey, over two-thirds of prostituted streetwalkers reported being the victims of repeated pimp perpetrated assaults[69]; with some prostitutes accusing their pimps of "severe violence, torture and attempted murder."[70]

According to former prostitute Rachel Lloyd, executive director of a New York City education and mentoring program for girl prostitutes, violence is a way of life for prostitution-involved youth:

> Sometimes I meet a girl who says, "I have a really good pimp — he beats me only with an open hand." ... Many of the girls see the pimps as boyfriends, but violence is integral to everything that happens in the sex industry.[71]

Prostituted youth may face the greatest risk for violence by a pimp when seeking to leave his stable and control. In describing what her pimp did when she tried to get out of the business, a girl prostitute recounted: "He told me to take my clothes off. I wouldn't so he punched me so hard he lifted me off the ground.... My skin split. Blood was spraying and it was like a horror movie."[72]

## Customers of Prostituted Girls

The child sex trade is fueled primarily by the men who sexually exploit them. Customers — also known as *johns, tricks,* and *clients*— of prostituted youth come in all ages, races, ethnic groups, sexual orientations, and income levels. Some are their pimps, others pornographers, pedophiles, and gang members, as well as anyone with a desire to prostitute underage females. They find these girls on street corners, referred to as "the track," in red light districts, industrial areas, through referrals, over the Internet, and other means. The unnatural attraction to young prostitutes, in particular, was noted by a reporter covering the low-income neighborhood of East New York, Brooklyn: "The youngest girls are so popular, their customers cause traffic jams."[73]

Though it is unknown precisely how many men (and some women and juveniles) seek the services of prostituted female youth, the indication is their numbers are far greater than the girls they sexually exploit and victimize. In one estimate, as many as 1.5 million men were said to pay for sex each week.[74] According to a Prostitution Task Force, in Minneapolis alone, roughly 1,500 prostituted females serviced between 15,300 and 30,000 male customers daily.[75] Researchers have approximated that up to anywhere from 69 to 84 percent of men in the United States may see female prostitutes.[76]

Customers typically demand of teenage streetwalkers acts ranging from fellatio to sexual intercourse. In one study, it was found that three in four prostituted girls' sexual contacts consisted mainly of oral copulation.[77] This was explained by an expert on teenage prostitution: "It is what [their] customers want and the most practical for working in cars. It's also quick, which is a concern, because street prostitution is illegal, and when the cops show up, it is sometimes necessary to run."[78]

Many prostituted girls engage in unprotected oral sex and sexual intercourse with multiple johns, leaving them susceptible to sexually transmitted infections. Prostitution-involved girls are also frequently the victims of customer-inflicted violence. Studies show that girl prostitutes experience a high rate of violence in the course of plying their trade, including rape, robbery, assault, verbal attacks, and threats.[79] One study suggested that customer violence is more dangerous to the prostitute than pimp violence.[80]

Prostituted youth are at high risk for becoming homicide victims. The murder rate for prostituted girls and women is well above that of people working in other dangerous occupations, with customers often the perpetrators, along with pimps, johns, drug addicts, homeless, and others encountered on the street in daily life.[81] Customers who are serial killers have long targeted prostitution-involved females, particularly those operating on the street level, often viewing them as worthless and unlikely to be missed by anyone.[82]

## Sexually Transmitted Diseases and AIDS

There is a high rate of sexually transmitted diseases (STDs) among prostitution-involved female youth as a result of the combination of unsafe survival sex, multiple anonymous sex partners, lack of condom use, and intravenous drug use along with sharing tainted needles. According to Walker, over 85 percent of prostituted teenagers have contracted an STD in the course of selling sex, such as gonorrhea, syphilis, herpes, and hepatitis B.[83] In the government publication *Prostitution and Child-Sex Tourism*, it was reported that nearly 84 percent of homeless youth participated in one or more high-risk behaviors for AIDS (Acquired Immune Deficiency Syndrome).[84] Another study found that more than half of sexually active homeless youth had contracted at least one STD.[85]

In the National Center for Missing and Exploited Children's report, *Female Juvenile Prostitution: Problem and Response*, STDs was noted as a common issue prostitution-involved girls were vulnerable to.[86] Researcher Clare Tattersall estimated that between one-half and two-thirds of prostituted youth become infected with an STD.[87] Other research has also shown a strong link between homeless prostituted female youth and sexually transmitted infections.[88]

The most serious STD girl prostitutes face is the Human Immunodeficiency Virus (HIV), which leads to AIDS. It has been reported that in Los Angeles, as many as 80 percent of homeless youth or street youth have been involved in prostitution, with 40 percent having injected drugs, the two most common means for HIV infection among homeless kids.[89] In San Francisco, an estimated one out four youth living on the street is infected with HIV.[90] One study reported that the HIV prevalence rate for homeless youth was up to ten times higher than other youth in the United States[91];

with homeless teenagers seven times as likely to die of AIDS and sixteen times more likely of being diagnosed with HIV than youth in the population at large.[92] Prostituted girls are especially at risk for HIV infection and other STDs "because of their youth, immaturity, and inability to resist customers who engage in unsafe, high risk, sexual practices."[93] In a study of streetwalkers and female intravenous drug addicts, 46 percent were HIV-positive.[94] Another study conducted by the University of Miami found that 41 percent of prostituted females carried the AIDS virus.[95] Covenant House, the largest New York City shelter for runaways estimated that girls who sold their bodies on regular basis could have a rate of HIV infection exceeding 50 percent.[96]

The clear dangers present for prostituted youth with respect to STDs and sexual relations was described by Pam Oliver in her study of child prostitution:

> Most children and young adolescents are not sufficiently developed physically to engage in penetrative sex. The physiologically immature reproductive tract in pre-menarchal girls is much less capable of resisting invasion and subsequent damage by sexually transmitted microorganisms. The sexual activity is often violent, and this can cause internal damage, destroying the normal vagina and infection barriers and putting children at greater risk than adults for contracting sexually transmitted disease.[97]

## Girl Prostitutes and Arrests

Most prostituted girls are runaways or thrownaways and often come into contact with the police through arrests for running away (see Chapter 6). In 2008, there were 47,149 arrests of females under the age of eighteen as runaways in the United States, according to the Justice Department's annual *Crime in the United States*.[98] By comparison, only 878 arrests of female minors occurred that year for prostitution and commercialized vice.[99] Though the research suggests that teenage girls constitute a high percentage of the hundreds of thousands or more youth who regularly offer their bodies for money across the country, they largely manage to avoid arrests for prostitution, in spite of the greater visibility of prostituted female youth as streetwalkers. This may be in part due to other crimes prostitution-involved girls are arrested for, such as sex offenses other than rape or prostitution, alcohol- and drug-related offenses, property offenses, vagrancy, and curfew and loitering law violations.[100] There is also evidence to indicate that some prostituted girls may be viewed by law enforcement more as victims than offenders and referred to social services or other child welfare agencies in lieu of arrest.[101]

That notwithstanding, prostitution-involved female youth are more likely to be arrested than their male counterparts for plying their trade. More than three times the number of females under eighteen were arrested for prostitution and commercialized vice as the number of males younger than eighteen in 2008, as shown in Figure 11.1. Moreover, the most current ten-year trends show an increase in arrests of prostituted girls (see Figure 11.2). Between 1999 and 2008, the number of female juvenile arrests for prostitution or commercialized vice rose nearly 65 percent (by comparison, male juvenile arrests for prostitution-related offenses declined almost 35 percent).[102]

Overall, prostituted girls appear to come into contact with the juvenile or criminal justice systems more often than prostituted boys. According to some studies, three-quarters of prostitution-involved female youth have had contact with law enforcement officers, juvenile courts, or other parts of the criminal justice system[103]; whereas it has been estimated that as many as seven out of ten prostitution-involved male youth have never come into contact with the juvenile or criminal justice systems.[104] Other researchers, though, have found a high rate of involvement by boy prostitutes with the justice system; with some suggesting male prostituted youth are more likely to have contact with police officers than prostitution-involved female youth.[105]

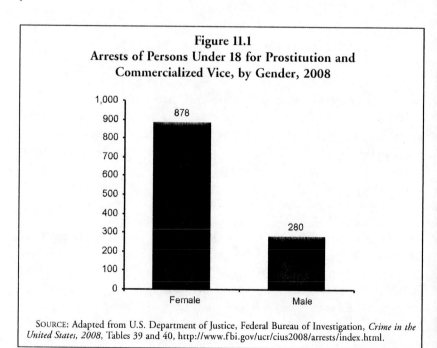

**Figure 11.1**
**Arrests of Persons Under 18 for Prostitution and Commercialized Vice, by Gender, 2008**

SOURCE: Adapted from U.S. Department of Justice, Federal Bureau of Investigation, *Crime in the United States, 2008*, Tables 39 and 40, http://www.fbi.gov/ucr/cius2008/arrests/index.html.

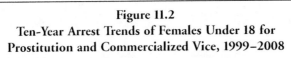

**Figure 11.2**
**Ten-Year Arrest Trends of Females Under 18 for**
**Prostitution and Commercialized Vice, 1999–2008**

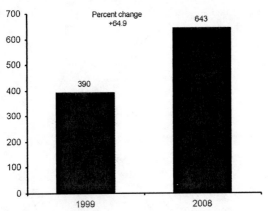

SOURCE: Adapted from U.S. Department of Justice, Federal Bureau of Investigation, *Crime in the United States, 2008,* Tables 39 and 40, http://www.fbi.gov/ucr/cius2008/arrests/index.html.

Even when arrested for prostitution-related offenses, most teenage prostitutes spend relatively little time in juvenile custody. According to Lois Lee, founder of Children of the Night, a shelter for homeless teenage prostitutes in Van Nuys, California: "Juvenile authorities turn these kids back onto the streets almost as fast as they are brought in," further suggesting that "social service agencies want little to do with street prostitutes."[106] As such, many prostitution-involved youth wind up back on the streets selling survival sex and participating in other high-risk activities until they become too sick to work or are arrested again.

Studies show that prostitutes are more likely to be arrested than their pimps or customers, by and large, with street level and drug addicted prostitutes having the highest rates of arrests.[107] Issues with self-incrimination, misguided love, and fear of or loyalty to a pimp have made it difficult for law enforcement to get prostituted youth to testify against pimps.[108] Recent crackdowns on pimps and johns have been somewhat successful in apprehending and prosecuting them, while freeing teenage prostitutes from that lifestyle.[109]

# 12

# Prostituted Male Youth

Male youth involvement in the sex trade industry is believed by many prostitution experts to be at least equal to that of female youth, if not greater. As discussed in the previous chapter on prostituted girls, boy prostitutes largely consist of runaways and thrownaways from home or juvenile care facilities. Most of these youth have been the victims of sexual and physical abuse and have mental health issues, problems with alcohol and/or drugs, and come from dysfunctional families. Many prostitution-involved male youth also experience sexual orientation or gender identity issues, often playing a big role in their leaving home voluntarily or against their wishes. Whether gay, bisexual, transgender, or unsure, these youth tend to be shunned by their families and discriminated against in their communities and schools. The result is they often strike out on their own. For those with nowhere else to go, they become street kids. This in turn leads to engaging in survival sex and prostitution, along with other dangerous patterns of behavior, such as intravenous drug use and sharing dirty needles.

Most prostituted boys operate without a controlling pimp, though some may still be manipulated in their actions by older, more street-wise individuals, or drug suppliers. The nature of their street activities places homeless prostituted male youth at high risk for sexually transmitted infections, including HIV; along with substance abuse, mental illness, and malnutrition. They are also susceptible to violence perpetrated by customers, other street people, hate offenders, drug addicts, and others; as well as involvement with the juvenile and criminal justice systems. Like their female counterparts, prostitution-involved male youth often have few viable means for breaking away from the street life, especially when in many instances there is no real home to go back to.

# The Extent of Male Youth Involved in Prostitution

How many male youth are engaging in selling sex? Precise figures are hard to come by, as much of the literature tends to focus on prostituted female youth or teenage prostitution in general. Moreover, unlike the typical out-in-the open streetwalking girl prostitutes, boy prostitutes are not always as visible, often plying their trade in parks, motels, bars, bathhouses, and other out-of-the-way places that make assessing their extent more challenging.

According to the *Encyclopedia of Sex and Sexuality*, the number of prostituted male youth in the United States could run into the tens of thousands.[1] High estimates of prostitution-involved youth in the United States range from about 300,000 to as many as three million at any given time.[2] Some data suggests that prostituted boys may represent half (and possibly an even higher percentage) of all teenagers active in the sex trade industry.[3] One study estimated the number of males among underage prostitutes in this country to be around 35 to 40 percent of the total.[4]

In the pioneering book *For Money or Love: Boy Prostitution in America*, Robin Lloyd estimated that there were 300,000 teenage males active in the sex trade industry nationwide.[5] Anne Rasmusson cited research to support this finding in her study of the commercial sexual exploitation of youth.[6] The proportion of prostitution-involved male youth seems to be higher in larger cities such as New York and San Francisco.[7] However, a rise in boy prostitution has also been seen in smaller cities.[8]

Other studies suggest that male youth are more or equally likely as runaways or thrownaways to become homeless, a key correlate in turning to prostituted sex for survival or as part of street life and drug addiction.[9] According to a government study, an estimated 1.6 million youth are runaways or homeless annually.[10] The Research Triangle Institute approximated that about 2.8 million youth between twelve and seventeen years of age had at least one episode of being homeless.[11] Some 300,000 runaway youth are seen as hard core runners who become street kids every year.[12] In one study, two in three full-time prostituted boys had run away from home before turning to prostitution.[13]

While there are no reliable figures on the number and breakdown of prostituted heterosexual gay, bisexual, or transgender male youth, per se, the indication is that as a group they "form a significant minority if not half of" juveniles in the sex-for-sale industry.[14] In a study of homeless teenagers, including sexual minorities, half the male youth reported being involved in survival sex.[15] A higher rate of prostitution involvement was found among homeless male youth than female youth. Another study found a high incidence of prostitution by transgender teenagers.[16]

## Entry into Prostitution

Though a boy can be initiated into the prostitution business at a very young age or as an older teenager, most prostituted male youth were in their preteens to early teens when they had their first paid sexual encounter.[17] Studies reveal that the average age of boys for entering prostitution is eleven to thirteen, including gay and transgender youth.[18] One study of male prostitution found that the average age for the first homosexual experience was 9.6 years.[19] Around six in ten of the prostituted boys reported receiving compensation for their sexual services. The male customer was, on average, at least five years older in a prostituted boy's first sexual experience.[20]

For most runaway and street male youth, their entrance into the world of commercial sexual exploitation comes quickly. A newly homeless youth will typically be solicited for sexual favors or enticed into prostituting themselves within thirty-six to forty-eight hours.[21] After living on the streets for two weeks, three-quarters of homeless youth will have engaged in some form of sexual exploitation, such as prostitution or pornography.[22] According to one study of prostituted boys whose first sexual experience was with a male, more than half reported being seduced, while two-thirds said they received payment to engage in sexual activity.[23]

In his study of homeless youth who were sexual minorities, Nicholas Ray quoted a typical homeless prostituted gay teenager and substance abuser, "Danny," and his entrance into prostitution for survival and shelter:

> I'd go to the library, I'd get on Craigslist, and Manhunt, and Gay.com, just to find somewhere to sleep for the night, not for money. I slept with them so I could have a place to stay.[24]

## Characterizing Prostituted Male Youth

The majority of prostitution-involved teenage males are runaways or thrownaways, similar to prostituted teenage females, who make their way to the streets and, finding no recourse, become homeless. Male prostituted youth come from various educational and socioeconomic backgrounds, racial and ethnic groups, and familial dynamics, including "delinquent school dropouts to well-educated, refined college students; they come from inner city projects and middle class suburbs; from completely disintegrated families and from effective loving families."[25]

Though prostituted boys cater primarily to homosexual customers, their sexual orientation or gender identity can be heterosexual, gay, bisexual, transgender, or undecided. In the first nationwide study of male teenage prostitution, the Urban and Rural Systems Associations of San Francisco characterized prostituted boys as follows[26]:

- Boy prostitutes sell sex largely for financial support, to explore their sexual orientation, or as a means to meet homosexual men.
- Money is the most significant factor in motivating adolescent males to enter prostitution and remain in the business.
- The average age of a prostituted boy is sixteen.
- Most prostitution-involved male youth are runaways/thrownaways.
- A high percentage of prostituted boys come from single parent or dysfunctional homes.
- The majority of boy prostitutes were sexually, physically, or mentally abused.
- A high rate of high school dropout or poor educational performance exists among male teenage prostitutes.
- Delinquent behavior is common among prostituted boys.
- Gay-identified boy prostitutes initially find the street lifestyle exciting.
- Pimps are rare in the male prostitution subculture.

Prostitution-involved male youth have a high rate of drug addiction, mental illnesses, and sexually transmitted diseases; and are at risk for violent victimization, verbal aggression, and involvement with law enforcement and the juvenile justice system.[27] Other studies have found that many boy prostitutes tend to be "self-destructive, unstable, immature, irresponsible, and have high levels of psychopathology."[28]

As many as half of all prostituted male youth are "thrown out of their houses because of sexual identity issues."[29] One study reported that two-thirds of prostitution-involved males considered themselves as either gay or bisexual.[30] However, other research suggests that most male prostitutes do not identify themselves as gay, but see their sexual involvement with other males as survival sex for money, food, shelter, or drugs.[31] According to sex therapist Ruth Westheimer:

> Many of these male homosexual prostitutes — often referred to as "hustlers" — do not consider themselves homosexuals because even though they may enjoy

the sexual contacts, they limit the activity to being fellated rather than perform-ing fellatio on a customer or engaging in anal intercourse.[32]

In a study where almost three-fourths of the prostitution-involved males were labeled as homosexuals, only 6 percent of the sample self-identified as gay.[33]

The majority of prostituted male youth are streetwalkers. In a study of adolescent prostitution, D. Kelly Weisberg found that more than nine in ten boy prostitutes worked on the streets.[34] However, boy brothels (also referred to as stables) do exist, in which prostituted male youth live and work. These are often operated and owned by pimps or madams. Teen prostitution researcher Joan Johnson pointed out that boy brothel prostitutes occupied the lowest level of the male prostitution-involved hierarchy.[35]

## Chickens and Chicken Hawks

Prostituted boys are, at times, referred to in the child sex trade indus-try as *chickens*, or "young boys or teenagers preferred by older men" who are known as *chicken hawks* (and also *chicken queens* or *chicken pluckers*).[36] The homosexual men who prey upon young male prostitutes are regarded by law enforcement and psychiatrists as child molesters and pedophiles.[37] Accord-ing to *Runaway Kids and Teenage Prostitution*, underage male prostitution often occurs in big cities with a large gay male population.[38] However, boy prostitutes can also be found selling sex in many suburbs and rural areas across the United States.[39] The following is an illustration of a typical chicken–chicken hawk encounter from the perspective of law enforcement:

> The boy will usually find a set of marble steps, sit, and observe passing cars. Eye contact is the key. The "chicken hawk" will stare at the boy he feels could be a "hustler." If a period of eye contact is made between both, the "chicken hawk" will still circle the block several times, making eye contact at each pass-ing. Finally the "chicken hawk" will nod and, if the boy returns the nod, a deal is in the making. At times, the "chickens" would work as teams, usually two together. If the customer wanted two boys, he would use hand signals, indicating how many boys he wanted and how much he was paying.[40]

Though most chicken hawks prefer young boy or teenage prostitutes, many will solicit prostituted males of any age. Some pedophiles favor chick-ens who fit within a certain age range and "will not pick up any boys who might be older or younger than he desires."[41]

A profile of the typical chicken hawk can be seen as follows:

- Usually middle aged.
- Relates to children often better than to adults.
- Regards the chicken victim of his desires as the sexual aggressor.
- Most often single, but can be married too.
- Typically nonviolent.
- Often associates with other pedophiles, child molesters, and chicken hawks.
- Was the victim of child molestation.
- Pretends to befriend the chicken.
- Often a white-collar worker.[42]

Gay clients of prostituted males tend to be mostly middle aged and physically unattractive, while desiring "bizarre and unusual sex acts which would not meet with acceptance in conventional gay society."[43] Experts on male prostitution have found that prostitution-involved males and the men who pay for their services often harbor a "deep hatred" towards one another, while struggling "with conflicting emotions during their time together, often creating fantasies that are acted out in the course of the sexual encounter."[44]

Some customers of male prostitutes do not consider themselves as gay, but still solicit the services of transgender prostituted boys, which include those referring to themselves as transsexuals, cross-dressers, butch, drag queens, etc. According to a review of child prostitution literature, in many countries, prostitution-involved male youth have reported that such men desire a "chick with a dick."[45] Garrett Prestage described further what motivates these male customers of boy prostitutes:

> Some simply like the sensibility and particular appeal of the "trannies"; some are attracted by the "kinkiness" of sex with a transsexual; some are attracted to the idea of sex with another man but are reluctant to choose a partner which is actually a man; and some enjoy particular sexual activities which require that their partner has a penis even though they prefer female partners.[46]

## Types of Prostituted Male Youth

Prostitution-involved male youth have been broken down into various types in the commercial sex trade industry, dependent upon what their services consist of or how they define themselves. Terms commonly used to refer to prostituted males include rentboys, escorts, hustlers, and gigolos. These are described as follows:[47]

- *Rentboys*—rent themselves out to clients, or pay rent from money earned through sex work.
- *Escorts*—do not identify themselves as gay, but engage in sex with male customers for payment (referred to as "gay for pay").
- *Hustlers*—involved in a sexual relationship while prostituting themselves or "hustling on the side."
- *Gigolos*—male prostitutes who service female clients.

Experts on male prostitution have created a number of typologies of prostitution-involved male youth. Johnson categorized most prostituted boys as street hustlers who were gay, bisexual[48]; and heterosexual; and others as transvestite prostitutes and upper class prostitutes.[49] She described upper class prostituted boys as often better looking and dressed, with more self-confidence than street hustler boy prostitutes. Many prostituted youth were found to be aggressive and addicted to drugs.

In a psychosocial study, S. E. Caukins and Neil Coombs identified four types of prostituted males: (1) street hustlers, (2) bar hustlers, (3) call boys, and (4) kept boys as follows[50]:

- *Street hustlers*—drifters who at times use prostitution as means to support family.
- *Bar hustlers*—drifters using prostitution to support a wife and/or children.
- *Call boys*—act as companions to upscale customers for social occasions, such as a party, in addition to providing prostitution services.
- *Kept boys*—houseboys who, along with prostituting themselves, carry out various nonsexual household chores.

The researchers asserted that a "gay sex market thrives in every big city ... a profit oriented street corner college for the recruiting, training, and selling of boys and men to older, affluent homosexuals."[51]

Dan Waldorf and Sheigla Murphy, in a study of prostitution-involved males and intravenous drug use, established two broad categories for prostituted boys: (1) hustlers and (2) call boys, subdividing each.[52] Hustlers were broken into three types:

- *Trade hustlers*—heterosexual or bisexual males who trade sexual favors for money, while not necessarily acknowledging being gay or enjoying paid gay sexual relations.
- *Drag queen hustlers*—transvestites and transsexual prostitutes specializing in oral copulation mostly in gay red-light districts.

- *Youth hustlers*—acknowledged homosexual males often appearing naive, but are often well experienced as prostituted youth.

Hustlers tended to locate clients in places typically frequented by chickens and chicken hawks such as gay bars and adult bookstores.

Waldorf and Murphy broke down call boys into four types[53]:

- *Call book boys*—identify themselves as gay or bisexual, while locating customers from a call book or maintaining a regular clientele. Drag queen call girls are transvestite males who work from a call book.

- *Models and escorts*—locate customers through advertising in general or special interest publications or over the Internet; often establish a network of steady clients and may also own a call book.

- *Erotic masseurs*—find new customers through advertising even while maintaining a regular client list; often certified by licensed massage schools; combine massages with sexual services at costs usually lower than that charged by call boys.

- *Porn industry stars*—elite or highest paid prostituted males, such as porn stars and erotic dancers; customers are usually propositioned at work with the sexual servicing outside the workplace.

Weisberg portrayed two distinct subcultures of prostitution-involved male youth: (1) peer-delinquent subculture and (2) gay subculture.[54] Peer-delinquent subculture prostitutes "engage indiscriminately in prostitution, drug dealing, panhandling, and petty criminal activity. They sell their sexual favors habitually as a way of making money."[55] Gay subculture prostitutes see the sex trade as "a means of identification and prostitution satisfies their needs for social interaction with gay persons and for sexual partners. Simultaneously, it provides a way of making money."[56]

These subcultures were subdivided into four types of boy prostitutes: (1) situational, (2) habitual, (3) vocational, and (4) avocational prostitutes[57]:

- *Situational prostitutes*—involved in prostitution only on certain occasions, while regarding it as merely an infrequent activity.

- *Habitual prostitutes*—active in inner city street life, such as prostitution, dealing in drugs, robbery, and petty theft.

- *Vocational prostitutes*—see prostitution as a vocation and themselves as professionals.

- *Avocational prostitutes*—vocational prostitutes who view the sex trade as strictly a part-time job.

## Prostituted Male Youth and Violence

Boy prostitutes face violence on a daily basis in the street environment. They are subject to beatings, rape, torture, robbery, verbal assaults, bias crimes, murder, and more.[58] One researcher described the "opportunities for bodily harm" to prostitution-involved male youth as rampant and violent and "endemic to this lifestyle."[59] Prostituted boys are thought to be at least as vulnerable to violent victimization while plying their trade as prostituted girls, particularly where it concerns violent customers.[60]

Gay, bisexual, transgender, or questioning (GBTQ) boy prostitutes have the highest risk for victimization. According to the National Runaway Switchboard, homeless youth identifying as sexual minorities are seven times more likely to be a victim of violence than heterosexual homeless youth.[61] A number of studies have found a high rate of assault, rape, and robbery among GBTQ homeless and prostituted youth.[62] One study suggested that homeless sexual minorities were at "increased risk for negative outcomes," compared to heterosexual homeless and non homeless youth[63]; while another associated assaultive and robbery violence against prostitution-involved GBTQ male youth with homophobic bystanders.[64] Mia Spangenberg found transgender prostitutes to be especially susceptible to victimization, pointing out that they "often deal with clients who are so ambivalent about their own gender identity that they lash out more violently than other clients."[65]

In *Drugs, Runaways, and Teen Prostitution*, Clare Tattersall described the violence experienced by one prostituted male youth named "Simon":

> Simon, a fifteen-year-old male prostitute from Texas, says, "I was repeatedly beaten up by johns. Twice I was taken to a field, raped at knifepoint, and kicked so badly that I couldn't work for days afterwards. I was often beaten up by johns who tried to get their money back after the act and I have been raped I don't know how many times."[66]

Runaway and homeless prostituted boys appear to be at a high risk for death by serial killers. Marcia Cohen found that such youth had been the victims of serial murders more often than their girl counterparts.[67] Another study reported a high rate of mortality for prostitution-involved males as a result of violence, AIDS, and drug overdose.[68]

## Sexually Transmitted Diseases

Prostituted male youth have a high rate of sexually transmitted diseases (STDs), including HIV (Human Immunodeficiency Virus) and its consequence, Acquired Immune Deficiency Syndrome (AIDS).[69] Infection is typically spread in two ways to the prostitution-involved male population: (1)

passing AIDS infected bodily fluids, often through anal intercourse, and (2) sharing dirty needles and tainted blood by intravenous (IV) drug users.[70] With frequent gay and bisexual relations with anonymous and unprotected customers and common IV drug use among prostituted boys, some believe their risk for exposure to the AIDS virus is greater than that of prostitution-involved girls.[71] The dangers of becoming infected with HIV are increased even further with promiscuity, substance abuse, unsanitary living conditions, and the street environment which invites risky behavior.

A plethora of studies illustrate the strong correlation between prostituted male youth and HIV/AIDS. In a study of prostitution-involved males in New York City, 53 percent of those engaging in homosexual prostitution activities tested HIV-seropositive, with 10 percent of males with a female clientele testing positive.[72] Another study by Edward Morse and associates of sexual patterns among customers of street prostituted males found a high HIV infection rate for the prostitutes, at 175 per 1,000, in spite of an awareness of HIV and its risks for exposure.[73] In a study of Manhattan prostituted male youth, with 50 percent gay, 26 percent bisexual, and 24 percent heterosexual, it was found that the risk for HIV infection was greatest as a result of "differential condom use" and other risky sexual activities.[74]

A Chicago survey of self-reported risk factors in contracting AIDS among homeless youth found that 87 percent of those responding had engaged in one or more of the following risk factors: having multiple sexual partners, high-risk sex partners, used condoms inconsistently, were involved in anal sex, prostitution, and/or IV drug use. The survey related the high-risk involvement with being male and having a history of sexual abuse.[75] In a study of male prostitutes and IV drug users, it was reported that 49 percent of the IV drug users and 11 percent of the prostitutes tested HIV-positive. A. R. Markos and colleagues noted the high rate of sexually transmitted diseases among prostitution-involved male youth, citing it as a strong risk factor in HIV infection.[76]

While the risk of contracting HIV and eventually AIDS is high for GBTQ prostitution-involved male youth, it may be even higher for transgender prostitutes. In one study, 20 percent of transgender runaways who became sex workers tested HIV-positive.[77] A study by Heather Worth also indicated a high risk of HIV among transgender prostitutes.[78]

## Boy Prostitutes and Arrests

Apart from the exposure to HIV and other diseases, violence, and various other dilemmas of daily street life, male youth involved in the sex trade industry face the risk to be arrested for prostitution-related offenses. There is conflicting data on prostituted boys, arrests, and other involvement with the juvenile and criminal justice systems. In a profile of juvenile prostitutes, based on information gathered from the Federal Bureau of Investigation's (FBI) National Incident-Based Reporting System, David Finkelhor and Richard Ormrod found that prostituted male youth were more likely to be arrested for prostitution activities than prostituted female youth, and more likely to be seen as offenders rather than victims of commercial sexual exploitation.[79] Weisberg found that there was a high rate of contact with the criminal and juvenile justice systems among boy prostitutes.[80] Two in three of the prostitution-involved male teens in her sample had been arrested one or more times, with prostitution-related offenses accounting for one in three arrests.

Other data indicates that prostituted boys are arrested less often than their female counterparts are and such arrests are on the decline, even while arrests of prostituted girls are on the rise. According to the FBI's annual publication *Crime in the United States*, as part of its annual Uniform Crime Reporting Program, in 2008 there were 1,359 arrests of males under the age of twenty-one for prostitution and commercialized vice. Of these, only 280 were arrests of juveniles or persons younger than eighteen (see Figure 12.1). By comparison, there were 6,405 arrests of females under twenty-one for prostitution and commercialized vice, of which 878 were younger than eighteen years of age. This indicates that were 4.7 females under twenty-one

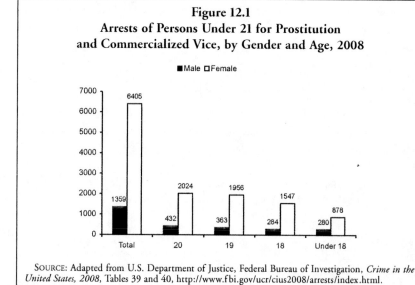

**Figure 12.1**
**Arrests of Persons Under 21 for Prostitution**
**and Commercialized Vice, by Gender and Age, 2008**

■ Male □ Female

SOURCE: Adapted from U.S. Department of Justice, Federal Bureau of Investigation, *Crime in the United States, 2008*, Tables 39 and 40, http://www.fbi.gov/ucr/cius2008/arrests/index.html.

arrested for every male under twenty-one for prostitution-related charges, with the ratio of 3.1 to 1 in arrests of female juveniles compared to male juveniles for prostitution and commercialized vice.

Moreover, between 1999 and 2008, arrests of males under eighteen for prostitution and commercialized vice fell almost 35 percent, while arrests rose nearly 65 percent for females under eighteen (see Figure 12.2). This disparity suggests that aside from prostituted girls being arrested more often (including as runaways), perhaps due to their greater exposure as streetwalkers and a stronger desire by law enforcement agencies to rescue them from the sex trade, more prostitution-involved boys may be arrested for related offenses. These include sex offenses other than forcible rape and prostitution, drug- and alcohol-related violations, property offenses, and curfew and loitering law violations — all of which considerably more male juveniles are arrested for in general than female juveniles.

Prostituted boys and girls tend to be arrested more often than their customers, pimps, pornographers, and others associated with the commercial sexual exploitation of children.[81] Recent busts by federal and local law enforcement have made gains in this imbalance, though juvenile arrests (or lack of) for prostitution and further involvement in the justice system continue to blur the lines between victim and offender in the child sex trade industry.[82]

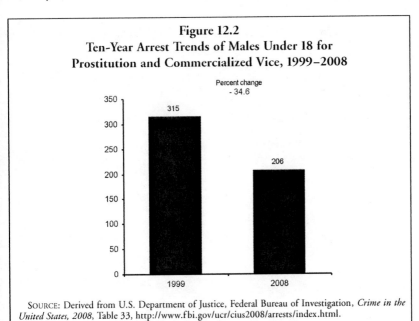

**Figure 12.2**
**Ten-Year Arrest Trends of Males Under 18 for**
**Prostitution and Commercialized Vice, 1999–2008**

Percent change
- 34.6

SOURCE: Derived from U.S. Department of Justice, Federal Bureau of Investigation, *Crime in the United States, 2008*, Table 33, http://www.fbi.gov/ucr/cius2008/arrests/index.html.

# PART VII

## COMBATING THE PROBLEM

# 13

# Responding to the Runaway and Thrownaway Homeless Youth Crisis

Understanding why youth run away or are thrown away and how they become street kids, prostituted, substance abusers, delinquents, or otherwise the victims of sexual exploitation, violence, homelessness and degradation, response to their crisis has come from the federal, state, and local level. Legislation has been aimed at protecting youth from child abuse and neglect, sexual exploitation and victimization, violence and vulnerabilities, substance abuse, and even themselves. Various programs have been focused on assisting runaways, thrownaways, prostitution-involved, and homeless youth in getting off the streets and into a safe environment. Efforts have been stepped up in recent years to go after pimps, customers, pornographers, and other sexual exploiters or victimizers of runaway and street youth. While there is no easy way to deal with the serious problem of youth who voluntarily or are forced to leave home or alternative care, and overall results have been mixed, the current approach has at least succeeded in recognizing the susceptibility and exploitation of this population group and addressing it to one degree or another.

## Federal Response to Runaway/Thrownaway and Homeless Youth

The federal government has responded to the problem of runaway, thrownaway, and homeless youth by enacting legislation and creating programs designed to address precursors and implications of leaving home for

157

life on the streets, making the transition back into a safe environment for such youth, as well as punish and prosecute those who sexually abuse, exploit, or victimize runaways and homeless youth.

## RUNAWAY AND HOMELESS YOUTH ACT

The Runaway and Homeless Youth Act (RHYA) was enacted in 1978 in response to the problem of runaway youth and its correlates such as child sexual abuse, teenage prostitution, juvenile delinquency and substance abuse, and homelessness.[1] It made available grant money to establish and maintain runaway shelters operated by states, localities, and nonprofit groups. In order to qualify for federal funding, criteria called for: (1) a reachable location to runaway youth, (2) a maximum capacity of twenty children, (3) an adequate staff to youth ratio, (4) satisfactory plans for contacting parents or family of runaways and providing for their safe return home, and (5) maintaining adequate records profiling runaway youth and their parents.

In 1980, the Act was amended to recognize that many runaway youth are, in fact, thrownaways, clarify requirements that allow access to shelter services for families of homeless runaways, and establishment of model programs designed to assist habitual runaway youth. The RHYA, reauthorized in 2003 under the Runaway, Homeless and Missing Children Protection Act,

> establishes and authorizes funding for a set of programs that offers a range of supports to runaway and homeless youth, including street-based outreach and education, youth and family counseling, emergency shelter, transitional housing, and services such as academic and employment preparation, life skills training, and health care.[2]

There are three major RHYA authorized service programs: (1) Basic Center Program, (2) Transitional Living Program, and (3) Street Outreach Program.

- Basic Center Program (BCP)—provides funding for short-term shelter and related services to youth under eighteen years of age and their families by way of community based public and nonprofit private centers. Among those eligible for BCP services are youth at risk for becoming runaways or homeless, and youth who are currently runaways, thrownaways, or street kids. The stay is for up to two weeks with a goal of reuniting homeless youth with their families or finding safe alternative housing.[3]
- Transitional Living Program (TLP)—provides funding for longer-term shelter and support through public and private organizations

for youth sixteen to twenty-one with the idea of establishing self-sufficiency. These youth are at risk for leaving or have already left home due to family conflict or instability, pregnancy, or other issues with little chance of ever returning home to live. TLP shelter residence can last for as long as eighteen months, and up to 180 more days for youth under or until they turn eighteen.[4]

- Street Outreach Program (SOP) — provides funding for services through public and private community based organizations in helping runaway and homeless street youth or those living in an environment that increases the risk for drug use, being sexually abused, prostituted, or otherwise sexually exploited or victimized. The goal of the program is to aid such youth as they transition to a safer, suitable place to live, including drug abuse prevention and survival assistance.[5]

Runaway and homeless youth who use these services represent only a small segment of the nearly two million such youth who are believed to run away, be tossed out of the house, or otherwise end up homeless each year. For example, in 2005, 51,680 youth received BCP services, 3,279 TLP services, and 515,000 connections with street youth were made by SOP organizations.[6]

## NATIONAL CENTER FOR MISSING AND EXPLOITED CHILDREN

As a result of public anxiety over the high rate of missing and sexually exploited youth each year, in 1984, legislation was enacted by Congress for establishing a permanent National Center for Missing and Exploited Children.[7] The Center hoped to organize a national effort to halt the wave of missing and exploited youth while addressing the implications related to the problem, such as child abuse, parental kidnapping, and prostitution.

The National Center was intended to act as a central contact point for parents or relatives of missing children and others who may have knowledge of their whereabouts or other information. Additional key components of the National Center include such things as providing expertise in legislation, education, advocacy, public awareness, and criminal justice system improvements.

## NATIONAL RUNAWAY SWITCHBOARD

The National Runaway Switchboard (NRS) is a BCP funded (since 1974) national communications system for runaway, thrownaway, homeless, and other youth in crisis and their families.[8] Located in Chicago, the NRS operates daily in all fifty states and U.S. territories. Its switchboard handles more than 100,000 calls per year, with around half the calls coming from youth. Within that group, 50 percent of the calls were made from youth on the street.

Among the services provided by the NRS are (1) a channel in which youth or parents can leave messages, (2) 24-hour referrals to resources in the community such as shelters, food banks, and social services agencies, and (3) crisis intervention counseling for youth. A family reunification service, HomeFree, has been in place since 1995 and provides bus tickets to persons ages twelve to twenty-one for returning home or other nearby placement (for example, independent living program) The NRS also has a website, www. 1800RUNAWAY.org, offering a host of information about and for runaway, thrownaway, and homeless youth.

## CHILD ABUSE PREVENTION AND TREATMENT ACT

The Child Abuse Prevention and Treatment Act was enacted in 1974 and amended in 1978 as a response to rising national concern about child abuse and neglect and its correlation to status offenders and juvenile delinquency. The Act provided for:

> (1) the establishment of a National Center on Child Abuse and Neglect, (2) increasing public awareness on child maltreatment, detection, and reporting, (3) assisting states and local communities in developing more effective mechanisms for delivery of services to families, (4) providing training and technical assistance to state and local communities in dealing with the problems of child abuse and neglect, and (5) supporting research into causal and preventative measures in child victimization.[9]

In order to qualify for federal funds, the following criteria must be met by a state: (1) have a standardized, comprehensive definition of child abuse and neglect, (2) investigate reports of child abuse, (3) maintain confidentiality of records, and (4) appoint guardians ad litem for youth involved in abuse or neglect court proceedings.

## NATIONAL CHILD ABUSE AND NEGLECT DATA SYSTEM

The National Child Abuse and Neglect Data System (NCANDS) was established in 1988 as required by the Child Abuse Prevention and Treatment Act.[10] The NCANDS is a voluntary nationwide data analysis system on abused and neglected children as known to state child protective services agencies. The Summary Data Component of NCANDS gathers microdata on the nature of reports of child maltreatment, characteristics of abuse and neglect victims and perpetrators, and response of state and local child protective services. This information is made accessible to policymakers, child welfare professionals, and researchers, as well as others interested in policy, identification, practice, and prevention of child abuse and neglect.

## JUVENILE JUSTICE AND DELINQUENCY PREVENTION ACT

The Juvenile Justice and Delinquency Prevention Act was enacted in 1974 and amended in 1996.[11] Its goal was to "identify and deinstitutionalize status offenders, dependent and neglected youth, and separate juvenile delinquents from adult criminals."[12] The act mandated: (1) a complete assessment of the efficiency of the juvenile justice system, (2) developing and implementing new options in delinquency prevention and diversion of status offenders from the criminal justice system, and (3) using resources in the juvenile justice system more effectively in dealing with juvenile delinquents. For states to receive funds under the provisions of the Act, they were required to submit plans that outlined their compliance with the requirements expressed.

## Federal Child Prostitution Laws

A number of statutes pertain to the prostitution of youth and those exploiting them, such as pimps, customers, pornographers, and online predators.

## THE MANN ACT

The White Slave Traffic Act, referred to as the Mann Act, was enacted in 1910 and first dealt on the federal level with the issues of prostitution-involved youth and the sexual exploitation of children.[13] The Act's design was combating white slavery, or forced selling of sex, and the trafficking of women and girls into prostitution. The Mann Act made it a federal crime to transport females across state lines for purposes of prostitution activities, and included "persuading, inducing, or coercing a woman or girl into making such a journey while using a 'common carrier' or the transportation of a female under the age of eighteen for prostitution or 'any immoral practice.'"[14]

In 1986, the Mann Act was revised by Congress to make it gender-neutral and to change "immoral practice" to "any sexual activity" in which any individual can be charged with a crime.[15] The revisions no longer made it a requirement that a commercial motive had to be present in the transportation of a juvenile across state lines. Section 2423 of the Act outlawed the "transportation with intent to engage in criminal sexual activity [and] travel with intent to engage in sexual acts with [a] juvenile."[16]

## PROTECTION OF CHILDREN AGAINST SEXUAL EXPLOITATION ACT

The Protection of Children Against Sexual Exploitation Act was enacted in 1978 after extensive hearings in the Senate and House of Representatives on child sexual abuse and sexual exploitation and how it relates to youth criminality and delinquent behavior.[17] The law aimed to stop the production and dissemination of child pornography by prohibiting the transportation of minors across state lines for purposes of sexual exploitation. The Act also expanded the federal government's power to prosecute producers and distributors of child pornographic material, providing:

> punishment for persons who use, employ, or persuade minors (defined as any persons under 16) to become involved in the production of visual or print materials that depict sexually explicit conduct if the producers know or have reasons to know that the materials will be transported in interstate or foreign commerce or mailed. Punishment is also specifically provided for parents, legal guardians, or other persons having custody or control of minors and who knowingly permit a minor to participate in the production of such material.[18]

## PROTECTION OF CHILDREN FROM SEXUAL PREDATORS ACT

The Protection of Children from Sexual Predators Act of 1998 increases penalties for violators of the Mann Act, while adding Section 2425 to the U.S. Code's Title 18, "prohibiting use of interstate or foreign commerce for transmitting information about a minor for purposes of enticing, encouraging, or soliciting anyone to participate in criminal sexual conduct."[19] The Act also provided for stiffer sentences to be imposed by the court through improvements such as for coercion, obstruction, and intentional misrepresentation.

## RACKETEER INFLUENCED AND CORRUPT ORGANIZATIONS ACT

The Racketeer Influenced and Corrupt Organizations Act (RICO) also addresses the commercial sexual exploitation of children, making it a federal crime to partake in an "enterprise" that affects interstate commerce and establishes a "pattern" of "racketeering activity."[20] Offenses applicable to the Mann Act are included among criminality as defined under such activity. The RICO statute allows prosecutors to file charges against individuals who are only indirectly controlling or involved in an interstate prostitution ring, while enabling victims to seek restitution by way of civil court.

## Federal Sex Trafficking Laws

With a rise in the interstate sex trafficking of minors in the United States, a number of federal laws pertain to sex trafficking and sex tourism. These include 18 U.S.C. §§ 1591, 2421, 2422, and 2423, which "prohibit sex tourism and the interstate and international sex trafficking of adults and children, as well as sex trafficking within a state."[21] An example is 18 U.S.C. § 1591, "as amended by the Trafficking Victims Protection Act of 2000, prohibits trafficking by making it illegal to recruit, entice, or obtain a person to engage in commercial sex acts, or to benefit from such activities."[22] Victims of sex trafficking are not required to have crossed state lines or international boundaries.

The federal laws also focus on patrons of prostituted and sexually exploited minors, as well as those benefiting from the arrangement of traveling to participate in the child sex trade. In 18 U.S.C. §, for instance,

> 2423(b) prohibits traveling across state lines or into the United States for the purpose of engaging in any illicit sexual conduct (which includes any commercial sex act with a person under 18) and carries a 30 year maximum sentence, while 18 U.S.C. § 2423(c) prohibits an American citizen or national engaging in illicit sexual conduct outside the United States and carries a 30 year maximum sentence.[23]

## Federal Child Pornography Laws

There are a number of federal laws regarding child pornography and the sexual exploitation of children. Sections 2251 and 2252 of Title 18 of the U.S. Code, for instance, prohibit child sex offenders such as pimps and procurers from photographing underage prostitutes, transporting or shipping in interstate or foreign commerce (this includes by mail or on the Internet), or receiving or distributing materials that visually depict minors in sexually explicit poses.[24] Under the statutes, it is not required to prove that a defendant intended to distribute such child pornographic materials.

The Child Protection, Restoration and Penalties Enhancement Act of 1990 increased Section 2252 prohibitions[25]; and under the Protection of Children From Sexual Predators Act of 1998, a jurisdictional foundation for prosecuting was added, assuming the "visual images were produced with materials transported by interstate or foreign commerce, including by mail or computer."[26]

The Child Pornography Prevention Act of 1996 (CPPA), in addressing child sexual exploitation, amends Section 2256 in defining conditions "for which visual images are or appear to be minors participating in sexually explicit acts, including through computer imagery."[27] The Constitutionality of the CPPA was upheld in *United States v. Hilton*[28] and *The Free Speech Coalition v. Reno.*[29]

## Child Exploitation and Obscenity Section

The U.S. Department of Justice's (DOJ) Child Exploitation and Obscenity Section (CEOS) enforces federal obscenity laws and is responsible for prosecuting persons violating federal law by the sexual exploitation of children. According to the DOJ, the:

> CEOS works in conjunction with the 93 United States Attorney Offices around the country to prosecute individuals who commit crimes in violation of federal statutes that encompass the sexual exploitation of children though the possession, receipt, distribution or manufacture of child pornography, the sexual abuse of children, and the trafficking of children for sexual activity. Additionally, with the assistance of its new High Tech Investigative Unit, CEOS places significant focus on crimes involving the use of the Internet to facilitate the sexual abuse of children or the trafficking of child pornography.[30]

Recent actions by the CEOS in relation to the sexual exploitation of youth include[31]:

- U.S. Department of Justice announces global effort in going after child pornographers.
- A Philadelphia man was sentenced to life in prison for the advertising, transporting, receiving, and possession of child porn.
- A Texas man was sentenced to seventy-six months behind bars for travel with intent to engage in sexual activity with minors.
- An Oregon man was given more than twenty-four months in prison for using a webcam to produce child porn.
- A Maryland man received a ten-year prison sentence for enticement of a minor.

- An Indiana man received an indictment as part of a nationwide probe in Internet child pornography.
- Six defendants were sentenced for involvement in an international child exploitation business enterprise.
- A Kentucky man received twenty years of imprisonment for producing child porn.
- A Mexican man received twenty-four years in prison for the sex trafficking of minors and transportation for purposes of commercial sex.
- An Idaho man pled guilty in an international child exploitation case.
- A Florida man was given ninety-seven months behind bars for travel to sexually exploit a minor.
- A former Indiana swim coach was sentenced in a child porn case.
- An Alaska man was given thirty years in prison for sex trafficking and drug offenses.

## State Child Prostitution and Sexual Exploitation Laws

In addition to federal statutes prohibiting the sexual exploitation of youth, most states have prostitution, pornography, and child sexual exploitation statutes that apply to johns, pimps, pedophiles, procurers, pornographers, and promoters of teenage prostitution and child pornography. Though the laws may vary from state to state, they generally apply to any sexual maltreatment, commercial exploitation, and victimization of prostitution-involved minors.

There are patron laws in most states that prohibit soliciting another for prostitution activities regardless of the prostitute's age.[32] A number of state statutes, though, are applicable to patronizing underage prostitutes. In Colorado, for instance, a statute prohibits being involved in prostitution with a person younger than eighteen years of age[33]; while there are three child prostitution patronizing laws in New York, varying in relation to the age of child victim.[34]

Though pimps play a large role in the prostitution of female youth, there are currently only four states with laws that apply specifically to the pimping of underage prostitutes: Illinois, Colorado, California, and West Virginia.[35] The Illinois statute applies to pimps who intentionally prostitute for money individuals age sixteen or younger[36]; whereas Colorado's law prohibits pimping by anyone who consciously "lives on or is supported ... by money or any other thing of value earned through prostitution involvement by a person under the age of eighteen."[37]

Pandering statutes generally pertain not only to pimping but also to other related child prostitution offenses, such as being responsible for a minor entering the prostitution business. In Iowa, for instance, a pandering law is applicable for anyone influencing or coercing a youth to enter prostitution, or using a place for the express function of teen prostitution, or receiving income from such place.[38] One need not receive cash payment or something of equal value for the sexual services of a minor to be convicted on pandering charges. The court ruled in *State v. Steer*,[39] for example, that such a provision was limited to the prostituted juvenile and not the person responsible for prostituting the minor.

Parents of prostitution-involved youth may also be criminally liable under some statutes. In a few states, there are prostitution laws that make the parents of underage prostitutes legally responsible for allowing their children to enter into prostitution or not putting forth enough effort to prevent such child prostitution.[40] In Louisiana, for instance, criminal liability of parents can apply if they willfully consent to their child's entry into the sex-for-sale business.[41] A comparable law exists in Montana.[42]

## Law Enforcement Crackdowns on the Sexual Exploitation of Runaway, Thrownaway, and Homeless Youth

As part of a nationwide effort to rescue prostituted runaway and thrownaway street kids, and reduce underage prostitution and child pornography, federal and local law enforcement agencies have worked separately and through joint task forces, strike forces, and professional networks such as The Pimp/Juvenile Prostitution Task Force, Law Enforcement Effort Against Child Harm (LEACH), Sexual Assault and Exploitation Felony Enforcement (SAFE) Team, and Runaway and Homeless Youth Network to combat the commercial sexual exploitation of youth.[43] The result has been a number of successful crackdowns on pimps, customers, pedophiles, pornographers and others who sexually exploit and victimize minors and young adults. This has led to highly publicized and not so publicized arrests, convictions, and incarceration of commercial sexual exploiters and victimizers of youth. Some recent examples are as follows: [44]

- In 2009, 571 adults were arrested nationwide, facing federal and state charges for the domestic trafficking of children or other offenses related to prostitution and commercial child sexual exploitation.
- In 2009, the FBI arrested over fifty alleged pimps and rescued forty-five prostitutes between the ages of thirteen and seventeen in a countrywide sweep dubbed Operation Cross Country.
- In June 2009, forty-five men and boys were arrested in Florida for downloading child porn off the Internet. They had collected in total as many as 15,000 images online.
- In February 2009, forty-four persons were arrested in Chicago on child prostitution charges, including a number as customers or for running a child prostitution ring.
- Between 2006 and 2009, at least 176 arrests were made in Polk County, Florida, on child pornography charges.
- In June 2008, 345 people were arrested by the FBI in a nationwide crackdown on child prostitution.
- In March 2006, twenty-seven people were charged in a child pornography Internet sting, with charges including child molestation and possession and manufacture of child porn.
- In a 2005 nationwide crackdown on child prostitution dubbed, Innocence Lost, law enforcement agencies arrested nineteen and charged more than thirty, while identifying thirty prostituted youth and confiscating child pornography images.

According to the Federal Bureau of Investigation, in 2008 there were 17,732 arrests of males age eighteen and over for prostitution and commercialized vice offenses in the United States.[45] Another 45,681 adult male arrests came for sex offenses other than prostitution and forcible rape.[46] Official data on prostitution-related arrests does not break down the number of persons arrested specifically for pimping, solicitation, and other crimes of sexual exploitation. Though overall arrests for prostitution and commercialized vice have been on the decline, a more aggressive pursuit by law enforcement agencies recently of those who sexually exploit runaway, thrownaway, and homeless youth suggests that their arrest and prosecution is on the rise and more prostituted youth are being taken off the street and placed in a safe environment.

This notwithstanding, given the hundreds of thousands of street kids who continue to be sexually exploited and victimized by pimps, pornographers, and other sexual predators, much more needs to be done to prevent running or being thrown away; as well as providing an alternative for homeless youth to prostituting themselves to survive or fit in. Finally, a greater focus by authorities and lawmakers on arresting, prosecuting, and stiffening penalties against those who take advantage of vulnerable youth for commercial sexual exploitation is imperative if the extent of runaways and thrownaways involved in prostitution, pornography, pedophilia, and other forms of profitable sexual victimization is to be reduced significantly.

# Chapter Notes

## Chapter 1

1. R. Barri Flowers, *Runaway Kids and Teenage Prostitution: America's Lost, Abandoned, and Sexually Exploited Children* (Westport, CT: Greenwood Press, 2001), pp. 3–6.

2. Alma C. Molino, "Characteristics of Help-Seeking Street Youth and Non-Street Youth," 2007 National Symposium on Homelessness Research, March 1–2, 2007, p. 7–2, http://aspe.hhs.gov/hsp/homelessness/symposium07/molino/index.htm.

3. U.S. Department of Justice, *Juvenile Offenders and Victims: 2006 National Report* (Washington, D.C.: Office of Juvenile Justice and Delinquency Prevention, 2006), p. 46.

4. Quoted in Thomas P. Gullotta, "Runaway: Reality or Myth," *Adolescence* 13, 52 (1978): 543–49. *See also* Ruby J. Martinez, "Understanding Runaway Teens," *Journal of Child and Adolescent Psychiatric Nursing* 19, 2 (2006): 77–88.

5. U.S. Department of Justice, *Law Enforcement Policies and Practices Regarding Missing Children and Homeless Youth: Research Project* (Washington, D.C.: Office of Juvenile Justice and Delinquency Prevention, 1993), p. 3.

6. *Ibid.*; Flowers, *Runaway Kids and Teenage Prostitution*; Natasha Slesnick, *Our Runaway and Homeless Youth: A Guide to Understanding* (Westport, CT: Praeger, 2004).

7. Heather Hammer, David Finkelhor, and Andrea J. Sedlak, *Runaway/Thrownaway Children: National Estimates and Characteristics*, NISMART Bulletin Series (Washington, D.C.: Office of Juvenile Justice and Delinquency Prevention, 2002), p. 2.

8. U.S. Department of Justice, Federal Bureau of Investigation, *Crime in the United States: Uniform Crime Reports 1998* (Washington, D.C.: Government Printing Office, 1999), p. 403.

9. Flowers, *Runaway Kids and Teenage Prostitution*; R. Barri Flowers, *Kids Who Commit Adult Crimes: A Study of Serious Juvenile Criminality and Delinquency* (Binghamton, NY: Haworth Press, 2002); Robert H. McNamara, *The Lost Population: Status Offenders in America* (Durham, NC: Carolina Academic Press, 2008); Cheryl L. Maxson, Margaret A. Little, Malcolm W. Klein, "Police Response to Runaway and Missing Children: A Conceptual Framework for Research and Policy," *Crime & Delinquency* 34, 1 (1988): 84–102.

10. *Law Enforcement Policies and Practices Regarding Missing Children and Homeless Youth*, p. 3; *Runaway/Thrownaway Children*, p. 2.

11. Molino, "Characteristics of Help-Seeking Street Youth and Non-Street Youth," p. 7–2. *See also* Runaway and Homeless Youth Act, U.S.C. §5701 (1978); Runaway, Homeless, and Missing Children Protection Act, P.L. 108–96 (2003).

12. Emilie Smeaton, *Living on the Edge: The Experiences of Detached Young Runaways* (Leeds, UK: The Children's Society, 2005), pp. 4, 6.

13. The National Network for Youth, "NN4Y Issue Brief: Unaccompanied Youth Overview," http://www.nn4youth.org/system/files/IssueBrief_Unaccompanyed_youth.pdf.

14. The National Network for Youth, "Who Are Runaway and Homeless Youth?" http://www.nn4youth.org/about–us/faqs-and-other-resources.

15. Office of Juvenile Justice and Delinquency Prevention, NISMART Bulletin, "National Estimates of Missing Children: An

Overview" (October 2002), http://www.ncjrs.gov/html/ojjdp/nismart/01/index.html.

16. Molino, "Characteristics of Help-Seeking Street Youth and Non-Street Youth." *See also* Les B. Whitbeck and Danny R. Hoyt, *Nowhere to Grow: Homeless and Runaway Adolescents and Their Families* (Hawthorne, NY: Aldine de Gruyter, 1999).

17. Focus Adolescent Services, "Why Teens Run Away," http://www.focusas.com/Runaways-WhyTeensRunAway.html.

18. Marilyn R. Zide and Andrew L. Cherry, "A Typology of Runaway Youths: An Empirically Based Definition," *Child and Adolescent Social Work Journal* 9 (1992): 155-68; Andrew L. Cherry, "Combining Cluster and Discriminant Analysis to Develop a Social Bond Typology of Runaway Youth," *Research on Social Work Practice* 3, 2 (1993): 175-90.

19. Clifford J. English, "Leaving Home: A Typology of Runaways," *Society* 10 (1973): 22-24.

20. David Finkelhor, Gerald Hotaling, and Andrea J. Sedlak, *Missing, Abducted, Runaway, and Thrownaway Children in America, First Report: Numbers and Characteristics, National Incidence Studies* (Washington, D.C.: Office of Juvenile Justice and Delinquency Prevention, 1990), pp. 174-77.

21. *Ibid.*, p. 176; Flowers, *Runaway Kids and Teenage Prostitution.*

22. Franklin Dunford and Tim Brennan, "A Taxonomy of Runaway Youth," *Social Service Review* 50, 3 (1976): 457-70.

23. Cited in Flowers, *Runaway Kids and Teenage Prostitution.*

24. *Ibid.*

25. *Ibid.*; National Runaway Switchboard, Keeping America's Runaway and At-Risk Youth Safe and Off The Streets, http://www.1800runaway.org.

26. *Missing, Abducted, Runaway, and Thrownaway Children in America*, pp. vii, 49.

27. Kelly Dedel, *Juvenile Runaways* (Washington, D.C.: Office of Community Oriented Policing Services, 2006), p. 3, http://www.ncjrs.gov/App/Publications/abstract.aspx?ID=235092.

28. *Ibid.*; Jim Wade and Nina Biehal, *Going Missing: Young People Absent from Care* (Chichester, UK: Wiley, 1998); Joe Piasecki, "Throwaway Kids," *Pasadena Weekly* (June 26, 2006), http://www.pasadenaweekly.com/cms/story/detail/?id=3559&IssueNum=25.

29. Caren Kaplan, *Children Missing from Care: An Issue Brief* (Washington, D.C.: Child Welfare League of America, 2004).

30. Wade and Biehal, *Going Missing: Young People Absent from Care.*

31. Dedel, *Juvenile Runaways*, p. 3; *Missing, Abducted, Runaway, and Thrownaway Children in America.*

32. Flowers, *Runaway Kids and Teenage Prostitution*; R. Barri Flowers, *The Prostitution of Women and Girls* (Jefferson, NC: McFarland, 2005), p. 89; R. Barri Flowers, *The Victimization and Exploitation of Women and Children: A Study of Physical, Mental and Sexual Maltreatment in the United States* (Jefferson, NC: McFarland, 1994), p. 36; Emilie Smeaton and Gwyther Rees, *Running Away in South Yorkshire: Research into the Incidence and Nature of the Problem in Sheffield, Rotherham, Barnsley, and Doncaster* (Sheffield, UK: Safe at Last, 2004).

33. Cited in Lindsay Crawford, "Troubled Teens Take to the Streets: Rebellious Youths with Nowhere to Run Away from Their Problems and Their Homes," Silver Chips Online (April 13, 2000), p. 1.

34. Cited in Runaway Teens.org, http://www.runawayteens.org/statistics.html.

35. Cited in Flowers, *Runaway Kids and Teenage Prostitution.*

36. Patricia Hersch, "Coming of Age on City Streets," *Psychology Today* 22, 1 (1988): 34.

37. Cited in Flowers, *The Victimization and Exploitation of Women and Children*, p. 36.

38. Cited in Flowers, *Runaway Kids and Teenage Prostitution*; Tim Brennan, *The Social Psychology of Runaways* (Toronto: Lexington Books, 1978), p. 5.

39. National Runaway Switchboard.

40. *Runaway/Thrownaway Children*, p. 2.

41. *Ibid.*, pp. 2-6.

42. Office of Applied Studies, *Results from the 2002 National Survey on Drug Use and Health: National Findings* (Rockville, MD: Substance Abuse and Mental Health Services Administration, 2003).

43. Cited in Runaway Teens.org.

44. *Missing, Abducted, Runaway, and Thrownaway Children in America*, pp. xvii-xix, 182-87.

45. *Ibid.*, pp. xix, 184-85.

46. *Ibid.*, p. 183.

47. *Ibid.*, pp. 174-272; Hammer, Finkelhor, and Sedlak, *Runaway/Thrownaway Children*, pp. 1-12.

## Chapter 2

1. Howard N. Snyder and Melissa Sickmund, *Juvenile Offenders and Victims: 1999 Na-*

*tional Report* (Washington, D.C.: Office of Juvenile Justice and Delinquency Prevention, 1999), p. 38.

2. R. Barri Flowers, *The Victimization and Exploitation of Women and Children: A Study of Physical, Mental and Sexual Maltreatment in the United States* (Jefferson, NC: McFarland, 1994), p. 37; S. Jorgenson, H. Thornburg, and J. Williams, "The Experience of Running Away: Perceptions of Adolescents Seeking Help in a Shelter Case Facility," *High School Journal* 12 (1980): 87–96.

3. David Finkelhor, Gerald Hotaling, and Andrea J. Sedlak, *Missing, Abducted, Runaway, and Thrownaway Children in America, First Report: Numbers and Characteristics, National Incidence Studies* (Washington, D.C.: Office of Juvenile Justice and Delinquency Prevention, 1990), p. 123.

4. Heather Hammer, David Finkelhor, and Andrea J. Sedlak, *Runaway/Thrownaway Children: National Estimates and Characteristics*, NISMART Bulletin Series (Washington, D.C.: Office of Juvenile Justice and Delinquency Prevention, 2002), p. 6.

5. Snyder and Sickmund, *Juvenile Offenders and Victims: 1999 National Report*, p. 58.

6. Les B. Whitbeck and Danny R. Hoyt, *Nowhere to Grow: Homeless and Runaway Adolescents and Their Families* (Hawthorne, NY: Aldine de Gruyter, 1999). *See also* Kimberly Kempf-Leonard and Pernilla Johansson, "Gender and Runaways: Risk Factors, Delinquency, and Juvenile Justice Experiences," *Youth Violence and Juvenile Justice* 5, 3 (2007): 308–27.

7. Les B. Whitbeck, Danny R. Hoyt, Kevin A. Yoder, Ana Mari Cauce, and Matt Paradise, "Deviant Behavior and Victimization Among Homeless and Runaway Adolescents," *Journal of Interpersonal Violence* 16 (2001): 1175–1204.

8. Alma C. Molino, "Characteristics of Help-Seeking Street Youth and Non-Street Youth," 2007 National Symposium on Homelessness Research, March 1–2, 2007, p. 7–2, http://aspe.hhs.gov/hsp/homelessness/sympo sium07/molino/index.htm; Rebecca P. Sanchez, Martha W. Waller, and Jody M. Greene, "Who Runs? A Demographic Profile of Runaway Youth in the United States," *Journal of Adolescent Health* 39, 5 (2006): 778–81.

9. Molino, "Characteristics of Help-Seeking Street Youth and Non-Street Youth."

10. U.S. Department of Justice, Federal Bureau of Investigation, *Crime in the United States, 2007*, Table 42, http://www.fbi.gov/ucr/cius 2007/data/table_42.html; R. Barri Flowers, *The*

*Adolescent Criminal: An Examination of Today's Juvenile Offender* (Jefferson, NC: McFarland, 2009), pp. 141–52; Jeanne G. Kaufman and Cathy S. Widom, "Childhood Victimization, Running Away, and Delinquency," *Journal of Research in Crime and Delinquency* 36, 4 (1999): 347–70.

11. R. Barri Flowers, *Runaway Kids and Teenage Prostitution: America's Lost, Abandoned, and Sexually Exploited Children* (Westport, CT: Greenwood Press, 2001), p. 8; "FBI Gives First Accounting of Missing U.S. Children," *Arizona Daily Star* (March 10, 2006), http://www.azs tarnet.com/sn/fromcomments/119396.php; Kevin A. Yoder, Les B. Whitbeck, and Danny R. Hoyt, "Event History Analysis of Antecedents to Running Away from Home and Being on the Street," *American Behavioral Scientist* 45 (2001): 51–65.

12. "FBI Gives First Accounting of Missing U.S. Children."

13. Flowers, *The Adolescent Criminal*; U.S. Department of Justice, Federal Bureau of Investigation, *Crime in the United States, 2007*, Table 33, http://www.fbi.gov/ucr/cius2007/data/table_33.html.

14. Hammer, Finkelhor, and Sedlak, *Runaway/Thrownaway Children*, p. 6.

15. Finkelhor, Hotaling, and Sedlak, *Missing, Abducted, Runaway, and Thrownaway Children in America, First Report*.

16. Cited in Lindsay Crawford, "Troubled Teens Take to the Streets: Rebellious Youths with Nowhere to Run Away from Their Problems and Their Homes," *Silver Chips Online* (April 13, 2000), p. 1.

17. Whitbeck and Hoyt, *Nowhere to Grow*.

18. Whitbeck, Hoyt, Yoder, Cauce, and Paradise, "Deviant Behavior and Victimization Among Homeless and Runaway Adolescents."

19. Snyder and Sickmund, *Juvenile Offenders and Victims: 1999 National Report*, p. 58.

20. Cited in Flowers, *Runaway Kids and Teenage Prostitution*, pp. 9–10.

21. R. Barri Flowers, *Children and Criminality: The Child as Victim and Perpetrator* (Westport, CT: Greenwood Press, 1986), p. 133.

22. Flowers, *The Victimization and Exploitation of Women and Children*, pp. 41–42.

23. Laurie Schaffner, "Searching For Connection: A New Look at Teenaged Runaways," *Adolescence* 33, 31 (1998): 619–28.

24. *Ibid.*; "FBI Gives First Accounting of Missing U.S. Children."

25. Finkelhor, Hotaling, and Sedlak, *Missing, Abducted, Runaway, and Thrownaway Children in America, First Report*.

26. Snyder and Sickmund, *Juvenile Offenders and Victims: 1999 National Report*, p. 58.

27. Whitbeck and Hoyt, *Nowhere to Grow*.

28. Whitbeck, Hoyt, Yoder, Cauce, and Paradise, "Deviant Behavior and Victimization Among Homeless and Runaway Adolescents."

29. "FBI Gives First Accounting of Missing U.S. Children."

30. Flowers, *Runaway Kids and Teenage Prostitution*.

31. R. Barri Flowers, *The Prostitution of Women and Girls* (Jefferson, NC: McFarland, 2005), pp. 91–93.

32. U.S. Department of Health and Human Services, Family Youth and Services Bureau, *Youth with Runaway, Throwaway, and Homeless Experiences: Prevalence, Drug Use, and Other At-Risk Behaviors* (Silver Springs, MD: National Clearinghouse on Families & Youth, 1995), p. 5.

33. Louise Homer, "Criminality Based Resource for Runaway Girls," *Social Casework* 10 (1973): 474.

34. James A. Hildebrand, "Why Runaways Leave Home," *Police Science* 54 (1963): 211–16.

35. Robert Shellow, "Suburban Runaways of the 60s," *Monographs of the Society for Research in Child Development* 32 (1967): 17.

36. Finkelhor, Hotaling, and Sedlak, *Missing, Abducted, Runaway, and Thrownaway Children in America, First Report*, p. 109.

37. R. Barri Flowers, *Female Crime, Criminals, and Cellmates: An Exploration of Female Criminality* (Jefferson, NC: McFarland, 1995), p. 144.

38. R. Barri Flowers, *Kids Who Commit Adult Crimes: A Study of Serious Juvenile Criminality and Delinquency* (Binghamton, NY: Haworth Press, 2002), p. 131.

39. Finkelhor, Hotaling, and Sedlak, *Missing, Abducted, Runaway, and Thrownaway Children in America, First Report*.

40. *Ibid.*, p. 108.

41. *Ibid.*, p. 124.

42. Rolf A. Loeber, Ann W. Weiher, and Carolyn Smith, "The Relationship Between Family Interaction and Delinquency and Substance Use," in David Huizinga, Rolf Loeber, and Terrence P. Thornberry, eds., *Urban Delinquency and Substance Abuse: Technical Report*, Vol. 1 (Washington, D.C.: Office of Juvenile Justice and Delinquency, 1991).

43. See, for example, David P. Farrington, "The Explanation and Prevention of Youthful Offending," in J. David Hawkins, ed., *Delinquency and Crime: Current Theories* (New York: Cambridge University Press, 1996); Flowers, *Children and Criminality*.

44. N. S. Johnson and Roxy Peck, "Sibship Composition and the Adolescent Runaway Phenomenon," *Journal of Youth and Adolescence* 7, 3 (1978): 301–05. *See also* Anton de Man, "Adolescent Runaways: Familial and Personal Correlates," *Social Behavior and Personaliy: An International Journal* 21, 2 (1993): 163–67; Loring P. Jones, "A Typology of Adolescent Runaways," *Child and Adolescent Social Work Journal* 5, 1 (1988): 16–29.

45. Israel Kolvin, Frederick J. Miller, Mary Fleeting, and Philip A. Kolvin, "Social and Parenting Factors Affecting Criminal-Offense Rates: Findings from the Newcastle Thousand Family Study (1947–1980)," *British Journal of Psychiatry* 152 (1988): 80–90.

46. John Newson, Elizabeth Newson, and Mike S. Adams, "The Social Origins of Delinquency," *Criminal Behavior and Mental Health* 3 (1993): 19–29.

47. Farrington, "The Explanation and Prevention of Youthful Offending;" Flowers, *The Adolescent Criminal*.

48. Farideh Hamidi, "A Study on Family Structure and Attachment Style of Runaway Girls and the Outcomes of Using Family and Supportive Therapy Interventions," http://en.sbu.ac.ir/Portals/0/Family/1.pdf.

49. Flowers, *Kids Who Commit Adult Crimes*, pp. 133–34; J. P. Lees and L. J. Newson, "Family or Sibship Position and Some of Juvenile Delinquency," *British Journal of Delinquency* 5 (1954): 46–55.

50. Flowers, *The Adolescent Criminal*.

51. CRS Report for Congress, *Runaway and Homeless Youth: Demographics, Programs, and Emerging Issues* (Washington, D.C.: Congressional Research Service, 2007), p. 27.

52. *Ibid.*, p. 28; Peter Edelman, Harry J. Holzer, and Paul Offner, *Reconnecting Disadvantaged Young Men* (Washington, D.C.: Urban Institute Press, 2006), p. 2.

53. *Runaway and Homeless Youth*, p. 28.

54. Edelman, Holzer, and Offner, *Reconnecting Disadvantaged Young Men*, p. 2.

55. Bob Reeg, "The Runaway and Homeless Youth Act and Disconnected Youth," in Jodie Levin-Epstein and Mark H. Greenberg, eds., *Leave No Youth Behind: Opportunities for Congress to Reach Disconnected Youth* (Washington, D.C.: Center for Law and Social Policy, 2003), pp. 56–63.

56. Flowers, *Runaway Kids and Teenage Prostitution*; Flowers, *The Adolescent Criminal*; Flowers, *Kids Who Commit Adult Crimes*.

57. *Runaway and Homeless Youth*, p. 28; Flowers, *Runaway Kids and Teenage Prostitution*.

# Chapter 3

1. The National Network for Youth, "Who Are Runaway and Homeless Youth?" http://www.nn4youth.org/about-us/faqs-and-other-resources.

2. Focus Adolescence Services, "Why Teens Run Away," http://www.focusas.com/Runaways-WhyTeensRunAway.html.

3. David Finkelhor, Gerald Hotaling, and Andrea J. Sedlak, *Missing, Abducted, Runaway, and Thrownaway Children in America, First Report: Numbers and Characteristics, National Incidence Studies* (Washington, D.C.: Office of Juvenile Justice and Delinquency Prevention, 1990), p. 135.

4. CRS Report for Congress, *Runaway and Homeless Youth: Demographics, Programs, and Emerging Issues* (Washington, D.C.: Congressional Research Service, 2007), p. 4.

5. *Ibid.*, p. 3; "Why Teens Run Away;" Joe Piasecki, "Throwaway Kids," *Pasadena Weekly* (June 26, 2006), http://www.pasadenaweekly.com/cms/story/detail/?id=3559&IssueNum=25; Samuel J. Fasulo, Theodore P. Cross, Peggy Mosley, and Joseph Leavey, "Adolescent Runaway Behavior in Specialized Foster Care," *Children and Youth Services Review* 24, 8 (2002): 623–640.

6. *Runaway and Homeless Youth*, p. 4.

7. R. Barri Flowers, *Runaway Kids and Teenage Prostitution: America's Lost, Abandoned, and Sexually Exploited Children* (Westport, CT: Greenwood Press, 2001), pp. 17–19.

8. Quoted in R. Barri Flowers, *The Victimization and Exploitation of Women and Children: A Study of Physical, Mental and Sexual Maltreatment in the United States* (Jefferson, NC: McFarland, 1994), p. 42.

9. National Runaway Switchboard, http://www.1800runaway.org/.

10. Heather Hammer, David Finkelhor, and Andrea J. Sedlak, *Runaway/Thrownaway Children: National Estimates and Characteristics*, NISMART Bulletin Series (Washington, D.C.: Office of Juvenile Justice and Delinquency Prevention, 2002), p. 2.

11. *Ibid.*, p. 8. *See also* Christopher L. Ringwalt, Jody M. Greene, and Marjorie J. Robertson, "Familial Backgrounds and Risk Behaviors of Youth with Thrownaway Experiences," *Journal of Adolescence* 21, 3 (1998): 241–52.

12. Finkelhor, Hotaling, and Sedlak, *Missing, Abducted, Runaway, and Thrownaway Children in America, First Report*, p. 140.

13. *Ibid.*

14. *Ibid.*, pp. 148–60.

15. Cited in Ross Atkin, "They Offer Help to Teens at the End of the Line," *Christian Science Monitor* (June 14, 2004), http://www.csmonitor.com/2004/0114/p14s02-lifp.html.

16. J. Kirk Felsman, "Abandoned Children: A Reconsideration," *Children Today* 13, 3 (1984): 13–18; Dodie Butler, *Runaway House: A Youth-run Project* (Washington, D.C.: Government Printing Office, 1974).

17. Jane L. Powers, Barbara Jaklitsch, and John Eckenrode, "Behavioral Indicators of Maltreatment Among Runaway and Homeless Youth," paper presented at the National Symposium on Child Victimization, Anaheim, CA, April 1988.

18. Renee S. Levine, Diane Metzendorf, and Kathryn A. Van Boskirk, "Runaway and Throwaway Youth: A Case for Early Intervention with Truants," *Social Work in Education* 8 (1986): 93–106; Gerald R. Adams, Thomas Gulotta, and Mary A. Clancy, "Homeless Adolescents: A Descriptive Study of Similarities and Differences Between Runaways and Throwaways," *Adolescence* 79 (1985): 715–24.

19. Cited in Carolyn Males and Julie Raskin, "The Children Nobody Wants," *Reader's Digest* (January 1984), p. 63.

20. Cited in "'Runaways,' 'Throwaways,' 'Bag Kids'—An Army of Drifter Teens," *U.S. News & World Report* (March 11, 1985), p. 53. *See also* Sally J. Hier, Paula J. Korboot, and Robert D. Schweitzer, "Social Adjustment and Symptomatology in Two Types of Homeless Adolescents: Runaways and Throwaways," *Adolescence* 25, 100 (1990): 761–71; James A. Inciardi, Ruth Horowitz, and Anne E. Pottieger, *Street Kids, Street Drugs, Street Crime* (Belmont, CA: Wadsworth, 1993).

21. Lynn Rew, Margaret Taylor-Seehafer, Nancy Thomas, and Ronald Yockey, "Correlates of Resilience in Homeless Adolescents," *Journal of Nursing Scholarship* 33, 1 (2001): 33–40.

22. U.S. Department of Health and Human Services, Family Youth and Services Bureau, *FYSB Update* (Silver Springs, MD: National Clearinghouse on Families & Youth, 1995), p. 2.

23. Opinion Research Corporation as cited in *Missing, Abducted, Runaway, and Thrownaway Children*, p. 136.

24. Males and Raskin, "The Children Nobody Wants," p. 63.

25. U.S. Department of Justice, *Juvenile Offenders and Victims: 1999 National Report* (Washington, D.C.: Office of Juvenile Justice and Delinquency Prevention, 1999), p. 38.

26. Finkelhor, Hotaling, and Sedlak, *Missing, Abducted, Runaway, and Thrownaway Children in America, First Report*, p. 136.

27. Hammer, Finkelhor, and Sedlak, *Runaway/Thrownaway Children*, p. 2.

28. Gil Griffin, "Running on Empty: Kids Take to the Streets When They Don't Feel Loved at Home," *San Diego Union-Tribune* (July 26, 1997), p. E1.

29. Gary J. Remafedi, "Adolescent Homosexuality: Issues for Pediatricians," *Clinical Pediatrics* 24, 9 (1985): 481–85; Monica E. Schneider and Robert E. Owens, "Concern for Lesbian, Gay, and Bisexual Kids: The Benefits for All Children," *Education and Urban Society* 32, 3 (2000): 349–67; Pierre J. Tremblay, "The Homosexuality Factor in the Youth Suicide Problem," presented at the Sixth Annual Conference of the Canadian Association for Suicide Prevention, Banff, Alberta (October 11–14, 1995), http://www.qrd.org/qrd/www/youth/tremblay/. *See also* Nicholas Ray, *Lesbian, Gay, Bisexual, and Transgender Youth: An Epidemic of Homelessness* (New York: National Gay and Lesbian Task Force Policy Institute and National Coalition for the Homeless, 2006); Gabe Kruks, "Gay and Lesbian Homeless/Street Youth: Special Issues and Concerns," *Journal of Adolescent Health* 12 (1991): 515–18.

30. Hammer, Finkelhor, and Sedlak, *Runaway/Thrownaway Children*, p. 6. *See also* Kelly Dedel, *Juvenile Runaways* (Washington, D.C.: Office of Community Oriented Policing Services, 2006), p. 2, http://www.ncjrs.gov/App/Publications/abstract.aspx?ID=235092; Alma C. Molino, "Characteristics of Help-Seeking Street Youth and Non-Street Youth," 2007 National Symposium on Homelessness Research, March 1–2, 2007, p. 7–3, http://aspe.hhs.gov/hsp/homelessness/symposium07/molino/index.htm.

31. Gil Griffin, "Running on Empty," p. E2.

32. Finkelhor, Hotaling, and Sedlak, *Missing, Abducted, Runaway, and Thrownaway Children in America, First Report*, p. 149.

33. *Ibid.*, p. 140.

34. Flowers, *Runaway Kids and Teenage Prostitution*, p. 22; Ringwalt, Greene, and Robertson, "Familial Backgrounds and Risk Behaviors of Youth with Thrownaway Experiences."

35. Hammer, Finkelhor, and Sedlak, *Runaway/Thrownaway Children*, p. 6.

36. Les B. Whitbeck and Danny R. Hoyt, *Nowhere to Grow: Homeless and Runaway Adolescents and Their Families* (Hawthorne, NY: Aldine de Gruyter, 1999). *See also* Michael E. Rohr, *Adolescent Runaway Behavior: Who Runs*

and *Why* (New York: Routledge, 1999); P. David Kurtz, Elizabeth W. Lindsey, Sara Jarvis, and Larry Nackerud, "How Runaway and Homeless Youth Navigate Troubled Waters: The Role of Formal and Informal Helpers," *Child and Adolescent Social Work Journal* 17, 5 (2000): 381–402.

37. Les B. Whitbeck, Danny R. Hoyt, Kevin A. Yoder, Ana Mari Cauce, and Matt Paradise, "Deviant Behavior and Victimization Among Homeless and Runaway Adolescents," *Journal of Interpersonal Violence* 16 (2001): 1175–1204. *See also* Natasha Slesnick, *Our Runaway and Homeless Youth: A Guide to Understanding* (Westport, CT: Praeger, 2004); Marlene Webber, *Street Kids: The Tragedy of Canada's Runaways* (Toronto: University of Toronto Press, 1991).

38. Emilie Smeaton, *Living on the Edge: The Experiences of Detached Young Runaways* (Leeds, UK: The Children's Society, 2005), p. 10. *See also* R. Barri Flowers, *The Prostitution of Women and Girls* (Jefferson, NC: McFarland, 2005), p. 96; Jennifer B. Unger, Thomas R. Simon, Traci L. Newman, Susanne B. Montgomery, Michele D. Kipke, and Michael Albomoz, "Early Adolescent Street Youth: An Overlooked Population with Unique Problems and Service Needs," *Journal of Early Adolescence* 18, 4 (1998): 325–48.

39. Finkelhor, Hotaling, and Sedlak, *Missing, Abducted, Runaway, and Thrownaway Children in America, First Report*.

40. *Ibid.*, p. 151.

41. The National Network for Youth, "NN4Y Issue Brief: Unaccompanied Youth Overview," http://www.nn4youth.org/system/files/IssueBrief_Unaccompanyed_youth.pdf.; U.S. Department of Health and Human Services, Family Youth and Services Bureau, *Youth with Runaway, Throwaway, and Homeless Experiences: Prevalence, Drug Use, and Other At-Risk Behaviors* (Silver Springs, MD: National Clearinghouse on Families & Youth, 1995).

42. *Youth with Runaway, Throwaway, and Homeless Experiences.*

43. Finkelhor, Hotaling, and Sedlak, *Missing, Abducted, Runaway, and Thrownaway Children in America, First Report*, p. 151.

44. *Ibid.*

45. *Ibid.*, p. 150.

## Chapter 4

1. Lynn Rew, Margaret Taylor-Seehafer, Nancy Thomas, and Ronald Yockey, "Corre-

lates of Resilience in Homeless Adolescents," *Journal of Nursing Scholarship* 33, 1 (2001): 33–40.

2. Westat, Inc., National Evaluation of Runaway and Homeless Youth (Washington, D.C.: U.S. Department of Health and Human Services, 1997).

3. Heather Hammer, David Finkelhor, and Andrea J. Sedlak, *Runaway/Thrownaway Children: National Estimates and Characteristics*, NISMART Bulletin Series (Washington, D.C.: Office of Juvenile Justice and Delinquency Prevention, 2002), p. 8.

4. P. David Kurtz, Gail L. Kurtz, and Sara Jarvis, "Problems of Maltreated Runaway Youth," *Adolescence* 26 (1991): 543–55.

5. Jacquelyn K. Warren, Faye Gary, and Jacquelyn Moorhead, "Self-Reported Experiences of Physical and Sexual Abuse Among Runaway Youths," *Perspectives in Psychiatric Care* 30, 1 (1994): 23–28.

6. Kimberly D. Ryan, Ryan Kilmer, Ana Mari Cauce, Haruko Watanabe, and Danny R. Hoyt, "Psychological Consequences of Child Maltreatment in Homeless Adolescents: Untangling the Unique Effects of Maltreatment and Family Environment," *Child Abuse and Neglect* 24 (2000): 333–52.

7. R. Barri Flowers, *The Adolescent Criminal: An Examination of Today's Juvenile Offender* (Jefferson, NC: McFarland, 2009), pp. 133–35; R. Barri Flowers, *Runaway Kids and Teenage Prostitution: America's Lost, Abandoned, and Sexually Exploited Children* (Westport, CT: Greenwood Press, 2001), pp. 41–47; Carol L. M. Caton, "The Epidemiology of Homelessness," in Carol L. M. Canton, ed., *Homeless in America* (New York: Oxford University Press, 1990).

8. Flowers, *Runaway Kids and Teenage Prostitution*; Study World, "Runaways: Victims at Home and On the Streets," http://www.studyworld.com/newsite/ReportEssay/SocialIssues/Political%5CRunaways_Victims_At_Home_and_On_the_Streets-32644.htm.

9. Flowers, *Runaway Kids and Teenage Prostitution*; Arlene R. Stiffman, "Physical and Sexual Abuse in Runaway Youths," *Child Abuse and Neglect* 13, 3 (1989): 417–26; Les B. Whitbeck, Danny R. Hoyt, and Kevin A. Ackley, "Abusive Family Backgrounds and Later Victimization Among Runaway and Homeless Youth," *Journal of Research on Adolescence* 7, 4 (1997): 375–92.

10. Caliber Associates, Analysis and Interpretation of New Information Concerning Runaway and Homeless Youth (Washington, D.C.: U.S. Department of Health and Human Services, 1997).

11. Stiffman, "Physical and Sexual Abuse in Runaway Youths;" R. Barri Flowers, *The Victimization and Exploitation of Women and Children: A Study of Physical, Mental and Sexual Maltreatment in the United States* (Jefferson, NC: McFarland, 1994); Mark D. Janus, Arlene McCormack, Ann W. Burgess, and Carol Hartman, *Adolescent Runaways: Causes and Consequences* (Lexington, MA: Lexington Books, 1987).

12. Sandra L. Ayerst, "Depression and Stress in Street Youth," *Adolescence* 34, 135 (1999): 567–75; Deborah Shelton, "Emotional Disorders in Young Offenders," *Journal of Nursing Scholarship* 33, 3 (2001): 259–63; About.com: Mental Health, "Study of Runaways Reveals Disturbing Data on Abuse, Mental Illness," (July 2002), http://mentalhealth.about.com/library/sci/0702/blrunaway702.htm.

13. Emilie Smeaton, *Living on the Edge: The Experiences of Detached Young Runaways* (Leeds, UK: The Children's Society, 2005), p. 9; Kelly Dedel, *Juvenile Runaways* (Washington, D.C.: Office of Community Oriented Policing Services, 2006), p. 6, http://www.ncjrs.gov/App/Publications/abstract.aspx?ID=235092.

14. Dedel, *Juvenile Runaways*, p. 6; Smeaton, *Living on the Edge*, p. 9; Natasha Slesnick, *Our Runaway and Homeless Youth: A Guide to Understanding* (Westport, CT: Praeger, 2004).

15. Emilie Smeaton and Gwyther Rees, *Running Away in South Yorkshire: Research into the Incidence and Nature of the Problem in Sheffield, Rotherham, Barnsley, and Doncaster* (Sheffield, UK: Safe at Last, 2004); National Association of Social Workers, *Helping Vulnerable Youth: Runaway and Homeless Adolescents in the United States* (Washington, D.C.: NASW Press, 1992).

16. Dedel, *Juvenile Runaways*, p. 6; Slesnick, *Our Runaway and Homeless Youth*; Caroline Abrahams and Roddy Mungal, *Runaways: Exploding the Myths* (London: National Children's Home, 1992).

17. Slesnick, *Our Runaway and Homeless Youth*; Abrahams and Mungal, *Runaways*; Dedel, *Juvenile Runaways*, p. 6; Debbie B. Riley, Geoffrey L. Greif, Debra L. Caplan, and K. M. Heather, "Common Themes and Treatment Approaches in Working with Families of Runaway Youths," *American Journal of Family Therapy* 32, 2 (2004): 139–53.

18. Dedel, *Juvenile Runaways*, p. 6; Abrahams and Mungal, *Runaways*; Slesnick, *Our Runaway and Homeless Youth*; Milton Greenblatt and Marjorie J. Robertson, "Life-Styles,

Adaptive Strategies, and Sexual Behaviors of Homeless Adolescents," *Hospital and Community Psychiatry* 44, 12 (1993): 1177–80; Gabe Kruks, "Gay and Lesbian Homeless/Street Youth: Special Issues and Concerns," *Journal of Adolescent Health* 12, 7 (1991): 515–18.

19. Flowers, *The Adolescent Criminal*; Dedel, *Juvenile Runaways*, p. 6; Slesnick, *Our Runaway and Homeless Youth*; Riley, Greif, Caplan, and Heather, "Common Themes and Treatment Approaches in Working with Families of Runaway Youths."

20. Smeaton, *Living on the Edge*, p. 10; Dedel, *Juvenile Runaways*, p. 6.

21. Flowers, *The Adolescent Criminal*; Flowers, *The Victimization and Exploitation of Women and Children*; Smeaton, *Living on the Edge*, p. 10; Gwyther Rees, *Working with Young Runaways: Learning from Practice* (London: The Children's Society, 2001).

22. Smeaton, *Living on the Edge*, p. 10; Flowers, *The Adolescent Criminal*; Geoff Newiss, *Missing Presumed..? The Police Response to Missing Persons* (London: Home Office, 1999).

23. Flowers, *The Adolescent Criminal*; R. Barri Flowers, *Kids Who Commit Adult Crimes: A Study of Serious Juvenile Criminality and Delinquency* (Binghamton, NY: Haworth, 2002); R. Barri Flowers, *Male Crime and Deviance: Exploring Its Cause, Dynamics, and Nature* (Springfield, IL: Charles C Thomas, 2003).

24. See, for example, Flowers, *Runaway Kids and Teenage Prostitution*; Stiffman, "Physical and Sexual Abuse in Runaway Youths," R. Barri Flowers, *Sex Crimes: Perpetrators, Predators, Prostitutes, and Victims*, 2nd ed. (Springfield, IL: Charles C Thomas, 2006); Richard Famularo, Robert Kinscherff, Terence Fenton, and Suzanne M. Bolduc, "Child Maltreatment Histories Among Runaway and Delinquent Children," *Clinical Pediatrics* 29 (1990): 713–18; Mary J. Rotheram-Borus, Karen A. Mahler, Cheryl Koopman, and Kris Langabeer, "Sexual Abuse History and Associated Multiple Risk Behavior in Adolescent Runaways," *American Journal of Orthopsychiatry* 66 (1996): 390–400; Mark D. Janus, Ann W. Burgess, and Arlene McCormack, "Histories of Sexual Abuse in Adolescent Male Runaways," *Adolescence* 22, 86 (1987): 405–17.

25. Flowers, *Runaway Kids and Teenage Prostitution*; Flowers, *The Victimization and Exploitation of Women and Children*.

26. U.S. Department of Health and Human Services, *Sexual Abuse Among Homeless Adolescents: Prevalence, Correlates, and Sequelae* (Washington, D.C.: Administration for Children and Families, 2002); R. Barri Flowers, *Children and Criminality: The Child as Victim and Perpetrator* (Westport, CT: Greenwood Press, 1986); Stiffman, "Physical and Sexual Abuse in Runaway Youths," pp. 417–26.

27. Kevin A. Yoder, "Comparing Suicide Attempters, Suicide Ideators, and Nonsuicidal Homeless and Runaway Adolescents," *Suicide & Life-Threatening Behavior* 29 (1999): 25–36.

28. Beth E. Molnar, Stanley B. Shade, Alex H. Kral, Robert E. Booth, and John K. Watters, "Suicidal Behavior and Sexual/Physical Abuse Among Street Youth," *Child Abuse and Neglect* 22 (1998): 213–22.

29. Ryan, Kilmer, Cauce, Watanabe, and Hoyt, "Psychological Consequences of Child Maltreatment in Homeless Adolescents."

30. Cited in Patricia Hersch, "Coming of Age on City Streets," *Psychology Today* 22, 1 (1988): 31.

31. Quoted in Stephanie Arbarbanel, "Women Who Make a Difference," *Family Circle* 107 (January 11, 1994), p. 11.

32. Kimberly A. Tyler, Danny R. Hoyt, and Les B. Whitbeck, "The Effects of Early Sexual Abuse on Later Sexual Victimization Among Female Homeless and Runaway Adolescents," *Journal of Interpersonal Violence* 15 (2000): 235–250.

33. Mimi H. Silbert, "Delancey Street Study: Prostitution and Sexual Assault," summary of results, Delancey Street Foundation, San Francisco, 1982, p. 3.

34. Kimberly A. Tyler, Danny R. Hoyt, Les B. Whitbeck, and Ana Mari Cauce, "The Impact of Childhood Sexual Abuse on Later Sexual Victimization Among Runaway Youth," *Journal of Research on Adolescence* 11, 2 (2001): 151–76.

35. Alex H. Kral, Beth E. Molnar, Robert E. Booth, and John K. Watters, "Prevalence of Sexual Risk Behaviour and Substance Use Among Runaway and Homeless Adolescents in San Francisco, Denver and New York City," *International Journal of STD and AIDS* 8 (1997): 109–17.

36. Nathanial E. Terrell, "Aggravated and Sexual Assault Among Homeless and Runaway Adolescents," *Youth & Society* 28 (1997): 267–90.

37. Les B. Whitbeck and Ronald L. Simons, "A Comparison of Adaptive Strategies and Patterns of Victimization Among Homeless Adolescents and Adults," *Violence and Victims* 8, 2 (1993): 135–52.

38. Arbarbanel, "Women Who Make a Difference," p. 11.

39. Laurie Schaffner, "Searching For Connection: A New Look At Teenaged Runaways," *Adolescence* 33, 31 (1998): 619–28.

40. The National Network for Youth, "NN4Y Issue Brief: Unaccompanied Youth Overview," http://www.nn4youth.org/system/files/IssueBrief_Unaccompanyed_youth.pdf.

41. CRS Report for Congress, *Runaway and Homeless Youth: Demographics, Programs, and Emerging Issues* (Washington, D.C.: Congressional Research Service, 2007), pp. 6–7.

42. Schaffner, "Searching For Connection."

43. Quoted in R. Barri Flowers, *Domestic Crimes, Family Violence and Child Abuse: A Study of Contemporary American Society* (Jefferson, NC: McFarland, 2000), p. 16.

44. *Ibid.*

45. Cited in Flowers, *The Victimization and Exploitation of Women and Children*, p. 30.

46. Flowers, *Runaway Kids and Teenage Prostitution*; R. Barri Flowers, *The Prostitution of Women and Girls* (Jefferson, NC: McFarland, 2005), pp. 48–52; Z. M. Lukman, "The Prevalence of Running Away from Home Among Prostituted Children in Malaysia," *Journal of Social Sciences* 5, 3 (2009): 158; Miriam Saphira, and Averil Herbert, "Victimization Among Those Involved in Underage Commercial Sexual Activity," *Women's Studies Journal* 19, 2 (2005): 32–40; Walter de Oliveira, *Working with Children on the Streets of Brazil: Politics and Practice* (Binghamton, NY: Haworth Press, 2000).

47. Gary L. Yates, Richard G. MacKenzie, Julia Pennbridge, and Avon Swofford, "A Risk Profile Comparison of Homeless Youth Involved in Prostitution and Homeless Youth Not Involved," *Journal of Adolescent Health* 12, 7 (1991): 545–48.

48. Les B. Whitbeck and, Danny R. Hoyt, *Nowhere to Grow: Homeless and Runaway Adolescents and Their Families* (Hawthorne, NY: Aldine De Gruyter, 1999).

49. Flowers, *The Victimization and Exploitation of Women and Children*; Flowers, *Runaway Kids and Teenage Prostitution*; Yates, MacKenzie, Pennbridge, and Swofford, "A Risk Profile Comparison of Homeless Youth Involved in Prostitution;" Lukman, "The Prevalence of Running Away from Home Among Prostituted Children in Malaysia," p. 158.

50. Quoted in Flowers, *Runaway Kids and Teenage Prostitution*, p. 43. *See also* Ray Johnson, "Dealing with Domestic Violence and Teen-age Runaways," *San Diego Union-Tribune* (October 22, 1997), p. B5.

51. National Survey on Drug Use and Health, *The NSDUH Report*, "Substance Abuse Among Youths Who Had Run Away from Home," (July 2, 2004), http://www.oas.samhsa.gov/2k4/runAways/runAways.htm.

52. *Ibid.*

53. Flowers, *The Victimization and Exploitation of Women and Children*, p. 44.

54. Joan J. Johnson, *Teen Prostitution* (Danbury, CT: Franklin Watts, 1992), p. 97.

55. Flowers, *The Prostitution of Women and Girls*, pp. 93–97.

56. Judianne Densen-Gerber and S. F. Hutchinson, "Medical-Legal and Societal Problems Involving Children-Child Prostitution, Child Pornography and Drug-Related Abuse; Recommended Legislation," in Selwyn M. Smith, ed., *The Maltreatment of Children* (Baltimore, MD: University Park Press, 1978), p. 322.

57. U.S. Department of Health and Human Services, Family Youth and Services Bureau, *Youth with Runaway, Throwaway, and Homeless Experiences: Prevalence, Drug Use, and Other At-Risk Behaviors* (Silver Springs, MD: National Clearinghouse on Families & Youth, 1995), pp. 4–5.

58. Lukman, "The Prevalence of Running Away from Home Among Prostituted Children in Malaysia," p. 160.

59. Flowers, *Runaway Kids and Teenage Prostitution*; Rotheram-Borus, Mahler, Koopman, and Langabeer, "Sexual Abuse History and Associated Multiple Risk Behavior in Adolescent Runaways;" Ruby J. Martinez, "Understanding Runaway Teens," *Journal of Child and Adolescent Psychiatric Nursing* 19, 2 (2006): 77–88; Molnar, Shade, Kral, Booth, and Watters, "Suicidal Behavior and Sexual/Physical Abuse Among Street Youth."

60. Cited in Hersch, "Coming of Age on City Streets," pp. 31–32.

61. *Ibid.*, p. 32.

62. "Study of Runaways Reveals Disturbing Data on Abuse, Mental Illness." *See also* Xiaojin Chen, Lisa Thrane, Les B. Whitbeck, Kurt D. Johnson, and Danny R. Hoyt, "Onset of Conduct Disorder, Use of Delinquent Subsistence Strategies, and Street Victimization Among Homeless and Runaway Adolescents in the Midwest," *Journal of Interpersonal Violence* 22, 9 (2007): 1156–83.

63. *Youth with Runaway, Throwaway, and Homeless Experiences*, p. 5.

64. Mary J. Rotheram-Borus, "Suicidal Behavior and Risk Factors Among Runaway Youths," *American Journal of Psychiatry* 150 (1993): 103–7.

65. *Sexual Abuse Among Homeless Adolescents.*

66. Jennifer B. Unger, Michele D. Kipke, Thomas R. Simon, Susanne B. Montgomery, and Christine J. Johnson, "Homeless Youths and Young Adults in Los Angeles: Prevalence of Mental Health Problems and the Relationship Between Mental Health and Substance Abuse Disorders," *American Journal of Community Psychology* 25, 3 (1997): 371–94.

67. *Sexual Abuse Among Homeless Adolescents*; Whitbeck and Hoyt, *Nowhere to Grow*; Ryan, Kilmer, Cauce, Watanabe, and Hoyt, "Psychological Consequences of Child Maltreatment in Homeless Adolescents."

68. P. David Kurtz, "Problems of Maltreated Runaway Youth," *Adolescence* 26,103 (1991): 543–55.

69. Dedel, *Juvenile Runaways*, p. 8; Slesnick, *Our Runaway and Homeless Youth*.

70. *Runaway and Homeless Youth*, p. 7. *See also* Mark E. Courtney, Ada Skyles, Gina Miranda, Andrew Zinn, Eboni Howard, and Robert M. Goerge, "Youth Who Run Away from Out-Of-Home Care," *Chaplin Hall Center for Children Issue Brief* 103 (2005): 2.

71. *Runaway and Homeless Youth*, p. 7; Joe Piasecki, "Throwaway Kids," *Pasadena Weekly* (June 26, 2006), http://www.pasadenaweekly.com/cms/story/detail/?id=3559&IssueNum=25.

72. Dedel, *Juvenile Runaways*, p. 7.

73. *Ibid.*, p. 8. *See also* Caren Kaplan, *Children Missing from Care: An Issue Brief* (Washington, D.C.: Child Welfare League of America, 2004); Vera Institute of Justice, *Youth Who Chronically AWOL from Foster Care: Why They Run, Where They Go, and What Can Be Done* (New York: NYC Administration for Children's Services, 2004), p. i.

74. *Helping Vulnerable Youth*.

75. *Youth with Runaway, Throwaway, and Homeless Experiences*.

76. "NN4Y Issue Brief: Unaccompanied Youth Overview."

77. Nicholas Ray, *Lesbian, Gay, Bisexual, and Transgender Youth: An Epidemic of Homelessness* (New York: National Gay and Lesbian Task Force Policy Institute and National Coalition for the Homeless, 2006), p. 13; Bryan N. Cochran, Angela J. Stewart, Joshua A. Ginzler, and Ana Mari Cauce, "Challenges Faced by Homeless Sexual Minorities: Comparison of Gay, Lesbian, Bisexual, and Transgender Homeless Adolescents with Their Heterosexual Counterparts," *American Journal of Public Health* 92, 5 (2005): 773.

78. Ray, *Lesbian, Gay, Bisexual, and Transgender Youth*, p. 13; Kruks, "Gay and Lesbian Homeless/Street Youth: Special Issues and Concerns," pp. 515–18; Linda M. Dame, "Queer Youth in Care in Manitoba: An Examination of Their Experiences Through Their Voices," *Canadian Online Journal of Queer Studies in Education* 1, 1 (2004): 1–28; Nicole D. K. Dylan, "City Enters Partnership to Assist Lesbian and Gay Homeless Youth," *Nation's Cities Weekly* 27, 10 (2004).

79. Safe Schools Coalition, "Homeless LGBT Youth and LGBT Youth in Foster Care," (July 6, 2009), http://www.safeschoolscoalition.org/RG-homeless.html.

80. Dame, "Queer Youth in Care in Manitoba;" Michael C. Clatts, W. Rees Davis, J. L. Sotheran, and Aylin Atillasoy, "Correlates and Distribution of HIV Risk Behaviors Among Homeless Youths in New York City: Implications for Prevention and Policy," *Child Welfare* 77, 2 (1998): 195–207.

81. Dylan, "City Enters Partnership to Assist Lesbian and Gay Homeless Youth."

82. Ray, *Lesbian, Gay, Bisexual, and Transgender Youth*, pp. 13–14.

83. *Ibid.*

84. Cited in "Homeless LGBT Youth and LGBT Youth in Foster Care."

85. Cited in Ray, *Lesbian, Gay, Bisexual, and Transgender Youth*, p. 16.

86. Jenny Gable, "Problems Faced by Homosexual Youth," (1995), http://www.lmsa.edu/jgable/lbg/paper.html.

87. Cited in Frank York and Robert H. Knight, "Reality Check on Homeless Gay Teens," *Family Policy* (1998), http://www.frc.org/fampol/fp98fcv.htm.

88. Cited in Ray, *Lesbian, Gay, Bisexual, and Transgender Youth*, p. 18.

89. *Ibid.*; Cochran, Stewart, Ginzler, and Cauce, "Challenges Faced by Homeless Sexual Minorities," p. 773.

90. Cited in Ray, *Lesbian, Gay, Bisexual, and Transgender Youth*, pp. 19–21; Justeen Hyde, "From Home to Street: Understanding Young People's Transitions into Homelessness," *Journal of Adolescence* 28, 2 (2005): 181–83; Bao Wan-Ning, Les B. Whitbeck, and Danny R. Hoyt, "Abuse, Support and Depression Among Homeless and Runaway Adolescents," *Journal of Health and Social Behavior* 41 (2000): 408–20.

91. Crawford, "Troubled Teens Take to the Streets," p. 1.

92. *Ibid.*

93. Hyde, "From Home to Street," p. 175.

94. Cited in Ray, *Lesbian, Gay, Bisexual, and Transgender Youth*, p. 20.

95. *Ibid.*

96. Smeaton, *Living on the Edge*, p. 10.

97. Cited in Bob Reeg, "The Runaway and Homeless Youth Act and Disconnected Youth," in Jodie Levin-Epstein and Mark H. Greenberg, eds., *Leave No Youth Behind: Opportunities for Congress to Reach Disconnected Youth* (Washington, D.C.: Center for Law and Social Policy, 2003), p. 58.

98. Hot Topics for School Administrators: School Dropout Prevention, "Identifying Students at High-Risk for School Drop-Out," http://www.educationalresourceservices.com/fil es/hot_topic_prinicipals.pdf. *See also* Patricia M. Sullivan and John F. Knutson, "The Prevalence of Disabilities and Maltreatment Among Runaway Children," *Child Abuse and Neglect* 24, 10 (2000): 1275–88.

99. Flowers, *Kids Who Commit Adult Crimes*, p. 60.

100. Ray, *Lesbian, Gay, Bisexual, and Transgender Youth*, p. 20; Pamela Miller, Peter Donahue, Dave Este, and Marvin Hofer, "Experiences of Being Homeless or at Risk of Being Homeless Among Canadian Youths," *Adolescence* 39, 156 (2004): 735–55; Daniel E. Bontempo and Anthony R. D'Augelli, "Effects of At-School Victimization and Sexual Orientation on Lesbian, Gay, or Bisexual Youths' Health Risk Behavior," *Journal of Adolescent Health* 30, 5 (2002): 364–74.

101. Miller, Donahue, Este, and Hofer, "Experiences of Being Homeless or at Risk of Being Homeless," p. 741; Ray, *Lesbian, Gay, Bisexual, and Transgender Youth*, p. 20.

102. Flowers, *The Prostitution of Women and Girls*, p. 97.

103. Quoted in Ray, *Lesbian, Gay, Bisexual, and Transgender Youth*, p. 20. *See also* Whitbeck and Hoyt, *Nowhere to Grow*, p. 86; Martinez, "Understanding Runaway Teens."

104. Robin Lloyd, *For Money or Love: Boy Prostitution in America* (New York: Ballantine, 1976), p. 58.

## Chapter 5

1. Heather Hammer, David Finkelhor, and Andrea J. Sedlak, *Runaway/Thrownaway Children: National Estimates and Characteristics*, NISMART Bulletin Series (Washington, D.C.: Office of Juvenile Justice and Delinquency Prevention, 2002), p. 7.

2. Laurie Schaffner, "Searching For Connection: A New Look at Teenaged Runaways," *Adolescence* 33, 31 (1998): 619–28.

3. Cited in Marjorie J. Robertson and Paul A. Toro, "Homeless Youth: Research, Intervention, and Policy," in Linda B. Fosburg and Deborah. L. Dennis, eds., *Practical Lessons: The 1998 National Symposium on Homelessness Research* (Washington, D.C.: U.S. Department of Housing and Urban Development and U.S. Department of Health and Human Services, 1998). *See also* Therese van Houten and Gary Golembiewski, *Adolescent Life Stress as a Predictor of Alcohol Abuse and/or Runaway Behavior* (Washington, D.C.: National Youth Alternatives Project, Inc., 1978); Robert H. McNamara, *The Lost Population: Status Offenders in America* (Durham, NC: Carolina Academic Press, 2008).

4. Wade Nkrumah, "Police Catch up with Runaway Forest Grove Boy," *Oregonian* (August 28, 2007), http://blog.oregonlive.com/ breakingnews/2007/08/police_spot_but_cant_ catch_run.html.

5. Schaffner, "Searching For Connection." *See also* Mark D. Janus, Arlene McCormack, Ann W. Burgess, and Carol Hartman, *Adolescent Runaways: Causes and Consequences* (Lexington, MA: Lexington Books, 1987).

6. Ruby J. Martinez, "Understanding Runaway Teens," *Journal of Child and Adolescent Psychiatric Nursing* 19, 2 (2006): 77–88; Michael E. Rohr, *Adolescent Runaway Behavior: Who Runs and Why* (New York: Routledge, 1999).

7. Robert M. Emerson, "On Last Resorts," *American Journal of Sociology* 87, 1 (1981):1–22.

8. Tim Brennan, Dave Huizinga, and Del Elliott, *The Social Psychology of Runaways* (Lexington, MA: Lexington Books, 1978).

9. Schaffner, "Searching For Connection."

10. Hammer, Finkelhor, and Sedlak, *Runaway/Thrownaway Children*, p. 7.

11. R. Barri Flowers, *Runaway Kids and Teenage Prostitution: America's Lost, Abandoned, and Sexually Exploited Children* (Westport, CT: Greenwood Press, 2001); Natasha Slesnick, *Our Runaway and Homeless Youth: A Guide to Understanding* (Westport, CT: Praeger, 2004); Andrew W. Safyer, Sanna J. Thompson, Elaine M. Maccio, Kimberley M. Zittel-Palamara, and Greg Forehand, "Adolescents' and Parents' Perceptions of Runaway Behavior: Problems and Solutions," *Child and Adolescent Social Work Journal* 21, 5 (2004): 495–512.

12. Kelly Dedel, *Juvenile Runaways* (Washington, D.C.: Office of Community Oriented Policing Services, 2006), p. 9, http://www.nc jrs.gov/App/Publications/abstract.aspx?ID= 235092; David Finkelhor, Gerald Hotaling, and Andrea J. Sedlak, *Missing, Abducted, Run-*

away, and Thrownaway Children in America, First Report: Numbers and Characteristics, National Incidence Studies (Washington, D.C.: Office of Juvenile Justice and Delinquency Prevention, 1990).

13. Flowers, Runaway Kids and Teenage Prostitution; Dedel, Juvenile Runaways, pp. 11–12; Marjorie Mayers, Street Kids and Streetscapes: Panhandling, Politics, and Prophecies (New York: Peter Lang, 2001); R. Barri Flowers, The Victimization and Exploitation of Women and Children: A Study of Physical, Mental and Sexual Maltreatment in the United States (Jefferson, NC: McFarland, 1994).

14. Lindsay Crawford, "Troubled Teens Take to the Streets: Rebellious Youths with Nowhere to Run Away from Their Problems and Their Homes," Silver Chips Online (April 13, 2000), p. 1.

15. Emilie Smeaton, Living on the Edge: The Experiences of Detached Young Runaways (Leeds, UK: The Children's Society, 2005), p. 13.

16. Dedel, Juvenile Runaways, p. 9; Hammer, Finkelhor, and Sedlak, Runaway/Thrownaway Children, p. 9.

17. Smeaton, Living on the Edge, p. 15.

18. Flowers, Runaway Kids and Teenage Prostitution; R. Barri Flowers, The Adolescent Criminal: An Examination of Today's Juvenile Offender (Jefferson, NC: McFarland, 2009), pp. 49–52; Gregory D. Zimet, Elisa J. Sobo, Teena Zimmerman, Joann Hackson, Joan Mortimer, Carlyn P. Yanda, and Rina Lazebnik, "Sexual Behavior, Drug Use, and Aids Knowledge Among Midwestern Runaways," Youth and Society 26, 4 (1995): 450–62.

19. R. Barri Flowers, The Prostitution of Women and Girls (Jefferson, NC: McFarland, 2005), pp. 96–98; Flowers, The Victimization and Exploitation of Women and Children; Evelyn Lau, Runaway: Diary of a Street Kid (Toronto: Harper and Collins, 1989).

20. Flowers, Runaway Kids and Teenage Prostitution; Dedel, Juvenile Runaways, p. 8; CBS/AP, "Runaway Teens Found Safe in Louisiana," (January 21, 2008), http://www.cbsnews.com/stories/2008/01/21/earlyshow/main3734447.shtml?tag=contentMain;contentBody. See also "Youth: The Runaways," Time.com (September 15, 1967), http://www.time.com/time/magazine/article/0,9171,941149-1,00.html; "Behavior: The Runaways A National Problem," Time.com (August 27, 1973), http://www.time.com/time/magazine/article/0,9171,907795,00.html.

21. Hammer, Finkelhor, and Sedlak, Runaway/Thrownaway Children, p. 6.

22. Study World, "Runaways: Victims at Home and On the Streets," http://www.studyworld.com/newsite/ReportEssay/SocialIssues/Political%5CRunaways__Victims_At_Home_and_On_the_Streets-32644.htm. See also Martin L. Forst and Martha E. Blomquist, Missing Children: Rhetoric and Reality (New York: Lexington Books, 1991).

23. Dedel, Juvenile Runaways, p. 9.

24. Sally Kestin and Megan O'Matz, "Runaways Face Tough Life on Streets," CYCNet.org, http://www.cyc-net.org/features/ft-runaways.html.

25. Flowers, Runaway Kids and Teenage Prostitution; Forst and Blomquist, Missing Children; Ronald L. Simons and Les B. Whitbeck, "Running Away During Adolescence as a Precursor to Adult Homelessness," Social Service Review 65, 2 (1991): 225–47; Michele D. Kipke, Susanne B. Montgomery, Thomas R. Simon, and Ellen F. Iverson, "Substance Abuse Disorders Among Runaway and Homeless Youth," Substance Use and Misuse 32 (1997): 969–86; Smeaton, Living on the Edge, p. 12.

26. Alma C. Molino, "Characteristics of Help-Seeking Street Youth and Non-Street Youth," 2007 National Symposium on Homelessness Research, March 1–2, 2007, p. 7–2, http://aspe.hhs.gov/hsp/homelessness/symposium07/molino/index.htm. See also Justeen Hyde, "From Home to Street: Understanding Young People's Transitions into Homelessness," Journal of Adolescence 28, 2 (2005): 171–83.

27. Martinez, "Understanding Runaway Teens."

28. Schaffner, "Searching For Connection."

29. Finkelhor, Hotaling, and Sedlak, Missing, Abducted, Runaway, and Thrownaway Children in America, First Report, p. 49.

30. Vera Institute of Justice, Youth Who Chronically AWOL from Foster Care: Why They Run, Where They Go, and What Can Be Done (New York: NYC Administration for Children's Services, 2004), p. i.

31. Ibid.

32. Schaffner, "Searching For Connection."

33. Dedel, Juvenile Runaways, p. 7; Samuel J. Fasulo, Theodore P. Cross, Peggy Mosley, and Joseph Leavey, "Adolescent Runaway Behavior in Specialized Foster Care," Children and Youth Services Review 24, 8 (2002): 623–640.

## Chapter 6

1. Heather Hammer, David Finkelhor, and Andrea J. Sedlak, Runaway/Thrownaway Chil-

*dren: National Estimates and Characteristics,* NISMART Bulletin Series (Washington, D.C.: Office of Juvenile Justice and Delinquency Prevention, 2002), p. 9.

2. *Ibid.*

3. Emilie Smeaton and Gwyther Rees, *Running Away in South Yorkshire: Research into the Incidence and Nature of the Problem in Sheffield, Rotherham, Barnsley, and Doncaster* (Sheffield, UK: Safe at Last, 2004).

4. David Finkelhor, Gerald Hotaling, and Andrea J. Sedlak, *Missing, Abducted, Runaway, and Thrownaway Children in America, First Report: Numbers and Characteristics, National Incidence Studies* (Washington, D.C.: Office of Juvenile Justice and Delinquency Prevention, 1990), p. 116.

5. U.S. Department of Justice, Office of Juvenile Justice and Delinquency Prevention, *Law Enforcement Policies and Practices Regarding Missing and Homeless Youth: Research Summary* (Washington, D.C.: Government Printing Office, 1993), p. 5.

6. R. Barri Flowers, *Runaway Kids and Teenage Prostitution: America's Lost, Abandoned, and Sexually Exploited Children* (Westport, CT: Greenwood Press, 2001), pp. 95–102; Marjorie Mayers, *Street Kids and Streetscapes: Panhandling, Politics, and Prophecies* (New York: Peter Lang, 2001); Kimberly Kempf-Leonard and Pernilla Johansson, "Gender and Runaways: Risk Factors, Delinquency, and Juvenile Justice Experiences," *Youth Violence and Juvenile Justice* 5, 3 (2007): 308–27.

7. Flowers, *Runaway Kids and Teenage Prostitution.*

8. *Ibid.*

9. *Law Enforcement Policies and Practices,* p. 9.

10. *Ibid.*

11. *Ibid.,* pp. 8–10.

12. *Ibid.,* p. 11.

13. Flowers, *Runaway Kids and Teenage Prostitution*; Kelly Dedel, *Juvenile Runaways* (Washington, D.C.: Office of Community Oriented Policing Services, 2006), p. 3.

14. *Law Enforcement Policies and Practices,* p. 12.

15. See for example, *In the Matter of Jennifer M.,* 509 N.Y.S. 2d 935, 937 (1986); *Lewis v. State* 288NE 2d 138 (1972); National Law Center on Homelessness and Poverty, *Alone Without a Home: A State-by-State Guide to Laws Affecting Unaccompanied Youth* (Washington, D.C.: National Law Center on Homelessness and Poverty, 2003); Thomas Hargrove, "Runaway Children Face Erratic Patchwork of State Laws," Stories in the News (June 5, 2005), http://www.sitnews.us/0605news/060505/060505_shns_missing.html.

16. *Law Enforcement Policies and Practices,* p. 14.

17. *Ibid.*

18. *Ibid.,* p. 17.

19. Flowers, *Runaway Kids and Teenage Prostitution*; Cheryl L. Maxson, Margaret A. Little, Malcolm W. Klein, "Police Response to Runaway and Missing Children: A Conceptual Framework for Research and Policy," *Crime & Delinquency,* 34, 1 (1988): 84–102; U.S. Department of Justice, Federal Bureau of Investigation, *Crime in the United States, 2007,* Table 38, http://www.fbi.gov/ucr/cius2007/data/table_38.html.

20. R. Barri Flowers, *The Adolescent Criminal: An Examination of Today's Juvenile Offender* (Jefferson, NC: McFarland, 2009); Charles Puzzanchera, *Trends in Justice System's Response to Status Offending: OJJDP Briefing Paper* (Pittsburgh, PA: National Center for Juvenile Justice, 2007).

21. *Crime in the United States, 2007,* http://www.fbi.gov/ucr/cius2007/data/table_29.html.

22. *Ibid.*; http://www.fbi.gov/ucr/cius2007/data/table_31.html.

23. Jason Zeidenberg and Vincent Schiraldi, *Runaway Juvenile Crime? The Context of Juvenile Crime Arrests in America* (Washington, D.C.: Justice Policy Institute, 1998), p. 1.

24. *Crime in the United States, 2007,* http://www.fbi.gov/ucr/cius2007/data/table_38.html.

25. *Ibid.*; http://www.fbi.gov/ucr/cius2007/data/table_42.html.

26. *Ibid.*

27. *Ibid.*

28. Flowers, *Runaway Kids and Teenage Prostitution*; Flowers, *The Adolescent Criminal*; Kempf-Leonard and Johansson, "Gender and Runaways;" Susan F. McClanahan, Gary M. McClelland, Karen M. Abram, and Linda A. Teplin, "Pathways Into Prostitution Among Female Jail Detainees and Their Implications for Mental Health Services," *Psychiatric Services* 50 (1999): 1606–13.

29. Arlene McCormack, Mark D. Janus, and Ann W. Burgess, "Runaway Youths and Sexual Victimization: Gender Differences in an Adolescent Runaway Population," *Child Abuse and Neglect* 10 (1986): 387–95. *See also* U.S. Department of Health and Human Services, Family and Youth Services Research, "Sexual Abuse Experiences of Runaway Youth, 2001–2002," http://www.acf.hhs.gov/programs/opre/fys/sex_abuse/index.html.

30. *Crime in the United States, 2007*, http://www.fbi.gov/ucr/cius2007/arrests/population_group.html.

31. R. Barri Flowers, *Minorities and Criminality* (Westport, CT: Praeger, 1990), pp. 131–34; Jerry Mandel, "Hispanics in the Criminal Justice System — The 'Nonexistent' Problem," *Agenda* 9, 3 (1979): 16–20; Don Dailey, "Stats: Arrest Rates in Line with Population," *The Morning News* (2007), http://www.nwaonline.net/projects/immigration/crime.html; Michigan State News Release, "Justice System Unfair, Unjust for Hispanics," About.com: Crime/Punishment, http://crime.about.com/od/issues/a/blmu041026.htm.

32. Hammer, Finkelhor, and Sedlak, *Runaway/Thrownaway Children*.

33. Lindsay Crawford, "Troubled Teens Take to the Streets: Rebellious Youths with Nowhere to Turn Run Away from Their Problems and Their Homes," *Silver Chips Online* (April 13, 2000), p. 18.

34. *Ibid.*

35. Flowers, *Runaway Kids and Teenage Prostitution*; Kempf-Leonard and Johansson, "Gender and Runaways;" R. Barri Flowers, *The Prostitution of Women and Girls* (Jefferson, NC: McFarland, 1998); Rebecca P. Sanchez, Martha W. Waller, and Jody M. Greene, "Who Runs? A Demographic Profile of Runaway Youth in the United States," *Journal of Adolescent Health* 39, 5 (2006): 778–81.

## Chapter 7

1. Heather Hammer, David Finkelhor, and Andrea J. Sedlak, *Runaway/Thrownaway Children: National Estimates and Characteristics*, NISMART Bulletin Series (Washington, D.C.: Office of Juvenile Justice and Delinquency Prevention, 2002), p. 6.

2. CRS Report for Congress, *Runaway and Homeless Youth: Demographics, Programs, and Emerging Issues* (Washington, D.C.: Congressional Research Service, 2007), p. 3.

3. U.S. Department of Health and Human Services, *Incidence and Prevalence of Homeless and Runaway Youth* (Washington, D.C.: Administration for Children and Families, 2003), p. 2. *See also* Michele D. Kipke, Thomas R. Simon, Susanne B. Montgomery, Jennifer B. Unger, and Ellen Iverson, "Homeless Youth and Their Exposure to and Involvement in Violence While Living on the Streets," *Journal of Adolescent Health* 20, 5 (1997): 360–67.

4. U.S. Department of Health and Human Services, *Sexual Abuse Among Homeless Adolescents: Prevalence, Correlates, and Sequelae* (Washington, D.C.: Administration for Children and Families, 2002).

5. Quoted in *Sexual Abuse Among Homeless Adolescents. See also* Kipke, Simon, Montgomery, Unger, and Iverson, "Homeless Youth and Their Exposure to Involvement in Violence," p. 361.

6. Beth E. Molnar, Alex H. Kral, and John K. Watters, *Street Youth at Risk for AIDS* (Rockville, MD: National Institute on Drug Abuse, 1994).

7. Les B. Whitbeck and Danny R. Hoyt, *Nowhere to Grow: Homeless and Runaway Adolescents and Their Families* (Hawthorne, NY: Aldine de Gruyter, 1999).

8. Kimberly D. Ryan, Ryan Kilmer, Ana Mari Cauce, Haruko Watanabe, and Danny R. Hoyt, "Psychological Consequences of Child Maltreatment in Homeless Adolescents: Untangling the Unique Effects of Maltreatment and Family Environment," *Child Abuse and Neglect* 24 (2000): 333–52.

9. *Incidence and Prevalence of Homeless and Runaway Youth*, p. 2–2; Josephine Ensign, "Reproductive Health of Adolescent Women in Seattle, Washington USA," *Women and Health* 31 (2000): 133–51; John Hagan and Bill McCarthy, *Mean Streets: Youth Crime and Homelessness* (Cambridge, MA: Cambridge University Press, 1998).

10. Alan R. Lifson and Linda L. Halcon, "Substance Abuse and High-Risk Needle-Related Behaviors Among Homeless Youth in Minneapolis: Implications for Prevention," *Journal of Urban Health* 78, 4 (2001): 690–98.

11. John Noell, Paul Rohde, John Seeley, and Linda Ochs, "Childhood Sexual Abuse, Adolescent Sexual Coercion and Sexually Transmitted Infection Acquisition Among Homeless Female Adolescents," *Child Abuse and Neglect* 25 (2001): 137–48.

12. *Runaway and Homeless Youth*, pp. 3–4.

13. *Incidence and Prevalence of Homeless and Runaway Youth*, p. 2–3. *See also* Missing, Exploited, and Runaway Children Protection Act, P.L. 106–71 (2000).

14. *Incidence and Prevalence of Homeless and Runaway Youth*, p. 2–3.

15. Colette L. Auerswald and Stephen L. Eyre, "Youth Homelessness in San Francisco: A Life Cycle Approach," *Social Science and Medicine* 54 (2002): 1497–1512.

16. CRS Report for Congress, *Runaway and Homeless Youth*, p. 4. *See also* Christopher L. Ringwalt, Jody M. Greene, Marjorie J. Robertson, and Melissa McPheeters, "The Prevalence of Homelessness Among Adolescents in the United States," *American Journal of Public Health* 88, 9 (1998): 1325–29.

17. *Runaway and Homeless Youth*, p. 4.

18. *Incidence and Prevalence of Homeless and Runaway Youth*, p. 1–1.

19. *Ibid.*, p. 1–2; Marjorie J. Robertson, *Homeless Youth on Their Own* (Berkley, CA: Alcohol Research Group, 1996).

20. *Incidence and Prevalence of Homeless and Runaway Youth*, p. 1–2; Lynn Rew, "Characteristics and Health Care Needs of Homeless Adolescents," *Nursing Clinics of North America* 37, 3 (2002): 423–32.

21. *Runaway and Homeless Youth*, p. 5; *Incidence and Prevalence of Homeless and Runaway Youth*, p. 1–1; Nicholas Ray, *Lesbian, Gay, Bisexual, and Transgender Youth: An Epidemic of Homelessness* (New York: National Gay and Lesbian Task Force Policy Institute and National Coalition for the Homeless, 2006), p. 12.

22. Ray, *Lesbian, Gay, Bisexual, and Transgender Youth*, p. 12; Ringwalt, Greene, Robertson, and McPheeters, "The Prevalence of Homelessness Among Adolescents in the United States," p. 1327; Marjorie J. Robertson and Paul A. Toro, "Homeless Youth: Research, Intervention, and Policy," http://aspe.hhs.gov/ProgSys/homeless/symposium/3-Youth.htm.

23. *Runaway and Homeless Youth*, pp. 6–7; Robertson and Toro, "Homeless Youth," pp. 1–2.

24. Ray, *Lesbian, Gay, Bisexual, and Transgender Youth*, p. 12; Sanna J. Thompson, Andrew W. Safyer, and David E. Pollio, "Differences and Predictors of Family Reunification Among Subgroups of Runaway Youths Using Shelter Services," *Social Work Research* 25, 3 (2001): 163–72.

25. Robertson and Toro, "Homeless Youth;" Ray, *Lesbian, Gay, Bisexual, and Transgender Youth*, p. 12.

26. U.S. Department of Health and Human Services, Family Youth and Services Bureau, *Youth with Runaway, Throwaway, and Homeless Experiences: Prevalence, Drug Use, and Other At-Risk Behaviors* (Silver Springs, MD: National Clearinghouse on Families and Youth, 1995), p. E6.

27. *Runaway and Homeless Youth*, p. 4; Robertson and Toro, "Homeless Youth," p. 4.

28. Cited in CRS Report for Congress, *The Runaway and Homeless Youth Program: Administration, Funding and Legislative Actions* (Washington, D.C.: Congressional Research Service, 2006), p. 2.

29. Hammer, Finkelhor, and Sedlak, *Runaway/Thrownaway Children*, p. 2.

30. Alma C. Molino, "Characteristics of Help-Seeking Street Youth and Non-Street Youth," 2007 National Symposium on Homelessness Research, March 1–2, 2007, p. 7–4, http://aspe.hhs.gov/hsp/homelessness/symposium07/molino/index.htm.

31. Z. M. Lukman, "The Prevalence of Running Away from Home Among Prostituted Youth in Malaysia," *Journal of Social Sciences* 5, 3 (2009): 157–62; Joan J. Johnson, *Teen Prostitution* (Danbury, CT: Franklin Watts, 1992); R. Barri Flowers, *Runaway Kids and Teenage Prostitution: America's Lost, Abandoned, and Sexually Exploited Children* (Westport, CT: Greenwood Press, 2001), pp. 42–47.

32. Les B. Whitbeck and Ronald L. Simons, "Life on the Streets: The Victimization of Runaway and Homeless Adolescents," *Youth and Society* 22, 1 (1990): 108–25.

33. *The Runaway and Homeless Youth Program*, p. 1; Hammer, Finkelhor, and Sedlak, *Runaway/Thrownaway Children*, pp. 1–12; National Runaway Switchboard, http://www.1800runaway.org/.

34. Flowers, *Runaway Kids and Teenage Prostitution*; Kipke, Simon, Montgomery, Unger, and Iverson, "Homeless Youth and Their Exposure to Involvement in Violence;" Danny R. Hoyt, Kimberly D. Ryan, and Ana Mari Cauce, "Personal Victimization in a High Risk Environment: Homeless and Runaway Adolescents," *Research in Crime and Delinquency* 36, 4 (1999): 371–91; Justeen Hyde, "From Home to Street: Understanding Young People's Transitions into Homelessness," *Journal of Adolescence* 28, 2 (2005): 171–83.

35. Pamela Miller, Peter Donahue, Dave Este, and Marvin Hofer, "Experiences of Being Homeless or at Risk of Being Homeless Among Canadian Youths," *Adolescence* 39, 156 (2004): 735–55.

36. Kimberly A. Tyler, Danny R. Hoyt, Les B. Whitbeck, and Ana Mari Cauce, "The Impact of Childhood Sexual Abuse on Later Sexual Victimization Among Runaway Youth," *Journal of Research on Adolescence* 11, 2 (2001): 164.

37. Flowers, *Runaway Kids and Teenage Prostitution*; R. Barri Flowers, *The Prostitution of Women and Girls* (Jefferson, NC: McFarland, 2005); Lukman, "The Prevalence of Running Away from Home Among Prostituted Youth;"

Augustine Brannigan and E. Gibbs Van Brunschot, "Youthful Prostitution and Child Sexual Trauma," *International Journal of Law and Psychiatry* 20 (1997): 337–54.

38. Stephen Gaetz, "Safe Streets for Whom? Homeless Youth, Social Exclusion, and Criminal Victimization," *Canadian Journal of Criminology and Criminal Justice* 46, 6 (2004): 423–55.

39. U.S. Department of Justice, Federal Bureau of Investigation, *Crime in the United States, 2007,* Table 38, http://www.fbi.gov/ucr/cius2007/data/table_38.html; Jason Zeidenberg and Vincent Schiraldi, *Runaway Juvenile Crime? The Context of Juvenile Crime Arrests in America* (Washington, D.C.: Justice Policy Institute, 1998), pp. 1–8.

40. Flowers, *Runaway Kids and Teenage Prostitution*; Whitbeck and Hoyt, *Nowhere to Grow*; Jeanne G. Kaufman and Cathy S. Widom, "Childhood Victimization, Running Away, and Delinquency," *Journal of Research in Crime and Delinquency* 36, 4 (1999): 347–70.

41. Kaufman and Widom, "Childhood Victimization, Running Away, and Delinquency."

42. *Ibid.*, p. 368. *See also* Molino, "Characteristics of Help-Seeking Street Youth and Non-Street Youth."

43. Ray, *Lesbian, Gay, Bisexual, and Transgender Youth*, p. 67.

44. Bao Wan-Ning, Les B. Whitbeck, and Danny R. Hoyt, "Abuse, Support and Depression Among Homeless and Runaway Adolescents," *Journal of Health and Social Behavior* 41 (2000): 408–20. *See also* Kimberly A. Tyler, "Social Network Characteristics and Risky Sexual and Drug Related Behaviors Among Homeless Young Adults," *Social Science Research* 37, 2 (2008): 673–85.

45. Flowers, *Runaway Kids and Teenage Prostitution*; Kaufman and Widom, "Childhood Victimization, Running Away, and Delinquency;" Molino, "Characteristics of Help-Seeking Street Youth and Non-Street Youth."

46. Vera Institute of Justice, *Youth Who Chronically AWOL from Foster Care: Why They Run, Where They Go, and What Can Be Done* (New York: NYC Administration for Children's Services, 2004), p. 23.

47. Ray, *Lesbian, Gay, Bisexual, and Transgender Youth*, p. 69; Gaetz, "Safe Streets for Whom?" p. 426.

48. Ray, *Lesbian, Gay, Bisexual, and Transgender Youth*, p. 70. *See also* John Hagan and Bill McCarthy, "Streetlife and Delinquency," *British Journal of Sociology* 43, 4 (1992): 533–61.

49. Hagan and McCarthy, "Streetlife and Delinquency," p. 556; Ray, *Lesbian, Gay, Bisexual, and Transgender Youth*, p. 70.

50. Ray, *Lesbian, Gay, Bisexual, and Transgender Youth*, p. 71; National Coalition for the Homeless, *Illegal to be Homeless: The Criminalization of Homelessness in the United States* (Washington, D.C.: National Coalition for the Homeless, 2004).

51. Ray, *Lesbian, Gay, Bisexual, and Transgender Youth*, p. 71; National Coalition for the Homeless and National Law Center on Homelessness and Poverty, *A Dream Denied: The Criminalization of Homelessness in U.S. Cities* (Washington, D.C.: National Coalition for the Homeless and National Law Center on Homelessness and Poverty, 2006).

52. Ray, *Lesbian, Gay, Bisexual, and Transgender Youth*, pp. 71–72.

53. Flowers, *Runaway Kids and Teenage Prostitution*; Ray, *Lesbian, Gay, Bisexual, and Transgender Youth*, p. 22; Zeidenberg and Schiraldi, *Runaway Juvenile Crime?*; Molino, "Characteristics of Help-Seeking Street Youth and Non-Street Youth;" R. Barri Flowers, *Kids Who Commit Adult Crimes: A Study of Serious Juvenile Criminality and Delinquency* (Binghamton, NY: Haworth Press, 2002); Norweeta G. Milburn, Mary Jane Rotheram-Borus, Philip Batterham, Babette Brumback, Doreen Rosenthal, and Shelley Mallett, "Predictors of Close Family Relationships Over One Year Among Homeless Young People," *Journal of Adolescence* 28, 2 (2005): 263–75.

54. Cited in Ray, *Lesbian, Gay, Bisexual, and Transgender Youth*, p. 23.

55. Molino, "Characteristics of Help-Seeking Street Youth and Non-Street Youth." *See also* Michael G. MacLean, Lara E. Embry, and Ana Mari Cauce, "Homeless Adolescents' Paths to Separation from Family: Comparison of Family Characteristics, Psychological Adjustment, and Victimization," *Journal of Community Psychology*, 27, 2 (1999): 179–87.

56. Hyde, "From Home to Street," p. 177.

57. Lukman, "The Prevalence of Running Away from Home Among Prostituted Youth," p. 158; Susan McIntyre, "The Youngest Profession — The Oldest Oppression: A Study of Sex. Work," in Christopher Bagley and Kanka Mallick, eds., *Child Sexual Abuse and Adult Offenders: New Theory and Research* (London: Ashgate, 1999), pp. 159–92.

58. Cited in Ray, *Lesbian, Gay, Bisexual, and Transgender Youth*, p. 22. *See also* Hyde, "From Home to Street," p. 180.

# Chapter 8

1. U.S. Department of Health and Human Services, Family and Youth Services Bureau, *Youth with Runaway, Throwaway, and Homeless Experiences: Prevalence, Drug Use, and Other At-Risk Behaviors* (Silver Springs, MD: National Clearinghouse on Families & Youth, 1995), p. 5. *See also* Deborah J. Sherman, "The Neglected Health Care Needs of Street Youth," *Public Health Reports* 107, 4 (1992): 433–40.

2. *Ibid. See also* R. Barri Flowers, *The Victimization and Exploitation of Women and Children: A Study of Physical, Mental and Sexual Maltreatment in the United States* (Jefferson, NC: McFarland, 1994), pp. 38–45.

3. Quoted in *Youth with Runaway, Throwaway, and Homeless Experiences*, pp. 5–6.

4. R. Barri Flowers, *Runaway Kids and Teenage Prostitution: America's Lost, Abandoned, and Sexually Exploited Children* (Westport, CT: Greenwood Press, 2001), pp. 53–55; Nicholas Ray, *Lesbian, Gay, Bisexual, and Transgender Youth: An Epidemic of Homelessness* (New York: National Gay and Lesbian Task Force Policy Institute and National Coalition for the Homeless, 2006), pp. 53–55; Kelly Dedel, *Juvenile Runaways* (Washington, D.C.: Office of Community Oriented Policing Services, 2006), p. 11, http://www.ncjrs.gov/App/Publications/ab stract.aspx?ID=235092; Susan T. Ennett, Susan L. Bailey, and E. Belle Federman, "Social Network Characteristics Associated with Risky Behaviors Among Runaway and Homeless Youth," *Journal of Health and Social Behavior* 40 (1999): 63–78.

5. Flowers, *Runaway Kids and Teenage Prostitution*; Wikipedia, the Free Encyclopedia, "Adolescent Sexuality in the United States," http://en.wikipedia.org/wiki/Adolescent_sexuality_in_the_United_States; Mary J. Rotheram-Borus, Heino Meyer-Bahlburg, Cheryl Koopman, Margaret Rosario, Theresa M. Exner, Ronald Henderson, Marjory Matthieu, and Rhoda Gruen, "Lifetime Sexual Behavior Among Runaway Males and Females," *Journal of Sex Research* 29, 1 (1992): 15–29.

6. See, for example, National Network for Youth, "HIV Risk of RHY," http://www.nn4 youth.org/our-work/cdc-grant/hiv-std; Ray, *Lesbian, Gay, Bisexual, and Transgender Youth*, pp. 53–57; Andrea L. Solarz, "Homelessness: Implications for Children and Youth," *Social Policy Report* 3, 4 (1988): 1–16; John Noell, Paul Rohde, John Seeley, and Linda Ochs, "Childhood Sexual Abuse, Adolescent Sexual Coercion and Sexually Transmitted Infection Acquisition Among Homeless Female Adolescents," *Child Abuse and Neglect* 25 (2001): 137–48; Doreen Rosenthal and Susan Moore, "Homeless Youths: Sexual and Drug-Related Behavior, Sexual Beliefs and HIV/AIDS Risk," *AIDS Care* 6, 1 (1994): 83–94.

7. Cited in "Adolescent Sexuality in the United States."

8. *Ibid.*

9. Laura S. Stepp, "Study: Half of All Teens Have Had Oral Sex," *Washington Post* (September 16, 2005). *See also* Jennie Yabroff, "The Oral Myth," *Newsweek* (May 23, 2008), http://www.newsweek.com/id/138444/output/print.

10. Cited in R. Barri Flowers, *The Adolescent Criminal: An Examination of Today's Juvenile Offender* (Jefferson, NC: McFarland, 2009), pp. 52–53.

11. Flowers, *Runaway Kids and Teenage Prostitution*.

12. Cited in Frank York and Robert H. Knight, "Reality Check on Homeless Gay Teens," *Family Policy* (1998) http://www.frc.org/fampol/fp98fcv.htm.

13. Cited in John Zaccaro, Jr., "Children of the Night," *Woman's Day* (March 29, 1988), p. 138.

14. Rosenthal and Moore, "Homeless Youths."

15. Cathy S. Widom and Joseph B. Kuhns, "Childhood Victimization and Subsequent Risk for Promiscuity, Prostitution and Teenage Pregnancy: A Prospective Study," *American Journal of Public Health* 86 (1996): 1607–12.

16. Cited in HealthHype.com, "Newly Homeless Youth Are at High Risk with Sexual Behavior," (January 11, 2008), http://www.healthhype.com/newly-homeless-youth-are-at-high-risk-with-sexual-behavior.html. *See also* Norweeta Milburn, Li-Jung Liang, Sung-Jae Lee, Mary J. Rotheram-Borus, Doreen Rosenthal, Shelley Mallett, Marguerita Lightfoot, and Patricia Lester, " Who Is Doing Well? A Typology of Newly Homeless Adolescents," *Journal of Community Psychology* 37, 2 (2009): 135–47.

17. Ennett, Bailey, and Federman, "Social Network."

18. Linda L. Halcon and Alan R. Lifson, "Prevalence and Predictors of Sexual Risks Among Homeless Youth," *Journal of Youth and Adolescence* 33, 1 (2004): 75–76.

19. Pam Oliver, "A Review of Literature on Child Prostitution," *Social Policy Journal of New Zealand* 19 (2002), http://www.thefreelibrary.com/_/print/PrintArticle.aspx?id=99849275.

*See also* Farquan Haq, "U.S. Children: Street Kids Turn to Sex to Survive," *Inter-Press Service* (March 27, 1996).

20. Cited in John E. Anderson, Thomas E. Freese, and Julia N. Pennbridge, "Sexual Risk Behavior and Condom Use Among Street Youth in Hollywood," *Family Planning Perspectives* 26, 1 (1994): 23. *See also* Lynn Rew, Rachel T. Fouladi, and Ronald D. Yockey, "Sexual Health Practices of Homeless Youth," *Journal of Nursing Scholarship* 34, 2 (2002): 139–45.

21. Jody M. Greene, Susan T. Ennett, and Christopher L. Ringwalt, "Prevalence and Correlates of Survival Sex Among Runaway and Homeless Youth," *American Journal of Public Health* 89, 9 (1999): 1406.

22. *Ibid. See also* Les B. Whitbeck and Ronald L. Simons, "Life on the Streets: The Victimization of Runaway and Homeless Adolescents," *Youth and Society* 22, 1 (1990): 108–25; David Barrett and William Beckett, "Child Prostitution: Reaching Out to Children Who Sell Sex to Survive," *British Journal of Nursing* 5 (1996): 1120–25.

23. Richard J. Estes and Neil A. Weiner, *The Commercial Sexual Exploitation of Children in the U.S., Canada, and Mexico* (Philadelphia, PA: University of Pennsylvania, 2002), p. 11.

24. Oliver, "A Review of Literature on Child Prostitution."

25. Flowers, *Runaway Kids and Teenage Prostitution*; R. Barri Flowers, *The Prostitution of Women and Girls* (Jefferson, NC: McFarland, 2005); Halcon and Lifson, "Prevalence and Predictors of Sexual Risk Among Homeless Youth;" R. Barri Flowers, *Male Crime and Deviance: Exploring Its Cause, Dynamics, and Nature* (Springfield, IL: Charles C Thomas, 2003); Jim Wade and Nina Biehal, *Going Missing: Young People Absent from Care* (Chichester, UK: Wiley, 1998); Task Force on Children Involved in Prostitution, *Children Involved in Prostitution* (Edmonton, Alberta: Ministry of Family and Social Services, 1997); Mimi H. Silbert, "Prostitution and Sexual Assault: Summary Results," *International Journal of Biosexual Research* 3 (1982): 69–71.

26. Greene, Ennett, and Ringwalt, "Prevalence and Correlates of Survival Sex;" Milton Greenblatt and Marjorie J. Robertson, "Life-Styles, Adaptive Strategies, and Sexual Behaviors of Homeless Adolescents," *Hospital and Community Psychiatry* 44, 12 (1993): 1177–80; Bill McCarthy and John Hagan, "Surviving on the Street: The Experience of Homeless Youth," *Journal of Adolescent Research* 7 (1992): 412–30.

27. Halcon and Lifson, "Prevalence and Pre-dictors of Sexual Risk Among Homeless Youth;" Greene, Ennett, and Ringwalt, "Prevalence and Correlates of Survival Sex," pp. 1406–09; Ray, *Lesbian, Gay, Bisexual, and Transgender Youth.*

28. Greene, Ennett, and Ringwalt, "Prevalence and Correlates of Survival Sex," p. 1408.

29. David Kihara, "Giuliani's Suppressed Report on Homeless Youth," *The Village Voice* 44, 33 (August 24, 1999), http://village voice.com.

30. Ray, *Lesbian, Gay, Bisexual, and Transgender Youth*, p. 56.

31. Cited in *Ibid.*

32. *Ibid.*, p. 57.

33. Estes and Weiner, *The Commercial Sexual Exploitation of Children*, p. 38. *See also* Silbert, "Prostitution and Sexual Assault;" Flowers, *The Victimization and Exploitation of Women and Children.*

34. Estes and Weiner, *The Commercial Sexual Exploitation of Children*, p. 38; Flowers, *The Victimization and Exploitation of Women and Children*; Flowers, *Runaway Kids and Teenage Prostitution.*

35. Flowers, *Male Crime and Deviance*; Flowers, *Runaway Kids and Teenage Prostitution*; Estes and Weiner, *The Commercial Sexual Exploitation of Children*; Evelina Giobbe, "A Comparison of Pimps and Batterers," *Michigan Journal of Gender and Law* 1, 1 (1993): 33–57; Richard J. Estes, *The Sexual. Exploitation of Children: A Working Guide to the. Empirical Literature* (Philadelphia, PA: University of Pennsylvania, 2001).

36. Lisa S. Wagner, Linda Carlin, Ana Mari Cauce, and Adam Tenner, "A Snapshot of Homeless Youth in Seattle: Their Characteristics, Behaviors and Beliefs About HIV Protective Strategies," *Journal of Community Health* 26, 3 (2001): 219–32.

37. Jody Miller and Martin D. Schwartz, "Rape Myths and Violence Against Street Prostitutes," *Deviant Behavior* 16, 1 (1995): 1–23.

38. See, for example, Ray, *Lesbian, Gay, Bisexual, and Transgender Youth*, p. 67; Pamela Miller, Peter Donahue, Dave Este, and Marvin Hofer, "Experiences of Being Homeless or at Risk of Being Homeless Among Canadian Youths," *Adolescence* 39, 156 (2004): 735–55; Jane L. Powers and Barbara Jaklitsch, *Understanding Survivors of Abuse: Stories of Homeless and Runaway Adolescents* (New York: Free Press, 1989); Deborah Bass, *Helping Vulnerable Youths: Runaway and Homeless Adolescents in the United States* (Washington, D.C.: National Association of Social Workers Press, 1992).

39. Nancy E. Walker, "Executive Summary:

How Many Teens Are Prostituted?" fce.msu.
edu/Family_Impact_Seminars/pdf/2002-2.
pdf.

40. National Center for Missing and Exploited Children, *Female Juvenile Prostitution: Problem and Response*, 2nd ed. (Alexandria, VA: National Center for Missing and Exploited Children, 2002), p. 5.

41. *Ibid.*, p. 7.

42. See, for example Emilie Smeaton, *Living on the Edge: The Experiences of Detached Young Runaways* (Leeds, UK: The Children's Society, 2005), p. 14; Michele D. Kipke, Susanne B. Montgomery, Thomas R. Simon, and Ellen F. Iverson, "Substance Abuse Disorders Among Runaway and Homeless Youth," *Substance Use and Misuse* 32 (1997): 969–86; Michael T. Windle, "Substance Use and Abuse Among Adolescent Runaways: A Four-Year Follow-up Study," *Journal of Youth and Adolescence* 18, 4 (1989): 331–43.

43. Flowers, *Runaway Kids and Teenage Prostitution*; Marjorie J. Robertson, *Homeless Youth in Hollywood: Patterns of Alcohol Use* (Berkley, CA: Alcohol Research Group, 1989); Colette L. Auerswald, and Stephen L. Eyre, "Youth Homelessness in San Francisco: A Life Cycle Approach," *Social Science and Medicine* 54 (2002): 1497–1512; Office of Applied Studies, *Substance Abuse Among Youth Who Had Run Away from Home* (Rockville, MD: Substance Abuse and Mental Health Services Administration, 2004).

44. Shelley Mallett, Doreen Rosenthal, and Deborah Keys, "Young People, Drug Use and Family Conflict: Pathways into Homelessness," *Journal of Adolescence* 28, 2 (2005): 185–99.

45. Cited in Ray, *Lesbian, Gay, Bisexual, and Transgender Youth*, p. 48.

46. Cited in June Wyman, "Drug Abuse Among Runaway and Homeless Youths Calls for Focused Outreach Solutions," *NIDA Notes* 12, 3 (1997), http://www.nida.nih.gov/NIDA_Notes/NNVol12N3/Runaway.html.

47. *Ibid.*

48. James M. Van Leeuwen, Susan Boyle, and Amber Yancy, "Urban Peak Public Health Survey Report, 2004: A Multi-City Collaborative," (December 2004), unpublished.

49. See, for example, Ray, *Lesbian, Gay, Bisexual, and Transgender Youth*, p. 49; Natasha Slesnick and Melissa Meade, "System Youth: A Subgroup of Substance-Abusing Homeless Adolescents," *Journal of Substance Abuse* 13 (2001): 367–84; Vera Institute of Justice, *Youth Who Chronically AWOL from Foster Care: Why They Run, Where They Go, and What Can Be Done* (New York: NYC Administration for Children's Services, 2004), pp. 12, 22–23.

50. Flowers, *Runaway Kids and Teenage Prostitution*; Kipke, Montgomery, Simon, and Iverson, "Substance Abuse Disorders Among Runaway and Homeless Youth;" National Center for Missing and Exploited Children, *Prostitution of Children and Child-Sex Tourism* (Alexandria, VA: National Center for Missing and Exploited Children, 1999), p. 9; R. Barri Flowers, *Drugs, Alcohol and Criminality in American Society* (Jefferson, NC: McFarland, 2008), pp. 99–111.

51. *Substance Abuse Among Youth Who Had Run Away from Home*; Flowers, *The Adolescent Criminal*; Flowers, *Drugs, Alcohol and Criminality in American Society*; Flowers, *Runaway Kids and Teenage Prostitution*; Robert M. Bray and May M. Marsden, eds., *Drug Use in Metropolitan America* (Thousand Oaks, CA: Sage, 1998).

52. *The Prostitution of Children and Child-Sex Tourism*, p. 9.

53. Flowers, *Runaway Kids and Teenage Prostitution*.

54. *The Prostitution of Children and Child-Sex Tourism*, p. 6. See also Flowers, *Runaway Kids and Teenage Prostitution*; Flowers, *The Prostitution of Women and Girls*.

55. *Prostitution of Children and Child-Sex Tourism*, p. 6; R. Barri Flowers, *Kids Who Commit Adult Crimes: A Study of Serious Juvenile Criminality and Delinquency* (Binghamton, NY: Haworth Press, 2002); Kevin A. Yoder, Les B. Whitbeck, and Danny R. Hoyt, "Gang Involvement and Membership Among Homeless and Runaway Youth," *Youth and Society* 34, 4 (2003): 441–67; Shay Bilchik, *1996 Youth Gang Survey: Summary* (Washington, D.C.: Office of Juvenile Justice and Delinquency Prevention, 1999); Kayleen Hazelhurst and Cameron Hazelhurst, eds., *Gangs and Youth Subcultures: International Explorations* (New Brunswick, NJ: Transaction Publishers, 1989).

56. Cited in Wyman, "Drug Abuse Among Runaway and Homeless Youths." *See also* Jody M. Greene, Susan T. Ennett, and Christopher L. Ringwalt, "Substance Use Among Runaway and Homeless Youth in Three National Samples," *American Journal of Public Health* 87, 2 (1997): 229–35.

57. Lynn Rew, Margaret Taylor-Seehafer, and Maureen L. Fitzgerald, "Sexual Abuse, Alcohol and Other Drug Use, and Suicidal Behaviors in Homeless Adolescents," *Issues in Comprehensive Pediatric Nursing* 24, 4 (2001): 225–40.

58. Ray, *Lesbian, Gay, Bisexual, and Transgender Youth*, p. 48.

59. *Youth with Runaway, Throwaway, and Homeless Experiences*, p. 7.

60. Cited in *Prostitution of Children and Child-Sex Tourism*, p. 9.

61. Estes and Weiner, *The Commercial Sexual Exploitation of Children*, p. 63.

62. The National Network for Youth, "NN4Y Issue Brief: Unaccompanied Youth Overview," http://www.nn4youth.org/system/files/IssueBrief_Unaccompanied_youth.pdf; James A. Farrow, Robert W. Deisher, Richard Brown, John W. Kulig, and Michele Kipke, "Health and Health Needs of Homeless and Runaway Youth," *Journal of Adolescent Health* 13 (1992): 717–26; Robert W. Deisher and William M. Rogers, "The Medical Care of Street Youth," *Journal of Adolescent Health* 12 (1991): 500–3.

63. *Prostitution of Children and Child-Sex Tourism*, p. 7.

64. Robertson, *Homeless Youth in Hollywood*.

65. Jennifer B. Unger, Michele D. Kipke, Thomas R. Simon, Susanne B. Montgomery, and Christine J. Johnson, "Homeless Youths and Young Adults in Los Angeles: Prevalence of Mental Health Problems and the Relationship Between Mental Health and Substance Abuse Disorders," *American Journal of Community Psychology* 25, 3 (1997): 371–94.

66. "NN4Y Issue Brief," p. 5.

67. Cited in *Prostitution of Children and Child-Sex Tourism*, p. 8.

68. Cited in Estes and Weiner, *The Commercial Sexual Exploitation of Children*, p. 63.

69. *Ibid.*

70. Cited in *Prostitution of Children and Child-Sex Tourism*, p. 8. *See also* Gary L. Yates, Richard G. MacKenzie, Julia Pennbridge, and Avon Swofford. "A Risk Profile Comparison of Homeless Youth Involved in Prostitution and Homeless Youth Not Involved," *Journal of Adolescent Health* 12, 7 (1991): 545–48.

71. Cited in *Prostitution of Children and Child-Sex Tourism*, p. 8.

72. *Ibid. See also* Beth E. Molnar, Stanley B. Shade, Alex H. Kral, Robert E. Booth, and John K. Watters, "Suicidal Behavior and Sexual/Physical Abuse Among Street Youth," *Child Abuse and Neglect*, 22 (1998): 213–22.

73. Mary J. Rotheram-Borus, "Suicidal Behavior and Risk Factors Among Runaway Youths," *American Journal of Psychiatry* 150 (1993): 103–7.

74. Molnar, Shade, Kral, Booth, and Watters, "Suicidal Behavior and Sexual/Physical Abuse Among Street Youth."

75. Ray, *Lesbian, Gay, Bisexual, and Transgender Youth*, p. 42; Benedict T. McWhirter,

"Loneliness: A Review of Current Literature, with Implications for Counseling and Research," *Journal of Counseling and Development* 68 (1990): 417–23.

76. Ami Rokach, "The Causes of Loneliness in Homeless Youth," *Journal of Psychology* 139, 5 (2005): 469–80.

77. Rew, Taylor-Seehafer, and Fitzgerald, "Sexual Abuse, Alcohol and Other Drug Use, and Suicidal Behaviors."

78. Cited in Zaccaro, Jr., "Children of the Night," p. 137.

79. *Prostitution of Children and Child-Sex Tourism*, p. 8; Flowers, *Runaway Kids and Teenage Prostitution*; Christine J. De Rosa, Susanne B. Montgomery, Justeen Hyde, Ellen F. Iverson, and Michele D. Kipke, "HIV Risk Behavior and HIV Testing: A Comparison of Rates and Other Associated Factors Among Homeless and Runaway Adolescents in Two Cities," *AIDS Education and Prevention* 13, 2 (2001): 131–48; Mary J. Rotheram-Borus, Cheryl Koopman, and Anke A. Ehrhardt, "Homeless Youth and HIV Infection," *American Psychologist* 46, 11 (1991): 1188–97; T. Richard Sullivan, "The Challenge of HIV Prevention Among High-Risk Adolescents," *Health and Social Work* 21 (1996): 58–65.

80. Wagner, Carlin, Cauce, and Tenner, "A Snapshot of Homeless Youth in Seattle," p. 227.

81. Rew, Fouladi, and Yockey, "Sexual Health Practices of Homeless Youth."

82. *Prostitution of Children and Child-Sex Tourism*, p. 8.

83. Flowers, *Runaway Kids and Teenage Prostitution*, pp. 54–55.

84. *Prostitution of Children and Child-Sex Tourism*, p. 8.

85. *Ibid.*

86. *Ibid.*

87. Lynn Rew, Tiffany A. Whittaker, Margaret Taylor-Seehafer, and Lorie R. Smith, "Sexual Health and Protective Resources in Gay, Lesbian, Bisexual, and Heterosexual Homeless Youth," *Journal for Specialists in Pediatric Nursing* 10, 1 (2005): 11–19.

88. Elizabeth M. Saewyc, Linda H. Bearinger, Robert W. Blum, and Michael D. Resnick, "Sexual Intercourse, Abuse and Pregnancy Among Adolescent Women: Does Sexual Orientation Make a Difference?" *Family Planning Perspectives* 31, 3 (1999): 127–31.

89. *Prostitution of Children and Child-Sex Tourism*, p. 8. *See also* Jim A. Cates, "Adolescent Male Prostitution by Choice," *Child and Adolescent Social Work* 6 (1989): 155–56.

90. *Ibid.*; Sullivan, "The Challenge of HIV

Prevention Among High-Risk Adolescents," p. 62.

91. "HIV Risk of RHY."

92. National Coalition for the Homeless, "Homeless Youth," *NCH Fact Sheet #13*, http: //www.nationalhomeless.org/factsheets/youth. html.

93. U.S. Department of Health and Human Services, *Program Assistance Letter: Understanding the Health Care Needs of Homeless Youth* (Washington, D.C.: Health Resources and Services Administration, 2001).

94. Cited in NN4Y Issue Brief, p. 5. See also R. W. Pfeifer and J. Oliver, "Study of HIV Seroprevalence in a Group of Homeless Youth in Hollywood, California," *Journal of Adolescent Health* 20, 5 (1997): 339–42.

95. Cited in Zaccaro, Jr., "Children of the Night," p. 137.

96. Cited in NN4Y Issue Brief, p. 5. See also Ray, *Gay, Bisexual, and Transgender Youth*, p. 54.

97. National Network for Youth, *Toolkit for Youth Workers: Fact Sheet. Runaway and Homeless Youth* (Washington, D.C.: National Network for Youth, 1998).

98. See for example *Prostitution of Children and Child-Sex Tourism*, pp. 8, 35–37; Rotheram-Borus, Koopman, and Ehrhardt, "Homeless Youth and HIV Infection;" Estes and Weiner, *The Commercial Sexual Exploitation of Children*, p. 68; Timothy P. Johnson, Jennie R. Aschkenasy, Mary R. Herbers, and Stephen A. Gillenwater, "Self-Reported Risk Factors for AIDS Among Homeless Youth," *AIDS Education and Prevention* 8 (1996): 308–22; Beth E. Molnar, Alex H. Kral, and John K. Watters, *Street Youth at Risk for AIDS* (Rockville, MD: National Institute on Drug Abuse, 1994).

99. *Prostitution of Children and Child-Sex Tourism*, p. 8; Johnson, Aschkenasy, Herbers, and Gillenwater, "Self-Reported Risk Factors for AIDS Among Homeless Youth."

100. Kihara, "Giuliani's Suppressed Report on Homeless Youth."

101. Patricia Hersch, "Coming of Age on City Streets," *Psychology Today* 22, 1 (1988): 35.

102. Rotheram-Borus, Meyer-Bahlburg, Koopman, Rosario, Exner, Henderson, Matthieu, and Gruen, "Lifetime Sexual Behavior Among Runaway Males and Females."

103. Cited in Study World, "Runaways: Victims At Home and On the Streets," http:// www.studyworld.com/newsite/ReportEssay/So cialIssues/Political%5CRunaways__Victims_At _Home_and_On_the_Streets-32644.htm.

104. *Prostitution of Children and Child-Sex Tourism*, pp. 8, 36; Steven Bittle, *Youth Involvement in Prostitution: A Literature Review and Annotated Bibliography* (Ottawa: Department of Justice Canada, 2002), pp. 25–26; Dan Allman, *M Is for MUTUAL, A Is for ACTS. Male Sex Work and AIDS in Canada* (Ottawa: Health Canada, 1999).

105. "HIV Risk of RHY."

106. *Youth with Runaway, Throwaway, and Homeless Experiences*, p. 7.

107. Robert W. Deisher, James A. Farrow, Kerry Hope, and Christina Litchfield, "The Pregnant Adolescent Prostitute," *American Journal of Diseases of Children* 143 (1989): 1162–65.

108. Halcon and Lifson, "Prevalence and Predictors of Sexual Risks Among Homeless Youth," p. 76.

109. Cited in "NN4Y Issue Brief," p. 5.

110. *Ibid.*; Deisher, Farrow, Hope, and Litchfield, "The Pregnant Adolescent Prostitute;" Widom and Kuhns, "Childhood Victimization and Subsequent Risk for Promiscuity, Prostitution and Teenage Pregnancy;" Lydia Bond, Rafael Mazin, and Maria V. Jiminez, "Street Youth and AIDS," *AIDS Education and Prevention* 4, 3 (1992): 14–23; Institute of Health Policy Studies, *Street Youth at Risk for AIDS* (San Francisco, CA: University of California, 1995).

111. Ray, *Lesbian, Gay, Bisexual, and Transgender Youth*, p. 58; Halcon and Lifson, "Prevalence and Predictors of Sexual Risks Among Homeless Youth."

112. *Youth with Runaway, Throwaway, and Homeless Experiences*, p. 7.

113. Wagner, Carlin, Cauce, and Tenner, "A Snapshot of Homeless Youth in Seattle," p. 227.

114. Cited in Zaccaro, Jr., "Children of the Night," p. 138.

115. Cited in Heather L. Bradley, "Crisis Intervention with Homeless and Sex-Working Youth," 3rd Annual Collaborative Crisis Centers Conference, Chicago, IL (May 6–8, 2005), http://www.uic.edu/orgs/convening/home less.htm.

116. Mary Manning, "Runaway Girl Found in Shallow Grave Identified," *Las Vegas Sun* (August 4, 2008), http://www.lasvegassun.com/ news/2008/aug/04/runaway-girl-found-shal low-grave-identified.

## Chapter 9

1. See for example R. Barri Flowers, *Runaway Kids and Teenage Prostitution: America's*

*Lost, Abandoned, and Sexually Exploited Children* (Westport, CT: Greenwood Press, 2001); CRS Report for Congress, *Runaway and Homeless Youth: Demographics, Programs, and Emerging Issues* (Washington, D.C.: Congressional Research Service, 2007), pp. 6–7; Marjorie. J. Robertson and Paul A. Toro, "Homeless Youth: Research, Intervention, and Policy," in Linda. B. Fosburg and Deborah. L. Dennis, eds., *Practical Lessons: The 1998 National Symposium on Homelessness Research* (Washington, D.C.: U.S. Department of Housing and Urban Development and U.S. Department of Health and Human Services; 1998); Bryan N. Cochran, Angela J. Stewart, Joshua A. Ginzler, and Ana Mari Cauce, "Challenges Faced by Homeless Sexual Minorities: Comparison of Gay, Lesbian, Bisexual, and Transgender Homeless Adolescents with Their Heterosexual Counterparts," *American Journal of Public Health* 92, 5 (2005): 773–77.

2. Heather Hammer, David Finkelhor, and Andrea J. Sedlak, *Runaway/Thrownaway Children: National Estimates and Characteristics*, NISMART Bulletin Series (Washington, D.C.: Office of Juvenile Justice and Delinquency Prevention, 2002), pp. 1–12.

3. Nicholas Ray, *Lesbian, Gay, Bisexual, and Transgender Youth: An Epidemic of Homelessness* (New York: National Gay and Lesbian Task Force Policy Institute and National Coalition for the Homeless, 2006), p. 12; Christopher L. Ringwalt, Jody M. Greene, Marjorie J. Robertson, and Melissa McPheeters, "The Prevalence of Homelessness Among Adolescents in the United States," *American Journal of Public Health* 88, 9 (1998): 1327; Marjorie J. Robertson and Paul A. Toro, "Homeless Youth: Research, Intervention, and Policy," http://aspe.hhs.gov/ProgSys/homeless/symposium/3-Youth.htm.

4. Cited in CRS Report for Congress, *The Runaway and Homeless Youth Program: Administration, Funding and Legislative Actions* (Washington, D.C.: Congressional Research Service, 2006), p. 2.

5. U.S. Department of Health and Human Services, Family Youth and Services Bureau, *Youth with Runaway, Throwaway, and Homeless Experiences: Prevalence, Drug Use, and Other At-Risk Behaviors* (Silver Springs, MD: National Clearinghouse on Families & Youth, 1995), p. E6.

6. Les B. Whitbeck and Ronald L. Simons, "Life on the Streets: The Victimization of Runaway and Homeless Adolescents," *Youth and Society* 22, 1 (1990): 108–25.

7. Ray, *Lesbian, Gay, Bisexual, and Transgender Youth*, p. 1; The National Network for Youth, "NN4Y Issue Brief: Unaccompanied Youth Overview," http://www.nn4youth.org/system/files/IssueBrief_Unaccompanyed_youth.pdf.

8. Michael C. Clatts, W. Rees Davis, J. L. Sotheran, and Aylin Atillasoy, "Correlates and Distribution of HIV Risk Behaviors Among Homeless Youths in New York City: Implications for Prevention and Policy," *Child Welfare* 77, 2 (1998): 195–207. *See also* Linda M. Dame, "Queer Youth in Care in Manitoba: An Examination of Their Experiences Through Their Voices," *Canadian Online Journal of Queer Studies in Education* 1, 1 (2004): 1–28.

9. Cited in Ray, *Lesbian, Gay, Bisexual, and Transgender Youth*, p. 13.

10. *Ibid.*

11. *Ibid.*

12. Nicole D. K. Dylan, "City Enters Partnership to Assist Lesbian and Gay Homeless Youth," *Nation's Cities Weekly* 27, 10 (2004).

13. Cited in Ray, *Lesbian, Gay, Bisexual, and Transgender Youth*, p. 13.

14. *Ibid. See also* Gabe Kruks, "Gay and Lesbian Homeless/Street Youth: Special Issues and Concerns," *Journal of Adolescent Health* 12 (1991): 515–18; Randall L. Sell, "Defining and Measuring Sexual Orientation: A Review," *Archives of Sexual Behavior* 26, 6 (1997): 643–58.

15. Safe Schools Coalition, "Homeless LGBT Youth and LGBT Youth in Foster Care," (July 6, 2009), http://www.safeschoolscoalition.org/RG-homeless.html.

16. Richard J. Estes and Neil A. Weiner, *The Commercial Sexual Exploitation of Children in the U.S., Canada, and Mexico* (Philadelphia, PA: University of Pennsylvania, 2002), p. 79.

17. Cited in Lisa Mottet and John M. Ohle, "Transitioning Our Shelters: A Guide to Making Homeless Shelters Safe for Transgender People," (2004), http://www.thetaskforce.org.

18. Ray, *Lesbian, Gay, Bisexual, and Transgender Youth*, p. 4; HCH Clinicians' Network, "Crossing to Safety: Transgender Health and Homelessness," *Healing Hands* 6 (2002): 1–6.

19. Cochran, Stewart, Ginzler, and Cauce, "Challenges Faced by Homeless Sexual Minorities," p. 773; Flowers, *Runaway Kids and Teenage Prostitution*; R. Barri Flowers, *College Crime: A Statistical Study of Offenses on American Campuses* (Jefferson, NC: McFarland, 2009), pp. 114–25; Martin. L. Forst, "A Substance Use Profile of Delinquent and Homeless Youths," *Journal of Drug Education* 24, 3 (1994): 219–31; Margaret Rosario, Joyce Hunter, and Marya

Gwadz, "Exploration of Substance Use Among Lesbian, Gay, and Bisexual Youth: Prevalence and Correlates," *Journal of Adolescent Research* 12, 4 (1997): 454–76.

20. Ray, *Lesbian, Gay, Bisexual, and Transgender Youth*, pp. 2–4; Cochran, Stewart, Ginzler, and Cauce, "Challenges Faced by Homeless Sexual Minorities," pp. 773–77; Ritch C. Savin-Williams, "Verbal and Physical Abuse as Stressors in the Lives of Lesbian, Gay Male and Bisexual Youths: Association with School Problems, Running Away, Substance Abuse, Prostitution, and Suicide," *Journal of Consulting and Clinical Psychology* 62, 2 (1994): 261–69.

21. Gary J. Remafedi, "Adolescent Homosexuality Issues for Pediatricians," *Clinical Pediatrics* 24, 9 (1985): 481–85; Monica E. Schneider and Robert E. Owens, "Concern for Lesbian, Gay, and Bisexual Kids: The Benefits for All Children," *Education and Urban Society* 32, 3 (2000): 349–67.

22. Remafedi, "Adolescent Homosexuality. Issues for Pediatricians;" Savin-Williams, "Verbal and Physical Abuse as Stressors in the Lives of Lesbian, Gay Male and Bisexual Youths;" Kruks, "Gay and Lesbian Homeless/Street Youth."

23. Cited in Ray, *Lesbian, Gay, Bisexual, and Transgender Youth*, p. 18.

24. *Ibid.*; Kruks, "Gay and Lesbian Homeless/Street Youth;" Doug Arey, "Gay Males and Sexual Child Abuse," in Lisa A. Fonte, ed., *Sexual Abuse in Nine North American Cultures: Treatment and Prevention* (Thousand Oaks, CA: Sage, 1995).

25. Cochran, Stewart, Ginzler, and Cauce, "Challenges Faced by Homeless Sexual Minorities," p. 773; James Lock and Hans Steiner, "Gay, Lesbian and Bisexual Youth Risks for Emotional, Physical, and Social Problems: Results from a Community-Based Survey," *Journal of the American Academy of Child and Adolescence Psychiatry* 38, 3 (1999): 297–304; John Hagan and Bill McCarthy, "Streetlife and Delinquency," *British Journal of Sociology* 43, 4 (1992): 533–61.

26. Frank York and Robert H. Knight, "Reality Check on Homeless Gay Teens," *Family Policy* (1998), http://www.frc.org/fampol/fp98 fcv.htm.

27. "Homeless LGBT Youth and LGBT Youth in Foster Care."

28. Cited in Ray, *Lesbian, Gay, Bisexual, and Transgender Youth*, p. 16.

29. Quoted in York and Robert H. Knight, "Reality Check on Homeless Gay Teens." *See also* Jenny Gable, "Problems Faced by Homosexual Youth," (1995), http://www.lmsa.edu/ jgable/lbg/paper.html.

30. Gil Griffin, "Running on Empty: Kids Take to the Streets When They Don't Feel Loved at Home," *San Diego Union-Tribune* (July 26, 1997), p. E1.

31. Sanna Thompson, Andrew W. Safyer, and David E. Pollio, "Examining Differences and Predictors of Family Reunification Among Subgroups of Runaway Youth Using Shelter Services," *Social Work Research* 25, 3 (2001): 163–72.

32. Ray, *Lesbian, Gay, Bisexual, and Transgender Youth*, p. 2.

33. *Ibid.*, pp. 41–64; Cochran, Stewart, Ginzler, and Cauce, "Challenges Faced by Homeless Sexual Minorities," pp. 773–77; Rashmi Gangamma, Natasha Slesnick, Paula Toviessi, and Julianne Serovich, "Comparison of HIV Risks Among Gay, Lesbian, Bisexual and Heterosexual Homeless Youth," *Journal of Youth and Adolescence* 37, 4 (2008): 456–64; Lisa M. Diamond, "Sexual Identity, Attractions, and Behavior Among Young Sexual-Minority Women Over a 2-Year Period," *Developmental Psychology* 36, 2 (2000): 241–50.

34. Gangamma, Slesnick, Toviessi, and Serovich, "Comparison of HIV Risks Among Gay, Lesbian, Bisexual and Heterosexual Homeless Youth." *See also* Margaret Rosario, Eric W. Schrimshaw, Joyce Hunter, and Marya Gwadz, "Gay-Related Stress and Emotional Distress Among Gay, Lesbian, and Bisexual Youths: A Longitudinal Examination," *Journal of Consulting and Clinical Psychology* 70, 4 (2002): 967–75; Margaret Rosario, Joyce Hunter, Shira Maguen, Marya Gwadz, and Raymond Smith, "The Coming-out Process and its Adaptational and Health-Related Associations Among Gay, Lesbian, and Bisexual Youths: Stipulation and Exploration of a Model," *American Journal of Community Psychology* 29 (2001): 133–60.

35. Gangamma, Slesnick, Toviessi, and Serovich, "Comparison of HIV Risks Among Gay, Lesbian, Bisexual and Heterosexual Homeless Youth." *See also* Rosario, Schrimshaw, Hunter, and Gwadz, "Gay-Related Stress and Emotional Distress Among Gay, Lesbian, and Bisexual Youths."

36. Steven A. Safren and Richard G. Heimberg, "Depression, Hopelessness, Suicidality, and Related Factors in Sexual Minority and Heterosexual Adolescents," *Journal of Consulting and Clinical Psychology* 67, 6 (1999): 859–66; Michael King, Joanna Semlyen, Sharon See Tai, Helen Killaspy, David Osborn, Dmitri

Popelyuk, and Irwin Nazareth, "A Systematic Review of Mental Disorder, Suicide, and Deliberate Self Harm in Lesbian, Gay and Bisexual People," *BMC Psychiatry* 8 (2008): 70; Les B. Whitbeck, Xiaojin Chen, Danny R. Hoyt, Kimberly A, Tyler, and Kurt D. Johnson, "Mental Disorder, Subsistence Strategies, and Victimization Among Gay, Lesbian, and Bisexual Homeless and Runaway Adolescents," *Journal of Sex Research* 41, 4 (2004): 329–42.

37. David M. Fergusson, L. John Horwood, and Annette L. Beautrais, "Is Sexual Orientation Related to Mental Health Problems and Suicidality in Young People?" *Archives of General Psychiatry* 56, 10 (1999): 876–80.

38. Whitbeck, Chen, Hoyt, Tyler, and Johnson, "Mental Disorder, Subsistence Strategies, and Victimization Among Gay, Lesbian, and Bisexual Homeless and Runaway Adolescents," p. 334.

39. Cited in Ray, *Lesbian, Gay, Bisexual, and Transgender Youth*, p. 43.

40. Whitbeck, Chen, Hoyt, Tyler, and Johnson, "Mental Disorder, Subsistence Strategies, and Victimization Among Gay, Lesbian, and Bisexual Homeless and Runaway Adolescents," p. 334.

41. Cited in Ray, *Lesbian, Gay, Bisexual, and Transgender Youth*, p. 43.

42. Gangamma, Slesnick, Toviessi, and Serovich, "Comparison of HIV Risks Among Gay, Lesbian, Bisexual and Heterosexual Homeless Youth;" Michelle Burden Leslie, Judith A. Stein, and Mary Jane Rotheram-Borus, "Sex Specific Predictors of Suicidality Among Runaway Youth," *Journal of Clinical Child and Adolescent Psychology* 31, 1 (2002): 27–40.

43. Whitbeck, Chen, Hoyt, Tyler, and Johnson, "Mental Disorder, Subsistence Strategies, and Victimization Among Gay, Lesbian, and Bisexual Homeless and Runaway Adolescents."

44. *Ibid.*, p. 334.

45. Natasha Slesnick and Jillian Prestopnik, "Dual and Multiple Diagnosis Among Substance Using Runaway Youth," *American Journal of Drug and Alcohol Abuse* 3, 1 (2005): 179–201.

46. Terceira A. Berdahl, Danny R. Hoyt, and Les B. Whitbeck, "Predictors of First Mental Health Service Utilization Among Homeless and Runaway Adolescents," *Journal of Adolescent Health* 37, 2 (2005): 145–54; Anna M. Avery, Ronald. E. Hellman, and Lori .K. Sudderth, "Satisfaction with Mental Health Services Among Sexual Minorities with Major

Mental Illness," *American Journal of Public Health* 91, 6 (2001): 990–91.

47. Gangamma, Slesnick, Toviessi, and Serovich, "Comparison of HIV Risks Among Gay, Lesbian, Bisexual and Heterosexual Homeless Youth;" Cochran, Stewart, Ginzler, and Cauce, "Challenges Faced by Homeless Sexual Minorities;" Lock and Steiner, "Gay, Lesbian and Bisexual Youth Risks for Emotional, Physical, and Social Problems;" Michele D. Kipke, Susanne B. Montgomery, Thomas R. Simon, and Ellen F. Iverson, "Substance Abuse Disorders Among Runaway and Homeless Youth," *Substance Use and Misuse* 32 (1997): 969–86.

48. Kruks, "Gay and Lesbian Homeless/ Street Youth;" Cochran, Stewart, Ginzler, and Cauce, "Challenges Faced by Homeless Sexual Minorities;" Ray, *Lesbian, Gay, Bisexual, and Transgender Youth*, pp. 49–51; Timothy P. Johnson, "Self-Reported Risk Factors for AIDS Among Homeless Youth," *AIDS Education Prevention* 8 (1996): 308–22.

49. Cochran, Stewart, Ginzler, and Cauce, "Challenges Faced by Homeless Sexual Minorities," p. 773.

50. *Ibid.*; Forst, "A Substance Use Profile of Delinquent and Homeless Youths;" Michael G. MacLean, Matthew J. Paradise, and Ana Mari Cauce, "Substance Use and Psychological Adjustment in Homeless Adolescents: A Test of Three Models," *American Journal of Community Psychology* 27 (1999): 405–27.

51. Cited in Ray, *Lesbian, Gay, Bisexual, and Transgender Youth*, p. 50.

52. Rosario, Hunter, and Gwadz, "Exploration of Substance Use Among Lesbian, Gay, and Bisexual Youth," pp. 462–63.

53. James M. Van Leeuwen, Susan Boyle, Stacy Salomonsen-Sautel, D. Nico Baker, J. T. Garcia, Allison Hoffman, and Christian J. Hopfer, "Lesbian, Gay, and Bisexual Homeless Youth: An Eight-City Public Health Perspective," *Child Welfare* 85, 2 (2006): 151–70.

54. Flowers, *Runaway Kids and Teenage Prostitution*; Cochran, Stewart, Ginzler, and Cauce, "Challenges Faced by Homeless Sexual Minorities," p. 773; Kruks, "Gay and Lesbian Homeless/Street Youth," pp. 515–18; Milton Greenblatt and Marjorie J. Robertson, "Life-Styles, Adaptive Strategies, and Sexual Behaviors of Homeless Adolescents," *Hospital and Community Psychiatry* 44, 12 (1993): 1177–80; Doreen Rosenthal and Susan Moore, "Homeless Youths: Sexual and Drug-Related Behavior, Sexual Beliefs and HIV/AIDS Risk," *AIDS Care* 6, 1 (1994): 83–94; Jody M. Greene, Susan T.

Ennett, and Christopher L. Ringwalt, "Prevalence and Correlates of Survival Sex Among Runaway and Homeless Youth," *American Journal of Public Health* 89, 9 (1999): 1406–9.

55. Flowers, *Runaway Kids and Teenage Prostitution*; R. Barri Flowers, *The Prostitution of Women and Girls* (Jefferson, NC: McFarland, 2005); R. Barri Flowers, *The Victimization and Exploitation of Women and Children: A Study of Physical, Mental and Sexual Maltreatment in the United States* (Jefferson, NC: McFarland, 1994); Caitlin Ryan and Ian Rivers, "Lesbian, Gay, Bisexual and Transgender Youth: Victimization and Its Correlates in the USA and UK," *Culture, Health, and Society* 5, 2 (2003): 103–19; Hagan and McCarthy, "Streetlife and Delinquency," pp. 533–61.

56. Greene, Ennett, and Ringwalt, "Prevalence and Correlates of Survival Sex Among Runaway and Homeless Youth," pp. 1406–9; Julia N. Pennbridge, Thomas Freese, and Richard G. MacKenzie, "High Risk Behaviors Among Street Youth in Hollywood, California," *AIDS Education and Prevention* (Fall 1992): 24–33; Susan T. Ennett, Susan L. Bailey, and E. Belle Federman, "Social Network Characteristics Associated with Risky Behaviors Among Runaway and Homeless Youth," *Journal of Health and Social Behavior* 40 (1999): 63–78.

57. Cited in Ray, *Lesbian, Gay, Bisexual, and Transgender Youth*, p. 56; Linda L. Halcon and Alan R. Lifson, "Prevalence and Predictors of Sexual Risks Among Homeless Youth," *Journal of Youth and Adolescence* 33, 1 (2004): 75–76.

58. Halcon and Lifson, "Prevalence and Predictors of Sexual Risks Among Homeless Youth;" John E. Anderson, Thomas E. Freese and Julia N. Pennbridge, "Sexual Risk Behavior and Condom Use Among Street Youth in Hollywood," *Family Planning Perspectives* 26, 1 (1994).

59. Stephen Gaetz, "Safe Streets for Whom? Homeless Youth, Social Exclusion, and Criminal Victimization," *Canadian Journal of Criminology and Criminal Justice* 46, 6 (2004): 423–55.

60. Nancy Haley, Elise Roy, Pascale Leclerc, and Jean-François Boivin, "HIV High Risk Profile of Male Street Youth Involved in Survival Sex," *Sexually Transmitted Infections* 80 (2004): 526–30.

61. Gaetz, "Safe Streets for Whom?"

62. Quoted in Robin Erb and Roberta de Boer, "Males Who Work as Prostitutes a Little-Known Part of Sex Iindustry," ToledoBlade. com (December 29, 2006), http://toledoblade. com/apps/pbcs.dll/article?AID=/20061229/ NEWS03/612290302.

63. See, for example, Ray, *Lesbian, Gay, Bisexual, and Transgender Youth*, p. 57; C. Pratt, "The Perilous Times of Transgender Youth," *New York Times* (June 18, 1995): CY7; Cochran, Stewart, Ginzler, and Cauce, "Challenges Faced by Homeless Sexual Minorities," p. 776; Elizabeth M. Saewyc, Carol Skay, Kimberly Richens, and Elizabeth Reis, "Sexual Orientation, Sexual Abuse, and HIV-Risk Related Behaviors Among Adolescents in the Pacific Northwest," *American Journal of Public Health* 96, 6 (2006).

64. "Crossing to Safety: Transgender Health and Homelessness," pp. 1–6; Ray, *Lesbian, Gay, Bisexual, and Transgender Youth*, p. 63.

65. Ray, *Lesbian, Gay, Bisexual, and Transgender Youth*, p. 3.

66. Lynn Rew, Tiffany A. Whittaker, Margaret Taylor-Seehafer, and Lorie R. Smith, "Sexual Health and Protective Resources in Gay, Lesbian, Bisexual, and Heterosexual Homeless Youth," *Journal for Specialists in Pediatric Nursing* 10, 1 (2005): 11–19; Margaret Rosario, Karen A. Mahler, Joyce Hunter, and Marya Gwadz, "Understanding the Unprotected Sexual Behaviors of Gay, Lesbian, and Bisexual Youths: An Empirical Test of the Cognitive-Environmental Model," *Health Psychology* 18 (1999): 272–80.

67. Elizabeth M. Saewyc, Linda H. Bearinger, Robert W. Blum, and Michael D. Resnick, "Sexual Intercourse, Abuse and Pregnancy Among Adolescent Women: Does Sexual Orientation Make a Difference?" *Family Planning Perspectives* 31, 3 (1999): 127–31. *See also* M. Rosa Solorio, Norweeta G. Milburn, Robert E. Weiss, and Philip J. Batterham, "Newly Homeless Youth STD Testing Patterns Over Time," *Journal of Adolescent Health* 39 (2006): 443e9–43e16.

68. Paul Gibson, "Gay Male and Lesbian Suicide," LAMBDA GLBT Community Services, http://www.lambda.org/youth_suicide. htm.

69. Michael C. Clatts, Lloyd A. Goldsamt, Huso Yi, and Marya V. Gwadz, "Homelessness and Drug Abuse Among Young Men Who Have Sex with Men in New York City: A Preliminary Epidemiological Trajectory," *Journal of Adolescence* 28, 2 (2005): 201–14.

70. Gangamma, Slesnick, Toviessi, and Serovich, "Comparison of HIV Risks Among Gay, Lesbian, Bisexual and Heterosexual Homeless Youth." *See also* T. Richard Sullivan, "The Challenge of HIV Prevention Among High-Risk Adolescents," *Health and Social*

*Work* 21 (1996): 58–65; M. L. O'Connor, "Unsafe Behaviors Place Street Youth, Especially Women, at Risk of HIV," *Family Planning Perspectives* 30, 1 (1998): 20–51.

71. Saewyc, Skay, Richens, and Reis, "Sexual Orientation, Sexual Abuse, and HIV-Risk Related Behaviors Among Adolescents."

72. Pratt, "The Perilous Times of Transgender Youth."

73. Gibson, "Gay Male and Lesbian Suicide."

## Chapter 10

1. R. Barri Flowers, *The Prostitution of Women and Girls* (Jefferson, NC: McFarland, 1998), p. 6.

2. Richard Goodall, *The Comfort of Sin: Prostitutes and Prostitution in the 1990s* (Kent, England: Renaissance Books, 1995), p. 1.

3. National Center for Missing and Exploited Children, *Prostitution of Children and Child-Sex Tourism* (Alexandria, VA: National Center for Missing and Exploited Children, 1999), p. 9.

4. See, for example, *U.S. v. Bitty*, 208 U.S. 393, 401 (1908); Charles Rosenbleet and Barbara J. Pariente, "The Prostitution of the Criminal Law," *American Criminal Law Review* 11 (1973): 373; R. Barri Flowers, *Runaway Kids and Teenage Prostitution: America's Lost, Abandoned, and Sexually Exploited Children* (Westport, CT: Greenwood Press, 2001).

5. R. Barri Flowers, *The Victimization and Exploitation of Women and Children: A Study of Physical, Mental, and Sexual Maltreatment in the United States* (Jefferson, NC: McFarland, 1994), p. 82. *See also* Teela Sanders, Maggie O'Neill, and Jane Pitcher, *Prostitution: Sex Work, Policy and Politics* (New York: Sage, 2009).

6. Pam Oliver, "A Review of Literature on Child Prostitution," *Social Policy Journal of New Zealand* 19 (2002), http://www.thefreelibrary.com/_/print/PrintArticle.aspx?id=99849275.

7. Mia Spangenberg, "Prostituted Youth in New York City: An Overview," (2001), http://www.libertadlatina.org/US_ECPAT_Child_Prostitution_NYC.htm.

8. Jody M. Greene, Susan T. Ennett, and Christopher L. Ringwalt, "Prevalence and Correlates of Survival Sex Among Runaway and Homeless Youth," *American Journal of Public Health* 89, 9 (1999): 1406–9; Milton Greenblatt

and Marjorie J. Robertson, "Life-Styles, Adaptive Strategies, and Sexual Behaviors of Homeless Adolescents," *Hospital and Community Psychiatry* 44, 12 (1993): 1177–80; Julia N. Pennbridge, Thomas Freese, and Richard G. MacKenzie, "High Risk Behaviors Among Street Youth in Hollywood, California," *AIDS Education and Prevention* (Fall 1992): 24–33.

9. Flowers, *Runaway Kids and Teenage Prostitution*; Joan J. Johnson, *Teen Prostitution* (Danbury, CT: Franklin Watts, 1992), p. 35.

10. Flowers, *Runaway Kids and Teenage Prostitution*; R. Barri Flowers, *Sex Crimes: Perpetrators, Predators, Prostitutes, and Victims*, 2nd ed. (Springfield, IL: Charles C Thomas, 2006), pp. 131–37; Steven Bittle, *Youth Involvement in Prostitution: A Literature Review and Annotated Bibliography* (Ottawa: Department of Justice Canada, 2002), pp. 4, 82; Laura A. Barnitz, *Commercial Sexual Exploitation of Children: Youth Involved in Prostitution, Pornography, and Sex Trafficking* (Washington, D.C.: Youth Advocate Program International, 1998); Daniel S. Campagna and Donald Poffenberger, *The Sexual Trafficking in Children: an Investigation of the Child Sex Trade* (Dover, MA: Auburn House, 1988).

11. Spangenberg, "Prostituted Youth in New York City;" Flowers, *Sex Crimes*; Klass Kids Foundation, "The HT Report," (February 2009), http://www.klaaskids.org/pg-ht-report.htm; Carey Goldberg, "Sex Slavery, Thailand to New York; Thousands of Indentured Asian Prostitutes May Be in U.S.," *New York Times* (September 11, 1995), p. B1; David J. Langum, *Crossing Over the Line: Legislating Morality and the Mann Act* (Chicago, IL: University of Chicago Press, 1995); Penny Venetis, "International Sexual Slavery," *Women's Rights Law Reporter* 18, 3 (1997): 268–70; Youngik Yoon, *International Sexual Slavery* (Washington, D.C.: CG Issue Overviews, 1997); William Booth, "13 Charged in Gang Importing Prostitutes," *Washington Post* (August 21, 1999), p. A3.

12. See, for example, Flowers, *Sex Crimes*; Spangenberg, "Prostituted Youth in New York City;" Eric M. Strauss, "Pimp Abducts Ohio Teens: Two Cousins Forced Into Having Sex for Money," ABC News (July 16, 2008), http://abcnews.go.com/TheLaw/story?id=5382645&page=1; "Teen Girls' Stories of Sex Trafficking in U.S.: International Sex Trafficking Is a Well-Known Problem, But It Happens Here as Well," ABC News (February 9, 2006), http://abcnews.go.com/print?id=1596778.

13. Flowers, *Runaway Kids and Teenage Prostitution*; Flowers, *The Prostitution of Women and*

*Girls*; Nancy E. Walker, "Executive Summary: How Many Teens Are Prostituted?" fce.msu. edu/Family_Impact_Seminars/pdf/2002-2.pdf ; General Accounting Office, *Sexual Exploitation of Children: A Problem of Unknown Magnitude* (Washington, D.C.: General Accounting Office, 1982); Michelle Stransky and David Finkelhor, *How Many Juveniles Are Involved in Prostitution in the United States?* (Durham, NC: Crimes Against Children Research Center, 2008).

14. Cited in Carol Smolenski, "Sex Tourism and the Sexual Exploitation of Children," *Christian Century* 112 (1995): 1079.

15. Flowers, *The Prostitution of Women and Girls*, p. 81.

16. Spangenberg, "Prostituted Youth in New York City."

17. Cited in Stransky and Finkelhor, *How Many Juveniles Are Involved in Prostitution in the United States?*, pp. 5–6. *See also* U.S. Department of Justice, Federal Bureau of Investigation, *Crime in the United States, 2008*, Table 38, http://www.fbi.gov/ucr/cius2008/data/table_38.html; Michael Satchel, "Kids for Sale: A Shocking Report on Child Prostitution Across America," *Parade Magazine* (July 20, 1986), p. 4.

18. Walker, "Executive Summary."

19. Flowers, *The Prostitution of Women and Girls*, p. 71; Stransky and Finkelhor, *How Many Juveniles Are Involved in Prostitution in the United States?*, p. 2.

20. R. Barri Flowers, *The Adolescent Criminal: An Examination of Today's Juvenile Offender* (Jefferson, NC: McFarland, 2009), pp. 54–55.

21. Cited in Stransky and Finkelhor, *How Many Juveniles Are Involved in Prostitution in the United States?*, p. 1. *See also* Richard J. Estes and Neil A. Weiner, *The Commercial Sexual Exploitation of Children in the U.S., Canada, and Mexico* (Philadelphia, PA: University of Pennsylvania, 2002), pp. 140–151.

22. Cited in Stransky and Finkelhor, *How Many Juveniles Are Involved in Prostitution in the United States?*, p. 4.

23. Heather J. Clawson, Mary Layne, and Kevonne Small, *Estimating Human Trafficking into the United States: Development of a Methodology* (Fairfax, VA: Caliber, 2006); Nancy A. Boxill, "Ending Sex Trafficking of Children in Atlanta," *Affilia* 22, 2 (2007): 138–49.

24. Flowers, *The Prostitution of Women and Girls*; Flowers, *Runaway Kids and Teenage Prostitution*; Gary L. Yates, Richard G. MacKenzie, Julia Pennbridge, and Avon Swofford, "A Risk Profile Comparison of Homeless Youth Involved in Prostitution and Homeless Youth Not Involved," *Journal of Adolescent Health* 12, 7 (1991): 545–48; Martha W. Moon, Diane Binson, Kimberly Page-Shafter, and Rafael Diaz, "Correlates of HIV Risk in a Random Sample of Street Youths in San Francisco," *Journal of the Association of Nurses in AIDS Care* 12, 6 (2001): 18–27; Walter de Oliveira, *Working with Children on the Streets of Brazil: Politics and Practice* (Binghamton, NY: Haworth Press,2000); Marlene Webber, *Street Kids: The Tragedy of Canada's Runaways* (Toronto: University of Toronto Press, 1991); David Barrett and William Beckett, "Child Prostitution: Reaching Out to Children Who Sell Sex to Survive," *British Journal of Nursing* 5 (1996): 1120–25.

25. Flowers, *Runaway Kids and Teenage Prostitution*; Rebecca P. Sanchez, "Facing Up to Homeless Youths," *Denver Post* (December 20, 2004): A1; U.S. Department of Health and Human Services, Family Youth and Services Bureau, *Youth with Runaway, Throwaway, and Homeless Experiences: Prevalence, Drug Use, and Other At-Risk Behaviors* (Silver Springs, MD: National Clearinghouse on Families and Youth, 1995), p. E6.

26. Cited in Marjorie J. Robertson and Paul A. Toro, "Homeless Youth: Research, Intervention, and Policy," in Linda B. Fosburg and Deborah L. Dennis, eds. *Practical Lessons: The 1998 National Symposium on Homelessness Research* (Washington, D.C.: U.S. Department of Housing and Urban Development and U.S. Department of Health and Human Services, 1998), http://aspe.hhs.gov/ProgSys/homeless/symposium/3-Youth.htm.

27. Christopher L. Ringwalt, Jody M. Greene, Marjorie J. Robertson, and Melissa McPheeters, "The Prevalence of Homelessness Among Adolescents in the United States," *American Journal of Public Health* 88, 9 (1998): 1325–29.

28. *Youth with Runaway, Throwaway, and Homeless Experiences*, p. E6.

29. Les B. Whitbeck and Ronald L. Simons, "Life on the Streets: The Victimization of Runaway and Homeless Adolescents," *Youth and Society* 22, 1 (1990): 108–25.

30. Flowers, *Runaway Kids and Teenage Prostitution*; *Prostitution of Children and Child-Sex Tourism*, pp. 2–5.

31. Suzanne Smalley, "Nationwide Increase in Teen Prostitution: Trends Show Kids Getting Younger, More from Middle Class Homes," *Newsweek* (August 10, 2003), http://www.couplescompany.com/Wireservice/Parenting/teen Prostitution.htm.

32. Heather Hammer, David Finkelhor, and Andrea J. Sedlak, *Runaway/Thrownaway Children: National Estimates and Characteristics*, NISMART Bulletin Series (Washington, D.C.: Office of Juvenile Justice and Delinquency Prevention, 2002), p. 2.

33. *Ibid.*, p. 8.

34. *Prostitution of Children and Child-Sex Tourism*, p. 3. *See also* Magnus J. Seng, "Child Sexual Abuse and Adolescent Prostitution: A Comparative Analysis," *Adolescence* 24 (1989): 671; Mary J. Rotheram-Borus, Karen A. Mahler, Cheryl Koopman, and Kris Langabeer, "Sexual Abuse History and Associated Multiple Risk Behavior in Adolescent Runaways," *American Journal of Orthopsychiatry* 66 (1996): 390–91.

35. Ruth Dean and Melissa Thomson, *Teen Prostitution: Teen Issues* (San Diego, CA: Lucent Books, 1997).

36. Walker, "Executive Summary."

37. "The HT Report."

38. Z. M. Lukman, "The Prevalence of Running Away from Home among Prostituted Children in Malaysia," *Journal of Social Sciences* 5, 3 (2009): 157.

39. David Barrett, "Young People and Prostitution: Perpetrators in Our Midst," *International Review of Law, Computers and Technology* 12, 3 (1998): 475–86.

40. *Prostitution of Children and Child-Sex Tourism*, p. 2. *See also* T. Richard Sullivan, "The Challenge of HIV Prevention Among High-Risk Adolescents," *Health and Social Work* 21 (1996): 58–60; Mimi H. Silbert and Ayala M. Pines, "Entrance Into Prostitution," *Youth and Society* 13 (1982): 471–73; Stephen Gaetz, Bill O'Grady, and Bryan Vaillancourt, *Making Money: The Shout Clinic Report on Homeless Youth and Employment* (Toronto: Central Toronto Community Health Centers, 1999); B. Schissel and K. Fedec, "The Selling of Innocence: The Gestalt of Danger in the Lives of Youth Prostitutes," *Canadian Journal of Criminology* 41, 1 (1999): 33–56.

41. "The HT Report;" Lukman, "The Prevalence of Running Away from Home Among Prostituted Children," p. 158; Flowers, *Runaway Kids and Teenage Prostitution.*

42. Lukman, "The Prevalence of Running Away from Home Among Prostituted Children," p. 158; Johnson, *Teen Prostitution.*

43. Susan M. Nadon, Catherine Koverola, and Eduard H. Schudermann, "Antecedents to Prostitution: Childhood Victimization," *Journal of Interpersonal Violence* 13 (1998): 206–21.

44. Martin L. Forst and Martha E. Blom-

quist, *Missing Children: Rhetoric and Reality* (NewYork: Lexington Books, 1991).

45. *Prostitution of Children and Child-Sex Tourism*, p. 2; Debra Whitcomb and Julie Eastin, *Joining Forces Against Child Sexual Exploitation: Models for a Multidisciplinary Team Effort* (Washington, D.C.: Office of Juvenile Justice and Delinquency Prevention, 1998), p. 36.

46. Silbert and Pines, "Entrance Into Prostitution," pp. 471–73; *Prostitution of Children and Child-Sex Tourism*, p. 2.

47. U.S. Department of Justice, Child Exploitation and Obscenity Section, "Child Prostitution: Domestic Trafficking of Minors," http://www.usdoj.gov/criminal/ceos/prostitution.html.

48. Flowers, *The Victimization and Exploitation of Women and Children*; Flowers, *Runaway Kids and Teenage Prostitution*; Flowers, *The Prostitution of Women and Girls*; National Center for Missing and Exploited Children, *Female Juvenile Prostitution: Problem and Response*, 2nd ed. (Alexandria, VA: National Center for Missing and Exploited Children, 2002), pp. 7, 14, 25, 42; Augustine Brannigan and E. Gibbs Van Brunschot, "Youthful Prostitution and Child Sexual Trauma," *International Journal of Law and Psychiatry* 20 (1997): 337–54; Ross Dawson, "Child Sexual Abuse, Juvenile Prostitution and Child Pornography: The Federal Response," *Journal of Child Care* 3, 2 (1987): 19–51; Jeanne G. Kaufman and Cathy S. Widom, "Childhood Victimization, Running Away, and Delinquency," *Journal of Research in Crime and Delinquency* 36, 4 (1999): 347–70; Mimi H. Silbert and Ayala M. Pines, "Sexual Child Abuse as an Antecedent to Prostitution," *Child Abuse and Neglect* 5 (1981): 407–11.

49. *Prostitution of Children and Child-Sex Tourism*, p. 2. *See also* Ronald L. Simons and Les B. Whitbeck, "Sexual Abuse as a Precursor to Prostitution and Victimization Among Adolescent and Adult Homeless Women," *Journal of Family Issues* 12, 3 (1991): 375.

50. Flowers, *Runaway Kids and Teenage Prostitution*; Simons and Whitbeck, "Sexual Abuse as a Precursor to Prostitution and Victimization," pp. 361–79; *Prostitution of Children and Child-Sex Tourism*, p. 3; Mark D. Janus, Ann W. Burgess, and Arlene McCormack, "Histories of Sexual Abuse in Adolescent Male Runaways," *Adolescence* 22, 86 (1987): 405–18.

51. Cited Oliver, "A Review of Literature on Child Prostitution."

52. K. Stewart, *Opportunistic Prostitution and Young People in Cairns City and Mulgrave*

*Shire* (Queensland, Australia: Youth Services, 1994).

53. Evelina Giobbe, "Confronting the Liberal Lies about Prostitution," in Dorchen Leidholdt and Janice G. Raymond, eds., *The Sexual Liberals and the Attack on Feminism* (New York: Pergamon Press, 1990).

54. Stephen Gaetz, "Safe Streets for Whom? Homeless Youth, Social Exclusion, and Criminal Victimization," *Canadian Journal of Criminology and Criminal Justice* 46, 6 (2004): 426. *See also* Yates, MacKenzie, Pennbridge, and Swofford, "A Risk Profile Comparison of Homeless Youth Involved in Prostitution;" Cathy S. Widom and M. Ashley Ames, "Criminal Consequences of Childhood Sexual Victimization," *Child Abuse and Neglect* 18, 4 (1994): 308–18.

55. Christina Hoag, "New Laws Treat Teen Prostitutes as Abuse Victims," ABC News (April 19, 2009), http://www.abcnews.go.com/US/WireStory?id=7370496&page=2.

56. Heather Worth, "Up on K Road on a Saturday Night: Sex, Gender and Sex Work in Auckland," *Venereology* 13, 1 (2000):15–24.

57. Barbara Gibson, *Male Order: Life Stories from Boys Who Sell Sex* (London: Cassell, 1990). *See also* Gabe Kruks, "Gay and Lesbian Homeless/Street Youth: Special Issues and Concerns," *Journal of Adolescent Health* 12 (1991): 515–18.

58. Nicholas Ray, *Lesbian, Gay, Bisexual, and Transgender Youth: An Epidemic of Homelessness* (New York: National Gay and Lesbian Task Force Policy Institute and National Coalition for the Homeless, 2006), p. 18; Sanna J. Thompson, Andrew W. Safyer, and David E. Pollio, "Differences and Predictors of Family Reunification Among Subgroups of Runaway Youths Using Shelter Services," *Social Work Research* 25, 3 (2001): 163–72.

59. Flowers, *Runaway Kids and Teenage Prostitution*; Flowers, *The Victimization and Exploitation of Women and Children*; *Prostitution of Children and Child-Sex Tourism*, pp. 6–7, 85; Spangenberg, "Prostituted Youth in New York City;" Whitbeck and Simons, "Life on the Streets," p. 111.

60. *Prostitution of Children and Child-Sex Tourism*, p. 7; Jean Faugier and Mary Sargeant, "Boyfriends, 'Pimps,' and Clients," in Graham Scambler and Annette Scambler, eds., *Rethinking Prostitution: Purchasing Sex in the 1990s* (London: Routledge, 1997), p. 124.

61. Jody Miller and Martin D. Schwartz, "Rape Myths and Violence Against Street Prostitutes," *Deviant Behavior* 16, 1 (1995): 1–23.

62. Quoted in Bittle, *Youth Involvement in Prostitution*, p. 23. *See also* John Lowman, "Street Prostitutes in Canada: An Evaluation of the Brannigan-Fleischman Opportunity Model," *Canadian Journal of Law and Society* 6 (1991): 137–64.

63. *Female Juvenile Prostitution*, p.xi; *Prostitution of Children and Child-Sex Tourism*, p. 7; R. Barri Flowers, *Male Crime and Deviance: Exploring Its Cause, Dynamics, and Nature* (Springfield, 1L: Charles C Thomas, 2003); John Lowman and Laura Fraser, *Violence Against Persons Who Are Prostitutes: The Experience in British Columbia* (Ottawa: Department of Justice Canada, 1996).

64. *Female Juvenile Prostitution*, p. xi; Wikipedia, the Free Encyclopedia, "Gary Ridgeway," http://en.wikipedia.org/wiki/Gary_Ridgeway; R. Barri Flowers and H. Loraine Flowers, *Murders in the United States: Crimes, Killers and Victims of the Twentieth Century* (Jefferson, NC: McFarland, 2004), pp. 96–97.

65. *Prostitution of Children and Child-Sex Tourism*, p. 7; Minouche Kandel, "Whores in Court: Judicial Processing of Prostitutes in the Boston Municipal Court in 1990," *Yale Journal of Law and Feminism* 4 (1992): 346.

66. Schissel and Fedec, "The Selling of Innocence," p. 51.

67. Cited in Steven Bittle, *Youth Involvement in Prostitution*, p. 24.

68. Flowers, *The Victimization and Exploitation of Women and Children*, p. 91. *See also* Howard Davidson and Gregory Loken, *Child Pornography and Prostitution: Background and Analysis* (Arlington, VA: National Center for Missing and Exploited Children, 1998); Rita Rooney, "Children for Sale: Pornography's Dark New World," *Reader's Digest* (July 1983), p. 53; Shirley O'Brien, *Child Pornography* (Dubuque, IA: Kendall/Hunt, 1983).

69. Flowers, *The Prostitution of Women and Girls*, p. 122; Flowers, *Runaway Kids and Teenage Prostitution*; Ethel Quayle, *Child Pornography: An Internet Crime* (New York: Routledge, 2003); Monique Ferraro and Eoghan Casey, *Investigating Child Exploitation and Pornography: The Internet, Law, and Forensic Science* (Maryland Heights, MO: Academic Press, 2004); "International Online Child Pornography Ring Busted," FoxNews.com (March 15, 2006), http://www.foxnews.com/story/0,2933,187977,00.html.

70. Flowers, *Runaway Kids and Teenage Prostitution*. *See also* Jason Ryan, "Mueller: 'We're Losing' the Child Porn War," ABC News (April 23, 2008), http://abcnews.go.com/TheLaw/FedCrimes/story?id=4712725&page=1; Jason

Ryan, "'Sophisticated' Child Porn Ring Busted," ABC News (March 4, 2008), http://abcnews.go.com/TheLaw/story?id=4388379.

71. "International Online Child Pornography Ring Busted;" Flowers, *Runaway Kids and Teenage Prostitution*; Herbert Bronwyn, "Child Pornography Arrests," ABC News (June 1, 2009), http://www.abc.net.au/am/content/2009/s2585864.htm; Terry Frieden, "170 Arrested in Global Child Porn Investigation," CNN.com (December 13, 2008), http://www.cnn.com/2008/CRIME/12/12/porn.arrests/index.html; "27 Charged in Child Porn Sting," CNN.com (March 16, 2006), http://www.cnn.com/2006/LAW/03/15/childporn.arrests/index.html; "Feds Arrest 125 People Nationwide in Child Porn Investigation," *USA Today* (October 19, 2006), http://www.usatoday.com/news/nation/2006-10-19-child-porn-arrests_x.htm; "Internet Sting Identifies 1,500 Suspected Child Pornographers," CNN Interactive (September 30, 1997), http://www.cnn.com/US/9709/30/cybersting/.

72. *Female Juvenile Prostitution*, pp. vii, 5, 7, 12, 14; Flowers, *Runaway Kids and Teenage Prostitution*; *Prostitution of Children and Child-Sex Tourism*, pp. 6–7; Simons and Whitbeck, "Sexual Abuse as a Precursor to Prostitution and Victimization," pp. 361–79; Kruks, "Gay and Lesbian Homeless/Street Youth," pp. 515–18; Brannigan and Van Brunschot, "Youthful Prostitution and Child Sexual Trauma," pp. 337–54; Patti Feuereisen and Caroline Pincus, *Invisible Girls: The Truth About Sexual Abuse*, 2nd ed. (Seattle, WA: Seal Press, 2009); Ann W. Burgess and Marieanne L. Clark, eds., *Child Pornography and Sex Rings* (New York: Free Press, 1984); Diana E. Russell, *Sex Exploitation* (Beverly Hills, Sage, 1984); Christopher Baley and Loretta Young, "Juvenile Prostitution and Child Sexual Abuse: A Controlled Study," *Canadian Journal of Community Mental Health* 6, 1 (1987): 5–26.

73. *Female Juvenile Prostitution*, pp. vii, 14; Rashmi Gangamma, Natasha Slesnick, Paula Toviessi, and Julianne Serovich, "Comparison of HIV Risks among Gay, Lesbian, Bisexual and Heterosexual Homeless Youth," *Journal of Youth and Adolescence* 37, 4 (2008); Nancy Haley, Elise Roy, Pascale Leclerc, and Jean-François Boivin, "HIV High Risk Profile of Male Street Youth Involved in Survival Sex," *Sexually Transmitted Infections* 80 (2004): 526–30; Doreen Rosenthal and Susan Moore, "Homeless Youths: Sexual and Drug-Related Behavior, Sexual Beliefs and HIV/AIDS Risk," *AIDS Care* 6, 1 (1994): 83–94; Priscilla M. Pyett and Deborah J. Warr, "Vulnerability on the Streets: Female Sex Workers and HIV Risk," *AIDS Care* 9, 5 (1997): 539–47; Mary J. Rotheram-Borus, Cheryl Koopman, and Anke A. Ehrhardt, "Homeless Youth and HIV Infection," *American Psychologist* 46, 11 (1991): 1188–97; Beth E. Molnar, Alex H. Kral, and John K. Watters, *Street Youth at Risk for AIDS* (Rockville, MD: National Institute on Drug Abuse, 1994); A. R. Markos, A. A. Wade, and M. Walzman, "The Adolescent Male Prostitute and Sexually Transmitted Diseases, HIV and AIDs," *Journal of Adolescence* 17 (1994): 123–30.

74. *Prostitution of Children and Child-Sex Tourism*, p. 6. See also Faugier and Sargeant, "Boyfriends, 'Pimps,' and Clients;" Donna Hughes, *Pimps and Predators on the Internet: Globalizing the Sexual Exploitation of Women and Children* (New York: ECPAT-US, 1999); Evelina Giobbe, "A Comparison of Pimps and Batterers," *Michigan Journal of Gender and Law* 1, 1 (1993): 33–57.

75. Hughes, *Pimps and Predators on the Internet*; *Prostitution of Children and Child-Sex Tourism*, p. 6; Cathy S. Widom and Joseph B. Kuhns, "Childhood Victimization and Subsequent Risk for Promiscuity, Prostitution and Teenage Pregnancy: A Prospective Study," *American Journal of Public Health* 86 (1996): 1607–12; U.S. Department of Justice, *Use of Computers in the Sexual Exploitation of Children* (Washington, D.C.: Office of Justice Programs, 1997).

76. Clare Tattersall, *Drugs, Runaways, and Teen Prostitution* (New York: Rosen, 1999), p. 38.

77. Cited in Johnson, *Teen Prostitution*, p. 91.

78. Spangenberg, "Prostituted Youth in New York City."

79. *Prostitution of Children and Child-Sex Tourism*, p. 10; Christina Hoag, "Teen Prostitutes Rescued, Not Arrested," *Tulsa World* (April 19, 2009), http://www.tulsaworld.com/news/article.aspx?subjectid=338&articleid=20090419_13_A10_Uietfe479338&archive=yes; Jim Patten, "Police: Teen Call Girls Grateful They Were Caught," *The Eagle Tribune* (September 13, 2007), http://www.eagletribune.com/punews/local_story_256115550; Kelly Dedel, *Juvenile Runaways* (Washington, D.C.: Office of Community Oriented Policing Services, 2006), pp. 3–5, http://www.ncjrs.gov/App/Publications/abstract.aspx?ID=235092.

80. *Prostitution of Children and Child-Sex Tourism*, p. 10; U.S. Department of Justice, Federal Bureau of Investigation, Uniform Crime

Reporting Program, http://www.fbi.gov/ucr/ ucr.htm; Flowers, *The Adolescent Criminal*; Howard N. Snyder, *Law Enforcement and Juvenile Crime* (Washington, D.C.: Office of Juvenile Justice and Delinquency Prevention, 2001).

81. R. Barri Flowers, *Minorities and Criminality* (Westport, CT: Praeger, 1990), pp. 95–103; Marie L. Talashek, Nilda Peragallo, Kathleen Norr, and Barbara L. Dancy, "The Context of Risky Behaviors for Latino Youth," *Journal of Transcultural Nursing* 15 (2004): 131–38; Claudia L. Moreno, "The Relationship Between Culture, Gender, Structural Factors, Abuse, Trauma, and HIV/AIDS For Latinas," *Qualitative Health Research* 17 (2007): 340–52; Celia Williamson and Gail Folaron, "Understanding the Experiences of Street Level Prostitutes," *Qualitative Social Work* 2 (2003): 271–87; Sherry Deren, Michele Shedlin, W. Rees Davis, Michael C. Clatts, Salvador Balcorta, Mark M. Beardsley, Jesus Sanchez, and Don Des Jarlais, "Dominican, Mexican, and Puerto Rican Prostitutes: Drug Use and Sexual Behaviors," *Hispanic Journal of Behavioral Sciences* 19 (1997): 202–13.

82. Flowers, *Runaway Kids and Teenage Prostitution*; Flowers, *The Prostitution of Women and Girls*; Flowers, *The Adolescent Criminal*.

83. *Crime in the United States, 2008*, Table 38.

84. *Ibid.*

85. Flowers, *The Prostitution of Women and Girls*; Spangenberg, "Prostituted Youth in New York City;" *Prostitution of Children and Child-Sex Tourism*, p. 2; "Survey Reveals Extent of Teen Prostitution," ABC News (August 9, 2006), http://abcnews.go.com/Health/story? id=2292336&page=1&CMP=OTC-RSS-Feeds0312; Geraldine Sealey, "Exposing America's Ugly Child Secret," ABC News (December 13, 2008), http://abcnews.go.com/US/story ?id=90557&page=1.

86. Flowers, *The Adolescent Criminal*; Flowers, *Runaway Kids and Teenage Prostitution*; *Prostitution of Children and Child-Sex Tourism*, p. 7; Widom and Ames, "Criminal Consequences of Childhood Sexual Victimization;" Brannigan and Van Brunschot, "Youthful Prostitution and Child Sexual Trauma;" R. Barri Flowers, *Kids Who Commit Adult Crimes: A Study of Serious Juvenile Criminality and Delinquency* (Binghamton, NY: Haworth Press, 2002).

87. See, for example, "Two Men Plead Guilty in Teen Prostitution Ring," Boston.com (September 15, 2009), http://www.boston.com/

news/local/maine/articles/2009/09/15/2_men_ plead_guilty_in_teen_prostitution_ring/; "Feds Rescue Suspected Teen Prostitutes in Sweep," KomoNews.com (Feburary 23, 2009), http: //www.komonews.com/news/40093317.html; Delvin Barrett, "FBI, Police Rescue Child Prostitutes Around U.S.," MyFoxPhoenix.com (February 23, 2009), http://www.myfoxphoe nix.com/dpp/news/child_prostitution_bust_02 2309; "Two Arizona Teens Accused of Pimping Other Girls," CNN.com/Crime (February 25, 2009), http://www.cnn.com/2009/CRIME/ 02/25/teen.pimp/index.html?imw=Y&iref=mp storyemail; Angela K. Brown, "Police: Teen Gang Ran Prostitution Ring," BreitBart TV (January 16, 2008), http://www.breitbart.com/ article.php?id=D8U70D9O0&show_article=1; David Schoetz, "Teen Sex For Sale: Middle School Madam Busted," ABC News (March 25, 2008), http://abcnews.go.com/GMA/story?id =4519538&page=1; Jason Ryan and Theresa Cook, "FBI Arrests 300 in Child Prostitution Sting," ABC News (June 25, 2008), http://abc news.go.com/TheLaw/FedCrimes/story?id=52 47386.

88. See, for example, "Teen Prostitution on Craigslist," CKNW News Talk Sports (June 29, 2009), http://www.cknw.com/Channels/Reg/ NewsLocal/Story.aspx/Story.aspx?ID=1107995; Greg Sandoval and Declan McCullagh, "Is Craigslist the World's Biggest Bordello?" CNET News (March 6, 2009), http://news.cnet.com/ is-craigslist-the-worlds-biggest-bordello/; Jane Minogue, "Prostitutes, the Internet, and Regulation, Part I," HuffPost Social News (March 25, 2009), http://www.huffingtonpost.com/ jane-minogue/part-i-prostitutes-the-in_b_ 178272.html; "7 Charged in Alleged Prostitution Ring on Craigslist," CNN.com (May 20, 2009), http://www.cnn.com/2009/CRIME/ 05/20/craigslist.prostitution/index.html?; Steven Musil, "Teen Suspected of Using Craigslist for Prostitution," CNET News (April 8, 2007), http://news.cnet.com/8301-10784_3-6174334-7.html; Jackson Holtz, "Craigslist Sex Ad Leads to 15 Arrests," HeraldNet (August 13, 2008), http://www.heraldnet.com/article/2008 0813/NEWS01/40977851&news01ad=1.

89. David Finkelhor and Richard Ormrod, *Prostitution of Juveniles: Patterns from NIBRS* (Washington, D.C.: Office of Justice Programs, 2004), pp. 1–12. *See also* Byran A. Fassett and Bill Walsh, "Juvenile Prostitution: An Overlooked Form of Child Abuse," *The APSAC Advisor* 7, 1 (1994): 9.

90. Finkelhor and Ormrod, *Prostitution of Juveniles*, pp. 6–7.

## Chapter 11

1. R. Barri Flowers, *The Adolescent Criminal: An Examination of Today's Juvenile Offender* (Jefferson, NC: McFarland, 2009), p. 55.

2. National Center for Missing and Exploited Children, *Prostitution of Children and Child-Sex Tourism* (Alexandria, VA: National Center for Missing and Exploited Children, 1999), p. 2; Mia Spangenberg, "Prostituted Youth in New York City: An Overview," (2001), http://www.libertadlatina.org/US_ECPAT_Ch ild_Prostitution_NYC.htm.

3. Nancy E. Walker, "Executive Summary: How Many Teens Are Prostituted?" fce.msu. edu/Family_Impact_Seminars/pdf/2002-2. pdf.

4. R. Barri Flowers, *Runaway Kids and Teenage Prostitution: America's Lost, Abandoned, and Sexually Exploited Children* (Westport, CT: Greenwood Press, 2001), pp. 107–8; Michelle Stransky and David Finkelhor, *How Many Juveniles Are Involved in Prostitution in the United States?* (Durham, NC: Crimes Against Children Research Center, 2008).

5. Spangenberg, "Prostituted Youth in New York City;" Flowers, *Runaway Kids and Teenage Prostitution*; Walker, "Executive Summary;" David Barrett, "Young People and Prostitution: Perpetrators in Our Midst," *International Review of Law, Computers and Technology* 12, 3 (1998): 475–86; R. Barri Flowers, *The Victimization and Exploitation of Women and Children: A Study of Physical, Mental and Sexual Maltreatment in the United States* (Jefferson, NC: McFarland, 1994), p. 37; S. Jorgenson, H. Thornburg, and J. Williams, "The Experience of Running Away: Perceptions of Adolescents Seeking Help in a Shelter Case Facility," *High School Journal* 12 (1980): 87–96.

6. Heather Hammer, David Finkelhor, and Andrea J. Sedlak, *Runaway/Thrownaway Children: National Estimates and Characteristics*, NISMART Bulletin Series (Washington, D.C.: Office of Juvenile Justice and Delinquency Prevention, 2002), pp. 2, 5.

7. National Runaway Switchboard, *Keeping America's Runaway and At-Risk Youth Safe and Off the Streets*, http://www.1800runaway.org/.

8. Patricia Hersch, "Coming of Age on City Streets," *Psychology Today* 22, 1 (1988): 34. *See also* Michael S. Scott and Kelly Dedel, *Street Prostitution*, 2nd ed. (Washington, D.C.: Office of Community Oriented Policing Services, 2006).

9. Flowers, *The Adolescent Criminal*, pp.

49–55; Clare Tattersall, *Drugs, Runaways, and Teen Prostitution* (New York: Rosen, 1999), p. 8; Anastasia Volkonsky, "Legalizing the 'Profession' Would Sanction the Abuse," *Insight on the News* 11 (1995): 21.

10. Flowers, *Runaway Kids and Teenage Prostitution*; Alma C. Molino, "Characteristics of Help-Seeking Street Youth and Non-Street Youth," 2007 National Symposium on Homelessness Research, March 1–2, 2007, p. 7–4; http://aspe.hhs.gov/hsp/homelessness/sympo sium07/molino/index.htm; Z. M. Lukman, "The Prevalence of Running Away from Home among Prostituted Youth in Malaysia," *Journal of Social Sciences* 5, 3 (2009): 157–62; CRS Report for Congress, *Runaway and Homeless Youth: Demographics, Programs, and Emerging Issues* (Washington, D.C.: Congressional Research Service, 2007), pp. 3–4; Jody M. Greene, Susan T. Ennett, and Christopher L. Ringwalt, "Prevalence and Correlates of Survival Sex Among Runaway and Homeless Youth," *American Journal of Public Health* 89, 9 (1999): 1406; Joan J. Johnson, *Teen Prostitution* (Danbury, CT: Franklin Watts, 1992).

11. *Runaway and Homeless Youth*, p. 5; Marjorie J. Robertson and Paul A. Toro, "Homeless Youth: Research, Intervention, and Policy," http://aspe.hhs.gov/ProgSys/homeless/sympo sium/3-Youth.htm.

12. *Runaway and Homeless Youth*, p. 5. *See also* Christopher L. Ringwalt, Jody M. Greene, Marjorie J. Robertson, and Melissa McPheeters, "The Prevalence of Homelessness Among Adolescents in the United States," *American Journal of Public Health* 88, 9 (1998): 1325–29.

13. Robertson and Toro, "Homeless Youth;" Nicholas Ray, *Lesbian, Gay, Bisexual, and Transgender Youth: An Epidemic of Homelessness* (New York: National Gay and Lesbian Task Force Policy Institute and National Coalition for the Homeless, 2006), p. 12.

14. U.S. Department of Health and Human Services, Family Youth and Services Bureau, *Youth with Runaway, Throwaway, and Homeless Experiences: Prevalence, Drug Use, and Other At-Risk Behaviors* (Silver Springs, MD: National Clearinghouse on Families and Youth, 1995), p. E6.

15. Les B. Whitbeck and Ronald L. Simons, "Life on the Streets: The Victimization of Runaway and Homeless Adolescents," *Youth and Society* 22, 1 (1990): 108–25.

16. Spangenberg, "Prostituted Youth in New York City;" Lukman, "The Prevalence of Running Away from Home Among Prostituted Youth," p. 158.

17. Martin L. Forst and Martha E. Blomquist, *Missing Children: Rhetoric and Reality* (NewYork: Lexington Books, 1991).

18. R. Barri Flowers, *The Prostitution of Women and Girls* (Jefferson, NC: McFarland, 2005); Suzanne Smalley, "Nationwide Increase in Teen Prostitution: Trends Show Kids Getting Younger, More from Middle Class Homes," *Newsweek* (August 10, 2003), http://www.cou plescompany.com/Wireservice/Parenting/teen Prostitution.htm.

19. Klass Kids Foundation, "The HT Report," (February 2009), http://www.klaaskids. org/pg-ht-report.htm; Richard J. Estes and Neil A. Weiner, *The Commercial Sexual Exploitation of Children in the U.S., Canada, and Mexico* (Philadelphia, PA: University of Pennsylvania, 2002), p. 92.

20. Susan K. Hunter, "Prostitution Is Cruelty and Abuse to Women and Children," *Michigan Journal of Gender and Law* 1, 91 (1993): 91–104.

21. D. Kelly Weisberg, *Children of the Night: A Study of Adolescent Prostitution* (Lexington, MA: Lexington Books, 1985), p. 94.

22. Mimi H. Silbert and Ayala M. Pines, "Occupational Hazards of Street Prostitutes," *Criminal Justice and Behavior* 8 (1981): 397; Mimi H. Silbert and Ayala M. Pines, "Entrance Into Prostitution," *Youth and Society* 13 (1982): 471–500.

23. Susan McIntyre, "The Youngest Profession — The Oldest Oppression: A Study of Sex Work," in Christopher Bagley and Kanka Mallick, eds., *Child Sexual Abuse and Adult Offenders: New Theory and Research* (London, Ashgate, 1999), pp. 159–92.

24. Cited in Anne Rasmusson, "Commercial Sexual Exploitation of Children: A Literature Review," Alliance for Speaking the Truths on Prostitution and Center for Urban and Regional Affairs (June 1, 1999), http://members. shaw.ca/pdg/exploitation_of_children.html #_Toc452540114.

25. Marica Cohen, *Juvenile Prostitution* (Washington, D.C.: National Association of Counties Research, Inc., 1987).

26. Miriam Saphira, *The Commercial Exploitation of Children* (Auckland, NZ: ECPAT, 2001).

27. Spangenberg, "Prostituted Youth in New York City."

28. *Ibid. See also* Karen E. Walker, "Exploitation of Children and Young People Through Prostitution," *Journal of Child Health Care* 6 (2002): 182–88.

29. Flowers, *Runaway Kids and Teenage Pros-titution*; Estes and Weiner, *The Commercial Sexual Exploitation of Children*, pp. 44–62; *Prostitution of Children and Child-Sex Tourism*, pp. 2–3; Flowers, *The Victimization and Exploitation of Women and Children*; National Center for Missing and Exploited Children, *Female Juvenile Prostitution: Problem and Response*, 2nd ed. (Alexandria, VA: National Center for Missing and Exploited Children, 2002), pp. 7, 14, 54; Daniel S. Campagna and Donald Poffenberger, *The Sexual Trafficking in Children: An Investigation of the Child Sex Trade* (Dover, MA: Auburn House, 1988), pp. 65–66; Ann W. Burgess, *The Sexual Victimization of Adolescents* (Rockville, MD: U.S. Department of Health and Human Services, 1985).

30. Rasmusson, "Commercial Sexual Exploitation of Children."

31. *Female Juvenile Prostitution*, p. 14; Flowers, *Runaway Kids and Teenage Prostitution*; Flowers, *The Victimization and Exploitation of Women and Children*; Jane A. Siegel and Linda M. Williams, "The Relationship Between Child Sexual Abuse and Female Delinquency and Crime: A Prospective Study," *Journal of Research in Crime and Delinquency* 40, 1 (2003): 71–94; Steven Bittle, *Youth Involvement in Prostitution: A Literature Review and Annotated Bibliography* (Ottawa: Department of Justice Canada, 2002), pp. vi, 15–16, 19–20; Mimi H. Silbert and Ayala M. Pines, "Sexual Child Abuse as an Antecedent to Prostitution," *Child Abuse and Neglect* 5 (1981): 407–11; Magnus J. Seng, "Child Sexual Abuse and Adolescent Prostitution: A Comparative Analysis," *Adolescence* 24 (1989): 665–75.

32. Sparky Harlan, Luanne L. Rodgers, and Brian Slattery, *Male and Female Adolescent Prostitution: Huckleberry House Sexual Minority Youth Services Project* (Washington, D.C.: U.S. Department of Health and Human Services, 1981), p. 21.

33. Mimi H. Silbert, "Delancey Street Study: Prostitution and Sexual Assault," summary of results, Delancey Street Foundation, San Francisco, 1982, p. 3.

34. Walker, "Executive Summary."

35. See, for example, Augustine Brannigan and E. Gibbs Van Brunschot, "Youthful Prostitution and Child Sexual Trauma," *International Journal of Law and Psychiatry* 20 (1997): 337–54; Cathy S. Widom and Joseph B. Kuhns, "Childhood Victimization and Subsequent Risk for Promiscuity, Prostitution and Teenage Pregnancy: A Prospective Study," *American Journal of Public Health* 86 (1996): 1607–10; Mary J. Rotheram-Borus, Karen A. Mahler, Cheryl Koopman, and Kris Langabeer, "Sexual Abuse

History and Associated Multiple Risk Behavior in Adolescent Runaways," *American Journal of Orthopsychiatry* 66 (1996): 390–400; Christopher M. Earls and Helene David, "Early Family and Sexual Experiences of Male and Female Prostitutes," *Canadian's Mental Health* 37/38 (1990): 7–11.

36. Evelina Giobbe, "Confronting the Liberal Lies about Prostitution," in Dorchen Leidholdt and Janice G. Raymond, eds., *The Sexual Liberals and the Attack on Feminism* (New York: Pergamon Press, 1990).

37. Dusti-S. Myers, "Generational Prostitution in the United States," *Associated Content Community* (December 2, 2008), http://www.associatedcontent.com/article/1239336/generational_prostitution_in_the_united.html?cat=9.

38. Campagna and Poffenberger, *The Sexual Trafficking in Children*, p.65. *See also* Susan M. Nadon, Catherine Koverola, and Eduard H. Schuderman, "Antecedents to Prostitution: Childhood Victimization," *Journal of Interpersonal Violence* 13 (1998): 206–21.

39. Ronald L. Simons and Les B. Whitbeck, "Sexual Abuse as a Precursor to Prostitution and Victimization Among Adolescent and Adult Homeless Women," *Journal of Family Issues* 12, 3 (1991): 361–79.

40. Weisberg, *Children of the Night*.

41. Flowers, *Runaway Kids and Teenage Prostitution*; Rotheram-Borus, Mahler, Koopman, and Langabeer, "Sexual Abuse History and Associated Multiple Risk Behavior in Adolescent Runaways;" Les B. Whitbeck, Danny R. Hoyt, and Kevin A. Ackley, "Abusive Family Backgrounds and Later Victimization Among Runaway and Homeless Youth," *Journal of Research on Adolescence* 7, 4 (1997): 375–92; Arlene R. Stiffman, "Physical and Sexual Abuse in Runaway Youths," *Child Abuse and Neglect* 13, 3 (1989): 417–26; Pam Oliver, "A Review of Literature on Child Prostitution," *Social Policy Journal of New Zealand* 19 (2002), http://www.thefreelibrary.com/_/print/PrintArticle.aspx?id=99849275.

42. Cited in Hersch, "Coming of Age on City Streets," p. 31. *See also* Kimberly A. Tyler, Les B. Whitbeck, Danny R. Hoyt, and Ana Mari Cauce, "Risk Factors for Sexual Victimization Among Male and Female Homeless and Runaway Youth," *Journal of Interpersonal Violence* 19 (2004): 503–20.

43. P. David Kurtz, Gail L. Kurtz, and Sara Jarvis, "Problems of Maltreated Runaway Youth," *Adolescence* 26 (1991): 543–55. *See also* Tyler, Whitbeck, Hoyt, and Cauce, "Risk Factors for Sexual Victimization Among Male and Female Homeless and Runaway Youth," pp. 503–20.

44. Susan F. McClanahan, Gary M. McClelland, Karen M. Abram, and Linda A. Teplin, "Pathways into Prostitution Among Female Jail Detainees and Their Implications for Mental Health Services," *Psychiatric Services* 50 (1999): 1606–13.

45. Lynn Rew, Margaret Taylor-Seehafer, Nancy Thomas, and Ronald Yockey, "Correlates of Resilience in Homeless Adolescents," *Journal of Nursing Scholarship* 33, 1 (2001): 33–40.

46. Westat, Inc., *National Evaluation of Runaway and Homeless Youth* (Washington, D.C.: U.S. Department of Health and Human Services, 1997).

47. Flowers, *Runaway Kids and Teenage Prostitution*, pp. 143–47.

48. Deborah R. Brock, *Making Work, Making Trouble: Prostitution as a Social Problem* (Toronto: University of Toronto Press, 1998).

49. Steven Bittle, Reconstructing "Youth Prostitution" as the "Sexual Procurement of Children": A Case Study, an unpublished Master's Thesis, (Burnaby, BC: Simon Fraser University, 1999).

50. Flowers, *Runaway Kids and Teenage Prostitution*; "The HT Report;" Kathleen Barry, *The Prostitution of Sexuality* (New York: New York University Press, 1995), p. 198; Kamika Dunlap and Barbara Grady, "City Comes to Grips with Teen Prostitution," *Oakland Tribune* (April 21, 2008), http://www.insidebayarea.com/teenprostitution/ci_9000424.

51. Flowers, *The Prostitution of Women and Girls*, p. 101; Flowers, *Runaway Kids and Teenage Prostitution*; *Prostitution of Children and Child-Sex Tourism*, p. 5.

52. Cited in Johnson, *Teen Prostitution*, p. 78. *See also* Celia Williamson and Terry Cluse-Tolar, "Pimp-Controlled Prostitution: Still an Integral Part of Street Life," *Violence Against Women* 8 (2002): 1074–92.

53. *Prostitution of Children and Child-Sex Tourism*, p. 4; Gregory A. Loken, "Child Prostitution," in U.S. Department of Justice, *Child Pornography and Prostitution: Background and Legal Analysis* (Alexandria, VA: National Center for Missing and Exploited Children, 1987).

54. Flowers, *Runaway Kids and Teenage Prostitution*, pp. 119–26.

55. Spangenberg, "Prostituted Youth in New York City."

56. Deborah Jones, "Pimped," *Chatelaine* 67 (November 1994), p. 111.

57. Flowers, *Runaway Kids and Teenage Pros-*

*titution*; Spangenberg, "Prostituted Youth in New York City;" George Gardner, "Hookers Go Hi-Tech, Advertize on Craigslist," Tech. Blorge (July 26, 2007), http://tech.blorge.com/Structure:%20/2007/07/26/hookers-go-hi-tech-advertise-on-craigslist/.

58. Spangenberg, "Prostituted Youth in New York City;" Nicholas D. Kristof, "The Pimps' Slaves," *New York Times* (March 16, 2008), http://www.nytimes.com/2008/03/16/opinion/16kristof.html?_r=2&oref=slogin&oref=slogin. *See also* "Study: Many Pimps Have Been Prostitutes," UPI.com (April 16, 2009), http://www.upi.com/Top_News/2009/04/16/Study-Many-pimps-have-been-prostitutes/UPI-94781239939726/.

59. Johnson, *Teen Prostitution*, pp. 76–77.

60. Rasmusson, "Commercial Sexual Exploitation of Children."

61. Flowers, *Runaway Kids and Teenage Prostitution*; R. Barri Flowers, *Female Crime, Criminals and Cellmates: An Exploration of Female Criminality and Delinquency* (Jefferson, NC: McFarland, 2009), p. 152; Russell Goldman, "Parents Who Pimp Their Children," ABC News (October 8, 2007), http://abcnews.go.com/US/story?id=3691604&page=1; Richard Dembo, Linda Williams, Werner Wothke, James Schmeidler, and C. Hendricks Brown, "The Role of Family Factors, Physical Abuse, and Sexual Victimization Experiences in High-Risk Youths' Alcohol and Other Drug Use and Delinquency: A Longitudinal Model," *Violence and Victims* 7, 3 (1992): 245–66.

62. Cited in Goldman, "Parents Who Pimp Their Children."

63. Spangenberg, "Prostituted Youth in New York City;" Vincent J. Webb, Charles M. Katz, and Scott H. Decker, "Assessing the Validity of Self-Reports by Gang Members: Results from the Arrest Drug Abuse Monitoring Program," *Crime and Delinquency* 52 (2006): 232–52; Amy Schalet, Geoffrey Hunt, and Karen Joe-Laidler, "Respectability and Autonomy: The Articulation and Meaning of Sexuality Among the Girls in the Gang," *Journal of Contemporary Ethnography* 32 (2003): 108–43; Kevin A. Yoder, Les B. Whitbeck, and Danny R. Hoyt, "Gang Involvement and Membership Among Homeless and Runaway Youth," *Youth and Society* 34, 4 (2003): 441–67; Kit R. Roane, "Gangs Turn to New Trade: Young Prostitutes," *New York Times* (July 11, 1999): 23; Shay Bilchik, *1996 Youth Gang Survey: Summary* (Washington, D.C.: Office of Juvenile Justice and Delinquency Prevention, 1999); Kayleen Hazelhurst and Cameron Hazelhurst, eds., *Gangs and Youth Subcultures: International Explorations* (New Brunswick, NJ: Transaction Publishers, 1989).

64. *See, for example* Dorothy H. Bracey, *"Baby-Pros": Preliminary Profiles of Juvenile Prostitutes* (New York: John Jay Press, 1979), p. 23; The Enablers," *Juvenile Prostitution in Minnesota: The Report of a Research Project* (St. Paul, MN: The Enablers, 1978), p. 57; Jennifer James, "Prostitute-Pimp Relationships," *Medical Aspects of Human Sexuality* 7 (1973): 147–63.

65. Flowers, *The Adolescent Criminal*, p. 58.

66. Rasmusson, "Commercial Sexual Exploitation of Children." *See also* Mimi H. Silbert and Ayala M. Pines, "Victimization of Street Prostitutes," *Victimology* 7 (1982): 122–33.

67. Flowers, *The Prostitution of Women and Girls*, p. 103. *See also* Kendra Nixon, Leslie Tutty, Pamela Downe, Kelly Gorkoff, and Jane Ursel, "The Everyday Occurrence: Violence in the Lives of Girls Exploited Through Prostitution," *Violence Against Women* 8 (2002): 1016–43.

68. Quoted in *Ibid.*, p. 51. *See also* Marg Csapo, "Juvenile Prostitution," *Canadian Journal of Special Education* 2, 2 (1986): 145–70.

69. Anastasia Volkonsky, "Legalizing the 'Profession' Would Sanction the Abuse," *Insight on the News* 11 (1995): 20. *See also* Minouche Kandel, "Whores in Court: Judicial Processing of Prostitutes in the Boston Municipal Court in 1990," *Yale Journal of Law and Feminism* 4 (1992): 329.

70. Volkonsky, "Legalizing the 'Profession' Would Sanction the Abuse," p. 20. *See also* John J. Potterat, Devon D. Brewer, Stephen Q. Muth, Richard B. Rothenberg, Donald E. Woodhouse, John B. Muth, Heather K. Stites, and Stuart Brody, "Mortality in a Long-term Open Cohort of Prostitute Women," *American Journal of Epidemiology* 159, 8 (2004): 778.

71. Quoted in Kristof, "The Pimps' Slaves."

72. Quoted in Jones, "Pimped," p. 112.

73. Quoted in Spangenberg, "Prostituted Youth in New York City." *See also* Neil P. McKeganey and Marina U. Barnard, *Sex Work on the Streets: Prostitutes and Their Clients* (Buckingham, UK: Open University Press, 1996).

74. Hunter, "Prostitution Is Cruelty and Abuse to Women and Children."

75. Cited in Spangenberg, "Prostituted Youth in New York City."

76. Hunter, "Prostitution Is Cruelty and Abuse to Women and Children."

77. Barbara Goldsmith, "Women on the

Edge: A Reporter at Large," *New Yorker* 69 (April 26, 1993): 65.

78. Adrian N. LeBlanc, "I'm a Shadow," *Seventeen* 52 (March 1993): 216. *See also* Walker, "Exploitation of Children and Young People Through Prostitution," pp. 182–88.

79. Flowers, *Runaway Kids and Teenage Prostitution*; Flowers, *The Prostitution of Women and Girls*; *Female Juvenile Prostitution*, pp. vii, 5, 14–15; HCH Clinicians' Network, "Crossing to Safety: Transgender Health and Homelessness," *Healing Hands* 6 (2002): 1–6; Walker, "Executive Summary;" Ray, *Lesbian, Gay, Bisexual, and Transgender Youth*, p. 385; Lisa S. Wagner, Linda Carlin, Ana Mari Cauce, and Adam Tenner, "A Snapshot of Homeless Youth in Seattle: Their Characteristics, Behaviors and Beliefs About HIV Protective Strategies," *Journal of Community Health* 26, 3 (2001): 219–32.

80. *Prostitution of Children and Child-Sex Tourism*, p. 7. *See also* Debra Whitcomb and Julie Eastin, *Joining Forces Against Child Sexual Exploitation: Models for a Multidisciplinary Team Effort* (Washington, D.C.: Office of Juvenile Justice and Delinquency Prevention, 1998), p. 37; Martin A. Monto, "Female Prostitution, Customers, and Violence," *Violence Against Women*, 10 (2004): 160–88.

81. R. Barri Flowers, *Male Crime and Deviance: Exploring Its Causes, Dynamics, and Nature* (Springfield, IL: Charles C Thomas, 2003); R. Barri Flowers, *Murder, at the End of the Day and Night: A Study of Criminal Homicide Offenders, Victims, and Circumstances* (Springfield, IL: Charles C Thomas, 2002), pp. 93–103; Potterat, Brewer, Muth, Rothenberg, Woodhouse, Muth, Stites, and Brody, "Mortality in a Longterm Open Cohort of Prostitute Women," pp. 778–85.

82. *Female Juvenile Prostitution*, p. xi; Flowers, *Murder, at the End of the Day and Night*; Ann Rule, *Green River, Running Red: The Real Story of the Green River Killer—America's Deadliest Serial Murderer* (New York: Pocket Star, 2005); Brian Lane and Wilfred Gregg, *The Encyclopedia of Serial Killers* (New York: Berkley, 1995); David Lester, *Serial Killers: The Insatiable Passion* (Philadelphia, PA: The Charles Press, 1995).

83. Walker, "Executive Summary." *See also* Claire E. Sterk, *Tricking and Tripping: Prostitution in the Era of AIDS* (Putnam Valley, NY: Social Change Press, 2000).

84. *Prostitution of Children and Child-Sex Tourism*, p. 8. *See also* Timothy P. Johnson, Jennie R. Aschkenasy, Mary R. Herbers, and Stephen A. Gillenwater, "Self-Reported Risk Factors for AIDS Among Homeless Youth," *AIDS Education and Prevention* 8 (1996): 308–22; Beth E. Molnar, Alex H. Kral, and John K. Watters, *Street Youth at Risk for AIDS* (Rockville, MD: National Institute on Drug Abuse, 1994).

85. Wagner, Carlin, Cauce, and Tenner, "A Snapshot of Homeless Youth in Seattle," p. 227.

86. *Female Juvenile Prostitution*, pp. x, 15.

87. Tattersall, *Drugs, Runaways, and Teen Prostitution*, p. 28.

88. Flowers, *Runaway Kids and Teenage Prostitution*; Spangenberg, "Prostituted Youth in New York City;" Campagna and Poffenberger, *The Sexual Trafficking in Children*, p. 64; Lynn Rew, Tiffany A. Whittaker, Margaret Taylor-Seehafer, and Lorie R. Smith, "Sexual Health and Protective Resources in Gay, Lesbian, Bisexual, and Heterosexual Homeless Youth," *Journal for Specialists in Pediatric Nursing* 10, 1 (2005): 16; Kevin Cwayna, *Knowing Where the Fountains Are: Stories and Realities of Homeless Youth* (Minneapolis, MN: Deaconess Press, 1993).

89. Cwayna, *Knowing Where the Fountains Are*, p. 72.

90. *Ibid.*

91. R. L. Sticof, L. F. Novick, and J. T. Kennedy, "HIV Seroprevalence in Facilities for Runaway and Homeless Adolescents in Four States: Florida, Texas, Louisiana and New York," paper presented at the Sixth International Conference on AIDS, San Francisco, CA, 1990.

92. Ray, *Lesbian, Gay, Bisexual, and Transgender Youth*, p. 54.

93. Flowers, *Runaway Kids and Teenage Prostitution*, pp. 113–14.

94. Goldsmith, "Women on the Edge," p. 74.

95. Cited in Flowers, *The Adolescent Criminal*, p. 63.

96. Hersch, "Coming of Age on City Streets," p. 37.

97. Oliver, "A Review of Literature on Child Prostitution." *See also* D. Lemmey and P. Tice, "Two Tragic Forms of Child Sexual Abuse: Are They Often Overlooked?" *Journal of Child Sexual Abuse* 9, 2 (2000): 86–106; A. Moscicki, B. Winkler, C. Irwin, and J. Schacter, "Differences in Biologic Maturation, Sexual Behavior, and Sexually Transmitted Disease Between Adolescents with and Without Cervical Intraepithelial Neoplasia," *Journal of Pediatrics* 115 (1989): 487–93.

98. U.S. Department of Justice, Federal Bureau of Investigation, *Crime in the United States,*

*2008*, Table 40, http://www.fbi.gov/ucr/cius 2008/arrests/index.html.

99. *Ibid.*

100. *Ibid.*; Flowers, *The Adolescent Criminal*; Flowers, *Female Crime, Criminals and Cellmates.*

101. Flowers, *Female Crime, Criminals and Cellmates*; Flowers, *The Adolescent Criminal*; David Finkelhor and Richard Ormrod, *Prostitution of Juveniles: Patterns from NIBRS* (Washington, D.C.: Office of Justice Programs, 2004), pp. 1–2.

102. *Crime in the United States, 2008*, Table 33.

103. Weisberg, *Children of the Night*, pp. 124–28.

104. Cited in Tamara Stieber, "The Boys Who Sell Sex to Men in San Francisco," *Sacramento Bee* (March 4, 1984), p. A22.

105. Weisberg, *Children of the Night*, p. 75.

106. Quoted in Bill Callahan, "Prisoners Without Chains: for Teen-agers Like Peaches, Coming Back Is an Uphill Battle," *San Diego Union-Tribune* (June 21, 1998), p. A19.

107. Flowers, *Runaway Kids and Teenage Prostitution*, p. 102–3; Flowers, *The Prostitution of Women and Girls*, p. 127; Spangenberg, "Prostituted Youth in New York City;" Laura Trujillo, "Escort Services Thriving Industry in Portland Area," *Oregonian* (June 7, 1996), p. B1.

108. Spangenberg, "Prostituted Youth in New York City;" Flowers, *The Adolescent Criminal.*

109. See, for example, "Oakland Battles Wave of Teenage Prostitution," KTVU (March 7, 2009), http://www.ktvu.com/news/19388 341/detail.html; Jodi Brooks, "FBI Makes Teen Sex Trade Busts in Denver: Child Prostitutes Rescued Across the Country," CBS4Denver.com (February 24, 2009), http://cbs4denver.com/crime/Child.Prostitutes.FBI.2.942679.ht ml; Federal Bureau of Investigation Portland, "Federal and Local Agencies Target Child Sex Trafficking as Part of National Effort," Press Release (February 23, 2009), http://portland.fbi.gov/pressrel/pressrel09/pd022309.htm; Kristin Pisarcik, "Miami Vice: Inside 'John Stings' and 'Escort Stings," ABC News (March 21, 2008); http://abcnews.go.com/2020/story?id=448866 7&page=1; Lara J. Jordan, "Kids Rescued, Pimps Arrested in Prostitution Busts," WSBT.com (June 25, 2008), http://www.wsbt.com/news/regional/21579334.html; "Deputies Break Up Beaverton Prostitution Ring," KATU.com (September 19, 2007), http://www.katu.com/news/9875602.html.

## Chapter 12

1. The Encyclopedia of Sex and Sexuality, "Prostitution," http://www.sexuality-encyclopedia.com/dr-ruth/Prostitution. *See also* Jim A. Cates, "Adolescent Male Prostitution by Choice," *Child and Adolescent Social Work* 6 (1989): 155–56.

2. R. Barri Flowers, *Runaway Kids and Teenage Prostitution: America's Lost, Abandoned, and Sexually Exploited Children* (Westport, CT: Greenwood Press, 2001); National Center for Missing and Exploited Children, *Prostitution of Children and Child-Sex Tourism* (Alexandria, VA: National Center for Missing and Exploited Children, 1999), p. 2; Nancy E. Walker, "Executive Summary: How Many Teens Are Prostituted?" fce.msu.edu/Family_Impact_Seminars/pdf/2002-2.pdf; Judianne Densen-Gerber and S. F. Hutchinson, "Medical-Legal and Societal Problems Involving Children, Child Prostitution, Child Pornography, and Drug-Related Abuse; Recommended Legislation," in Selwyn M. Smith, ed., *The Maltreatment of Children* (Baltimore, MD: University Park Press, 1978), p. 318.

3. Flowers, *Runaway Kids and Teenage Prostitution*; R. Barri Flowers, *The Victimization and Exploitation of Women and Children: A Study of Physical, Mental and Sexual Maltreatment in the United States* (Jefferson, NC: McFarland, 1994), p. 82; Mia Spangenberg, "Prostituted Youth in New York City: An Overview," (2001), http://www.libertadlatina.org/US_ECPAT_Child_Pr ostitution_NYC.htm.

4. Connie Sponsler, "Juvenile Prostitution Prevention Project," *WHISPER* 13, 2 (1993): 3–4. *See also* Robin Erb and Roberta de Boer, "Males who Work as Prostitutes: A Little-Known Part of Sex Industry," ToledoBlade.com (December 29, 2006), http://toledoblade.com/apps/pbcs.dll/article?AID=/20061229/NEWS 03/612290302.

5. Robin Lloyd, *For Money or Love: Boy Prostitution in America* (New York: Ballantine, 1976), pp. 58–72. *See also* Matthew Rettenmund, *Boy Culture* (New York: St. Martin's Press, 1997).

6. Cited in Anne Rasmusson, "Commercial Sexual Exploitation of Children: A Literature Review," Alliance for Speaking the Truths on Prostitution and Center for Urban and Regional Affairs (June 1, 1999), http://members.shaw.ca/pdg/exploitation_of_children.html#_Toc 452540114.

7. Spangenberg, "Prostituted Youth in New

York City;" U.S. Department of Justice, Office of Juvenile Justice and Delinquency Prevention, *Prostitution of Children and Child-Sex Tourism* (Alexandria, VA: National Center for Missing and Exploited Children, 1999), p. 2.

8. *Prostitution of Children and Child-Sex Tourism*, p. 2.

9. CRS Report for Congress, *Runaway and Homeless Youth: Demographics, Programs, and Emerging Issues* (Washington, D.C.: Congressional Research Service, 2007), pp. 5–6; Nicholas Ray, *Lesbian, Gay, Bisexual, and Transgender Youth: An Epidemic of Homelessness* (New York: National Gay and Lesbian Task Force Policy Institute and National Coalition for the Homeless, 2006), p. 12; Marjorie J. Robertson and Paul A. Toro, "Homeless Youth: Research, Intervention, and Policy," http://aspe.hhs.gov/ProgSys/homeless/symposium/3-Youth.htm; Christopher L. Ringwalt, Jody M. Greene, Marjorie J. Robertson, and Melissa McPheeters, "The Prevalence of Homelessness Among Adolescents in the United States," *American Journal of Public Health* 88, 9 (1998): 1327.

10. Ray, *Lesbian, Gay, Bisexual, and Transgender Youth*, p. 12; Ringwalt, Greene, Robertson, and McPheeters, "The Prevalence of Homelessness Among Adolescents in the United States," p. 1327; Robertson and Toro, "Homeless Youth."

11. U.S. Department of Health and Human Services, Family Youth and Services Bureau, *Youth with Runaway, Throwaway, and Homeless Experiences: Prevalence, Drug Use, and Other At-Risk Behaviors* (Silver Springs, MD: National Clearinghouse on Families and Youth, 1995), p. E6.

12. Patricia Hersch, "Coming of Age on City Streets," *Psychology Today* 22, 1 (1988): 3–4.

13. Flowers, *Runaway Kids and Teenage Prostitution*; Donald M. Allen, "Young Male Prostitutes: A Psychosocial Study," *Archives of Sexual Behavior* 9 (1980): 409–18; Wikipedia, the Free Encyclopedia, "Male Prostitution," http://en.wikipedia.org/wiki/Rent_boy.

14. Spangenberg, "Prostituted Youth in New York City."

15. Linda L. Halcon and Alan R. Lifson, "Prevalence and Predictors of Sexual Risks Among Homeless Youth," *Journal of Youth and Adolescence* 33, 1 (2004): 75–76; John E. Anderson, Thomas E. Freese and Julia N. Pennbridge, "Sexual Risk Behavior and Condom Use Among Street Youth in Hollywood," *Family Planning Perspectives* 26, 1 (1994): 23.

16. Heather Worth, "Up on K Road on a Saturday Night: Sex, Gender and Sex Work in Auckland," *Venereology* 13, 1 (2000): 15–24.

17. Flowers, *Runaway Kids and Teenage Prostitution*; David F. Luckenbill, "Entering Male Prostitution," *Journal of Contemporary Ethnography* 14 (1985): 131–53.

18. Klass Kids Foundation, "The HT Report," (February 2009), http://www.klaaskids.org/pg-ht-report.htm; Richard J. Estes and Neil A. Weiner, *The Commercial Sexual Exploitation of Children in the U.S., Canada, and Mexico* (Philadelphia, PA: University of Pennsylvania, 2002), p. 92.

19. Neil R. Coombs, "Male Prostitution: A Psychosocial View of Behavior," *American Journal of Orthopsychiatry* 44 (1974): 782–89.

20. Christopher M. Earls and Helene David, "A Psychosocial Study of Male Prostitution," *Archives of Sexual Behavior* 18 (1989): 401–19.

21. Spangenberg, "Prostituted Youth in New York City;" Z. M. Lukman, "The Prevalence of Running Away from Home Among Prostituted Children in Malaysia," *Journal of Social Sciences* 5, 3 (2009): 158.

22. Study World, "Runaways: Victims at Home and On the Streets," http://www.studyworld.com/newsite/ReportEssay/SocialIssues/Political%5CRunaways_Victims_At_Home_and_On_the_Streets-32644.htm.

23. Allen, "Young Male Prostitutes," pp. 409–18.

24. Ray, *Lesbian, Gay, Bisexual, and Transgender Youth*, p. 52.

25. Allen, "Young Male Prostitutes," p. 418. *See also* John Scott, Victor Minichiello, Rodrigo Mariño, Glenn P. Harvey, Maggie Jamieson, and Jan Browne, "Understanding the New Context of the Male Sex Work Industry," *Journal of Interpersonal Violence* 20 (2005): 320–42.

26. Cited in Hilary Abramson, "Sociologists Try to Reach Young Hustlers," *Sacramento Bee* (September 3, 1984), p. A8.

27. Flowers, *Runaway Kids and Teenage Prostitution*, S. E. Caukins and Neil R. Coombs, "The Psychodynamics of Male Prostitution," *American Journal of Psychotherapy* 30 (1976): 446, 450; Ray, *Lesbian, Gay, Bisexual, and Transgender Youth*, pp. 41–44, 59, 66–67; Bryan N. Cochran, Angela J. Stewart, Joshua A. Ginzler, and Ana Mari Cauce, "Challenges Faced by Homeless Sexual Minorities: Comparison of Gay, Lesbian, Bisexual, and Transgender Homeless Adolescents with Their Heterosexual Counterparts," *American Journal of Public Health* 92, 5 (2005): 773–77; Clare Tattersall, *Drugs, Runaways, and Teen Prostitution* (New York: Rosen, 1999), p. 31.

28. Flowers, *The Prostitution of Women and Girls*, p. 138; Cudore L. Snell, *Young Men in the Street: Help-Seeking Behavior of Young Male Prostitutes* (Westport, CT: Praeger, 1995); Jan Browne and Victor Minichiello, "Research Directions in Male Sex Work," *Journal of Homosexuality* 31, 4 (1996): 29–56; Robert P. McNamara, *The Times Square Hustler: Male Prostitution in New York City* (Westport, CT: Praeger, 1994); Caukins and Coombs, "The Psychodynamics of Male Prostitution," pp. 446, 450; Donald H. Russell, "On the Psychopathology of Boy Prostitutes," *International Journal of Offender Therapy and Comparative Criminology* 15 (1971): 49–52; Donald MacNamara, "Male Prostitution in American Cities: A Socioeconomic or Pathological Phenomenon?" *American Journal of Orthopsychiatry* 35 (1965): 204.

29. Ray, *Lesbian, Gay, Bisexual, and Transgender Youth*, p. 2; Tamar Stieber, "The Boys Who Sell Sex to Men in San Francisco," *Sacramento Bee* (March 4, 1984), p. A22.

30. Earls and David, "A Psychosocial Study of Male Prostitution," pp. 401–19.

31. Caukins and Coombs, "The Psychodynamics of Male Prostitution," p. 446; Richard Green, *Sexual Science and the Law* (Cambridge, MA: Harvard University Press, 1992), p. 194.

32. "Prostitution."

33. Coombs, "Male Prostitution," pp. 782–89.

34. D. Kelly Weisberg, *Children of the Night: A Study of Adolescent Prostitution* (Lexington, MA: Lexington Books, 1985), p. 61. *See also* R. Barri Flowers, "The Sex Trade Industry's Worldwide Exploitation of Children," *The ANNALS of the American Academy of Political and Social Science* 575 (2001): 147–57.

35. Joan J. Johnson, *Teen Prostitution* (Danbury, CT: Franklin Watts, 1992), p. 100.

36. "Prostitution;" Wikipedia, the Free Encyclopedia, "Chickenhawk," http://en.wikipedia.org/wiki/Chickenhawk_(sexuality).

37. Flowers, *Runaway Kids and Teenage Prostitution. See also* Kenneth V. Lanning, *Child Sex Rings: A Behavioral Analysis, for Criminal Justice Professionals Handling Cases of Child Sexual Exploitation* (Alexandria, VA: National Center for Missing and Exploited Children, 1992); Kenneth V. Lanning, *Child Molesters: A Behavioral Analysis for Law Enforcement Officers Investigating Cases of Child Sexual Exploitation* (Arlington, VA: National Center for Missing and Exploited Children, 1992).

38. Flowers, *The Prostitution of Women and Girls*, p. 140.

39. *Ibid.*

40. Quoted in Alfred Danna, "Juvenile Male Prostitution: How Can We Reduce the Problem?" *USA Today* 113 (May 1988), p. 87.

41. *Ibid.*, p. 88.

42. Flowers, *The Victimization and Exploitation of Women and Children*, p. 87.

43. Green, *Sexual Science and the Law*, p. 194; Caukins and Coombs, "The Psychodynamics of Male Prostitution," pp. 446, 450.

44. Johnson, *Teen Prostitution*, p. 11.

45. Pam Oliver, "A Review of Literature on Child Prostitution," *Social Policy Journal of New Zealand* 19 (2002), http://www.thefreelibrary.com/_/print/PrintArticle.aspx?id=99849275.

46. Garrett Prestage, "Male and Transsexual Prostitution," in Roberta Perkins, Garrett Prestage, Rachel Sharp, and Frances Lovejoy, eds., *Sex Work and Sex Workers in Australia* (Sydney: University of New South Wales Press, 1994), p. 177.

47. "Male Prostitution;" Flowers, *Runaway Kids and Teenage Prostitution*; Timothy M. Hall, "Rent-Boys, Barflies, and Kept Men: Men Involved in Sex with Men for Compensation in Prague," *Sexualities* 10 (2007): 457–72; Gary Indiana, *Rent Boy* (Baltimore, MD: Serpent's Tail, 1994); Mark Adams, *Hustlers, Escorts, and Porn Stars: An Insider's Guide to Male Prostitution in America* (Las Vegas, NV: Insiders Guide, 1999).

48. Johnson, *Teen Prostitution*, p. 110.

49. *Ibid.*

50. Caukins and Coombs, "The Psychodynamics of Male Prostitution," pp. 441–51.

51. *Ibid.*, p. 441.

52. Dan Waldorf and Sheigla Murphy, "Intravenous Drug Use and Syringe-Sharing Practices of Call Men and Hustlers," in Martin A. Plant, ed., *AIDS, Drugs, and Prostitution* (London: Routledge, 1990), pp. 109–31.

53. *Ibid.*

54. Weisberg, *Children of the Night*, p. 19

55. *Ibid.*

56. *Ibid.*

57. *Ibid.*, p. 40.

58. Flowers, *Runaway Kids and Teenage Prostitution*; Sponsler, "Juvenile Prostitution Prevention Project;" *Prostitution of Children and Child-Sex Tourism*, pp. 6–7; Ray, *Lesbian, Gay, Bisexual, and Transgender Youth*, pp. 67–69; Pamela Miller, Peter Donahue, Dave Este, and Marvin Hofer, "Experiences of Being Homeless or at Risk of Being Homeless Among Canadian Youths," *Adolescence* 39, 156 (2004): 735–55; Kimberly A. Tyler, Danny R. Hoyt, Les B. Whitbeck, and Ana Mari Cauce, "The Impact

of Childhood Sexual Abuse on Later Sexual Victimization Among Runaway Youth," *Journal of Research on Adolescence* 11, 2 (2001): 151–76.

59. Rasmusson, "Commercial Sexual Exploitation of Children." *See also* Stephen W. Baron, "Street Youth Violence and Victimization," *Trauma, Violence, and Abuse* 4 (2003): 22–44.

60. Flowers, *Runaway Kids and Teenage Prostitution*; Tattersall, *Drugs, Runaways, and Teen Prostitution*, p. 23; Spangenberg, "Prostituted Youth in New York City."

61. Cited in Ray, *Lesbian, Gay, Bisexual, and Transgender Youth*, p. 3.

62. *Ibid.*, p. 67; Cochran, Stewart, Ginzler, and Cauce, "Challenges Faced by Homeless Sexual Minorities," p. 773; Michele D. Kipke, Thomas R. Simon, Susanne B. Montgomery, Jennifer B. Unger, and Ellen Iverson, "Homeless Youth and Their Exposure to and Involvement in Violence While Living on the Streets," *Journal of Adolescent Health* 20, 5 (1997): 360–67.

63. Cochran, Stewart, Ginzler, and Cauce, "Challenges Faced by Homeless Sexual Minorities," p. 773.

64. John Lowman, "Street Prostitution," in Vincent Sacco, ed., *Deviance Conformity and Control in Canadian Society*, 2nd ed. (Scarborough: Prentice-Hall Canada, 1992); Dan Allman, *M Is for MUTUAL, A Is for ACTS. Male Sex Work and AIDS in Canada* (Ottawa: Health Canada, 1999).

65. Spangenberg, "Prostituted Youth in New York City."

66. Tattersall, *Drugs, Runaways, and Teen Prostitution*, p. 23.

67. Marcia Cohen, *Juvenile Prostitution* (Washington, D.C.: National Association of Counties Research, Inc., 1987).

68. Sponsler, "Juvenile Prostitution Prevention Project."

69. *Ibid.*; Flowers, *Runaway Kids and Teenage Prostitution*; Waldorf and Murphy, "Intravenous Drug Use and Syringe-Sharing Practices of Call Men and Hustlers," pp. 109–27; Cochran, Stewart, Ginzler, and Cauce, "Challenges Faced by Homeless Sexual Minorities," p. 773; Elizabeth M. Saewyc, Carol Skay, Kimberly Richens, and Elizabeth Reis, "Sexual Orientation, Sexual Abuse, and HIV-Risk Related Behaviors Among Adolescents in the Pacific Northwest," *American Journal of Public Health* 96, 6 (2006); Anderson, Freese and Pennbridge, "Sexual Risk Behavior and Condom Use Among Street Youth in Hollywood," p. 23; Lynn Rew, Rachel T. Fouladi, and Ronald D.

Yockey, "Sexual Health Practices of Homeless Youth," *Journal of Nursing Scholarship* 34, 2 (2002): 139–45; James A. Inciardi, Anne E. Pottieger, Mary Ann Forney, Dale D. Chitwood, and Duane C. McBride, "Prostitution, IV Drug Use, and Sex for Crack Exchanges Among Serious Delinquents: Risks for HIV Infection," *Criminology* 29 (1991): 221–35.

70. Flowers, *Runaway Kids and Teenage Prostitution*.

71. Flowers, *The Prostitution of Women and Girls*, p. 143; *Prostitution of Children and Child-Sex Tourism*, p. 8.

72. Mary Ann Chiasson, Alan R. Lifson, Rand L. Stoneburner, William E. Ewing, Deborah S. Hildebrandt, and Harold W. Jaffe, "HIV-1 Seroprevalence in Male and Female Prostitutes in New York City," Abstracts from the Sixth International Conference on AIDS, Stockholm, Sweden, June 1988.

73. Edward V. Morse, Patricia M. Simon, and Paul M. Balson, "Sexual Behavior Patterns of Customers of Male Street Prostitutes," *Archives of Sexual Behavior* 21, 4 (1992): 347–57.

74. Richard R. Pleak and Heino Meyer-Bahlburg, "Sexual Behavior and AIDS Knowledge of Young Male Prostitutes in Manhattan," *Journal of Sex Research* 27 (1990): 557–88.

75. Timothy P. Johnson, "Self-Reported Risk Factors for AIDS Among Homeless Youth," *AIDS Education Prevention* 8 (1996): 308–22.

76. A. R. Markos, A. A. Wade, and M. Walzman, "The Adolescent Male Prostitute and Sexually Transmitted Diseases, HIV and AIDs," *Journal of Adolescence* 17 (1994): 123–30.

77. C. Pratt, "The Perilous Times of Transgender Youth," *New York Times* (June 18, 1995): CY7.

78. Worth, "Up on K Road on a Saturday Night."

79. David Finkelhor and Richard Ormrod, *Prostitution of Juveniles: Patterns from NIBRS* (Washington, D.C.: Office of Justice Programs, 2004), pp. 1–2.

80. Weisberg, *Children of the Night*, p. 75.

81. Flowers, *The Prostitution of Women and Girls*, p. 127; Spangenberg, "Prostituted Youth in New York City;" Laura Trujillo, "Escort Services Thriving Industry in Portland Area," *Oregonian* (June 7, 1996), p. B1.

82. See, for example, Abby Simons, "Minneapolis to Go After Johns to Fight Prostitution," StarTribune.com (March 12, 2009), http://www.startribune.com/local/41084482.html; "Oakland Battles Wave of Teenage Prostitution," KTVU (March 7, 2009), http://www.

ktvu.com/news/19388341/detail.html; Jodi Brooks, "FBI Makes Teen Sex Trade Busts in Denver: Child Prostitutes Rescued Across the Country," CBS4Denver.com (February 24, 2009), http://cbs4denver.com/crime/Child. Prostitutes.FBI.2.942679.html; Federal Bureau of Investigation Portland, "Federal and Local Agencies Target Child Sex Trafficking as Part of National Effort," Press Release (February 23, 2009), http://portland.fbi.gov/pressrel/press rel09/pd022309.htm; Barbara Grady, "Prose cutor Targets Pimps Not Girls," *Oakland Tribune* (April 23, 2008), http://www.insidebay area.com/search/ci_9024565?IADID=Search-www.insidebayarea.com-www.insidebayarea. com; Kristin Pisarcik, "Miami Vice: Inside 'John Stings' and 'Escort Stings," ABC News (March 21, 2008), http://abcnews.go.com/ 2020/story?id=4488667&page=1; Lara J. Jordan, "Kids Rescued, Pimps Arrested in Prostitution Busts," WSBT.com (June 25, 2008), http://www.wsbt.com/news/regional/21579 334.html.

## Chapter 13

1. U.S.C. § 5701–5702 Supp. II (1978).

2. Bob Reeg, "The Runaway and Homeless Youth Act and Disconnected Youth," in Jodie Levin-Epstein and Mark H. Greenberg, eds., *Leave No Youth Behind: Opportunities for Congress to Reach Disconnected Youth* (Washington, D.C.: Center for Law and Social Policy, 2003), pp. 53. See also Runaway, Homeless, and Missing Children Protection Act of 2003, P.L. 108–96 (2003).

3. Reeg, "The Runaway and Homeless Youth Act," p. 54; CRS Report for Congress, *Runaway and Homeless Youth: Demographics, Programs, and Emerging Issues* (Washington, D.C.: Congressional Research Service, 2007), pp. 15–18.

4. Runaway and Homeless Youth, pp. 19–21; Reeg, "The Runaway and Homeless Youth Act," p. 54.

5. Reeg, "The Runaway and Homeless Youth Act," pp. 54–55; *Runaway and Homeless Youth*, p. 21.

6. Runaway and Homeless Youth, pp. 17–19.

7. National Center for Missing and Exploited Children, http://www.missingkids. com/missingkids/servlet/PublicHomeServlet?LanguageCountry=en_US; R. Barri Flowers, *The Adolescent Criminal: An Examination of Today's*

*Juvenile Offender* (Jefferson, NC: McFarland, 1990), p. 203.

8. National Runaway Switchboard, www. 1800runaway.org; *Runaway and Homeless Youth*, pp. 21–22; Wikipedia, the Free Encyclopedia, "National Runaway Switchboard," http://en. wikipedia.org/wiki/National_Runaway_Switch board.

9. The Office on Child Abuse and Neglect, P.L. 100–294; 42 U.S.C. § 5101–5106 (1974), as amended by the Child Abuse Prevention and Treatment and Adoption Reform Act of 1978, P.L. 95–266, 92 Stat. 205 (1978).

10. U.S. Department of Health and Human Services, Administration for Children and Families, Federal and State Reporting Systems, National Child Abuse and Neglect Data System (NCANDS), http://www.acf.hhs.gov/program s/cb/systems/index.htm.

11. Juvenile Justice and Delinquency Prevention Act of 1974, P.L. 93–415.

12. R. Barri Flowers, *Kids Who Commit Adult Crimes: A Study of Serious Juvenile Criminality and Delinquency* (Binghamton, NY: Haworth Press, 2002), p. 178.

13. Act of June 25, 1910, ch. 395, 36 Stat. 825, codified as amended, 18 U.S.C. §§ 2421–2424 (1998).

14. R. Barri Flowers, *Runaway Kids and Teenage Prostitution: America's Lost, Abandoned, and Sexually Exploited Children* (Westport, CT: Greenwood Press, 2001), pp. 168–69.

15. Child Sexual Abuse and Pornography Act of 1986, P.L. 99–628, § 5.

16. 18 U.S.C. § 2423, Transportation of Minors, as amended by Protection of Children from Sexual Predators Act, § 103, P.L. 105–314, 112 Stat. 2974 (1998).

17. Criminal Forfeiture, 18 U.S.C. § 2253 (1978); Civil Forfeiture 18 U.S.C. § 2254 (1978).

18. *Ibid.*

19. Flowers, *Runaway Kids and Teenage Prostitution*, p. 169; See also Protection of Children from Sexual Predators Act of 1998, P.L. 105–314, 101, 112 Stat. 2974 (1998).

20. Prohibited Activities, 18 U.S.C. § 1962 (1982).

21. U.S. Department of Justice, Child Exploitation and Obscenity Section (CEOS), "Trafficking and Sex Tourism," http://www. usdoj.gov/criminal/ceos/trafficking.html.

22. *Ibid.*

23. *Ibid.*

24. Sexual Exploitation of Children, 18 U.S.C. § 2251 et seq.

25. The Victims of Child Abuse Act of 1990,

P.L. 101–647, § 323, 104 Stat. 4789, 4818 (1990).

26. Flowers, *Runaway Kids and Teenage Prostitution*, p. 170. *See also* 18 U.S.C. § 2251 (a), as amended by Protection of Children from Sexual Predators Act, § 201.

27. Flowers, *Runaway Kids and Teenage Prostitution*, p. 170. *See also* The Omnibus Consolidated Appropriations Act of 1997, P.L. 104–208, § 121, 110 stat. 3009, 3009–26 (1997).

28. *United States v. Hilton*, No. 98–513, slip op. at 3 (1st Cir. Jan. 27, 1999).

29. 1997 WL 487758 (N.D. Cal.).

30. U.S. Department of Justice, Child Exploitation and Obscenity Section (CEOS), "Citizens Guide to United States Federal Exploitation Laws," http://www.usdoj.gov/criminal/ceos/citizensguide.html.

31. U.S. Department of Justice, Child Exploitation and Obscenity Section (CEOS), Press Releases 2008 and 2009, http://www.usdoj.gov/criminal/ceos/pressreleases.html.

32. National Center for Missing and Exploited Children, *Prostitution of Children and Child-Sex Tourism* (Alexandria, VA: National Center for Missing and Exploited Children, 1999), pp. 11–12.

33. Colorado Rev. Stat. Ann. § 18-7-406.

34. New York Penal Code §§ 230.04, 230.05, 230.06.

35. Illinois Ann. Stat. ch. 720, para. 5/11-19.1; Colorado Rev. Stat. Ann. § 18-7-405; California Penal Code § 266h; West Virginia Code § 61-8-8.

36. Illinois Ann. Stat. ch. 720, para. 5/11-19.1.

37. Quoted in *Prostitution of Children and Child-Sex Tourism*, p. 12. *See also* Colorado Rev. Stat. Ann. § 18-7-40.

38. Iowa Code Ann. § 725.3.

39. *State v. Steer*, 517 A, 2d 797 (N.H. 1986).

40. *See, for example*, Nevada Rev. Stat. § 201.360; Oregon Rev. Stat. § 167.017; South Dakota Codified Laws Ann. § 22–23–2.

41. Louisiana Rev. Stat. Ann. § 14:82.1.

42. Montana Code Ann. § 45-5-603.

43. *Prostitution of Children and Child-Sex Tourism*, pp. 26–28.

44. "Child Porn Arrests: 'Shooting Fish in a Barrel,'" KVAL.com (October 5, 2009), http://www.kval.com/news/national/63547752.html; Aisha Ali, "Washington DC A Sexual Playground for Pimps and Johns: Exposing Child Prostitution Rings in DC," Examiner.com (March 17, 2009); "Child Prostitution Crackdown, 44 Arrested Locally," CBS2 (February 23, 2009), http://cbs2chicago.com/local/child.prostitution.44.2.941974.html; Terry Frieden, "FBI Arrests Hundreds in Child Sex Crackdown," CNN.com (June 25, 2008), http://www.cnn.com/2008/CRIME/06/25/child.prostitutes/index.html; "Twenty-Seven Charged in Child Porn Sting," CNN.com (March 16, 2006), http://www.cnn.com/2006/LAW/03/15/childporn.arrests/index.html; Christine Lagorio, "Crackdown on Child Prostitution: Justice Department Charges More than Thirty Across Several States," CBS News (December 16, 2005), http://www.cbsnews.com/stories/2005/12/16/national/main1133570.shtml.

45. U.S. Department of Justice, Federal Bureau of Investigation, *Crime in the United States, 2008*, Table 39, http://www.fbi.gov/ucr/cius2008/data/table_39.html.

46. *Ibid. See also* "FBI Rescues Dozens of Teen Prostitutes," The Star.com (February 23, 2009), http://www.thestar.com/News/World/article/591827; Barbara Grady, "Prosecutor Targets Pimps, Not Girls," *Oakland Tribune* (April 23, 2008), http://www.insidebayarea.com/search/ci_9024565?IADID=Search-www.insidebayarea.com-www.insidebayarea.com.

# Bibliography

ABC News. (August 9, 2006) "Survey Reveals Extent of Teen Prostitution." http://abcnews.go.com/Health/story?id=2292336&page=1&CMP=OTC-RSSFeeds0312.

_____. (February 9, 2006) "Teen Girls' Stories of Sex Trafficking in U.S.: International Sex Trafficking Is a Well-Known Problem, but It Happens Here as Well." http://abcnews.go.com/print?id=1596778.

About.com: Mental Health. (July 2002) "Study of Runaways Reveals Disturbing Data on Abuse, Mental Illness." http://mentalhealth.about.com/library/sci/0702/blrunaway702.htm.

Abrahams, Caroline, and Roddy Mungal. (1992) *Runaways: Exploding the Myths*. London: National Children's Home.

Abramson, Hilary. (September 3, 1984) "Sociologists Try to Reach Young Hustlers." *Sacramento Bee*, p. A8.

Adams, Gerald R., Thomas Gulotta, and Mary A. Clancy. (1985) "Homeless Adolescents: A Descriptive Study of Similarities and Differences Between Runaways and Throwaways." *Adolescence* 79: 715–24.

Adams, Mark. (1999) *Hustlers, Escorts, and Porn Stars: An Insider's Guide to Male Prostitution in America*. Las Vegas, NV: Insiders Guide.

Ali, Aisha. (March 17, 2009) "Washington DC a Sexual Playground for Pimps and Johns: Exposing Child Prostitution Rings in DC." Examiner.com.

Allen, Donald M. (1980) "Young Male Prostitutes: A Psychosocial Study." *Archives of Sexual Behavior* 9: 409–18.

Allman, Dan. (1999) *M Is for MUTUAL, A Is for ACTS. Male Sex Work and AIDS in Canada*. Ottawa: Health Canada.

Anderson, John E., Thomas E. Freese and Julia N. Pennbridge. (1994) "Sexual Risk Behavior and Condom Use Among Street Youth in Hollywood." *Family Planning Perspectives* 26, 1: 23.

Arbarbanel, Stephanie. (January 11, 1994) "Women Who Make a Difference." *Family Circle* 107: 11.

Arey, Doug. (1995) "Gay Males and Sexual Child Abuse." In Lisa A. Fonte, ed. *Sexual Abuse in Nine North American Cultures: Treatment and Prevention*. Thousand Oaks, CA: Sage.

*Arizona Daily Star*. (March 10, 2006) "FBI Gives First Accounting of Missing U.S. Children." http://www.azstarnet.com/sn/from comments/119396.php.

Atkin, Ross. (June 14, 2004) "They Offer Help to Teens at the End of the Line." *Christian Science Monitor*. http://www.csmonitor.com/2004/0114/p14s02-lifp.html.

Auerswald, Colette L., and Stephen L. Eyre. (2002) "Youth Homelessness in San Francisco: A Life Cycle Approach." *Social Science and Medicine* 54: 1497–1512.

Avery, Anna M., Ronald E. Hellman, and Lori K. Sudderth. (2001) "Satisfaction with Mental Health Services Among Sexual Minorities with Major Mental Illness." *American Journal of Public Health* 91, 6: 990–91.

Ayerst, Sandra L. (1999) "Depression and Stress in Street Youth." *Adolescence* 34, 135: 567–75.

Baley, Christopher, and Loretta Young. (1987) "Juvenile Prostitution and Child Sexual Abuse: A Controlled Study." *Canadian Journal of Community Mental Health* 6, 1: 5–26.

Barnitz, Laura A. (1998) *Commercial Sexual Ex-*

ploitation of Children: Youth Involved in Pros-
titution, Pornography, and Sex Trafficking.
Washington, D.C.: Youth Advocate Program
International.

Baron, Stephen W. (2003) "Street Youth Violence and Victimization." *Trauma, Violence,
and Abuse* 4: 22–44.

Barrett, David. (1998) "Young People and Prostitution: Perpetrators in Our Midst." *International Review of Law, Computers and Technology* 12, 3: 475–86.

_____, and William Beckett. (1996) "Child
Prostitution: Reaching Out to Children Who
Sell Sex to Survive." *British Journal of Nurs-
ing* 5: 1120–25.

Barrett, Delvin. (February 23, 2009) "FBI, Police Rescue Child Prostitutes Around U.S."
MyFoxPhoenix.com. http://www.myfoxph
oenix.com/dpp/news/child_prostitution_
bust_022309.

Barry, Kathleen. (1995) *The Prostitution of Sexuality*. New York: New York University Press.

Bass, Deborah. (1992) *Helping Vulnerable
Youths: Runaway and Homeless Adolescents in
the United States*. Washington, D.C.: National Association of Social Workers Press.

Berdahl, Terceira A., Danny R. Hoyt, and Les
B. Whitbeck. (2005) "Predictors of First
Mental Health Service Utilization Among
Homeless and Runaway Adolescents." *Jour-
nal of Adolescent Health* 37, 2: 145–54.

Bilchik, Shay. (1999) *1996 Youth Gang Survey:
Summary*. Washington, D.C.: Office of Juvenile Justice and Delinquency Prevention.

Bittle, Steven. (1999) Reconstructing "Youth
Prostitution" as the "Sexual Procurement of
Children": A Case Study. Unpublished Master's Thesis. Burnaby, BC: Simon Fraser University.

_____. (2002) *Youth Involvement in Prostitu-
tion: A Literature Review and Annotated Bibliography*. Ottawa: Department of Justice
Canada.

Bond, Lydia, Rafael Mazin, and Maria V.
Jiminez. (1992) "Street Youth and AIDS,"
*AIDS Education and Prevention* 4, 3: 14–23.

Bontempo, Daniel E., and Anthony R.
D'Augelli. (2002) "Effects of At-School Victimization and Sexual Orientation on Lesbian, Gay, or Bisexual Youths' Health Risk
Behavior." *Journal of Adolescent Health* 30,
5: 364–74.

Booth, William. (August 21, 1999) "13 Charged
in Gang Importing Prostitutes." *Washington
Post*, p. A3.

Boston.com. (September 15, 2009) "Two Men
Plead Guilty in Teen Prostitution Ring."

http://www.boston.com/news/local/maine/
articles/2009/09/15/2_men_plead_guilty_in
_teen_prostitution_ring/.

Boxill, Nancy A. (2007) "Ending Sex Trafficking of Children in Atlanta." *Affilia* 22, 2:
138–49.

Bracey, Dorothy H. (1979) "*Baby-Pros*": Preliminary Profiles of Juvenile Prostitutes. New York:
John Jay Press.

Bradley, Heather L. (May 6–8, 2005) "Crisis
Intervention with Homeless and Sex-Working Youth." 3rd Annual Collaborative Crisis
Centers Conference. Chicago, IL. http://
www.uic.edu/orgs/convening/homeless.htm.

Brannigan, Augustine, and E. Gibbs Van Brunschot. (1997) "Youthful Prostitution and
Child Sexual Trauma." *International Journal
of Law and Psychiatry* 20: 337–54.

Bray, Robert M., and May M. Marsden, eds.
(1998) *Drug Use in Metropolitan America*.
Thousand Oaks, CA: Sage.

Brennan, Tim. (1978) *The Social Psychology of
Runaways*. Toronto: Lexington Books.

_____, Dave Huizinga, and Del Elliott. (1978)
*The Social Psychology of Runaways*. Lexington, MA: Lexington Books.

Brock, Deborah R. (1998) *Making Work, Making Trouble: Prostitution as a Social Problem*.
Toronto: University of Toronto Press.

Bronwyn, Herbert. (June 1, 2009) "Child
Pornography Arrests." ABC News. http://
www.abc.net.au/am/content/2009/s258586
4.htm.

Brooks, Jodi. (February 24, 2009) "FBI Makes
Teen Sex Trade Busts in Denver: Child Pros-
titutes Rescued Across the Country." CBS4
Denver.com. http://cbs4denver.com/crime/
Child.Prostitutes.FBI.2.942679.html.

Brown, Angela K. (January 16, 2008) "Police:
Teen Gang Ran Prostitution Ring." Breit-
Bart TV. http://www.breitbart.com/article.
php?id=D8U70D9O0&show_article=1.

Browne, Jan, and Victor Minichiello. (1996)
"Research Directions in Male Sex Work."
*Journal of Homosexuality* 31, 4: 29–56.

Burgess, Ann W. (1985) *The Sexual Victimization of Adolescents*. Rockville, MD: U.S. Department of Health and Human Services.

_____, and Marieanne L. Clark, eds. (1984)
*Child Pornography and Sex Rings*. New York:
Free Press.

Butler, Dodie. (1974) *Runaway House: A Youth-
run Project*. Washington, D.C.: Government
Printing Office.

Caliber Associates. (1997) Analysis and Interpretation of New Information Concerning
Runaway and Homeless Youth. Washington,

D.C.: U.S. Department of Health and Human Services.

California Penal Code. § 266h.

Callahan, Bill. (June 21, 1998) "Prisoners Without Chains: For Teen-agers Like Peaches, Coming Back Is an Uphill Battle." *San Diego Union-Tribune*, p. A19.

Campagna, Daniel S., and Donald Poffenberger. (1988) *The Sexual Trafficking in Children: An Investigation of the Child Sex Trade.* Dover, MA: Auburn House.

Cates, Jim A. (1989) "Adolescent Male Prostitution by Choice." *Child and Adolescent Social Work* 6: 155–56.

Caton, Carol L. M. (1990) "The Epidemiology of Homelessness." In Carol L. M. Canton, ed. *Homeless in America.* New York: Oxford University Press.

Caukins, S. E., and Neil R. Coombs. (1976) "The Psychodynamics of Male Prostitution." *American Journal of Psychotherapy* 30: 446, 450.

CBS/AP. (January 21, 2008) "Runaway Teens Found Safe in Louisiana." http://www.cbs news.com/stories/2008/01/21/earlyshow/mai n3734447.shtml?tag=contentMain;content Body.

CBS2. (February 23, 2009) "Child Prostitution Crackdown, 44 Arrested Locally." http://cbs 2chicago.com/local/child.prostitution.44. 2.941974.html.

Chen, Xiaojin, Lisa Thrane, Les B. Whitbeck, Kurt D. Johnson, and Danny R. Hoyt. (2007) "Onset of Conduct Disorder, Use of Delinquent Subsistence Strategies, and Street Victimization Among Homeless and Runaway Adolescents in the Midwest." *Journal of Interpersonal Violence* 22, 9: 1156–83.

Cherry, Andrew L. (1993) "Combining Cluster and Discriminant Analysis to Develop a Social Bond Typology of Runaway Youth." *Research on Social Work Practice* 3, 2: 175–90.

Chiasson, Mary Ann, Alan R. Lifson, Rand L. Stoneburner, William E. Ewing, Deborah S. Hildebrandt, and Harold W. Jaffe. (June 1988) "HIV-1 Seroprevalence in Male and Female Prostitutes in New York City." Abstracts from the Sixth International Conference on AIDS, Stockholm, Sweden.

Child Abuse Prevention, Adoption and Family Services Act. (1988) P.L. 100–294.

Child Abuse Prevention and Treatment and Adoption Reform Act. (1978) P.L. 95–266, 92 Stat. 205.

Child Sexual Abuse and Pornography Act. (1986) P.L. 99–628, § 5.

Civil Forfeiture. (1978) 18 U.S.C. §§ 2254.

CKNW News Talk Sports. (June 29, 2009) "Teen Prostitution on Craigslist." http:// www.cknw.com/Channels/Reg/NewsLocal/ Story.aspx/Story.aspx?ID=1107995.

Clatts, Michael C., Lloyd A. Goldsamt, Huso Yi, and Marya V. Gwadz. (2005) "Homelessness and Drug Abuse Among Young Men Who Have Sex with Men in New York City: A Preliminary Epidemiological Trajectory." *Journal of Adolescence* 28, 2: 201–14.

_____, W. Rees Davis, J. L. Sotheran, and Aylin Atillasoy. (1998) "Correlates and Distribution of HIV Risk Behaviors Among Homeless Youths in New York City: Implications for Prevention and Policy." *Child Welfare* 77, 2: 195–207.

Clawson, Heather J., Mary Layne, and Kevonne Small. (2006) *Estimating Human Trafficking into the United States: Development of a Methodology.* Fairfax, VA: Caliber.

CNN.com. Crime. (May 20, 2009) "7 Charged in Alleged Prostitution Ring on Craigslist." http://www.cnn.com/2009/CRIME/05/20/ craigslist.prostitution/index.html?

_____. (March 16, 2006) "Twenty-Seven Charged in Child Porn Sting." http://www. cnn.com/2006/LAW/03/15/childporn.ar rests/index.html.

_____. (February 25, 2009) "Two Arizona Teens Accused of Pimping Other Girls." http://www.cnn.com/2009/CRIME/02/25/ teen.pimp/index.html?imw=Y&iref=mpsto ryemail.

CNN Interactive. (September 30, 1997) "Internet Sting Identifies 1,500 Suspected Child Pornographers." http://www.cnn.com/US/ 9709/30/cybersting/.

Cochran, Bryan N., Angela J. Stewart, Joshua A. Ginzler, and Ana Mari Cauce. (2005) "Challenges Faced by Homeless Sexual Minorities: Comparison of Gay, Lesbian, Bisexual, and Transgender Homeless Adolescents with Their Heterosexual Counterparts." *American Journal of Public Health* 92, 5: 773–77.

Cohen, Marcia. (1987) *Juvenile Prostitution.* Washington, D.C.: National Association of Counties Research, Inc.

Colorado Rev. Stat. Ann. § 18–7–405, 406.

Coombs, Neil R. (1974) "Male Prostitution: A Psychosocial View of Behavior." *American Journal of Orthopsychiatry* 44: 782–89.

Courtney, Mark E., Ada Skyles, Gina Miranda, Andrew Zinn, Eboni Howard, and Robert M. Goerge. (2005) "Youth Who Run Away from Out-of-Home Care." *Chaplin Hall Center for Children Issue Brief* 103: 2.

Crawford, Lindsay. (April 13, 2000) "Troubled Teens Take to the Streets: Rebellious Youths with Nowhere to Run Away from Their Problems and Their Homes." Silver Chips Online, pp. 1, 18.

Criminal Forfeiture. (1978) 18 U.S.C. §§ 2253.

CRS Report for Congress.. (2007) Runaway and Homeless Youth: Demographics, Programs, and Emerging Issues. Washington, D.C.: Congressional Research Service.

_____. (2006) The Runaway and Homeless Youth Program: Administration, Funding and Legislative Actions. Washington, D.C.: Congressional Research Service.

Csapo, Marg. (1986) "Juvenile Prostitution." Canadian Journal of Special Education 2, 2: 145–70.

Cwayna, Kevin. (1993) Knowing Where the Fountains Are: Stories and Realities of Homeless Youth. Minneapolis, MN: Deaconess Press.

Dailey, Don. (2007) "Stats: Arrest Rates in Line with Population." The Morning News. http://www.nwaonline.net/projects/immigration/crime.html.

Dame, Linda M. (2004) "Queer Youth in Care in Manitoba: An Examination of Their Experiences Through Their Voices." Canadian Online Journal of Queer Studies in Education 1, 1: 1–28.

Danna, Alfred. (May 1988) "Juvenile Male Prostitution: How Can We Reduce the Problem?" USA Today 113: 87.

Davidson, Howard, and Gregory Loken. (1998) Child Pornography and Prostitution: Background and Analysis. Arlington, VA: National Center for Missing and Exploited Children.

Dawson, Ross. (1987) "Child Sexual Abuse, Juvenile Prostitution and Child Pornography: The Federal Response." Journal of Child Care 3, 2: 19–51.

de Man, Anton. (1993) "Adolescent Runaways: Familial and Personal Correlates." Social Behavior and Personaliy: An International Journal 21, 2: 163–67.

de Oliveira, Walter. (2000) Working with Children on the Streets of Brazil: Politics and Practice. Binghamton, NY: Haworth Press.

De Rosa, Christine J., Susanne B. Montgomery, Justeen Hyde, Ellen F. Iverson, and Michele D. Kipke. (2001) "HIV Risk Behavior and HIV Testing: A Comparison of Rates and Other Associated Factors Among Homeless and Runaway Adolescents in Two Cities." AIDS Education and Prevention 13, 2: 131–48.

Dean, Ruth, and Melissa Thomson. (1997) Teen Prostitution: Teen Issues. San Diego, CA: Lucent Books.

Dedel, Kelly. (2006) Juvenile Runaways. Washington, D.C.: Office of Community Oriented Policing Services. http://www.ncjrs.gov/App/Publications/abstract.aspx?ID=23 5092.

Deisher, Robert W., James A. Farrow, Kerry Hope, and Christina Litchfield. (1989) "The Pregnant Adolescent Prostitute." American Journal of Diseases of Children 143: 1162–65.

_____, and William M. Rogers. (1991) "The Medical Care of Street Youth," Journal of Adolescent Health 12: 500–3.

Dembo, Richard, Linda Williams, Werner Wothke, James Schmeidler, and C. Hendricks Brown. (1992) "The Role of Family Factors, Physical Abuse, and Sexual Victimization Experiences in High-Risk Youths' Alcohol and Other Drug Use and Delinquency: A Longitudinal Model." Violence and Victims 7, 3: 245–66.

Densen-Gerber, Judianne, and S. F. Hutchinson. (1978) "Medical-Legal and Societal Problems Involving Children-Child Prostitution, Child Pornography and Drug-Related Abuse; Recommended Legislation." In Selwyn M. Smith, ed. The Maltreatment of Children. Baltimore, MD: University Park Press.

Deren, Sherry, Michele Shedlin, W. Rees Davis, Michael C. Clatts, Salvador Balcorta, Mark M. Beardsley, Jesus Sanchez, and Don Des Jarlais. (1997) "Dominican, Mexican, and Puerto Rican Prostitutes: Drug Use and Sexual Behaviors." Hispanic Journal of Behavioral Sciences 19: 202–13.

Diamond, Lisa M. (2000) "Sexual Identity, Attractions, and Behavior Among Young Sexual-Minority Women Over a 2-Year Period." Developmental Psychology 36, 2: 241–50.

Dunford, Franklin, and Tim Brennan. (1976) "A Taxonomy of Runaway Youth." Social Service Review 50, 3: 457–70.

Dunlap, Kamika, and Barbara Grady. (April 21, 2008) "City Comes to Grips with Teen Prostitution." Oakland Tribune. http://www.insidebayarea.com/teenprostitution/ci_90004 24.

Dylan, Nicole D. K. (2004) "City Enters Partnership to Assist Lesbian and Gay Homeless Youth." Nation's Cities Weekly 27, 10.

Earls, Christopher M., and Helene David. (1990) "Early Family and Sexual Experiences of Male and Female Prostitutes." Canadian's Mental Health 37/38: 7–11.

_____, and _____. (1989) "A Psychosocial

Study of Male Prostitution." *Archives of Sexual Behavior* 18: 401–19.

Edelman, Peter, Harry J. Holzer, and Paul Offner. (2006) *Reconnecting Disadvantaged Young Men.* Washington, D.C.: Urban Institute Press.

Emerson, Robert M. (1981) "On Last Resorts," *American Journal of Sociology* 87, 1: 1–22.

"The Enablers." (1978) *Juvenile Prostitution in Minnesota: The Report of a Research Project.* St. Paul, MN: The Enablers.

Encyclopedia of Sex and Sexuality. "Prostitution." http://www.sexuality-encyclopedia.com/dr-ruth/Prostitution.

English, Clifford J. (1973) "Leaving Home: A Typology of Runaways." *Society* 10: 22–24.

Ennett, Susan T., Susan L. Bailey, and E. Belle Federman. (1999) "Social Network. Characteristics Associated with Risky Behaviors Among Runaway and Homeless Youth." *Journal of Health and Social Behavior* 40: 63–78.

Ensign, Josephine. (2000) "Reproductive Health of Adolescent Women in Seattle, Washington USA." *Women and Health* 31: 133–51.

Erb, Robin, and Roberta de Boer. (December 29, 2006) "Males Who Work as Prostitutes a Little-Known Part of Sex Iindustry." ToledoBlade.com. http://toledoblade.com/apps/pbcs.dll/article?AID=/20061229/NEWS03/612290302.

Estes, Richard J. (2001) *The Sexual. Exploitation of Children: A Working Guide to the Empirical Literature.* Philadelphia, PA: University of Pennsylvania.

_____, and Neil A. Weiner. (2002) *The Commercial Sexual Exploitation of Children in the U.S., Canada, and Mexico.* Philadelphia, PA: University of Pennsylvania.

Famularo, Richard, Robert Kinscherff, Terence Fenton, and Suzanne M. Bolduc. (1990) "Child Maltreatment Histories Among Runaway and Delinquent Children." *Clinical Pediatrics* 29: 713–18.

Farrington, David P. (1996) "The Explanation and Prevention of Youthful Offending." In J. David Hawkins, ed. *Delinquency and Crime: Current Theories.* New York: Cambridge University Press.

Farrow, James A., Robert W. Deisher, Richard Brown, John W. Kulig, and Michele Kipke. (1992) "Health and Health Needs of Homeless and Runaway Youth." *Journal of Adolescent Health* 13: 717–26.

Fassett, Byran A., and Bill Walsh. (1994) "Ju-

venile Prostitution: An Overlooked Form of Child Abuse." *The APSAC Advisor* 7, 1: 9.

Fasulo, Samuel J., Theodore P. Cross, Peggy Mosley, and Joseph Leavey. (2002) "Adolescent Runaway Behavior in Specialized Foster Care." *Children and Youth Services Review* 24, 8: 623–640.

Faugier, Jean, and Mary Sargeant. (1997) "Boyfriends, 'Pimps,' and Clients." In Graham Scambler and Annette Scambler, eds. *Rethinking Prostitution: Purchasing Sex in the 1990s.* London: Routledge.

Federal Bureau of Investigation Portland. (February 23, 2009) "Federal and Local Agencies Target Child Sex Trafficking as Part of National Effort." Press Release. http://portland.fbi.gov/pressrel/pressrel09/pd022309.htm.

Felsman, J. Kirk. (1984) "Abandoned Children: A Reconsideration." *Children Today* 13, 3: 13–18.

Fergusson, David M., L. John Horwood, and Annette L. Beautrais. (1999) "Is Sexual Orientation Related to Mental Health Problems and Suicidality in Young People?" *Archives of General Psychiatry* 56, 10: 876–80.

Ferraro, Monique, and Eoghan Casey. (2004) *Investigating Child Exploitation and Pornography: The Internet, Law, and Forensic Science.* Maryland Heights, MO: Academic Press.

Feuereisen, Patti, and Caroline Pincus. (2009) *Invisible Girls: The Truth About Sexual Abuse.* 2nd ed. Seattle, WA: Seal Press.

Finkelhor, David, Gerald Hotaling, and Andrea J. Sedlak. (1990) *Missing, Abducted, Runaway, and Thrownaway Children in America, First Report: Numbers and Characteristics, National Incidence Studies.* Washington, D.C.: Office of Juvenile Justice and Delinquency Prevention.

_____, and Richard Ormrod. (2004) *Prostitution of Juveniles: Patterns from NIBRS.* Washington, D.C.: Office of Justice Programs.

Flowers, R. Barri. (2009) *The Adolescent Criminal: An Examination of Today's Juvenile Offender.* Jefferson, NC: McFarland.

_____. (1986) *Children and Criminality: The Child as Victim and Perpetrator.* Westport, CT: Greenwood Press.

_____. (2009) *College Crime: A Statistical Study of Offenses on American Campuses.* Jefferson, NC: McFarland.

_____. (2000) *Domestic Crimes, Family Violence and Child Abuse: A Study of Contemporary American Society.* Jefferson, NC: McFarland.

_____. (2008) *Drugs, Alcohol and Criminality in American Society.* Jefferson, NC: McFarland.

_____. (1995) *Female Crime, Criminals, and Cellmates: An Exploration of Female Criminality.* Jefferson, NC: McFarland.

_____. (2002) *Kids Who Commit Adult Crimes: A Study of Serious Juvenile Criminality and Delinquency.* Binghamton, NY: Haworth Press.

_____. (2003) *Male Crime and Deviance: Exploring Its Cause, Dynamics, and Nature.* Springfield, IL: Charles C Thomas.

_____. (1990) *Minorities and Criminality.* Westport, CT: Praeger.

_____. (2002) *Murder, at the End of the Day and Night: A Study of Criminal Homicide Offenders, Victims, and Circumstances.* Springfield, IL: Charles C Thomas.

_____. (2005) *The Prostitution of Women and Girls.* Jefferson, NC: McFarland.

_____. (2001) *Runaway Kids and Teenage Prostitution: America's Lost, Abandoned, and Sexually Exploited Children.* Westport, CT: Greenwood Press.

_____. (2006) *Sex Crimes: Perpetrators, Predators, Prostitutes, and Victims.* 2nd ed. Springfield, IL: Charles C Thomas.

_____. (2001) "The Sex Trade Industry's Worldwide Exploitation of Children." *The ANNALS of the American Academy of Political and Social Science* 575: 147–57.

_____. (1994) *The Victimization and Exploitation of Women and Children: A Study of Physical, Mental and Sexual Maltreatment in the United States.* Jefferson, NC: McFarland.

_____, and H. Loraine Flowers. (2004) *Murders in the United States: Crimes, Killers and Victims of the Twentieth Century.* Jefferson, NC: McFarland.

Focus Adolescence Services. "Why Teens Run Away." http://www.focusas.com/Runaways-WhyTeensRunAway.html.

Forst, Martin. L. (1994) "A Substance Use Profile of Delinquent and Homeless Youths." *Journal of Drug Education* 24, 3: 219–31.

_____, and Martha E. Blomquist. (1991) *Missing Children: Rhetoric and Reality.* New York: Lexington Books.

FoxNews.com. (March 15, 2006) "International Online Child Pornography Ring Busted." http://www.foxnews.com/story/0,2933,18797 7,00.html.

Frieden, Terry. (June 25, 2008) "FBI Arrests Hundreds in Child Sex Crackdown." CNN. com. http://www.cnn.com/2008/CRIME/06/25/child.prostitutes/index.html.

_____. (December 13, 2008) "170 Arrested in Global Child Porn Investigation." CNN. com. http://www.cnn.com/2008/CRIME/12/12/porn.arrests/index.html.

Gable, Jenny. (1995) "Problems Faced by Homosexual Youth." http://www.lmsa.edu/jgable/lbg/paper.html.

Gaetz, Stephen. (2004) "Safe Streets for Whom? Homeless Youth, Social Exclusion, and Criminal Victimization." *Canadian Journal of Criminology and Criminal Justice* 46, 6: 423–55.

_____, Bill O'Grady, and Bryan Vaillancourt. (1999) *Making Money: The Shout Clinic Report on Homeless Youth and Employment.* Toronto: Central Toronto Community Health Centers.

Gangamma, Rashmi, Natasha Slesnick, Paula Toviessi, and Julianne Serovich. (2008) "Comparison of HIV Risks Among Gay, Lesbian, Bisexual and Heterosexual Homeless Youth." *Journal of Youth and Adolescence* 37, 4: 456–64.

Gardner, George. (July 26, 2007) "Hookers Go Hi-Tech, Advertize on Craigslist." Tech. Blorge. http://tech.blorge.com/Structure:%20/2007/07/26/hookers-go-hi-tech-advertise-on-craigslist/.

General Accounting Office. (1982) *Sexual Exploitation of Children: A Problem of Unknown Magnitude.* Washington, D.C.: General Accounting Office.

Gibson, Barbara. (1990) *Male Order: Life Stories from Boys Who Sell Sex.* London: Cassell.

Gibson, Paul. "Gay Male and Lesbian Suicide." LAMBDA GLBT Community Services. http://www.lambda.org/youth_suicide.htm.

Giobbe, Evelina. (1993) "A Comparison of Pimps and Batterers." *Michigan Journal of Gender and Law* 1, 1: 33–57.

_____. (1990) "Confronting the Liberal Lies About Prostitution." In Dorchen Leidholdt and Janice G. Raymond, eds. *The Sexual Liberals and the Attack on Feminism.* New York: Pergamon Press.

Goldberg, Carey. (September 11, 1995) "Sex Slavery, Thailand to New York; Thousands of Indentured Asian Prostitutes May Be in U.S." *New York Times,* p. B1.

Goldman, Russell. (October 8, 2007) "Parents Who Pimp Their Children." ABC News. http://abcnews.go.com/US/story?id=3691604&page=1.

Goldsmith, Barbara. (April 26, 1993) "Women on the Edge: A Reporter at Large." *New Yorker* 69: 65.

Goodall, Richard. (1995) *The Comfort of Sin: Prostitutes and Prostitution in the 1990s.* Kent, England: Renaissance Books.

Grady, Barbara. (April 23, 2008) "Prosecutor Targets Pimps Not Girls." *Oakland Tribune.*

http://www.insidebayarea.com/search/ci_90
24565?IADID=Search-www.insidebayarea.
com-www.insidebayarea.com.

Green, Richard. (1992) *Sexual Science and the Law.* Cambridge, MA: Harvard University Press.

Greenblatt, Milton, and Marjorie J. Robertson. (1993) "Life-Styles, Adaptive Strategies, and Sexual Behaviors of Homeless Adolescents." *Hospital and Community Psychiatry* 44, 12: 1177–80.

Greene, Jody M., Susan T. Ennett, and Christopher L. Ringwalt. (1999) "Prevalence and Correlates of Survival Sex Among Runaway and Homeless Youth." *American Journal of Public Health* 89, 9: 1406–9.

_____, _____, and _____. (1997) "Substance Use Among Runaway and Homeless Youth in Three National Samples." *American Journal of Public Health* 87, 2: 229–35.

Griffin, Gil. (July 26, 1997) "Running on Empty: Kids Take to the Streets When They Don't Feel Loved at Home." *San Diego Union-Tribune,* p. E1.

Gullotta, Thomas P. (1978) "Runaway: Reality or Myth." *Adolescence* 13, 52: 543–49.

Hagan, John, and Bill McCarthy. (1998) *Mean Streets: Youth Crime and Homelessness.* Cambridge, MA: Cambridge University Press.

_____, and _____. (1992) "Streetlife and Delinquency." *British Journal of Sociology* 43, 4: 533–61.

Halcon, Linda L., and Alan R. Lifson. (2004) "Prevalence and Predictors of Sexual Risks Among Homeless Youth." *Journal of Youth and Adolescence* 33, 1: 75–76.

Haley, Nancy, Elise Roy, Pascale Leclerc, and Jean-François Boivin. (2004) "HIV High Risk Profile of Male Street Youth Involved in Survival Sex." *Sexually Transmitted Infections* 80: 526–30.

Hall, Timothy M. (2007) "Rent-Boys, Barflies, and Kept Men: Men Involved in Sex with Men for Compensation in Prague." *Sexualities* 10: 457–72.

Hamidi, Farideh. "A Study on Family Structure and Attachment Style of Runaway Girls and the Outcomes of Using Family and Supportive Therapy Interventions." http://en.sbu.ac.ir/Portals/0/Family/1.pdf.

Hammer, Heather, David Finkelhor, and Andrea J. Sedlak. (2002) *Runaway/Thrownaway Children: National Estimates and Characteristics.* NISMART Bulletin Series. Washington, D.C.: Office of Juvenile Justice and Delinquency Prevention.

Haq, Farquan. (March 27, 1996) "U.S. Children: Street Kids Turn to Sex to Survive." *Inter-Press Service.*

Hargrove, Thomas. (June 5, 2005) "Runaway Children Face Erratic Patchwork of State Laws." Stories in the News. http://www.sitnews.us/0605news/060505/060505_shns_missing.html.

Harlan, Sparky, Luanne L. Rodgers, and Brian Slattery. (1981) *Male and Female Adolescent Prostitution: Huckleberry House Sexual Minority Youth Services Project.* Washington, D.C.: U.S. Department of Health and Human Services.

Hazelhurst, Kayleen, and Cameron Hazelhurst, eds. (1989) *Gangs and Youth Subcultures: International Explorations.* New Brunswick, NJ: Transaction Publishers.

HCH Clinicians' Network. (2002) "Crossing to Safety: Transgender Health and Homelessness." *Healing Hands* 6: 1–6.

HealthHype.com. (January 11, 2008) "Newly Homeless Youth Are at High Risk with Sexual Behavior." http://www.healthhype.com/newly-homeless-youth-are-at-high-risk-with-sexual-behavior.html.

Hersch, Patricia. (1988) "Coming of Age on City Streets." *Psychology Today,* 22, 1: 28–37.

Hier, Sally J., Paula J. Korboot, and Robert D. Schweitzer. (1990) "Social Adjustment and Symptomatology in Two Types of Homeless Adolescents: Runaways and Throwaways." *Adolescence* 25, 100: 761–71.

Hildebrand, James A. (1963) "Why Runaways Leave Home." *Police Science* 54: 211–16.

Hoag, Christina. (April 19, 2009) "New Laws Treat Teen Prostitutes as Abuse Victims." ABC News. http://www.abcnews.go.com/US/WireStory?id=7370496&page=2.

_____. (April 19, 2009) "Teen Prostitutes Rescued, Not Arrested." *Tulsa World.* http://www.tulsaworld.com/news/article.aspx?subjectid=338&articleid=20090419_13_A10_U ietfe479338&archive=yes.

Holtz, Jackson. (August 13, 2008) "Craigslist Sex Ad Leads to 15 Arrests." HeraldNet. http://www.heraldnet.com/article/20080813/NEWS01/40977851&news0lad=1.

Homer, Louise (1973) "Criminality Based Resource for Runaway Girls." *Social Casework* 10: 474.

Hot Topics for School Administrators: School Dropout Prevention. "Identifying Students at High-Risk for School Drop-Out." http://www.educationalresourceservices.com/files/hot_topic_prinicipals.pdf.

Hoyt, Danny R., Kimberly D. Ryan, and Ana Mari Cauce. (1999) "Personal Victimization in a High Risk Environment: Homeless and Runaway Adolescents." *Research in Crime and Delinquency* 36, 4: 371–91.

Hughes, Donna. (1999) *Pimps and Predators on the Internet: Globalizing the Sexual Exploitation of Women and Children*. New York: ECPAT-US.

Hunter, Susan K. (1993) "Prostitution Is Cruelty and Abuse to Women and Children." *Michigan Journal of Gender and Law* 1, 91: 91–104.

Hyde, Justeen. (2005) "From Home to Street: Understanding Young People's Transitions into Homelessness." *Journal of Adolescence* 28, 2: 171–83.

Illinois Ann. Stat. ch. 720, para. 5/11–19.1.

*In the Matter of Jennifer M.* (1986) 509 N.Y.S. 2d 935, 937.

Inciardi, James A., Anne E. Pottieger, Mary Ann Forney, Dale D. Chitwood, and Duane C. McBride. (1991) "Prostitution, IV Drug Use, and Sex for Crack Exchanges Among Serious Delinquents: Risks for HIV Infection." *Criminology* 29: 221–35.

_____, Ruth Horowitz, and Anne E. Pottieger. (1993) *Street Kids, Street Drugs, Street Crime*. Belmont, CA: Wadsworth.

Indiana, Gary. (1994) *Rent Boy*. Baltimore, MD: Serpent's Tail.

Institute of Health Policy Studies. (1995) *Street Youth at Risk for AIDS*. San Francisco, CA: University of California.

Iowa Code Ann. § 725.3.

James, Jennifer. (1973) "Prostitute-Pimp Relationships." *Medical Aspects of Human Sexuality* 7: 147–63.

Janus, Mark D., Ann W. Burgess, and Arlene McCormack. (1987) "Histories of Sexual Abuse in Adolescent Male Runaways." *Adolescence* 22, 86: 405–18.

_____, _____, _____, and Carol Hartman. (1987) *Adolescent Runaways: Causes and Consequences*. Lexington, MA: Lexington Books.

Johnson, Joan J. (1992) *Teen Prostitution*. Danbury, CT: Franklin Watts.

Johnson, N. S., and Roxy Peck. (1978) "Sibship Composition and the Adolescent Runaway Phenomenon." *Journal of Youth and Adolescence* 7, 3: 301–05.

Johnson, Ray. (October 22, 1997) "Dealing with Domestic Violence and Teen-age Runaways." *San Diego Union-Tribune*, p. B5.

Johnson, Timothy P. (1996) "Self-Reported Risk Factors for AIDS Among Homeless Youth." *AIDS Education Prevention* 8: 308–22.

_____, Jennie R. Aschkenasy, Mary R. Herbers, and Stephen A. Gillenwater. (1996) "Self-Reported Risk Factors for AIDS Among Homeless Youth." *AIDS Education and Prevention* 8: 308–22.

Jones, Deborah. (November 1994) "Pimped." *Chatelaine* 67: 111.

Jones, Loring P. (1988) "A Typology of Adolescent Runaways." *Child and Adolescent Social Work Journal* 5, 1: 16–29.

Jordan, Lara J. (June 25, 2008) "Kids Rescued, Pimps Arrested in Prostitution Busts." WSBT.com. http://www.wsbt.com/news/regional/21579334.html.

Jorgenson, S., H. Thornburg, and J. Williams. (1980) "The Experience of Running Away: Perceptions of Adolescents Seeking Help in a Shelter Case Facility." *High School Journal* 12: 87–96.

Juvenile Justice and Delinquency Prevention Act. (1974) P.L. 93–415.

Kandel, Minouche. (1992) "Whores in Court: Judicial Processing of Prostitutes in the Boston Municipal Court in 1990." *Yale Journal of Law and Feminism* 4: 329–346.

Kaplan, Caren. (2004) *Children Missing from Care: An Issue Brief*. Washington, D.C.: Child Welfare League of America.

KATU.com. (September 19, 2007) "Deputies Break Up Beaverton Prostitution Ring." http://www.katu.com/news/9875602.html.

Kaufman, Jeanne G., and Cathy S. Widom. (1999) "Childhood Victimization, Running Away, and Delinquency." *Journal of Research in Crime and Delinquency* 36, 4: 347–70.

Kempf-Leonard, Kimberly, and Pernilla Johansson. (2007) "Gender and Runaways: Risk Factors, Delinquency, and Juvenile Justice Experiences." *Youth Violence and Juvenile Justice* 5, 3: 308–27.

Kestin, Sally, and Megan O'Matz. "Runaways Face Tough Life on Streets." CYCNet.org. http://www.cyc-net.org/features/ft-runaways.html.

Kihara, David. (August 24, 1999) "Giuliani's Suppressed Report on Homeless Youth." *The Village Voice* 44, 33. http://village voice.com.

King, Michael, Joanna Semlyen, Sharon See Tai, Helen Killaspy, David Osborn, Dmitri Popelyuk, and Irwin Nazareth. (2008) "A Systematic Review of Mental Disorder, Suicide, and Deliberate Self Harm in Lesbian, Gay and Bisexual People." *BMC Psychiatry* 8: 70.

Kipke, Michele D., Susanne B. Montgomery, Thomas R. Simon, and Ellen F. Iverson. (1997) "Substance Abuse Disorders Among

Runaway and Homeless Youth." *Substance Use and Misuse* 32: 969–86.

_____, Thomas R. Simon, Susanne B. Montgomery, Jennifer B. Unger, and Ellen Iverson. (1997) "Homeless Youth and Their Exposure to and Involvement in Violence While Living on the Streets." *Journal of Adolescent Health* 20, 5: 360–67.

Klass Kids Foundation. (February 2009) "The HT Report." http://www.klaaskids.org/pght-report.htm.

Kolvin, Israel, Frederick J. Miller, Mary Fleeting, and Philip A. Kolvin. (1988) "Social and Parenting Factors Affecting Criminal-Offense Rates: Findings from the Newcastle Thousand Family Study (1947–1980)." *British Journal of Psychiatry* 152: 80–90.

Komonews.com. (February 23, 2009) "Feds Rescue Suspected Teen Prostitutes in Sweep." http://www.komonews.com/news/40093317.html.

Kral, Alex H., Beth E. Molnar, Robert E. Booth, and John K. Watters. (1997) "Prevalence of Sexual Risk Behaviour and Substance Use Among Runaway and Homeless Adolescents in San Francisco, Denver and New York City." *International Journal of STD and AIDS* 8: 109–17.

Kristof, Nicholas D. (March 16, 2008) "The Pimps' Slaves." *New York Times.* http://www.nytimes.com/2008/03/16/opinion/16kristof.html?_r=2&oref=slogin&oref=slogin.

Kruks, Gabe. (1991) "Gay and Lesbian Homeless/Street Youth: Special Issues and Concerns." *Journal of Adolescent Health* 12, 7: 515–18.

KTVU. (March 7, 2009) "Oakland Battles Wave of Teenage Prostitution." http://www.ktvu.com/news/19388341/detail.html.

Kurtz, P. David. (1991) "Problems of Maltreated Runaway Youth." *Adolescence* 26,103: 543–55.

_____, Elizabeth W. Lindsey, Sara Jarvis, and Larry Nackerud. (2000) "How Runaway and Homeless Youth Navigate Troubled Waters: The Role of Formal and Informal Helpers." *Child and Adolescent Social Work Journal* 17, 5: 381–402.

_____, Gail L. Kurtz, and Sara Jarvis. (1991) "Problems of Maltreated Runaway Youth." *Adolescence* 26: 543–55.

KVAL.com. (October 5, 2009) "Child Porn Arrests: 'Shooting Fish in a Barrel.'" http://www.kval.com/news/national/63547752.html.

Lagorio, Christine. (December 16, 2005) "Crackdown on Child Prostitution: Justice Department Charges More than Thirty Across Several States." CBS News. http://www.cbsnews.com/stories/2005/12/16/national/main1133570.shtml.

Lane, Brian, and Wilfred Gregg. (1995) *The Encyclopedia of Serial Killers.* New York: Berkley.

Langum, David J. (1995) *Crossing Over the Line: Legislating Morality and the Mann Act.* Chicago, IL: University of Chicago Press.

Lanning, Kenneth V. (1992) *Child Molesters: A Behavioral Analysis for Law Enforcement Officers Investigating Cases of Child Sexual Exploitation.* Arlington, VA: National Center for Missing and Exploited Children.

_____. (1992) *Child Sex Rings: A Behavioral Analysis, for Criminal Justice Professionals Handling Cases of Child Sexual Exploitation.* Alexandria, VA: National Center for Missing and Exploited Children.

Lau, Evelyn. (1989) *Runaway: Diary of a Street Kid.* Toronto: Harper and Collins.

LeBlanc, Adrian N. (March 1993) "I'm a Shadow." *Seventeen* 52: 216.

Lees, J. P., and L. J. Newson. (1954) "Family or Sibship Position and Some of Juvenile Delinquency." *British Journal of Delinquency* 5: 46–55.

Lemmey, D., and P. Tice. (2000) "Two Tragic Forms of Child Sexual Abuse: Are They Often Overlooked?" *Journal of Child Sexual Abuse* 9, 2: 86–106.

Leslie, Michelle Burden, Judith A. Stein, and Mary Jane Rotheram-Borus. (2002) "Sex Specific Predictors of Suicidality Among Runaway Youth." *Journal of Clinical Child and Adolescent Psychology* 31, 1: 27–40.

Lester, David (1995) *Serial Killers: The Insatiable Passion.* Philadelphia, PA: The Charles Press.

Levine, Renee S., Diane Metzendorf, and Kathryn A. Van Boskirk. (1986) "Runaway and Throwaway Youth: A Case for Early Intervention with Truants." *Social Work in Education* 8: 93–106.

*Lewis v. State.* (1972) 288NE 2d 138.

Lifson, Alan R., and Linda L. Halcon. (2001) "Substance Abuse and High-Risk Needle-Related Behaviors Among Homeless Youth in Minneapolis: Implications for Prevention." *Journal of Urban Health* 78, 4: 690–98.

Lloyd, Robin. (1976) *For Money or Love: Boy Prostitution in America.* New York: Ballantine.

Lock, James, and Hans Steiner. (1999) "Gay, Lesbian and Bisexual Youth Risks for Emotional, Physical, and Social Problems: Results from a Community-Based Survey." *Journal of the American Academy of Child and Adolescence Psychiatry* 38, 3: 297–304.

Loeber, Rolf A., Ann W. Weiher, and Carolyn Smith. (1991) "The Relationship Between Family Interaction and Delinquency and Substance Use." In David Huizinga, Rolf Loeber, and Terrence P. Thornberry, eds. *Urban Delinquency and Substance Abuse: Technical Report*, Vol. 1. Washington, D.C.: Office of Juvenile Justice and Delinquency.

Loken, Gregory A. (1987) "Child Prostitution." In U.S. Department of Justice. *Child Pornography and Prostitution: Background and Legal Analysis*. Alexandria, VA: National Center for Missing and Exploited Children.

Louisiana Rev. Stat. Ann. § 14:82.1.

Lowman, John. (1991) "Street Prostitutes in Canada: An Evaluation of the Brannigan-Fleischman Opportunity Model." *Canadian Journal of Law and Society* 6: 137–64.

_____. (1992) "Street Prostitution." In Vincent Sacco, ed. *Deviance Conformity and Control in Canadian Society*. 2nd ed. Scarborough: Prentice-Hall Canada.

_____, and Laura Fraser. (1996) *Violence Against Persons Who Are Prostitutes: The Experience in British Columbia*. Ottawa: Department of Justice Canada.

Luckenbill, David F. (1985) "Entering Male Prostitution." *Journal of Contemporary Ethnography* 14: 131–53.

Lukman, Z. M. (2009) "The Prevalence of Running Away from Home Among Prostituted Youth in Malaysia." *Journal of Social Sciences* 5, 3: 157–62.

MacLean, Michael G., Lara E. Embry, and Ana Mari Cauce. (1999) "Homeless Adolescents' Paths to Separation from Family: Comparison of Family Characteristics, Psychological Adjustment, and Victimization." *Journal of Community Psychology*, 27, 2: 179–87.

_____, Matthew J. Paradise, and Ana Mari Cauce. (1999) "Substance Use and Psychological Adjustment in Homeless Adolescents: A Test of Three Models." *American Journal of Community Psychology* 27: 405–27.

MacNamara, Donald. (1965) "Male Prostitution in American Cities: A Socioeconomic or Pathological Phenomenon?" *American Journal of Orthopsychiatry* 35: 204.

Males, Carolyn, and Julie Raskin. (January 1984) "The Children Nobody Wants." *Reader's Digest*, p. 63.

Mallett, Shelley, Doreen Rosenthal, and Deborah Keys. (2005) "Young People, Drug Use and Family Conflict: Pathways into Homelessness." *Journal of Adolescence* 28, 2: 185–99.

Mandel, Jerry. (1979) "Hispanics in the Criminal Justice System—The 'Nonexistent' Problem." *Agenda* 9, 3: 16–20.

Manning, Mary. (August 4, 2008) "Runaway Girl Found in Shallow Grave Identified." *Las Vegas Sun*. http://www.lasvegassun.com/news/2008/aug/04/runaway-girl-found-shallow-grave-identified.

Markos, A. R., A. A. Wade, and M. Walzman. (1994) "The Adolescent Male Prostitute and Sexually Transmitted Diseases, HIV and AIDs." *Journal of Adolescence* 17: 123–30.

Martinez, Ruby J. (2006) "Understanding Runaway Teens." *Journal of Child and Adolescent Psychiatric Nursing* 19, 2: 77–88.

Maxson, Cheryl L., Margaret A. Little, and Malcolm W. Klein. (1988) "Police Response to Runaway and Missing Children: A Conceptual Framework for Research and Policy." *Crime & Delinquency* 34, 1: 84–102.

Mayers, Marjorie. (2001) *Street Kids and Streetscapes: Panhandling, Politics, and Prophecies*. New York: Peter Lang.

McCarthy, Bill, and John Hagan. (1992) "Surviving on the Street: The Experience of Homeless Youth." *Journal of Adolescent Research* 7: 412–30.

McClanahan, Susan F., Gary M. McClelland, Karen M. Abram, and Linda A. Teplin. (1999) "Pathways Into Prostitution Among Female Jail Detainees and Their Implications for Mental Health Services." *Psychiatric Services* 50: 1606–13.

McCormack, Arlene, Mark D. Janus, and Ann W. Burgess. (1986) "Runaway Youths and Sexual Victimization: Gender Differences in an Adolescent Runaway Population." *Child Abuse and Neglect* 10: 387–95.

McIntyre, Susan. (1999) "The Youngest Profession—The Oldest Oppression: A Study of Sex. Work." In Christopher Bagley and Kanka Mallick, eds. *Child Sexual Abuse and Adult Offenders: New Theory and Research*. London: Ashgate.

McKeganey, Neil P., and Marina U. Barnard. (1996) *Sex Work on the Streets: Prostitutes and Their Clients*. Buckingham, UK: Open University Press.

McNamara, Robert H. (2008) *The Lost Population: Status Offenders in America*. Durham, NC: Carolina Academic Press.

McNamara, Robert P. (1994) *The Times Square Hustler: Male Prostitution in New York City*. Westport, CT: Praeger.

McWhirter, Benedict T. (1990) "Loneliness: A Review of Current Literature, with Implications for Counseling and Research." *Journal of Counseling and Development* 68: 417–23.

Michigan State News Release. "Justice System Unfair, Unjust for Hispanics." About.com: Crime/Punishment, http://crime.about.com/od/issues/a/blmu041026.htm.

Milburn, Norweeta G., Li-Jung Liang, Sung-Jae Lee, Mary J. Rotheram-Borus, Doreen Rosenthal, Shelley Mallett, Marguerita Lightfoot, and Patricia Lester. (2009) " Who Is Doing Well? A Typology of Newly Homeless Adolescents." *Journal of Community Psychology* 37, 2: 135–47.

_____, Mary J. Rotheram-Borus, Philip Batterham, Babette Brumback, Doreen Rosenthal, and Shelley Mallett. (2005) "Predictors of Close Family Relationships Over One Year Among Homeless Young People." *Journal of Adolescence* 28, 2: 263–75.

Miller, Jody, and Martin D. Schwartz. (1995) "Rape Myths and Violence Against Street Prostitutes." *Deviant Behavior* 16, 1: 1–23.

Miller, Pamela, Peter Donahue, Dave Este, and Marvin Hofer. (2004) "Experiences of Being Homeless or at Risk of Being Homeless Among Canadian Youths." *Adolescence* 39, 156: 735–55.

Minogue, Jane. (March 25, 2009) "Prostitutes, the Internet, and Regulation, Part I." *Huff-Post Social News.* http://www.huffingtonpost.com/jane-minogue/part-i-prostitutes-the-in_b_178272.html.

Missing, Exploited, and Runaway Children Protection Act. (2000) P.L. 106–71.

Molino, Alma C. (March 1–2, 2007) "Characteristics of Help-Seeking Street Youth and Non-Street Youth." 2007 National Symposium on Homelessness Research, p. 7–4. http://aspe.hhs.gov/hsp/homelessness/symposium07/molino/index.htm.

Molnar, Beth E., Alex H. Kral, and John K. Watters. (1994) *Street Youth at Risk for AIDS.* Rockville, MD: National Institute on Drug Abuse.

_____, Stanley B. Shade, Alex H. Kral, Robert E. Booth, and John K. Watters. (1998) "Suicidal Behavior and Sexual/Physical Abuse Among Street Youth." *Child Abuse and Neglect,* 22: 213–22.

Montana Code Ann. § 45-5-603.

Monto, Martin A. (2004) "Female Prostitution, Customers, and Violence." *Violence Against Women,* 10: 160–88.

Moon, Martha W., Diane Binson, Kimberly Page-Shafter, and Rafael Diaz. (2001) "Correlates of HIV Risk in a Random Sample of Street Youths in San Francisco." *Journal of the Association of Nurses in AIDS Care* 12, 6: 18–27.

Moreno, Claudia L. (2007) "The Relationship Between Culture, Gender, Structural Factors, Abuse, Trauma, and HIV/AIDS for Latinas." *Qualitative Health Research* 17: 340–52.

Morse, Edward V., Patricia M. Simon, and Paul M. Balson. (1992) "Sexual Behavior Patterns of Customers of Male Street Prostitutes." *Archives of Sexual Behavior* 21, 4: 347–57.

Moscicki, A., B. Winkler, C. Irwin, and J. Schacter. (1989) "Differences in Biologic Maturation, Sexual Behavior, and Sexually Transmitted Disease Between Adolescents with and Without Cervical Intraepithelial Neoplasia." *Journal of Pediatrics* 115: 487–93.

Mottet, Lisa, and John M. Ohle. (2004) "Transitioning Our Shelters: A Guide to Making Homeless Shelters Safe for Transgender People." http://www.thetaskforce.org.

Musil, Steven. (April 8, 2007) "Teen Suspected of Using Craigslist for Prostitution." CNET News. http://news.cnet.com/8301-10784_3-6174334-7.html.

Myers, Dusti-S. (December 2, 2008) "Generational Prostitution in the United States." *Associated Content Community.* http://www.associatedcontent.com/article/1239336/generational_prostitution_in_the_united.html?cat=9.

Nadon, Susan M., Catherine Koverola, and Eduard H. Schudermann. (1998) "Antecedents to Prostitution: Childhood Victimization." *Journal of Interpersonal Violence* 13: 206–21.

National Association of Social Workers. (1992) *Helping Vulnerable Youth: Runaway and Homeless Adolescents in the United States.* Washington, D.C.: NASW Press.

National Center for Missing and Exploited Children. (2002) *Female Juvenile Prostitution: Problem and Response.* 2nd ed. Alexandria, VA: National Center for Missing and Exploited Children.

_____. (1999) *Prostitution of Children and Child-Sex Tourism.* Alexandria, VA: National Center for Missing and Exploited Children.

National Coalition for the Homeless. "Homeless Youth." *NCH Fact Sheet #13.* http://www.nationalhomeless.org/factsheets/youth.html.

_____. (2004) *Illegal to Be Homeless: The Criminalization of Homelessness in the United States.* Washington, D.C.: National Coalition for the Homeless.

_____, and National Law Center on Homelessness and Poverty. (2006) *A Dream Denied: The Criminalization of Homelessness in U.S. Cities.* Washington, D.C.: National Coalition for the Homeless and National Law Center on Homelessness and Poverty.

National Law Center on Homelessness and Poverty. (2003) *Alone Without a Home: A State-by-State Guide to Laws Affecting Unaccompanied Youth.* Washington, D.C.: National Law Center on Homelessness and Poverty.

National Network for Youth. "HIV Risk of RHY." http://www.nn4youth.org/our-work/cdc-grant/hiv-std.

_____. "NN4Y Issue Brief: Unaccompanied Youth Overview." http://www.nn4youth.org/system/files/IssueBrief_Unaccompanyed_youth.pdf.

_____. (1998) *Toolkit for Youth Workers: Fact Sheet. Runaway and Homeless Youth.* Washington, D.C.: National Network for Youth.

_____. "Who Are Runaway and Homeless Youth?" http://www.nn4youth.org/about-us/faqs-and-other-resources.

National Runaway Switchboard. Keeping America's Runaway and At-Risk Youth Safe and Off the Streets. http://www.1800runaway.org.

National Survey on Drug Use and Health. (July 2, 2004) *The NSDUH Report.* "Substance Abuse Among Youths Who Had Run Away from Home." http://www.oas.samhsa.gov/2k4/runAways/runAways.htm.

Nevada Rev. Stat. § 201.360.

New York Penal Code §§ 230.04, 230.05, 230.06.

Newiss, Geoff. (1999) *Missing Presumed...? The Police Response to Missing Persons.* London: Home Office.

Newson, John, Elizabeth Newson, and Mike S. Adams. (1993) "The Social Origins of Delinquency." *Criminal Behavior and Mental Health* 3: 19–29.

Nixon, Kendra, Leslie Tutty, Pamela Downe, Kelly Gorkoff, and Jane Ursel. (2002) "The Everyday Occurrence: Violence in the Lives of Girls Exploited Through Prostitution." *Violence Against Women* 8: 1016–43.

Nkrumah, Wade. (August 28, 2007) "Police Catch Up with Runaway Forest Grove Boy." *Oregonian.* http://blog.oregonlive.com/breakingnews/2007/08/police_spot_but_cant_catch_run.html.

Noell, John, Paul Rohde, John Seeley, and Linda Ochs. (2001) "Childhood Sexual Abuse, Adolescent Sexual Coercion and Sexually Transmitted Infection Acquisition Among Homeless Female Adolescents." *Child Abuse and Neglect* 25: 137–48.

O'Brien, Shirley. (1983) *Child Pornography.* Dubuque, IA: Kendall/Hunt.

O'Connor, M. L. (1998) "Unsafe Behaviors Place Street Youth, Especially Women, at Risk of HIV." *Family Planning Perspectives* 30, 1: 20–51.

Office of Applied Studies. (2003) *Results from the 2002 National Survey on Drug Use and Health: National Findings.* Rockville, MD: Substance Abuse and Mental Health Services Administration.

_____. (2004) *Substance Abuse Among Youth Who Had Run Away from Home.* Rockville, MD: Substance Abuse and Mental Health Services Administration.

Office of Juvenile Justice and Delinquency Prevention. (October 2002) NISMART Bulletin, "National Estimates of Missing Children: An Overview." http://www.ncjrs.gov/html/ojjdp/nismart/01/index.html.

The Office on Child Abuse and Neglect. (1974) 42 U.S.C. § 5101–5106.

Oliver, Pam. (2002) "A Review of Literature on Child Prostitution." *Social Policy Journal of New Zealand* 19. http://www.thefreelibrary.com/_/print/PrintArticle.aspx?id=998492 75.

The Omnibus Consolidated Appropriations Act. (1997) P.L. 104–208, § 121, 110 stat. 3009, 3009–26.

Oregon Rev. Stat. § 167.017.

Patten, Jim. (September 13, 2007) "Police: Teen Call Girls Grateful They Were Caught." *The Eagle Tribune.* http://www.eagletribune.com/punews/local_story_256115550.

Pennbridge, Julia N., Thomas Freese, and Richard G. MacKenzie. (Fall 1992) "High Risk Behaviors Among Street Youth in Hollywood, California." *AIDS Education and Prevention,* pp. 24–33.

Pfeifer, R. W., and J. Oliver. (1997) "Study of HIV Seroprevalence in a Group of Homeless Youth in Hollywood, California." *Journal of Adolescent Health* 20, 5: 339–42.

Piasecki, Joe. (June 26, 2006) "Throwaway Kids." *Pasadena Weekly.* http://www.pasadenaweekly.com/cms/story/detail/?id=3559&IssueNum=25.

Pisarcik, Kristin. (March 21, 2008) "Miami Vice: Inside 'John Stings' and 'Escort Stings.'" ABC News. http://abcnews.go.com/2020/story?id=4488667&page=1.

Pleak, Richard R., and Heino Meyer-Bahlburg. (1990) "Sexual Behavior and AIDS Knowledge of Young Male Prostitutes in Manhattan." *Journal of Sex Research* 27: 557–88.

Potterat, John J., Devon D. Brewer, Stephen Q. Muth, Richard B. Rothenberg, Donald E. Woodhouse, John B. Muth, Heather K. Stites, and Stuart Brody. (2004) "Mortality in a Long-term Open Cohort of Prostitute Women." *American Journal of Epidemiology* 159, 8: 778.

Powers, Jane L., and Barbara Jaklitsch. (1989) *Understanding Survivors of Abuse: Stories of Homeless and Runaway Adolescents.* New York: Free Press.

_____, _____, and John Eckenrode. (April 1988) "Behavioral Indicators of Maltreatment Among Runaway and Homeless Youth." Paper presented at the National Symposium on Child Victimization, Anaheim, CA.

Pratt, C. (June 18, 1995) "The Perilous Times of Transgender Youth." *New York Times*, p. CY7.

Prestage, Garrett. (1994) "Male and Transsexual Prostitution." In Roberta Perkins, Garrett Prestage, Rachel Sharp, and Frances Lovejoy, eds. *Sex Work and Sex Workers in Australia.* Sydney: University of New South Wales Press.

Prohibited Activities. (1982) 18 U.S.C. § 1962.

Protection of Children from Sexual Predators Act of 1998. (1998) P.L. 105–314, 101, 112 Stat. 2974.

Puzzanchera, Charles. (2007) *Trends in Justice System's Response to Status Offending: OJJDP Briefing Paper.* Pittsburgh, PA: National Center for Juvenile Justice.

Pyett, Priscilla M., and Deborah J. Warr. (1997) "Vulnerability on the Streets: Female Sex Workers and HIV Risk." *AIDS Care* 9, 5: 539–47.

Quayle, Ethel. (2003) *Child Pornography: An Internet Crime.* New York: Routledge.

Rasmusson, Anne. (June 1, 1999) "Commercial Sexual Exploitation of Children: A Literature Review." Alliance for Speaking the Truths on Prostitution and Center for Urban and Regional Affairs. http://members.shaw. ca/pdg/exploitation_of_children.html#_Toc452540114.

Ray, Nicholas. (2006) *Lesbian, Gay, Bisexual, and Transgender Youth: An Epidemic of Homelessness.* New York: National Gay and Lesbian Task Force Policy Institute and National Coalition for the Homeless.

Reeg, Bob. (2003) "The Runaway and Homeless Youth Act and Disconnected Youth." In Jodie Levin-Epstein and Mark H. Greenberg, eds. *Leave No Youth Behind: Opportunities for Congress to Reach Disconnected Youth.* Washington, D.C.: Center for Law and Social Policy.

Rees, Gwyther. (2001) *Working with Young Runaways: Learning from Practice.* London: The Children's Society.

Remafedi, Gary J. (1985) "Adolescent Homosexuality: Issues for Pediatricians." *Clinical Pediatrics* 24, 9: 481–85.

Rettenmund, Matthew. (1997) *Boy Culture.* New York: St. Martin's Press.

Rew, Lynn. (2002) "Characteristics and Health Care Needs of Homeless Adolescents." *Nursing Clinics of North America* 37, 3: 423–32.

_____, Margaret Taylor-Seehafer, and Maureen L. Fitzgerald. (2001) "Sexual Abuse, Alcohol and Other Drug Use, and Suicidal Behaviors in Homeless Adolescents." *Issues in Comprehensive Pediatric Nursing* 24, 4: 225–40.

_____, Margaret Taylor-Seehafer, Nancy Thomas, and Ronald Yockey. (2001) "Correlates of Resilience in Homeless Adolescents." *Journal of Nursing Scholarship* 33, 1: 33–40.

_____, Rachel T. Fouladi, and Ronald D. Yockey. (2002) "Sexual Health Practices of Homeless Youth." *Journal of Nursing Scholarship* 34, 2: 139–45.

_____, Tiffany A. Whittaker, Margaret Taylor-Seehafer, and Lorie R. Smith. (2005) "Sexual Health and Protective Resources in Gay, Lesbian, Bisexual, and Heterosexual Homeless Youth." *Journal for Specialists in Pediatric Nursing* 10, 1: 11–19.

Riley, Debbie B., Geoffrey L. Greif, Debra L. Caplan, and K. M. Heather. (2004) "Common Themes and Treatment Approaches in Working with Families of Runaway Youths." *American Journal of Family Therapy* 32, 2: 139–53.

Ringwalt, Christopher L., Jody M. Greene, and Marjorie J. Robertson. (1998) "Familial Backgrounds and Risk Behaviors of Youth with Thrownaway Experiences." *Journal of Adolescence* 21, 3: 241–52.

_____, _____, _____, and Melissa McPheeters. (1998) "The Prevalence of Homelessness Among Adolescents in the United States." *American Journal of Public Health* 88, 9: 1325–29.

Roane, Kit R. (July 11, 1999) "Gangs Turn to New Trade: Young Prostitutes." *New York Times*, p. 23.

Robertson, Marjorie J. (1989) *Homeless Youth in Hollywood: Patterns of Alcohol Use.* Berkley, CA: Alcohol Research Group.

_____. (1996) *Homeless Youth on Their Own.* Berkley, CA: Alcohol Research Group.

_____. (1998) "Homeless Youth: Research, Intervention, and Policy." In Linda B. Fosburg and Deborah. L. Dennis, eds. *Practical Lessons: The 1998 National Symposium on Homelessness Research.* Washington, D.C.: U.S. Department of Housing and Urban Development and U.S. Department of Health and Human Services.

_____, and Paul A. Toro. "Homeless Youth: Research, Intervention, and Policy." http://aspe.hhs.gov/ProgSys/homeless/symposium/3-Youth.htm.

Rohr, Michael E. (1999) *Adolescent Runaway Behavior: Who Runs and Why.* New York: Routledge.

Rokach, Ami. (2005) "The Causes of Loneliness in Homeless Youth." *Journal of Psychology* 139, 5: 469–80.

Rooney, Rita. (July 1983) "Children for Sale: Pornography's Dark New World." *Reader's Digest*, p. 53.

Rosario, Margaret, Eric W. Schrimshaw, Joyce Hunter, and Marya Gwadz. (2002) "Gay-Related Stress and Emotional Distress Among Gay, Lesbian, and Bisexual Youths: A Longitudinal Examination." *Journal of Consulting and Clinical Psychology* 70, 4: 967–75.

_____, Joyce Hunter, and Marya Gwadz. (1997) "Exploration of Substance Use Among Lesbian, Gay, and Bisexual Youth: Prevalence and Correlates." *Journal of Adolescent Research* 12, 4: 454–76.

_____, Joyce Hunter, Shira Maguen, Marya Gwadz, and Raymond Smith. (2001) "The Coming-out Process and its Adaptational and Health-Related Associations Among Gay, Lesbian, and Bisexual Youths: Stipulation and Exploration of a Model." *American Journal of Community Psychology* 29: 133–60.

_____, Karen A. Mahler, Joyce Hunter, and Marya Gwadz. (1999) "Understanding the Unprotected Sexual Behaviors of Gay, Lesbian, and Bisexual Youths: An Empirical Test of the Cognitive-Environmental Model." *Health Psychology* 18: 272–80.

Rosenbleet, Charles, and Barbara J. Pariente. (1973) "The Prostitution of the Criminal Law," *American Criminal Law Review* 11: 373.

Rosenthal, Doreen and Susan Moore. (1994) "Homeless Youths: Sexual and Drug-Related Behavior, Sexual Beliefs and HIV/AIDS Risk." *AIDS Care* 6, 1: 83–94.

Rotheram-Borus, Mary J. (1993) "Suicidal Behavior and Risk Factors Among Runaway Youths." *American Journal of Psychiatry* 150: 103–7.

_____, Cheryl Koopman, and Anke A. Ehrhardt. (1991) "Homeless Youth and HIV Infection." *American Psychologist* 46, 11: 1188–97.

_____, Heino Meyer-Bahlburg, Cheryl Koopman, Margaret Rosario, Theresa M. Exner, Ronald Henderson, Marjory Matthieu, and Rhoda Gruen. (1992) "Lifetime Sexual Behavior Among Runaway Males and Females." *Journal of Sex Research* 29, 1: 15–29.

_____, Karen A. Mahler, Cheryl Koopman, and Kris Langabeer. (1996) "Sexual Abuse History and Associated Multiple Risk Behavior in Adolescent Runaways." *American Journal of Orthopsychiatry* 66: 390–400.

Rule, Ann. (2005) *Green River, Running Red: The Real Story of the Green River Killer — America's Deadliest Serial Murderer.* New York: Pocket Star.

Runaway and Homeless Youth Act. (1978) U.S.C. §5701.

Runaway, Homeless, and Missing Children Protection Act. (2003) P.L. 108–96.

Russell, Diana E. (1984) *Sex Exploitation.* Beverly Hills, Sage.

Russell, Donald H. (1971) "On the Psychopathology of Boy Prostitutes." *International Journal of Offender Therapy and Comparative Criminology* 15: 49–52.

Ryan, Caitlin, and Ian Rivers. (2003) "Lesbian, Gay, Bisexual and Transgender Youth: Victimization and Its Correlates in the USA and UK." *Culture, Health, and Society* 5, 2: 103–19.

Ryan, Jason. (April 23, 2008) "Mueller: 'We're Losing' the Child Porn War." ABC News. http://abcnews.go.com/TheLaw/FedCrimes/story?id=4712725&page=1.

_____. (March 4, 2008) "'Sophisticated' Child Porn Ring Busted." ABC News. http://abcnews.go.com/TheLaw/story?id=4388379.

_____, and Theresa Cook. (June 25, 2008) "FBI Arrests 300 in Child Prostitution Sting." ABC News. http://abcnews.go.com/TheLaw/FedCrimes/story?id=5247386.

Ryan, Kimberly D., Ryan Kilmer, Ana Mari Cauce, Haruko Watanabe, and Danny R. Hoyt. (2000) "Psychological Consequences of Child Maltreatment in Homeless Adolescents: Untangling the Unique Effects of Maltreatment and Family Environment." *Child Abuse and Neglect* 24: 333–52.

Saewyc, Elizabeth M., Carol Skay, Kimberly Richens, and Elizabeth Reis. (2006) "Sexual Orientation, Sexual Abuse, and HIV-Risk

Related Behaviors Among Adolescents in the Pacific Northwest." *American Journal of Public Health* 96, 6.

_____, Linda H. Bearinger, Robert W. Blum, and Michael D. Resnick. (1999) "Sexual Intercourse, Abuse and Pregnancy Among Adolescent Women: Does Sexual Orientation Make a Difference?" *Family Planning Perspectives* 31, 3: 127–31.

Safe Schools Coalition. (July 6, 2009) "Homeless LGBT Youth and LGBT Youth in Foster Care." http://www.safeschoolscoalition. org/RG-homeless.html.

Safren, Steven A., and Richard G. Heimberg. (1999) "Depression, Hopelessness, Suicidality, and Related Factors in Sexual Minority and Heterosexual Adolescents." *Journal of Consulting and Clinical Psychology* 67, 6: 859–66.

Safyer, Andrew W., Sanna J. Thompson, Elaine M. Maccio, Kimberley M. Zittel-Palamara, and Greg Forehand. (2004) "Adolescents' and Parents' Perceptions of Runaway Behavior: Problems and Solutions." *Child and Adolescent Social Work Journal* 21, 5: 495–512.

Sanchez, Rebecca P. (December 20, 2004) "Facing Up to Homeless Youths." *Denver Post*, p. A1.

_____, Martha W. Waller, and Jody M. Greene. (2006) "Who Runs? A Demographic Profile of Runaway Youth in the United States." *Journal of Adolescent Health* 39, 5: 778–81.

Sanders, Teela, Maggie O'Neill, and Jane Pitcher. (2009) *Prostitution: Sex Work, Policy and Politics.* New York: Sage.

Sandoval, Greg, and Declan McCullagh. (March 6, 2009) "Is Craigslist the World's Biggest Bordello?" CNET News. http://news.cnet.com/is-craigslist-the-worlds-biggest-bordello/.

Saphira, Miriam. (2001) *The Commercial Exploitation of Children.* Auckland, NZ: ECPAT.

_____, and Averil Herbert. (2005) "Victimization Among Those Involved in Underage Commercial Sexual Activity." *Women's Studies Journal* 19, 2: 32–40.

Satchel, Michael. (July 20, 1986) "Kids for Sale: A Shocking Report on Child Prostitution Across America." *Parade Magazine*, p. 4.

Savin-Williams, Ritch C. (1994) "Verbal and Physical Abuse as Stressors in the Lives of Lesbian, Gay Male and Bisexual Youths: Association with School Problems, Running Away, Substance Abuse, Prostitution, and Suicide." *Journal of Consulting and Clinical Psychology* 62, 2: 261–69.

Schaffner, Laurie. (1998) "Searching for Connection: A New Look at Teenaged Runaways." *Adolescence* 33, 31: 619–28.

Schalet, Amy, Geoffrey Hunt, and Karen Joe-Laidler. (2003) "Respectability and Autonomy: The Articulation and Meaning of Sexuality Among the Girls in the Gang." *Journal of Contemporary Ethnography* 32: 108–43.

Schissel, B., and K. Fedec. (1999) "The Selling of Innocence: The Gestalt of Danger in the Lives of Youth Prostitutes." *Canadian Journal of Criminology* 41, 1: 33–56.

Schneider, Monica E., and Robert E. Owens. (2000) "Concern for Lesbian, Gay, and Bisexual Kids: The Benefits for All Children." *Education and Urban Society* 32, 3: 349–67.

Schoetz, David. (March 25, 2008) "Teen Sex for Sale: Middle School Madam Busted." ABC News. http://abcnews.go.com/GMA/story?id=4519538&page=1.

Scott, John, Victor Minichiello, Rodrigo Mariño, Glenn P. Harvey, Maggie Jamieson, and Jan Browne. (2005) "Understanding the New Context of the Male Sex Work Industry." *Journal of Interpersonal Violence* 20: 320–42.

Scott, Michael S., and Kelly Dedel. (2006) *Street Prostitution.* 2nd ed. Washington, D.C.: Office of Community Oriented Policing Services.

Sealey, Geraldine. (December 13, 2008) "Exposing America's Ugly Child Secret." ABC News. http://abcnews.go.com/US/story?id=90557&page=1.

Sell, Randall L. (1997) "Defining and Measuring Sexual Orientation: A Review." *Archives of Sexual Behavior* 26, 6: 643–58.

Seng, Magnus J. (1989) "Child Sexual Abuse and Adolescent Prostitution: A Comparative Analysis." *Adolescence* 24: 665–75.

Sexual Exploitation of Children. 18 U.S.C. § 2251 (a). As amended by Protection of Children from Sexual Predators Act. § 201.

Shellow, Robert. (1967) "Suburban Runaways of the 60s." *Monographs of the Society for Research in Child Development* 32: 17.

Shelton, Deborah. (2001) "Emotional Disorders in Young Offenders." *Journal of Nursing Scholarship* 33, 3: 259–63.

Sherman, Deborah J. (1992) "The Neglected Health Care Needs of Street Youth." *Public Health Reports* 107, 4: 433–40.

Siegel, Jane A., and Linda M. Williams. (2003) "The Relationship Between Child Sexual Abuse and Female Delinquency and Crime: A Prospective Study." *Journal of Research in Crime and Delinquency* 40, 1: 71–94.

Silbert, Mimi H. (1982) "Delancey Street

Study: Prostitution and Sexual Assault." Summary of results. Delancey Street Foundation, San Francisco, p. 3.

_____. (1982) "Entrance Into Prostitution." *Youth and Society* 13: 471–500.

_____. (1982) "Prostitution and Sexual Assault: Summary Results." *International Journal of Biosexual Research* 3: 69–71.

_____. (1981) "Sexual Child Abuse as an Antecedent to Prostitution." *Child Abuse and Neglect* 5: 407–11.

_____. (1982) "Victimization of Street Prostitutes." *Victimology* 7: 122–33.

_____, and Ayala M. Pines. (1981) "Occupational Hazards of Street Prostitutes." *Criminal Justice and Behavior* 8: 397.

Simons Abby. (March 12, 2009) "Minneapolis to Go After Johns to Fight Prostitution." StarTribune.com. http://www.startribune.com/local/41084482.html.

Simons, Ronald L., and Les B. Whitbeck. (1991) "Running Away During Adolescence as a Precursor to Adult Homelessness." *Social Service Review* 65, 2: 225–47.

_____, and _____. (1991) "Sexual Abuse as a Precursor to Prostitution and Victimization Among Adolescent and Adult Homeless Women." *Journal of Family Issues* 12, 3: 361–79.

Slesnick, Natasha. (2004) *Our Runaway and Homeless Youth: A Guide to Understanding.* Westport, CT: Praeger.

_____, and Jillian Prestopnik. (2005) "Dual and Multiple Diagnosis Among Substance Using Runaway Youth." *American Journal of Drug and Alcohol Abuse* 3, 1: 179–201.

_____, and Melissa Meade. (2001) "System Youth: A Subgroup of Substance-Abusing Homeless Adolescents." *Journal of Substance Abuse* 13: 367–84.

Smalley, Suzanne. (August 10, 2003) "Nationwide Increase in Teen Prostitution: Trends Show Kids Getting Younger, More from Middle Class Homes." *Newsweek.* http://www.couplescompany.com/Wireservice/Parenting/teenProstitution.htm.

Smeaton, Emilie. (2005) *Living on the Edge: The Experiences of Detached Young Runaways.* Leeds, UK: The Children's Society.

_____, and Gwyther Rees. (2004) *Running Away in South Yorkshire: Research into the Incidence and Nature of the Problem in Sheffield, Rotherham, Barnsley, and Doncaster.* Sheffield, UK: Safe at Last.

Smolenski, Carol. (1995) "Sex Tourism and the Sexual Exploitation of Children." *Christian Century* 112: 1079.

Snell, Cudore L. (1995) *Young Men in the Street: Help-Seeking Behavior of Young Male Prostitutes.* Westport, CT: Praeger.

Snyder, Howard N. (2001) *Law Enforcement and Juvenile Crime.* Washington, D.C.: Office of Juvenile Justice and Delinquency Prevention.

_____, and Melissa Sickmund. (1999) *Juvenile Offenders and Victims: 1999 National Report.* Washington, D.C.: Office of Juvenile Justice and Delinquency Prevention.

Solarz, Andrea L. (1988) "Homelessness: Implications for Children and Youth." *Social Policy Report* 3, 4: 1–16.

Solorio, M. Rosa, Norweeta G. Milburn, Robert E. Weiss, and Philip J. Batterham. (2006) "Newly Homeless Youth STD Testing Patterns Over Time." *Journal of Adolescent Health* 39: 443e9–43e16.

South Dakota Codified Laws Ann. § 22–23–2.

Spangenberg, Mia. (2001) "Prostituted Youth in New York City: An Overview." http://www.libertadlatina.org/US_ECPAT_Child_Prostitution_NYC.htm.

Sponsler, Connie. (1993) "Juvenile Prostitution Prevention Project." *WHISPER* 13, 2: 3–4.

The Star.com. (February 23, 2009) "FBI Rescues Dozens of Teen Prostitutes." http://www.thestar.com/News/World/article/591827.

*State v. Steer.* (1986) 517 A, 2d 797.

Stepp, Laura S. (September 16, 2005) "Study: Half of All Teens Have Had Oral Sex." *Washington Post.*

Sterk, Claire E. (2000) *Tricking and Tripping: Prostitution in the Era of AIDS.* Putnam Valley, NY: Social Change Press.

Stewart, K. (1994) *Opportunistic Prostitution and Young People in Cairns City and Mulgrave Shire.* Queensland, Australia: Youth Services.

Sticof, R. L., L. F. Novick, and J. T. Kennedy. (1990) "HIV Seroprevalence in Facilities for Runaway and Homeless Adolescents in Four States: Florida, Texas, Louisiana and New York." Paper presented at the Sixth International Conference on AIDS, San Francisco, CA.

Stieber, Tamar. (March 4, 1984) "The Boys Who Sell Sex to Men in San Francisco." *Sacramento Bee*, p. A22.

Stiffman, Arlene R. (1989) "Physical and Sexual Abuse in Runaway Youths." *Child Abuse and Neglect* 13, 3: 417–26.

Stransky, Michelle, and David Finkelhor. (2008) *How Many Juveniles Are Involved in Prostitution in the United States?* Durham, NC: Crimes Against Children Research Center.

Strauss, Eric M. (July 16, 2008) "Pimp Abducts Ohio Teens: Two Cousins Forced Into Having Sex for Money." ABC News. http://abc news.go.com/TheLaw/story?id=5382645& page=1.

Study World. "Runaways: Victims at Home and on the Streets." http://www.studyworld. com/newsite/ReportEssay/SocialIssues/Polit ical%5CRunaways_Victims_At_Home_and _On_the_Streets-32644.htm.

Sullivan, Patricia M., and John F. Knutson. (2000) "The Prevalence of Disabilities and Maltreatment Among Runaway Children." *Child Abuse and Neglect* 24, 10: 1275–88.

Sullivan, T. Richard. (1996) "The Challenge of HIV Prevention Among High-Risk Adolescents." *Health and Social Work* 21: 58–65.

Talashek, Marie L., Nilda Peragallo, Kathleen Norr, and Barbara L. Dancy. (2004) "The Context of Risky Behaviors for Latino Youth." *Journal of Transcultural Nursing* 15: 131–38.

Task Force on Children Involved in Prostitution. (1997) *Children Involved in Prostitution.* Edmonton, Alberta: Ministry of Family and Social Services.

Tattersall, Clare. (1999) *Drugs, Runaways, and Teen Prostitution.* New York: Rosen.

Terrell, Nathanial E. (1997) "Aggravated and Sexual Assault Among Homeless and Runaway Adolescents." *Youth & Society* 28: 267–90.

Thompson, Sanna J., Andrew W. Safyer, and David E. Pollio. (2001) "Differences and Predictors of Family Reunification Among Subgroups of Runaway Youths Using Shelter Services." *Social Work Research* 25, 3: 163–72.

Time.com. (August 27, 1973) "Behavior: The Runaways a National Problem." http://www. time.com/time/magazine/article/0,9171, 907795,00.html.

_____. (September 15, 1967) "Youth: The Runaways." http://www.time.com/time/maga zine/article/0,9171,941149-1,00.html.

Transportation of Minors. 18 U.S.C. § 2423.

Tremblay, Pierre J. (October 11–14, 1995) "The Homosexuality Factor in the Youth Suicide Problem." Presented at the Sixth Annual Conference of the Canadian Association for Suicide Prevention, Banff, Alberta. http:// www.qrd.org/qrd/www/youth/tremblay/.

Trujillo, Laura. (June 7, 1996) "Escort Services Thriving Industry in Portland Area." *Oregonian,* p. B1.

Tyler, Kimberly A. (2008) "Social Network Characteristics and Risky Sexual and Drug Related Behaviors Among Homeless Young Adults." *Social Science Research* 37, 2: 673–85.

_____, Danny R. Hoyt, and Les B. Whitbeck. (2000) "The Effects of Early Sexual Abuse on Later Sexual Victimization Among Female Homeless and Runaway Adolescents." *Journal of Interpersonal Violence* 15: 235–250.

_____, _____, _____, and Ana Mari Cauce. (2001) "The Impact of Childhood Sexual Abuse on Later Sexual Victimization Among Runaway Youth." *Journal of Research on Adolescence* 11, 2: 151–76.

_____, Les B. Whitbeck, Danny R. Hoyt, and Ana Mari Cauce. (2004) "Risk Factors for Sexual Victimization Among Male and Female Homeless and Runaway Youth." *Journal of Interpersonal Violence* 19: 503–20.

U.S. Department of Health and Human Services. Administration for Children and Families. Federal and State Reporting Systems. National Child Abuse and Neglect Data System (NCANDS). http://www.acf.hhs.gov/ programs/cb/systems/index.htm.

_____. (1995) Family Youth and Services Bureau. *FYSB Update.* Silver Springs, MD: National Clearinghouse on Families & Youth.

_____. (1995) Family Youth and Services Bureau. *Youth with Runaway, Throwaway, and Homeless Experiences: Prevalence, Drug Use, and Other At-Risk Behaviors.* Silver Springs, MD: National Clearinghouse on Families & Youth.

_____. (2001–2002) Family and Youth Services Research. "Sexual Abuse Experiences of Runaway Youth, 2001–2002." http://www.acf. hhs.gov/programs/opre/fys/sex_abuse/in dex.html.

_____. (2003) *Incidence and Prevalence of Homeless and Runaway Youth.* Washington, D.C.: Administration for Children and Families.

_____. (2001) *Program Assistance Letter: Understanding the Health Care Needs of Homeless Youth.* Washington, D.C.: Health Resources and Services Administration.

_____. (2002) *Sexual Abuse Among Homeless Adolescents: Prevalence, Correlates, and Sequelae.* Washington, D.C.: Administration for Children and Families.

U.S. Department of Justice. Child Exploitation and Obscenity Section (CEOS). "Child Prostitution: Domestic Trafficking of Minors." http://www.usdoj.gov/criminal/ceos/ prostitution.html.

_____. Child Exploitation and Obscenity Section (CEOS). "Citizens Guide to United States Federal Exploitation Laws." http://

www.usdoj.gov/criminal/ceos/citizensguide.
html.

_____. (2009) Child Exploitation and Obscenity Section (CEOS). Press Releases 2008 and 2009. http://www.usdoj.gov/criminal/ceos/pressreleases.html.

_____. Child Exploitation and Obscenity Section (CEOS). "Trafficking and Sex Tourism." http://www.usdoj.gov/criminal/ceos/trafficking.html.

_____. (2009) Federal Bureau of Investigation. *Crime in the United States, 2007.* http://www.fbi.gov/ucr/cius2007/arrests/population_group.html.

_____. (1999) Federal Bureau of Investigation. *Crime in the United States: Uniform Crime Reports 1998.* Washington, D.C.: Government Printing Office.

_____. Federal Bureau of Investigation. Uniform Crime Reporting Program. http://www.fbi.gov/ucr/ucr.htm.

_____. (1999) *Juvenile Offenders and Victims: 1999 National Report.* Washington, D.C.: Office of Juvenile Justice and Delinquency Prevention.

_____. (2006) *Juvenile Offenders and Victims: 2006 National Report.* Washington, D.C.: Office of Juvenile Justice and Delinquency Prevention.

_____. (1993) *Law Enforcement Policies and Practices Regarding Missing Children and Homeless Youth: Research Project.* Washington, D.C.: Office of Juvenile Justice and Delinquency Prevention.

_____. (1993) Office of Juvenile Justice and Delinquency Prevention. *Law Enforcement Policies and Practices Regarding Missing and Homeless Youth: Research Summary.* Washington, D.C.: Government Printing Office.

_____. (1999) Office of Juvenile Justice and Delinquency Prevention. *Prostitution of Children and Child-Sex Tourism.* Alexandria, VA: National Center for Missing and Exploited Children.

_____. (1997) *Use of Computers in the Sexual Exploitation of Children.* Washington, D.C.: Office of Justice Programs.

U.S. *News & World Report.* (March 11, 1985) "'Runaways,' 'Throwaways,' 'Bag Kids'—An Army of Drifter Teens," p. 53.

*U.S. v. Bitty.* (1908) 208 U.S. 393, 401.

Unger, Jennifer B., Michele D. Kipke, Thomas R. Simon, Susanne B. Montgomery, and Christine J. Johnson. (1997) "Homeless Youths and Young Adults in Los Angeles: Prevalence of Mental Health Problems and the Relationship Between Mental Health and

Substance Abuse Disorders." *American Journal of Community Psychology* 25, 3: 371–94.

_____, Thomas R. Simon, Traci L. Newman, Susanne B. Montgomery, Michele D. Kipke, and Michael Albomoz. (1998) "Early Adolescent Street Youth: An Overlooked Population with Unique Problems and Service Needs." *Journal of Early Adolescence* 18, 4: 325–48.

*United States v. Hilton.* (January 27, 1999) No. 98-513, slip op. at 3.

UPI.com. (April 16, 2009) "Study: Many Pimps Have Been Prostitutes." http://www.upi.com/Top_News/2009/04/16/Study-Many-pimps-have-been-prostitutes/UPI-94781239939726/.

USA *Today.* (October 19, 2006) "Feds Arrest 125 People Nationwide in Child Porn Investigation." http://www.usatoday.com/news/nation/2006-10-19-child-porn-arrests_x.htm.

van Houten, Therese, and Gary Golembiewski. (1978) *Adolescent Life Stress as a Predictor of Alcohol Abuse and/or Runaway Behavior.* Washington, D.C.: National Youth Alternatives Project, Inc.

Van Leeuwen, James M., Susan Boyle, and Amber Yancy. (December 2004) "Urban Peak Public Health Survey Report, 2004: A Multi-City Collaborative." Unpublished.

_____, _____, Stacy Salomonsen-Sautel, D. Nico Baker, J. T. Garcia, Allison Hoffman, and Christian J. Hopfer. (2006) "Lesbian, Gay, and Bisexual Homeless Youth: An Eight-City Public Health Perspective." *Child Welfare* 85, 2: 151–70.

Venetis, Penny. (1997) "International Sexual Slavery." *Women's Rights Law Reporter* 18, 3: 268–70.

Vera Institute of Justice. (2004) *Youth Who Chronically AWOL from Foster Care: Why They Run, Where They Go, and What Can Be Done.* New York: NYC Administration for Children's Services.

The Victims of Child Abuse Act. (1990) P.L. 101-647, § 323, 104 Stat. 4789, 4818.

Volkonsky, Anastasia. (1995) "Legalizing the 'Profession' Would Sanction the Abuse." *Insight on the News* 11: 20.

Wade, Jim, and Nina Biehal. (1998) *Going Missing: Young People Absent from Care.* Chichester, UK: Wiley.

Wagner, Lisa S., Linda Carlin, Ana Mari Cauce, and Adam Tenner. (2001) "A Snapshot of Homeless Youth in Seattle: Their Characteristics, Behaviors and Beliefs About HIV Protective Strategies." *Journal of Community Health* 26, 3: 219–32.

Waldorf, Dan, and Sheigla Murphy. (1990) "Intravenous Drug Use and Syringe-Sharing Practices of Call Men and Hustlers." In Martin A. Plant, ed. *AIDS, Drugs, and Prostitution*. London: Routledge.

Walker, Karen E. (2002) "Exploitation of Children and Young People Through Prostitution." *Journal of Child Health Care* 6: 182–88.

Walker, Nancy E. (2002) "Executive Summary: How Many Teens Are Prostituted?" fce.msu. edu/Family_Impact_Seminars/pdf/2002-2. pdf.

Wan-Ning, Bao, Les B. Whitbeck, and Danny R. Hoyt. (2000) "Abuse, Support and Depression Among Homeless and Runaway Adolescents." *Journal of Health and Social Behavior* 41: 408–20.

Warren, Jacquelyn K., Faye Gary, and Jacquelyn Moorhead. (1994) "Self-Reported Experiences of Physical and Sexual Abuse Among Runaway Youths." *Perspectives in Psychiatric Care* 30, 1: 23–28.

Webb, Vincent J., Charles M. Katz, and Scott H. Decker. (2006) "Assessing the Validity of Self-Reports by Gang Members: Results from the Arrest Drug Abuse Monitoring Program." *Crime and Delinquency* 52: 232–52.

Webber, Marlene. (1991) *Street Kids: The Tragedy of Canada's Runaways*. Toronto: University of Toronto Press.

Weisberg, D. Kelly. (1985) *Children of the Night: A Study of Adolescent Prostitution*. Lexington, MA: Lexington Books.

West Virginia Code § 61-8-8.

Westat, Inc. (1997) National Evaluation of Runaway and Homeless Youth. Washington, D.C.: U.S. Department of Health and Human Services.

Whitbeck, Les B., and Danny R. Hoyt. (1999) *Nowhere to Grow: Homeless and Runaway Adolescents and Their Families*. Hawthorne, NY: Aldine de Gruyter.

_____, _____, and Kevin A. Ackley. (1997) "Abusive Family Backgrounds and Later Victimization Among Runaway and Homeless Youth." *Journal of Research on Adolescence* 7, 4: 375–92.

_____, _____, Kevin A. Yoder, Ana Mari Cauce, and Matt Paradise. (2001) "Deviant Behavior and Victimization Among Homeless and Runaway Adolescents." *Journal of Interpersonal Violence* 16: 1175–1204.

_____, and Ronald L. Simons. (1993) "A Comparison of Adaptive Strategies and Patterns of Victimization Among Homeless Adolescents

and Adults." *Violence and Victims* 8, 2: 135–52.

_____, and _____. (1990) "Life on the Streets: The Victimization of Runaway and Homeless Adolescents." *Youth and Society* 22, 1: 108–25.

_____, Xiaojin Chen, Danny R. Hoyt, Kimberly A, Tyler, and Kurt D. Johnson. (2004) "Mental Disorder, Subsistence Strategies, and Victimization Among Gay, Lesbian, and Bisexual Homeless and Runaway Adolescents." *Journal of Sex Research* 41, 4: 329–42.

Whitcomb, Debra, and Julie Eastin. (1998) *Joining Forces Against Child Sexual Exploitation: Models for a Multidisciplinary Team Effort*. Washington, D.C.: Office of Juvenile Justice and Delinquency Prevention.

Widom, Cathy S., and Joseph B. Kuhns. (1996) "Childhood Victimization and Subsequent Risk for Promiscuity, Prostitution and Teenage Pregnancy: A Prospective Study." *American Journal of Public Health* 86: 1607–12.

_____, and M. Ashley Ames. (1994) "Criminal Consequences of Childhood Sexual Victimization." *Child Abuse and Neglect* 18, 4: 308–18.

Wikipedia, the Free Encyclopedia. "Adolescent Sexuality in the United States." http://en. wikipedia.org/wiki/Adolescent_sexuality_in _the_United_States.

_____. "Chickenhawk." http://en.wikipedia. org/wiki/Chickenhawk_(sexuality).

_____. "Gary Ridgeway." http://en.wikipedia. org/wiki/Gary_Ridgeway.

_____. "Male Prostitution." http://en.wiki pedia.org/wiki/Rent_boy.

_____. "National Runaway Switchboard." http://en.wikipedia.org/wiki/National_Runaway_Switchboard.

Williamson, Celia, and Gail Folaron. (2003) "Understanding the Experiences of Street Level Prostitutes." *Qualitative Social Work* 2: 271–87.

_____, and Terry Cluse-Tolar. (2002) "Pimp-Controlled Prostitution: Still an Integral Part of Street Life." *Violence Against Women* 8: 1074–92.

Windle, Michael T. (1989) "Substance Use and Abuse Among Adolescent Runaways: A Four-Year Follow-up Study." *Journal of Youth and Adolescence* 18, 4: 331–43.

Worth, Heather. (2000) "Up on K Road on a Saturday Night: Sex, Gender and Sex Work in Auckland." *Venereology* 13, 1:15–24.

Wyman, June. (1997) "Drug Abuse Among Runaway and Homeless Youths Calls for Focused Outreach Solutions." *NIDA Notes* 12,

3. http://www.nida.nih.gov/NIDA_Notes/ NNVol12N3/Runaway.html.

Yabroff, Jennie. (May 23, 2008) "The Oral Myth," *Newsweek*. http://www.newsweek. com/id/138444/output/print.

Yates, Gary L., Richard G. MacKenzie, Julia Pennbridge, and Avon Swofford. (1991) "A Risk Profile Comparison of Homeless Youth Involved in Prostitution and Homeless Youth Not Involved." *Journal of Adolescent Health* 12, 7: 545–48.

Yoder, Kevin A. (1999) "Comparing Suicide Attempters, Suicide Ideators, and Nonsuicidal Homeless and Runaway Adolescents." *Suicide & Life-Threatening Behavior* 29: 25–36.

_____. (2003) "Gang Involvement and Membership Among Homeless and Runaway Youth." *Youth and Society* 34, 4: 441–67.

_____, Les B. Whitbeck, and Danny R. Hoyt. (2001) "Event History Analysis of Antecedents to Running Away from Home and Being on the Street." *American Behavioral Scientist* 45: 51–65.

Yoon, Youngik. (1997) *International Sexual Slavery*. Washington, D.C.: CG Issue Overviews.

York, Frank, and Robert H. Knight. (1998) "Reality Check on Homeless Gay Teens." *Family Policy*. http://www.frc.org/fampol/fp 98fcv.htm.

Zaccaro, John, Jr. (March 29, 1988) "Children of the Night." *Woman's Day*, p. 138.

Zeidenberg, Jason, and Vincent Schiraldi. (1998) *Runaway Juvenile Crime? The Context of Juvenile Crime Arrests in America*. Washington, D.C.: Justice Policy Institute.

Zide, Marilyn R., and Andrew L. Cherry. (1992) "A Typology of Runaway Youths: An Empirically Based Definition." *Child and Adolescent Social Work Journal* 9: 155–68.

Zimet, Gregory D., Elisa J. Sobo, Teena Zimmerman, Joann Hackson, Joan Mortimer, Carlyn P. Yanda, and Rina Lazebnik. (1995) "Sexual Behavior, Drug Use, and Aids Knowledge Among Midwestern Runaways." *Youth and Society* 26, 4: 450–62.

# Index